Walkin' on the
Happy Side of Misery

Walkin' on the Happy Side of Misery

A SLICE OF LIFE
ON THE APPALACHIAN TRAIL

J. R. 'Model-T' Tate

STACKPOLE
BOOKS

Cover design by Tessa J. Sweigert
Cover photograph courtesy of Shutterstock

Cataloging-in-Publication data is on file with the Library of Congress

ISBN 978-0-8117-1284-2

*This book is lovingly dedicated to my grandchildren,
Lauren, Jesalyn, Joshua, Rebekah, Nathan, Sarah,
Shaelee, Jacob, and wee Carson.
May you find the true joy that comes with
"walking on the happy side of misery"!*

Memories

Stand atop the mountains and let your spirit soar
With the hawks and the clouds and the freshening wind.
Stand and gaze in awe at God's gift to His creatures,
Great and small. Bask in the sunshine of His majesty.
Stand and marvel at this earthly gem,
which shines with splendor
And casts its aura of blue-green beauty
into the endless universe.
Stand and see that all is within His control
And know that it is good to be alive!

—J.R. 'MODEL-T' TATE, AFTER CLIMBING MT. KATAHDIN, SEPTEMBER 1990

Oh! I'm just a piece of tin;
Nobody knows what shape I'm in.
Got four wheels and a runnin' board.
Oh! I'm a four-door; I'm a Ford!

The rust keeps on a-sucking,
But I keep on a-trucking!
Honk, honk, rattle, rattle; settin' forth;
Honk, honk, Tin Lizzie headin' North!

—ANDREA TATE POUSSON TO HER DAD, APRIL 1990

May the Trail rise to meet you;
May the wind be always at your back;
May the sun shine warmly on your bod'.
Until we meet again, my friend,
May the "Trail Goddess" hold
You in the palm of her hand!

(Variation on a traditional Irish Blessing)

—A WISH FROM NOEL DECAVALCANTE, "THE SINGING HORSEMAN",
MARCH 1990

Contents

Preface

In early spring each year, an exodus takes place in this country. A cross section of humankind makes its way, singly or by two's or three's, to an isolated mountaintop in northeast Georgia. These sojourners—weird-looking creatures burdened with huge loads and wearing strange garments—are linked by their appearance and behavior. The connection? They share a common purpose: to hike the Appalachian Trail from Georgia's Springer Mountain to Mount Katahdin in Maine in a single season. These creatures call themselves "thru-hikers."

Like lemmings rushing to the sea, thru-hikers scurry northward, following a torturous, winding footpath for months, as if pulled along by an invisible, unfathomable force. They seem willing to endure immense hardship and pain to fulfill the near maniacal passion that drives them toward Katahdin. Spirit-sapping wetness becomes the norm; stinking, sweaty, tattered clothing and body odor that brings to mind the smell of rotting swamp muck are accepted as commonplace. With numb fingers and pinched faces, the early birds chance the howling, arctic-like winds and drifting snows of the southern Appalachians, while the slowpokes dare Katahdin's icy wrath by trying winter's patience. In another season, when the sun transforms the mountains into vast saunas, it seems these intrepid souls must surely dissolve into soggy pools of filthy DNA. Plagued by calorie deficit, gnawing hunger, and voracious appetites, thru-hikers gobble down innumerable meals of cheap macaroni and cheese, instant oatmeal, peanut butter, and anything else they can get their hands on to fill empty bellies and help them eke out a few more miles.

In fact, thru-hikers will put up with almost anything that Mother Nature or her mischievous sidekicks, Fate and Chance, decide to dish out, for they are wholly dedicated to their purpose. Everything becomes subservient to the Trail and their determination to stand atop Katahdin. But, as often happens, Fate decrees otherwise . . .

The Appalachian Trail is a leveler of society—a catalyst that reduces all who walk its rugged path to a stratum of sameness. The great and the small, the rich and the poor, the famous and the ordinary—those who seek "nirvana" in the guise of "thru-hiker"—are reduced to a common denominator by the Trail. Each must grind out the miles, suffer the bone-crushing exhaustion and desolate loneliness, and deal with the lesser evils—gut-wrenching hunger, blisters, bugs, snakes, sullen rain-filled days, and a balky mind that keeps harping, "You don't have to do this. Go home!"

But, ahh! The rewards! To lie on a sun-drenched carpet of wild flowers in an alpine meadow and build fluffy kingdoms in the sky; or to dangle fiery feet in a burbling mountain stream and let its seductive melody caress the senses; or to gaze on a sunset so filled with the colors of creation that words will not come; or even the exquisite soothing of a parched throat with a cold soda given in kindness by a stranger—the heart leaps and the mind rejoices at such simple pleasures that abound on the "happy side of misery." The soul feasts, the spirit is replenished, and the footsteps continue toward Katahdin.

But be warned! There are few shortcuts if the hiker is true to his or her conscience. The mountains between Springer and Katahdin are littered with the dashed dreams of those who sought to cheat the Trail of its toll; for, like dandelion fluff blowing across a manicured lawn, the seeds of lax purpose and sloppy intent can proliferate into rationalized disregard of the white blazes, which ultimately lead to the sacred summit. For once the seeds of discontent are scattered, the double-dealing mind goads, "These next hundred miles are a bummer. Let's skip this section and hole up for a few days at . . ."; and having gained a toehold, the mind then finds it easy going. Another giant car hop north, and then another; and one morning the mind suddenly asks, "What the heck am I doing out here anyway? It's not fun anymore." The "Dream" has become like soured milk, and the hiker fades into obscurity.

Each journey is a storehouse of memories, whether it lasts only a mile or ends atop Mt. Katahdin. My first "slice of life on the Appalachian Trail," chronicled within the pages of this book, became a turning point in my existence—so life-altering that the journey still remains vividly real. The people, places (as they were in 1990), and happenings are true to my memory, although some remembrances may be tainted or tarnished by my pesky alter-ego, Model-T, who "duct-taped" himself to my psyche several years ago and has insisted on "top billing" in the telling of this journey. I apologize in advance for any errors, and for the few occasions when I limped along leaning on the crutch of "literary license"; and if called for, I will don sackcloth liberally dusted with ashes in penance for any egos traumatized by my wordy stomping. Too, I have deigned to use "trail names" in place of actual names—mainly because that is the way of the Trail.

Model-T and I have walked on the "Happy Side of Misery" twice more since that first glorious trip. And still, on balmy spring days when the awakening redbuds race the March lilies onto Nature's canvas; when the first robins flutter across last fall's leaving of brown, now splotched with delicate green; I feel the Trail calling, and its echo haunts my soul . . .

J.R. Tate
(Georgia to Maine, 1990, 1994, 1998)

Acknowledgments

With grateful appreciation to Bettye Pinter, my erstwhile editor, friend, and guru, who kept my pen from running away; to Verda Napier, whose pizzazz kept my nose to the grindstone; to my Trail family, who nurtured me when the going got tough; and to my wonderful wife, Judith, without whose love, support, encouragement, and grass cutting, there wouldn't be a book!

CHAPTER 1

Horns or Tits

I gave the pack a tentative tug. It didn't feel as heavy now as it had when I pushed it into the trunk of our aged blue Buick Skylark eight hours earlier, back at Roanoke. Encouraged, I hoisted it up to the big hook on the truth teller, letting it dangle, and smirked for the benefit of my backwoods sidekick, David Jones.

"Fifty-two pounds!" I raised my voice for the benefit of two young hikers—younger than David—who stood close by waiting to weigh their packs. "And that includes two quarts of water and four days of food. Not bad for a six-month walk in the woods, huh?"

David said, "Heck Model-T, I can beat that." Grunting, he heaved his pack onto the hook and watched while the pointer wobbled and finally steadied at the "fifty-one" mark. We both verified the reading and he chuckled, "See. And that pound difference, multiplied by five million steps, is going to save me tons."

I accepted my lot, tempted to ditch one of my quart water bottles—two pounds—to give me a leg up, but that might put us in a food-toss race, and I had just enough supplies to last the four days to Neels Gap, my first resupply point. Instead, I swallowed my pride, grumbling, "Old age and treachery's gonna clean your young clock before we get to Maine."

My voice, lacking vinegar, betrayed the words and David grinned. Still, the generation gap was like a spreading sinkhole, threatening to swallow my resolve in a swift gulp, and I wondered for the umpteenth time at my sanity. At fifty-three, I teetered under a load of years twice David's springy, exuberant twenty-five. It would take a lot more than treachery to push me up the Appalachian Trail! With effort, I shoved the worry out of my mind, and we moved our packs aside to make room for the next hiker.

Judith, J.R.'s wife-turned-chauffeur for today, shook her head. "You two need to have your heads examined. It's bad enough that you're going to walk to Maine, but to carry over fifty pounds on your back . . . Crazy."

We'd been down *that* path already, at least two dozen times. David shifted uncomfortably and I blathered an innocuous rebuttal, hoping to avert an embarrassing squabble. "Gee, Honey, it's only a little over 2100 miles. A piece of cake, really. Come on, let's check out the Visitor Center." THE LOOK, a nasty piece of business, raced across her face—an ominous cloud that briefly threatened to rain on our day—and brought on a pregnant silence. I held my breath and pulled my mind toward the nearby roar of Amicalola Falls, filling it with the crescendo of the cascading water. THE LOOK, ever a chameleon, changed into a grimace and retreated to lock horns another day. Without another word, Judith turned toward the door of the rustic building that housed Amicalola Falls State Park Visitor Center.

David and I propped our backpacks against the wall and followed her inside, listening to a loud groan that followed us through the door: "Holy cow! Eighty-six pounds." Discordant chortling from another hiker turned into a gasping "Gawd Almighty! Seventy-eight! Damn, this thing can't be right!" David and I, smugly satisfied that we were in a down-and-dirty-no-frills mode, smiled knowingly at each other—the truth teller didn't lie.

J.R., the obdurate, complaining "ego" that perpetuated my status as an "alter", cut into my thoughts. "Don't be so all-fired complacent, Big Shot. It's a long haul to Maine." I gritted my teeth and retorted, "Going any-where with you is a long haul." This promised to be a long trip with J.R. dogging my thoughts, but it was the only way . . .

When we went back outside, David and I posed by the large bronze Appalachian Trail marker at the front of the Visitor Center, smiling into Judith's camera with confidence and anticipation although my belly churned with the fluttering of a gazillion busy butterflies. Did David's?

Pictures taken, nothing remained to be said; the moment of truth stared us squarely in the eyes. Judith hugged David, and then he discreetly walked off, leaving the moment to Judith and J.R. (The Ego's wife was one thing I refused to share!) Oblivious to the milling tourists, they embraced, clinging to one another in the ageless ritual of man about to step across the threshold, leaving wife and family to hope and luck as he begins a long journey toward the unknown. As a military wife, she knew the routine, though that didn't make it any easier.

She: "Write and call every chance you get."

He: "Every chance. I'll be fine. David will keep an eye out."

After a last brief kiss, I collected J.R. and we followed David into the woods. I gave in to J.R.'s urging for a final glimpse before the forest swallowed us. She stood like a statue, forlorn and unmoving, frozen in time, her image blurred by the soft drizzle that started to fall from the fuzzy Georgia overcast, magnifying the aura of loneliness that seemed to hover around her like a casket shroud. J.R. growled, "We don't have to do this, you know. There's still time to call it off—" I cut him off. "Maine, we agreed, and Maine it's gonna be, even if we have to crawl."

Blowing her a kiss, I strengthened my resolve, cinched the hip belt until it hurt, and pushed into the forest. But the image of Judith remained, a searing picture permanently branded on my memory.

I picked up the pace and followed David up the Approach Trail toward Springer Mountain, the southern terminus of the Appalachian Trail, eight miles away. The trip had begun!

From what I had read, many aspiring thru-hikers are intimidated by the Approach Trail, which has the dubious reputation of chewing up eager "wannabe's" and spitting out mangled dreams. Many opt to ride up a forest service road to Springer's vicinity; in fact, one original thinker parachuted onto Springer to begin his trek and was quickly tagged with the trail name "Jump Start". Early on, David and I (against J.R.'s protest, for he wanted to ride) decided the Approach Trail was an essential part of the whole, and if we bypassed it, we somehow cheated ourselves and lost in the deal.

So, inflated with good intentions, with me leading our two-man parade, we bantered and joked the miles away in an on-again, off-again drizzle, bragging about how easy the trail was and how light our packs felt. (Actually, my muscles burned like the fury of Hell, and I wondered if the truth teller hadn't lied after all!) The pack felt like a huge tumor growing out of my back—a thief that sapped my energy and deformed me into a wobbly hunchback.

J.R. fumed at my fakery: "You are a bald-faced liar. Why don't you just admit that you're hurting. You had better take a break before you blow a gasket." I snorted, "Not on your life. There'll be icicles in July before I let this young whippersnapper think he can outdo me."

Five minutes later, long enough to save face with The Ego, I announced, "About break time, isn't it?" and tossed my pack against a tree, thinking that "replacement gaskets" might be hard to come by out here! David followed my lead, and we sat facing one another on opposite sides of the muddy path, grinning like possums at our new lease on life. I gulped at the water bottle, and my thoughts regressed . . .

David Jones had walked into my life one cool November Saturday the previous fall. I had joined a group of ten hikers from the Roanoke (Virginia) Appalachian Trail Club for a twelve-mile day hike. During the lunch break, I mentioned something about hoping to thru-hike the Appalachian Trail, adding with a twist of flip, "maybe next spring."

David jumped into the conversation. "That's been a dream of mine for a long time, and I've been thinking about doing it, too. Now would be a good time because my job's not going anywhere. Maybe it's time for a career change. If you'd like some company, maybe we could go together."

Jeepers! This was an unexpected push toward an awesome precipice! I considered the possibility. At a glance we appeared as opposite as Mutt and Jeff: Gray-bearded and tending toward crown baldness; barely reaching five feet, nine inches; I had recently turned fifty-three and was retired. David, single and half my age, sported a thick shock of unruly red hair—a legacy of Scottish genes. He needed two yardsticks to fully measure his height; made his keep as foreman of a local furniture shop (although with his good looks, polite manner, and innocent, youthful charm, he could easily have been a model for men's clothing). Criminy! I had children older than David! I even had grandchildren! What could we have in common? Six months with an incompatible partner could extend to eternity!

"Yeah, maybe," I replied, and pushed the idea out of my mind, thinking that Judith would jinx it anyway.

We crossed paths again a few weeks later. David asked, "Have you thought any more about doing a thru-hike?"

"Not much. To be truthful, I haven't figured out a way to get around the boss."

"I've mulled it over a lot. It would be a lot of fun," he said, and a faraway gleam crept into his eyes.

That it would! Excitement built as I thought of new vistas that shimmered just out of reach. With the power I now wielded over The Ego, he was like putty, but Judith would be another matter. We both dreaded her main weapon of attack—THE LOOK. "Yeah," I said wistfully, "it would be the trip of a lifetime. Let me think about it, and I'll call you in a few days."

About J.R. and me: I'm an alter ego, although to J.R.'s way of thinking, I exist only as a figment of his imagination, like a maverick headache (or pain in the rumpus, since that's where he does most of his thinking).

Oddly, I haven't the slightest idea about my origin. One day I just *was*, and I've been here ever since.

He almost had me convinced that I really was a figment when I first began bouncing around inside his noggin. But soon I became aware that, like J.R., I hungered and thirsted and slept; more astoundingly, I had a mind of my own!

Early in our roller coaster relationship, he handled me like a new toy—a plaything when he got bored or fancied some entertainment; a ruddy discard when fun time was finished. Like a child, as the years passed I grew, until one day he found it impossible to shut me out. Suddenly, he faced the stark realization: I had become an ENTITY, a force to be reckoned with, and we were stuck together for the duration.

Oddly, J.R. and I make strange bedfellows to be bound in such intimacy. In a word, he is a *bore*! His qualifications: Piddler extraordinaire; Grand Huzzini of the status-quo school; a veteran couch potato, always reading a book or immersed in some nonsensical sitcom on TV. By my reckoning, the only thing the poor dufus has going for himself: He is a retired Marine. Somehow, he managed to storm the shores of Gitchi-gummi and got through his twenty years without sending the Marine Corps into an "esprit" tailspin! J.R., blissful in his ignorance, flaps along with Society's turkeys.

On the other hand, I am an unfettered spirit, intertwined with Nature. I thrill when the storm rages; the music of the sunrise haunts my day; I commune with the spirit of the earth and am mellowed by the tasting. I'm *out there*, aching to soar to soul-stirring heights where only eagles nest.

Over the years, in order to survive we have learned to coexist in an uneasy truce (which is often violated as we struggle to carry out different agendas); yet, somehow we have always managed to patch the holes with fragile apologies. Always though, the highest item on my agenda has been to yank J.R. out of his rut!

One mellow spring evening last year while we were engaged in a tug of war over dessert—chocolate ice cream (J.R.'s favorite) or a Snickers bar (mine)—I made a startling discovery! My will had become stronger than his! Which gave me *unlimited power* over the schmook!

I chewed contentedly on the Snickers and tweaked his cerebrum. "Hey J.R. Ol' Buddy, it's about time you and me had a little powwow." He groaned and said to Judith, who stood at the sink washing supper dishes, "Jeez! All of a sudden I have a terrific headache. I'm going to bed."

The idea of spending six months on the Appalachian Trail festered like an abscessed sore, until it became a spiritual malaise that filled my days with restless desire and turned me into a disgruntled cur. J.R., happy with his status quo, fought me tooth and nail, while I constantly nipped at his peace of mind. Vindictively, I planned ambushes to land the target of my discontent in hot water with Judith. One such occasion:

Dawn. I smack his libido, sending his dream parade of cute little girlies scuttling. "Time to wake up, Gobbler. Your turkey friends are waiting."

J.R., lying on his back, mumbles aloud in a low, sleep-choked voice, "Leave me alone, Dummy. How many times have I got to tell you that you're the turkey, not me?"

Judith, just beginning to stir beside him, picks up on his barely audible words. "Did you just call me a turkey?" Hostility stirs the air.

J.R. opens his eyes, realizes he's glitched big time, and tries to cover the slip. "Sorry, bad dream. These late night Snickers bars, I guess," and he pulls the pillow over his head, pretending to go back to sleep.

Judith: "You've been talking a lot in your sleep lately. Are you okay? Maybe you'd better lay off the Snickers."

I rattle him again. "Katahdin calls; do you have the balls? Hee hee hee!"

He growls, his voice muffled by the pillow, "For cryin' out loud, just get off my back and leave me alone!"

Judith has excellent hearing. "What! What did you just say?" Not waiting for a reply, she rolls out THE LOOK—that withering, mind-numbing piece of voodoo with which all women are armed at birth; that vindictive subjugator, which makes strong men cringe and turns them into namby-pamby, milquetoast, miserable wretches—as J.R. now becomes. It's not a pretty sight!

J.R., busted, peeps from beneath his pillowy refuge, squints against THE LOOK, and croaks, "Sorry, dear. I meant to say, 'I gotta get off my back.'"

"You are lying through your teeth," she snarls. "I heard what you said." She zaps him with another dose of THE LOOK and stomps off toward the bathroom. J.R. is in for a hard day—again—the miserable schmook. But he's got to cave sooner or later!

J.R. finally waved the white flag. "Okay, if you can do an end run around THE LOOK, count me in. But," (J.R. always had a "but" or two tucked away.) "if things get too hairy out there, we come home. Agreed?" I hid my crossed fingers and promised, "You got it. Okay, Ego, here's the game plan . . ." and I explained. "Just let me do the talking."

That evening the stage was set. After supper, Judith immersed herself in a book, while J.R., in a sincere move of cooperation, gave up his nightly dose of CNN (repeated four times in succession—one of Judith's pet peeves) and watched a Lawrence Welk rerun instead. The mood, soft and relaxed for a change, seemed just right. I nudged him. "Okay, Marine, I've got the podium. Stand by for heavy rolls," and I spoke, the first time ever, directly to Judith. It felt kinky, like I had suddenly been caught up in a weird, bigamous triangle.

"Honey, I'm bored." J.R. cringed, for *that* word was a "no-no" in this house, sure to bring on THE LOOK. I saw its nasty reflection stirring in her eyes and rushed on. "What I meant is, I need a change, like maybe a life-style makeover."

No mercy showed, but then I didn't expect any—yet. She snapped, "Why don't you get a job?"

"Naw. That'd be too *boring*." THE LOOK armed itself, ready for a lightning strike. Chancy! "What I'd really like to do is get out and about more; try some new things."

"Like what, exactly? And don't try to tell me a job would be boring!" J.R. shivered beneath her icy stare.

I tossed the baited hook in the water. "I was thinking about trading the old Skylark in for something with a little more pizzazz."

"Pizzazz? What's wrong with the Skylark?"

"Well, nothing really, except it's getting quite a few miles on the chassis, just like me. I could get one of those little Mazda Miata's. A red convertible, maybe."

Her voice tore through the air like a revved-up chain saw. "I think not!"

I went on, as if she'd never spoken, retrieving the bait slowly, teasingly. "But that would be sooo cool. I could grow a beard, maybe go down to the local bistro and mix it up with the locals."

She nibbled, and her expression gradually changed from hostility to sympathy. I could almost see the psychedelic-colored words flashing on the big screen behind her eyes: "*midlife crisis!*" and hear her thoughts: "Ohmigosh! He's fifty-three. Is it already time for *that*? And that little ditzy blonde a couple of doors down has been making eyes at him!"

I got ready to set the hook. "You know what I might just do? I was talking with a fellow the other day who plans to do a six-month hike from Georgia to Maine on the Appalachian Trail, leaving in a couple of months. Now, *that* might be a lot of fun."

The gears meshed: Midlife crisis with a blonde, or a monastic six-month cooling off period in the woods?

She never had a chance! I let her swallow the bait slowly, painlessly, tastefully, and set the hook. "Of course, when I finished, you would have to come to Maine and get me." A chance to visit New England in the fall, when the leaves peaked with color! She loved to travel.

"Maybe a few weeks in the mountains *would* do you good. You could surely use the exercise." I reeled in the line!

"I'll call David tonight. Oh, by the way, I'm going to need a FEW items for the trip, like a backpack and tent and sleeping bag and . . .", but she didn't seem to hear me. Her eyes had the same faraway gleam that David had gotten!

J.R.: "Damn, Alter-man, but you're good!"

"Yeah, I am. Why don't you go on to bed? Everything's gonna be just fine."

"I think I will—Honey, I'm going to bed. I've got another blasted headache." The poor schmook!

The drizzle started again, more earnest this time, and brought me back to the trail. "Are you ready to roll?" I asked, rising to my feet and flexing muscles that had stiffened into tight rubber bands during the break. "I've got to loosen up. Go on ahead and I'll be along shortly." David nodded and started up the path. Afraid we might get separated, I called, "If I don't catch you by the time you get to that spring at the base of Springer Mountain, wait for me there. It's the one you circled on your map." He gave me a thumbs-up and disappeared around a bend.

I walked slowly, resisting the urge to pick up items that had been discarded along the way by overly ambitious hikers. Among the items David and I had seen since leaving Amicalola Falls: A full gallon can of Coleman fuel; a 16 x 20 foot polytarp—probably eight pounds worth; a full bag of food, enough for at least a week; assorted sweaters and jackets; a pair of boots, slightly used; and the crowning jewel, a six-quart cast iron Dutch oven! David had commented, "The locals must love thru-hikers. I wonder how often they come up here and cart this stuff away?"

I had replied, "Dadgum! I could have outfitted myself if I'd only known. They must do a good business, if this is any indication." After all, it was estimated that about 2000 aspiring thru-hikers would pass this way between early March and May; and, today being the tenth of April, we figured to be somewhere in the middle of the pack.

Silence pressed in, tomblike, alleviated only by the soft padding of my footsteps and the gentle rustle of the drizzle. Hiking by myself wasn't a problem though. David and I had agreed early on that we would not be tied to one another's apron strings. Partners for mutual support and companion-

ship when needed, yes, but not chained together in an unbreakable bond—
like The Ego and me!

A twig snapped behind me. I turned around and stepped to the side so
that "Mr. Eighty-six Pounds" and his buddy, "Mr. Seventy-eight," could get
by. Both huffed and puffed like a steam engine at full throttle. "How you
boys doin'?" I asked.

"Eighty-six," chunky build and no neck, maybe twenty, his tee shirt
sweated and splattered with mud, grunted, "Truckin' on to Maine." His
slight limp and wry grin told me otherwise. "Seventy-eight," a skinny
replica with acne blotches on his face, didn't even try to hide his misery and
growled an epithet that rhymed with "spit."

"Well, ya'll have fun, ya hear," I called as they faded into the mist.
J.R.: "We'll see those two again."

We did, sooner than expected. Within the hour, I passed both hikers.
They had emptied their packs and each was sorting his stuff into two
piles—one to carry, the other to leave for the admiring locals. As I slogged
past, "Eighty-six" called, "Hey mister! Help yerself if you need anything."
They had to be kidding!

"Thanks, fellers, but no thanks. I've already done this drill. See you up
the trail." But I never saw either of them again.

As promised, David waited at the spring, a small crystal pool fed by
seepage from beneath a large rock. The drizzle had stopped, and he sat on
a log in the small, flat clearing, looking rested as he swigged water and
snacked on trail mix. If he hurt anywhere it didn't show, and I felt a twinge
of jealousy because I ached all over; worse, I felt exhausted. One more
mile to Springer Mountain Shelter—home for the night. It would be a long
pull though, all uphill.

David pointed at the northwest sky. "It looks like a storm's heading
this way." His blue-gray eyes showed concern but not fear. During the
weeks we had trained together, I had gotten to know the inner David and
glimpsed the maturity and strength that lurked beneath the facade of his
twenty-five years. David was solid as a rock, a fact that hadn't gone unnoticed by J.R., who had paid David what to his mind was the ultimate compliment: "Damn shame he wasn't a Marine."

I looked up beyond Springer Mountain. The low-hanging, lead-gray
clouds retreated before a billowing cauldron of dark-greenish wrath that
rose above the mountain like a colossal, angry genie and pushed its caustic
sheen our way. Even as we watched, the first rumble rolled across the bleak
forest like a muted kettledrum, ominous, warning of impending disaster,
its hollow echo bouncing between sullen mountaintops and the growing

maelstrom as if it were a helpless pawn. The thunder resonated again, louder this time, and lightning flickered at the horizon's edge.

"Yeah, it's coming on faster'n a freight train," I said, trying to keep the alarm out of my voice. "Think we can beat it?" Suddenly, I felt weak—the afternoon's toil or an adrenalin rush because of the storm? Thinking a sugar boost might help, I reached into the camera pouch on my hip belt and got two "brownies" (Judith's parting gift) and stuffed one in my mouth, chewing hard.

David scratched his head. "Maybe, but it'll be close. We could pitch our tents right here and ride it out, and then hike on up Springer Mountain in the morning."

I crammed the other brownie in my mouth and thought about it: Wet tent to deal with in the morning? Probably. The day was mild, enough so that I had been comfortable hiking in shorts and tee shirt, even with the drizzle. If this beast ushered in a cold front, which it probably did, I'd rather start tomorrow morning from a dry shelter. I glanced at my watch—5:30—and tried to judge the storm's nearness.

David waited for an answer. I swallowed the sticky glob and drained my water bottle. "The shelter looks like the best bet right now. I'm gonna go for it, just as soon's I fill my water bottles." A mile in thirty minutes should be a piece of cake! "How about you?"

"Yeah, sounds good. That storm's a good thirty minutes away. I think we can beat it." He began rummaging through his pack for his rain gear.

The storm rapidly spread its vicious tentacles across the sky—noxious streaks of churning gray that striated the metallic darkness—while in a display of unearthly power, long sheets of flame zigzagged through the malevolent sea and thunderous mayhem rattled the heavens. Without warning, the mountains groaned with the anguish of a thousand hell-bent souls, a devilish keening that sent a chill down my spine. David said, "The wind's picking up."

I shuddered. "Scary." I screwed on the tops and put the bottles in my pack, forcing my hands to make slow, deliberate moves as I sought to repress the rising panic. "I'll put my rain gear on later, if I have to. See you at the shelter." I rushed up the trail, spurred on by the approaching menace. The clock was running!

"Dang, J.R.! Time's running out!" I had been climbing for forty minutes, pushing beyond limits never before tested. My feet dragged like I had on booted anvils, and my chest heaved like a blacksmith's billows, causing me to gasp like a fish flopping on a bank as I tried to satisfy screaming lungs. J.R. said testily, "Pap would say that you're trying to milk the cow's horns instead of the tits. In other words, you don't have the foggiest idea what you're doing." (Pap, J.R.'s paternal granddad, now deceased for five years, had lived a full life as a tobacco farmer in the knobs that edge Kentucky's bluegrass utopia, where he picked up the dubious reputation as a grass roots philosopher—in a crusty sort of way. During J.R.'s childhood, he and Pap had become closer than fish and chips, and the relationship endured until Pap's death.)

I wheezed, "Well, I happen to know which end is which, and I'm NOT squeezing horns. Dang it all, we've got to be near the top."

A brilliant flash, followed by the inevitable explosion, caused me to flinch, putting a halt to our bickering. Immediately, fat drops of rain smelling of dust swept in on the wings of a gust, and the fleeting wet coolness brought bittersweet relief before scudding off the mountain. Then, an eerie quiet fell on the mountain. The calm before the storm!

"We've lost the race," I muttered. Resigned to what would follow next, I shrugged out of my pack and slipped into my rain gear.

Immediately, the storm swept in like a throng of wailing banshees, filling the air with a wild, maniacal howl, which overwhelmed the blinding deluge that fell from the convulsing heavens. "Holy Jesus! We're in for it now!" J.R.'s oath or mine? Impossible to tell in the roar. Whipped into a frenzy by the wind, the cold rain beat against my skin like thousands of vicious, stinging bees. Beneath the rain gear, I felt drenched. Leaky jacket or sweat? Whatever the cause, water soaked my clothing, making a mockery of "protection" and giving new meaning to "miserable." All around, barren trees slashed and swayed like gremlins in a macabre dance of anguished torment as they scourged the storm with leafless limbs, groaning and gyrating in an effort to break their rooted shackles and take flight. J.R.: "Eerie." I: "No, ghostly." My heart raced at the bizarre performance and I pushed on.

Thoughts filled my head, competing with the chaos: Where is David? If I hear the thunder, then the lightning missed! Do rubber boot soles act as insulators? How many of these (storms) will I encounter between here and Maine? And the big one—is my sleeping bag still dry? (At least I'd had enough sense to wrap it in a plastic garbage bag!)

A tremendous explosion directly overhead—the worst yet—and I went to my knees. Accident or Act of God? I said a quick "Our Father" while I was down, and then skittered up the trail. After a few panicky steps, the spurt dwindled and became the wheezing shuffle of a hundred year-old man and I thought, "Tits or horns? Maybe J.R. is right. Maybe I have dug a hole far deeper than I can climb out of."

Frustrated and desperate to escape the beating, I yelled into the storm, "Dammit! I need a miracle! Where's the top?" The trees, seeming to ridicule my outburst, flailed me with their branches. The Marine said, "Suck it up, Alter-man. This is no place to tarry. We have to go on." I gritted my teeth. "Yeah, we've got to get off this mountain," and I took a few steps—counting off five, gasping a few times, counting off five more, over and over, too exhausted now to duck the lightning jolts.

Suddenly the storm pitched me against a tree, almost throwing me to the ground as it clawed and grabbed, shoved and buffeted, slashed and kicked with a show of force beyond anything I had ever known. I wrestled to regain my balance and tried to push against the fierce flow, but I had nothing left to give. It had all been squandered on the futile race to beat the storm. Beyond caring, I wobbled like an unbalanced high wire performer and thought dully, "What next?"

The Ego's snarl penetrated my zombie-like state. "How long are you going to stand here enjoying the view, Ace? We've reached the summit. And for gosh sake, quit your gibberish. You're slobbering like a mad dog."

Had I been jabbering nonsense? A horrendous explosion brought me to my senses, and I resumed the wheezing, tottering walk toward the next blue blaze, now dulled to a hazy gray by the torrent.

"There's the mailbox," J.R. said, breaking through my misery. A few yards ahead, barely visible in the sheeting rain, a dented white mailbox tilted atop a weathered post. Exhaustion momentarily gave way to euphoria and I squawked, "Dang, J.R.! The Appalachian Trail and the first white blaze! We made it, man!"

I tried to dance a little jig but my legs refused to participate, so I slapped the mailbox a good lick and immediately wished I could take it back; after all, the battered talisman looked as if it had suffered enough already. If only David were here to share the moment!

Where was he? I peered into the storm, straining, hoping to catch a glimpse of him striding through the downpour. I yelled, "David!" and then again, "David, you out there?" but the wind muffled my cries and threw the words back. Where had that boy got off to?

The disappointment brought on a quandary: To sign the hiker register supposedly tucked inside the mailbox, or run for the shelter, still a few hundred yards down the other side of the summit? J.R. purred, enticing and smooth as Eve's snake, "Do it now, and then you won't have to come back in the morning. David wouldn't let a little rain stop him." Ha! A little rain! The storm raged like a fighting tiger! Impulsively, I said, "Okay, Ego. This'll be for posterity, so that all who come after us will know that the Model-T is on the Trail!"

Another quandary: What to write? Certainly, something profound; some catchy, mind-warping phrases to embellish my leap toward fame; words that would serve as a beacon to others who would follow! Thinking hard, I reached for the register. At my touch, the heavens exploded in a gigantic convulsion of flame and deafening noise—an omen from the Almighty? The mountaintop seemed to groan in protest as smoke and the acrid smell of ozone rushed in on the heels of the nearby strike. I jerked my hand away, the register forgotten. (Had I touched holy ground without permission?) I scrambled over to a large tree and hunkered down to wait for David.

Terrified, I buffered the storm with my pack as best I could. J.R. said tersely, "Damnation! Who did you piss off Up There?" Trembling, I squeaked, "That tree sacrificed itself for us! That strike was meant for US!" The Marine retorted, "A worthy sacrifice. Darn shame trees don't qualify for medals." I took several deep breaths and tried to get a handle on my runaway heart, cringing and flinching at each explosion. The Marine, exhilarated, bellowed, "It's just like being back in Th' Nam (South Vietnam)!" I, wondering if I had peed in my shorts, countered, "You're nuts!"

A blurred movement caught my eye and I blinked away the water. David wavered above me like an apparition, yelling and pointing up the Trail, but I couldn't make out what he said because of the roar. He yelled again, this time into my ear, "Let's get to the shelter! Sign the register in the morning!" Relieved, I nodded and followed him through the swirling, gusting fury of crazed elements and trees gone mad.

We hadn't gotten far when the storm suddenly slackened, seeming to lose interest, and relinquished its hold on the mountain as it moved off to the southeast, leaving in its stead a skinny drizzle and dripping trees, and a water-logged world. The storm's legacy oozed out of my hair, down through my beard, and seeped into my mouth—a sweat-brine taste that reminded me of oysters on the half shell and kept me constantly flicking my tongue across my lips for more. The Trail gushed like a mountain brook and tried to force its liquid cargo into my boots—long since filled to the tops. As we went, our footsteps added their "squishy-sloppy" sounds to the "tap-splat" noise of the forest.

An unsettling thought occurred: What if the shelter was full? I grimaced at the thought of putting up a tent in the rain, especially with exhaustion weighing so heavily. What if there wasn't anyplace to pitch a tent? What if we had to slog through this mess to the next shelter, another two and a half miles? Darkness was coming on fast! J.R. cut through my anxiety: "Enough of the 'what if's'. What if dogs rooted and hogs barked and cats laid eggs? Nothing ever came from 'what if's'." Another of Pap's crusty insights?

Concentrating on a suitable comeback to J.R., while at the same time keeping my eyes on the slippery path, I ran smack into David, who had abruptly stopped. "Jeez, I'm sorry!"

My apology went unnoticed. "There! See it?" He pointed at a blue blaze beneath a small, white sign cut into the shape of an arrow with the magic word, "Shelter." "We're almost home!"

This shelter, like most of the others, was a three-sided structure with the front opened to Nature, and was built to sleep six hikers on its elevated plank floor. Even with the tin roof (hopefully intact!) and brown clapboard walls, no motel had ever looked sweeter! Drenched and shivering now—the temperature was fast dropping—David and I walked across the small clearing through the rain-tarnished twilight to the open front and peered inside.

Four hikers, already cocooned in sleeping bags for the night and somehow resembling over-sized gnomes, stared at us. Eerily, their faces seemed to float like unattached whitish ovals out of the shadowy recess of the back wall. Wet clothing hung from every nail and peg, and scattered gear covered each inch of unused floor space. Alarmingly, at first glance the shelter seemed full. David's eyes spoke, and I nodded: Room for two more. Only, we had to claim it!

During our tenuous relationship, I had learned a thing or two from The Marine, and now it paid off. I counted, pointing at each cocoon: "One, two, three, four. Hot dang, David, there's room! Howdy folks. I'm Model-T. Y'all thru-hikers?" A confused nod from one of the white blobs. "So are we. Heck of a storm, wasn't it? Glad there's still room for two late arrivals. Which side do you want, David?" The words tumbled out in a rush, sizzling the silence. ("Marines always attack! Marines *never* retreat!" J.R. always said, but I suppose that excluded THE LOOK.)

David grinned at the brazen effrontery, but the blobs slowly attached to necks and became faces as the gnomes unzipped sleeping bags and began to put in order the chaos they had created.

After quick thanks and short introductions, we peeled off soggy clothes, trusting the dark to preserve a thimbleful of modesty, and pulled on long johns, which had suffered only slight dampness in spite of the storm's malicious intent. The deep dusk made it difficult to see, and we felt and whispered our way through this first supper, quickly eating sandwiches and chips, courtesy of Judith, and then hanging our food bags from the rafter.

I crawled into the warm snugness of a world better understood—amazingly, still dry—and whispered, "See you in the morning. "Heck of a way to start the Trail, huh?"

"Yeah, interesting. Tomorrow it begins!" David's voice was charged with a full measure of Scottish genes roiling just below the boiling point with excitement. The exuberance of youth!

"Yeah," I grunted, trying to sound enthusiastic through the hodge-podge sludge of aches and uncertainty. "Tomorrow." But my thoughts revolved around a long-horned cow with low-hanging teats.

I lay awake, staring into the darkness, listening to the soft cadence of rain on the tin roof and the distant sound of thunder, by now far off to the southeast. Night noises and strange surroundings kept sleep at bay. Some-where close by, the patter of a busy mouse merged with the drizzly rooftop symphony as the wily creature began a night of foraging in some careless hiker's food bag—a hard lesson soon to be learned by the light of day. I relaxed, for David and I had already attended *that* class, and our bags dan-gled in safety beneath tuna-can mouse guards.

David, next to me, slept peacefully, his breathing deep and steady like a comforting salve. Outside the shelter, a night varmint rattled metal against a rock—a skunk? Would the night noises, now so alien, become part of the evening serenade, soothing and consoling, a sleep potion? Now, each scratch, each scurrying noise became something going "bump in the night." Until I made friends with the darkness, each unknown sound would cause the pulse to spurt and the adrenalin to flow, would conjure up images of monsters lurking beneath the shelter or just out of sight in the trees.

J.R. snorted, "Childhood fantasies. Monsters under the bed. Boogey man in the closet. Get a grip." I thought he had gone to sleep.

"Yeah, you're right." I covered my head to get away from the night spooks and told myself, "I'll shake hands with the dark another time."

Daylight pushed through the small opening of my sleeping bag, driving a wedge into my brain. Momentarily confused, I waited for the fatigue-induced stupor to dissipate and then rubbed the sleep-gremlins from my eyes. Wincing at the pain—yesterday's payback—I slowly poked my head out and nearly fainted! The woods sparkled and shimmered with fiery glit-ter, both beautiful and terrifying in one anxious rush. Uninvited, the word "ICE!" exploded in my head and escaped out of my mouth, cleaving the early morning silence like a butcher's knife. "Dang, J.R., when it rains, it pours! Boy! Are the others gonna be surprised when they wake up." Fully awake now, I unzipped my bag and scooted to the edge of the shelter for a closer look, keen to see if the ice posed a threat to hiking. J.R. snickered, "You'd better think about getting glasses, Alter-man." Feeling foolish, I realized the glittering beauty came from infinite reflections of the early morning rays on rain-cloaked branches—Nature's penance for yesterday's tantrum! I breathed an immense sigh of relief!

My eyes flicked around the shelter. Last night's gnomes, now transformed into people through the magic of daylight, lay side by side like giant cocoons awaiting metamorphosis. One of the bags stirred, tried to roll over, and then gave up with a stifled moan. I slowly stood up, careful of the tight muscles as I checked for damage and inwardly groaned away the soreness. A tingle of excitement smothered the pain as I glanced at my watch. "Holy cow! It's almost eight o'clock! We've got to get out of here, J.R., or we'll never get to Maine."

Beside me, David's soft, muffled snores floated out of a tiny hole in his bag. I gave him a gentle shake and whispered, "David, it's eight o'clock. We need to get moving." No response . . . I shook again, harder this time. "Katahdin's waiting for us."

That must have punched the right button, because the easy seesawing stopped and his head emerged, the red hair tousled like a red clover haymow, and a huge grin twisted his face with anticipation. "Yeah, let's do it!" he blurted, his voice filled with excitement and purpose.

Smells of breakfast—grits for me and oatmeal for David—slowly brought the others to life. One by one, amid groans, protests, and a few epithets, they came awake. A boyish face timidly appeared out of the sleeping bag to my right and sniffed the air. "Yum. Smells good," he said, puffing up into a mammoth stretch and running his hands through short, blondish-brown hair. He held out his hand. "Hi. My name's Volunteer, and I'm from Tennessee." His eyes glistened with pride, as shiny as the watery reflection of the nearby trees, as he added, "I just graduated from the University of Tennessee at Knoxville." He seemed pretty young—or maybe J.R. was getting old. (Myself, I'm perennial!)

Down the row of bags, just beyond David at my left, a gray-haired man, on the short side of seventy, smiled and said, "I'm Bill, no trail name, and the one with her head still covered up is my wife, Celia."

He shook her bag and got a grouchy, "What time is it?" for his effort. Bill jerked his hand back like he had touched a red-hot stove, which caused me to wonder if Celia had long ago "conditioned" him with THE LOOK. J.R. shuddering: "Of course she has. Just look at his eyes, all panicky, ready to hightail it out of here."

J.R. should know! (In fact, he and I had often discussed THE LOOK and had finally arrived at the conclusion that this curse on mankind was all

Eve's fault. Our irrefutable logic: When Eve offered Adam the "apple" and he refused, telling her it was nothing but big trouble, she must have instinctively zapped him with THE LOOK, causing him to wimp out and eat the blasted thing, which gave her a taste of raw power! At that moment, we figured, THE LOOK must have taken up residence in women's genes, reproducing itself down through the ages, generation to generation, mother to daughter, lurking hidden until the last ding-dong of the wedding bells, eager to leap forth at its master's slightest call to make another poor sap's life miserable—at least that was the conclusion we reached.)

Yeah, Ol' Bill knew about THE LOOK all right! He started to shake her again but thought better of it. A wise man, him, not unleashing THE LOOK inside the shelter, and I sent him a nod of thanks sprinkled with sympathy.

Bill continued, "We're from Texas and believe it or not, we've not done any hiking before, except for the mile we did yesterday." (They must have driven up the Forest Service Road and walked back here to the terminus.) "Celia and I read about the Appalachian Trail in the National Geographic a few years back, and we decided right then to hike it some day. I recently retired, so we decided to do a thru-hike, sort of on a whim I suppose." He glanced at Celia's immobile form and said, "Yesterday wasn't too bad. Heck, it couldn't be all that difficult." (I knew right then I was looking at "trail fodder.") Bill went on, speaking with the authority of a seasoned hiker, "We even set everything up in our back yard and it all worked fine."

I barely managed to hold back the rib-cracking horselaugh that convulsed my innards. He would get his reality check soon enough. (Plus it was *their* thru-hike—no business of mine.) I sneaked a glance at David. One small pinprick and he would have exploded!

The hiker against the far wall, next to Celia, finally woke up, scratched deeply into his large mass of scraggly brown hair, and then raked his hand down a decrepit ponytail, ending at the rubber band that kept the act together. Finished with that part of his morning ritual, he turned and smiled broadly. I guessed his age at somewhere between twenty and forty. "Hi guys. My name's Hippy Man. I'm from Pennsylvania." He said it with an odd touch of apology (or perhaps it was his Yankee accent falling on southern ears). A full-size guitar hung from a nail above his head.

"Yours?" I queried.

"Yep." As though he were reading my thoughts, he added, "I'm gonna play it all the way to Maine." Sure he was—NOT! David shook his head in disbelief, and I guessed the guitar would be history well before Hippy Man got to Damascus (Virginia), 452 miles up the Trail.

David and I finished breakfast, packed, and headed back up to Springer's summit to complete yesterday afternoon's unfinished business. The early sun had finally given way to a band of high clouds after a futile struggle to dominate the sky, and the morning quickly chilled, aided by a cutting north wind. My pack thermometer read a mere 32 degrees—yesterday afternoon's whopper had become today's cold front.

The mailbox, still tilted, had weathered the storm, as undoubtedly it had many others. I reached inside for the register and asked David, "Have you decided on a trail name yet?"

I had been after him for weeks to pick one, since trail names had become a tradition over the past couple of decades. Mine had come easy, and I now wore it like an old, comfortable jacket. (A friend, exasperated at my slow pace on a day hike, had muttered to another hiker, "He's as slow as an old Model T." I couldn't help but overhear, but I let it slide and took it as a compliment. After all, those old Model T's were slow, steady, seldom broke down, and were easily repaired—a perfect comparison—and I told J.R., "We've got a trail name!") One thing I knew for certain: If David didn't pick a trail name, the Trail family would give him one, and it might not be complimentary. I surely didn't want to have a hiking partner called "Stinky Feet" or "Barf Bucket"!

"Maybe," David replied hesitantly. "I'm not sure yet. I'll just see how it plays. What are you going to write?" he asked, peering over my shoulder.

J.R. piped up. "Yeah, what?" Good question! Pen poised between numb fingers, I shivered from the wind's bite and waited for lofty adjectives and profound words to flow from my fingers onto the waiting lines. It had all seemed so simple yesterday, in spite of the storm's punch. Today, with the moment at hand, my brain seemed as slow as cold molasses and nothing flowed. Feeling like an idiot, I slowly scrawled, "Model-T, Northbound to Katahdin," meekly passed the pen to David, and then backed away before he could comment on my creativity. However, The Ego couldn't pass up the opportunity: "Wow, Scriptus, that's deep. Ed Garvey will probably want to use it."

(J.R.'s snide comment referred to a well-known trail personality who, at age 55, had completed a thru-hike in 1970, becoming one of six—out of the ten who started—to finish that year. Subsequently, Ed had written *Appalachian Hiker: Adventure of a Lifetime*, which became a reference for aspiring thru-hikers, including David and me. Word had filtered through the hiking community that Ed planned a twentieth anniversary thru-hike starting April thirteenth, three days hence. Ed was a role model, and I hoped to meet him somewhere on the Trail.)

David scribbled in the register and finished his entry by snarling, "Rats! I messed that up." However, I was stomping around like an Indian on the warpath, trying to bring some feeling back into my numbed extremities and didn't bother to ask him what he had "messed up."

Volunteer strode up the path whistling a bouncy tune, his face aglow as his breath stroked the air like a puffing calliope. David handed him the register. He gave our entries a cursory once over, added his own brief commentary, and then the three of us walked to a nearby bronze plaque—the official marker for the southern terminus of the Trail and guardian of the *first* of countless white blazes—the 2x6 inch rectangles that blaze the path for thru-hikers on the long trek to Katahdin. (The plaque, dated 1934, depicts a vintage 1930's hiker walking toward his destiny.)

Volunteer read the inscription aloud: "A Footpath for Those who seek Fellowship with the Wilderness." The words, stilted and hollow, fluttered away with the stiff breeze. Would our dreams falter among the mountains and go the same way?

We took pictures to freeze (literally) our likenesses at this hallowed shrine, slapped one another on the back a few times, vowing to be one of the "one in ten" who would finish the entire Trail during the next six months to claim the title, "thru-hiker." Hyped up, we beat a hasty retreat back to the shelter to collect our equipment. Mount Katahdin was waiting!

Things had heated up when we returned to the shelter. Bill fiddled with his gear, sneaking furtive glances at Celia's back as he implored her to rise and face the day. So far, he had managed to get her head out of the goose-down bag, and he now coaxed her to go "all the way" with a cup of steaming chocolate. It didn't work.

Hippy Man, oblivious to the withering daggers Celia cast at poor Bill—any married man could tell that Hippy Man had never been snared—happily hummed a hard rock medley and crammed things in his pack as he got ready to rock-and-roll his way to Katahdin with the help of his trusted sidekick, El Senor Guitar.

Bill upped the ante with a pop tart, which brought Celia to the sitting position. J.R., the voice of experience, snickered, "It's going to take a lot more than bribes to scoot her out into the cold." No bet! Besides, from what I'd already seen, these two were definitely trying to milk horns!

I sneaked a glance at their gear: They had brand name equipment, state of the art stuff that I would have gladly swapped J.R. for. Bill whined, "Celia Honey, the day's wasting." The imperious, immovable Celia refused to be pressured and turned THE LOOK on full power, which caused poor Bill to sullenly retreat to the far wall of the shelter, a

befuddled, helpless expression on his face, beaten before the first steps
had been taken.

Shortly, another crisis developed. Señor Guitar refused to cooperate.
No matter what position Hippy Man tied the guitar, it managed to end up
as an ungainly hump on the humongous pack—nearly half again as large
as mine. Watching him struggle, I revised my estimate: El Señor would be
off the Trail before Fontana Dam, a mere 164 miles away.

David and Volunteer stood outside the shelter with packs on and
watched the antics. David said, "Are you ready to leave?"

I whispered, "Naw. This is the best show I've seen in ages. I'll catch
up with you guys later," and watched them walk away.

Abruptly, Hippy Man exploded. "Bastard!" Totally losing it, he
snorted like an angry bull, stomped the floor, and spit out a string of expletives as he began flinging gear from his pack. Most ended up on the
ground, but a few items landed on Celia, who had again snuggled down
inside her bag and turned her back to the world. Bill and I caught our
breaths, half expecting the bag to explode and THE LOOK to spring forth
and make mush out of Hippy Man, but nothing happened. I exhaled loudly
and Bill murmured, "That boy leads a charmed life."

That part of his plan finished, Hippy Man frowned and further vented
his frustration with a swift kick at the now-empty pack. As if nothing had
happened, he smiled benignly at his audience of two and started all over. I
pointed at El Señor and asked Hippy Man, "Have you ever thought about
taking up the harmonica?"

He laughed. "I almost took up bass fiddle. Wouldn't that be a trick?"

J.R. fretted, "C'mon Alter, let's go. This could be an all-day event." Or
longer!

I went over and shook the beaten man's hand. "Good luck, 'Bill-on-a-
whim'," I told him, and I truly meant it! "See you up the Trail."

As I hurried after David and Volunteer, J.R. snickered, "What's the
rush? If we don't catch them, we can always team up with Bill and Celia."
I: "That'll be the day!"

At the Trail intersection, I gazed at the "Footpath of Fellowship" and
felt the excitement build. "J.R., this is a momentous occasion! Do you want
to say anything?" I played it big. "We are a footstep away from the greatest
journey of our lives, a commitment of six months and over 2100-plus miles
of pure adventure. Once we start, there will be no turning back. This
moment deserves a fitting commemoration to mark the occasion, something to aggrandize the Trail and make this a day to remember."

The Marine offered, "How about we sing, 'From the Halls of Montezuma'?" I grimaced, "Naw, it's not the Marine Corps Birthday. We need something more akin to Nature, like a little of Walt Whitman's A Song of the Open Road? That would be neat." (J.R. had to memorize the whole poem in the fifth grade but had forgotten most of it.) "Sure," he replied with as much enthusiasm as a muddy dog about to get a bath, "anything that heats your woolies." Feeling more than a little foolish, I sneaked a quick look around to make sure no one was watching, and then I shouted in a loud voice: "Afoot and lighthearted, I take to the open road. Healthy, free, the world before me; the long, brown path before me leading wherever I choose." (That was the extent of J.R.'s retention, but it was enough.) The mountains seemed to swell with pride; the trees silently applauded; and I took a bow.

I hesitated. "One more thing to do, Ol' Buddy," and I performed a final ritual by picking a small pebble from the muddy path to carry to Katahdin's summit, carefully tucking it away inside my camera pouch. "Maybe we'd better have a back up, too," I told J.R., grabbing another pebble, this one even smaller, explaining, "It's a long way to Katahdin."

Satisfied, I let my soul electrify with excitement, squared my shoulders, and took the first steps toward Maine—and the unknown. Life couldn't have been more wonderful!

Ten minutes into the journey, Hippy Man breezed past in a frenzied rush, the guitar now a docile passenger bobbing up and down in vigorous rhythm with its master's powerful stride. A brief twitch of his lips substituted for a smile. He scooted past, chirping, "Gotta make some miles; gotta eat some trail! Gonna do twenty miles today!" And then he bounded out of sight, a hare streaking for a distant finish line. I shook my head. "The poor guy. Everyone knows the tortoise won the race. We'll see him again."

Thirty minutes (and one mile) later, I crossed gravelly USFS Road 42, where it intersects the Trail at Big Stamp Gap, and halted in the middle of the road, swiped at the sweat that streamed down my face, and cursed the 52 pounds on my back. Chuckling wryly, I told The Marine, "One mile down. Only 2142 left." The Marine: "I don't find that amusing at all."

I caught up with David at Stover Creek Shelter, a replica of the shelter on Springer Mountain, after just two and a half miles. The sun, launching a major offensive against the clouds, had at last broken free, giving the day warmth and turning the wind into an ally. David dawdled at a warped picnic table just outside the shelter, soaking up the sun's rays while he munched on trail mix and thumbed through a soiled, somewhat mutilated spiral notebook that served as the shelter register. He had spread his sleeping bag and skimpy foam sleep pad across some rhododendron bushes in a sunny spot beside the shelter to dry. The pad, I noticed, had long ago given up its status as an item of comfort; now thin as new ice, it only paid lip service to usefulness.

David glanced up at the sound of my footsteps. Shading his eyes against the sun's brightness, he said, "I wondered if you'd make it this far for lunch."

I looked at my watch: 12:05. "Jeez, this was a fast morning. I'm not all that hungry, but maybe I'd better get started on this ramen just as soon as I lay my gear out to dry. Thanks to my friend, The Singing Horseman, I could open a thriving ramen supermarket!" David knew the story behind the ramen and smiled wryly at my dilemma.

I first met the Singing Horseman—a literal translation of his Italian name, for he neither sang nor rode, as far as I knew—in 1989 when I happened on a group of thru-hikers north of the James River (Virginia). I had managed to drag J.R. off his couch by convincing him that a hundred miles of backpacking would help him in his battle against the small but persistent paunch that threatened to take up permanent residence below his beltline. J.R., on discovering that Horseman was a retired Air Force officer, immediately engaged in the inevitable friendly inter-service rivalry that seems to naturally come into play when two people from different services meet. In the two weeks that Horseman and I/J.R. hiked together, we became close friends.

The Singing Horseman was well known on the Trail. Brandishing a heavy load of Italian genes, he reminded me of Marlon Brando trying to portray The Godfather; on the other hand, he could as easily have been a bedraggled, barrel-chested, well-fed opera singer. Short, broad (in both dimensions!), gregarious and out-going, sporting a thick, dark, matted carpet of chest hair (always visible through the deep V-necked shirt he continually wore), he snacked on dry ramen as he hiked—mile after mile, day after day, until he finally munched his way to Katahdin. As he munched the miles away—a modern day Hansel leaving a trace in the wilderness for others to follow—ramen crumbs would fall like tiny flakes of snow onto the Trail and into the black forest on his chest, sprinkling the dark hair with patches of white. And each evening, a grateful mouse population would descend from the shelter rafters to feast on the bountiful manna while

Horseman blissfully slept. When we hikers shared a shelter with Horseman, we never worried about our food bags—the mice had far easier pickings!

After Judith had given her blessing to the thru-hike, I called Horseman. "I'm going to do it! I'm leaving on April 10ᵗʰ!"

Horseman: "Great! Tell you what, I'm going to send you my data book (*Appalachian Trail Data Book-1989*) with all the notes I made on my trip, like where the hard climbs and water sources are, plus some info that really helped me get ready for the hike. But the best advice I can give you, the thing that carried me through, is to eat three packs of ramen every day. Eat it dry while you walk, and then drink the seasoning packets in the evening to put salt back in your system."

He lost me. After a doubtful silence I asked, "Did I understand you to say *three* packs a day? *every day?*" He had to be joking. Nobody could eat *that* much ramen.

"Yeah, three packs. If you don't get it all down while you're hiking, eat the rest as an after-dinner snack." He was absolutely serious!

"Uh, okay, if you say so." After we hung up, J.R. growled, "That guy's been in the woods too long, or else the Air Force addled his brain." Horseman's "three-pack advice" lingered like a bad taste: Trying to convince myself, I retorted, "Possibly. But just remember, he did make it all the way. That was the voice of experience talking!"

"Where's Volunteer?" I asked as I draped my inflatable Therm-a-Rest—a healthy piece of work compared to the pitiful thing David slept on—and sleeping bag over some bushes.

"He went on ahead. Said he wanted to eat lunch at the Falls." (Long Creek Falls was another 2.5 miles up the Trail.) "You know how kids are."

I chuckled, and then determined to follow Horseman's advice, I opened the first pack of ramen and bit off a hunk. The dry noodles crunched between my teeth like crushed Styrofoam, gritty and tasteless. I smiled bravely at David's screwy look, (which reminded J.R. of the time his Granny, Pap's feisty, diminutive wife, gave him a healthy dose of castor oil for an unknown stomach ailment). J.R. launched a string of expletives to let me know what he thought of Horseman and ramen in general. "Needs some lubrication," I said, reaching for the peanut butter. The next bite turned into a gooey glob and caught in my throat. I barely averted a gagging catastrophe by pushing it down into the bottomless pit with a huge gulp of water. Blinking back tears, I said, "Darn! I guess it's an acquired taste, like dipping snuff."

J.R., with admiration: "Damnation, Horseman must be one tough hombre if he can stomach this cardboard! He shoulda been a Marine!"

David: "Man! You've got a cast iron stomach! How can you eat that stuff?"

I: "You don't know the half of it," thinking of the other eleven packs of ramen in my food bag, plus the twenty-four waiting at Neels Gap, plus the twenty-one that Judith would soon mail to Fontana Dam Village for the trek through the Smokies—ad infinitum . . . Three packs times 180 days— 540 packs of the accursed stuff between Springer and Katahdin! Dang! My teeth would be ground down to nubs by the time I finished the trip! I sighed wearily and said, "David, it's gotta be an Italian thing."

"Here," he said, handing me the register, "take a look at this." He nearly gagged as I attempted to push another glob down."

I set Horseman's curse aside for the time being, determined to try again later, and flipped backwards through the scribbled pages. The earliest entry had been made on the first day of January—weekenders enjoying the backwoods in twelve inches of snow. "Some hardy souls out roaming the Blue Ridge," I mused, wondering what it must be like to pit oneself against winter in these mountains. J.R. piped up, "I'd say 'stupid souls'—like us." I ignored him and turned the pages back to more recent entries, hoping to get a feel for who was immediately ahead of us. Time wise, we figured we were close to the middle of the thru-hiker pack, but there didn't seem to be all that many entries before today.

The register reflected the world of hikers. Their woes, hopes, anger, pain, frustration, philosophical views, attempts at levity, praises to Nature, curses against Nature; all had been recorded, forming an ex officio history of the Trail.

The latest entry, dated today, had been signed, "Wahoola." "Who's Wahoola?" I asked, for as far as I knew, no one by that name had signed the register back on Springer Mountain.

"That's me," David said, a sheepish smile slowly breaking across his face, more embarrassed than proud.

Delighted, I slapped his back and shook his hand, as if he'd just announced the birth of a baby boy—which in a way he had—rejoicing that his dilemma had finally been solved and that we no longer had to wade through this briar patch. Then the name overtook my excitement and I asked, "What's a 'Wahoola' anyway?"

"You remember that pretty creek we crossed yesterday after we left the Interstate? The one before Dahlonega, on the way to Amicalola Falls?"

I nodded, conjuring up an image of the rippling, rocky stream, well on the way to becoming a river as it rushed toward the ocean.

"The name sort of jumped out at me, the Yahoola River. I liked the sound of it, so I decided to take it for my trail name." A blush flamed his cheeks and he chuckled, "But this morning when I signed the register, I got excited and wrote 'Wahoola.' So I guess that's going to be my trail name."

"I like it." But I couldn't help wondering if, as with J.R. and me, an alter ego had spawned in David's noggin!

The day remained pleasantly warm, and Wahoola (aka David) and I hiked together along Stover Creek, today only listless and in no hurry to go anywhere. Soon we entered a towering cathedral of virgin hemlocks and became as dwarfs in the presence of mighty, ancient titans. Here and there, brilliant lasers streamed down though holes in the high canopy and formed patterns on the forest floor that faded into the dark, shadowy limits of our vision and bespoke of things hidden and mysterious. Awed by beauty far removed from the artist's brush, we talked in hushed tones and reveled in the moment.

Long Creek Falls, fat from yesterday's storm, tumbled down the mountainside in a stairway of descending cascades. Each miniature cataract tossed its own aura of shimmering, misting colors into the air, sparkling like small dancing rainbows as the stream frantically shot over the ledges and, roaring louder than a dozen lions, plunged into a maelstrom of frothy white and spritzed the air with mist.

Volunteer sat on a large rock just beyond the reach of the spray and dangled his feet in a smaller pool while he flipped small sticks, one at a time, into the current. He watched the stick-boat swirl around the eddy and immediately launched a replacement when the stout current captured the small craft and swept it out of sight. J.R. said, "He reminds me of a little boy playing in a large puddle of water after a thunderstorm." I chuckled, "It looks like fun."

Wahoola tapped his shoulder and yelled above the din, "Are you having a good time?"

Startled, Volunteer turned around, wide-eyed, almost slipping off the rock, and blurted, "Cripes! I thought you were a bear!" He flashed us a guilty look, like a youngster caught with his hand in the forbidden cookie jar, blushed furiously beneath the beginnings of trail grime, and then wiped the slate clean with a boyish grin and a shout of glee. "I'm busted! You all want to play, too?" Without waiting for a reply, he scooted over to make room.

Wahoola and I gathered our own fleet of ships and then removed our boots and dangled our feet in the refreshing cold torrent. Three grown kids, we frittered away the afternoon, putting Katahdin on hold for a few hours as we launched ships and shouted encouragement at our entries, hoping for the honor of having the first competitor in each race to cross the imaginary finish line before floating out of sight. The Marine grumbled, "Those sticks are making a lot better time than we are." I replied, "What's the hurry? Katahdin's not going anywhere."

Late in the afternoon, our feet now unshriveled by three miles of hiking, we climbed a sloping ridge high on a mountain crest. The sun seemed to swell into a gigantic red orb that momentarily rested on the earth's shoulders as it prepared for its nightly plunge into darkness. Wahoola, in the lead, paused. "It's going to be dark soon. We'd better start looking for a spot." Hawk Mountain Shelter, two miles back, had been clogged with members of an outdoor club, and the next shelter, Gooch Gap, was six miles away—far beyond my reach, for the day's effort lay on me like tainted meat.

"Yeah, it's been a 'long-short' day," I said. We had come a whopping ten miles today, about what we had planned to average these first three days to Neels Gap. "No need to get into tomorrow's mileage." Volunteer seemed relieved.

The slope gradually broadened into a thinly wooded plateau, fairly level and blemished with enough small openings to accommodate a company of Marines. "How about this?" I asked, heading for the nearest spot, not waiting to see if the others followed. "Pick your partners, gents. Plenty to go around."

Wahoola and I, old pros after several practice weekends, had the routine down pat: Tents up first, and then string a clothesline; off with the wet and on with the dry; cook; eat; clean up; hang food bag; relax and enjoy the night; all as smooth as a greased axle. Volunteer followed our lead, watching closely, emulating our prowess, but he hadn't attended the University of Nature, so Wahoola and I had the mac-n-cheese boiling by the time he finished putting up his tent.

Mac-n-cheese is a thru-hiker's dream: Inexpensive, lightweight, loaded with calories, a no-brainer (if you could boil water!), and versatile—it mixed well with all kinds of tasty things, like canned tuna, Vienna sausage (and probably grubs, if one fell on really hard times!). Wahoola and I carried a cheap generic brand, five for a dollar, and truth be known, not being a connoisseur, all mac-n-cheese was pretty much the same— cheap calories in a box.

As was ramen! Guilt nagged at me as I slurped soupy mac-n-cheese. (I hadn't yet quite mastered the water proportion.) Now and then my eyes strayed to the food bag where the uneaten part of ramen pack number one, plus packs two and three—this day's quota—awaited their fate, along with the other nine packs. Seeking an easy way out, I asked Volunteer, "You eat ramen?"

"Not if I can help it. I had enough of that stuff in college. Why?" To prove his point, he held up a box of classy mac-n-cheese and grinned, which led me to believe that boy had discriminating taste buds!

"No reason, just curious." Dang Horseman and his cursed ramen! Maybe a bear would wander into camp during the night and carry it off if I made things easy.

We joked and bantered our way through the meal, rehashing the day's highlights, spinning yarns, falling into an easy pattern of camaraderie. Had Hippy Man made his twenty miles? Had Bill and Celia made two? Would we make ten again tomorrow?

The day cooled rapidly as the shadows deepened, but not having a water source nearby and no way to put a fire out if the wind got up, we decided against a campfire. A noise down the Trail, and a scout troop, maybe twenty teens with a sprinkling of adults, filed past us, a mélange of exuberance at the front and desperation of the damned at the rear. We returned their half-hearted waves with jubilant calls of encouragement.

The talk turned serious. Curious, I inquired, "Volunteer, what are you going to do after the Trail?"

He shrugged. "I don't know. What I would really like to do is become a Marine aviator. I applied for the flight program last fall but got turned down."

J.R.'s attention immediately peaked. "If you please," he requested, so I yielded the podium. "It's the Corps' loss," The Marine said. "Why don't you reapply after the hike? Sometimes a yearly quota gets filled, but the next year it could be wide open. The Corps is always looking for a few good men, and I'll be glad to write you a glowing letter of recommendation. By the way, are you married?"

The old goat! He had just been waiting for an opening! (His and Judith's daughter, Alyson, 20 and unmarried, still lived at home while she attended college. J.R. had become obsessed with the search for a fitting son-in-law—someone who didn't eat at the table with a baseball cap on; preferably a person who knew the difference between "ain't" and "isn't"; and (tossing me a crumb), someone who enjoyed hiking. He had already tried to work up a match between Wahoola and Alyson, but the veteran sidestepper easily skirted the scheme.)

Wahoola immediately caught the drift and choked on a fit of coughing. I turned off J.R.'s microphone before he could mess up a good thing, quickly adding, "Not that it matters."

Volunteer looking confused, gave Wahoola a strange look. "No, but I'm engaged." Bummer! He would have made a fine prospect. "Thanks for the offer. I'll think about it."

The night chill nipped through my jacket. Beyond our clearing, maybe a couple of hundred yards up the Trail, the dim glow of a large campfire softened the dark, and the shouts and laughter of youngsters, now rejuvenated, floated over the forest on gentle, fair weather zephyrs. I got up and stretched. "Enough excitement for the first day. I need my beauty sleep. See you in the morning." Glancing at a sudden shower of sparks that rose above the trees and quickly faded into the blackness, I snorted, "Or sooner, if the woods catch on fire!"

Several yards from my tent, I hung a plastic grocery bag—recently used to protect my extra pair of long johns from the weather but now stuffed with eleven packs (plus) of ramen—on a low hanging limb. "Pray for a bear, Ego!"

I relaxed in the sleeping bag and listened to the frolicking of the scouts, envious of their youthful zest, their jubilant shouts. "Dang it, J.R., where did it all go?" He thought for a minute. "Time is like a pickpocket. It takes your life and leaves an empty pocket without you knowing it." I: "Yeah, and life is like milking Pap's cow—you mean to squeeze the tits, but sometimes all you can find are the horns." What would the morrow bring?

CHAPTER 2

Garter Snake Soup Is Good for the Soul

I slowly came awake and stretched, carefully easing into the protesting muscles as I tuned in to the outside world and strained to pick up any indication of feisty weather, but all seemed quiet. I checked the time—6:30. A lot better than yesterday! No use lying here any longer, for I had to pee; plus, I could hardly wait to see if Horseman's curse had disappeared. "Up and at'em, Marine. The day's awastin'." I crawled out of the bag and stuck my head out of the tent into the frosty dawn, which vacillated between light and dark as high cirrus bands played tag with the sun. Night unfinished, or day beginning? A solitary ray pushed through the wispy veil and painted a narrow swatch of gold on the forest floor. Promising!

I wiggled swollen feet into stubborn boots and made the obligatory pit stop, and then hobbled across the clearing to see if Dame Fortune had smiled. Alas! She hadn't even simpered, and the bag still dangled like an annoying habit that refused to go away. "Rats, Ego, even the danged bears won't eat this stuff!" He retorted, "It's probably bear repellent in disguise." I carried the bag back to the tent and told him, "Well, you can't expect to catch fish every time you go fishing. Maybe we'll have better luck today."

It was *cold*—28 degrees by my pack thermometer! From the other two tents, sounds of easy slumber drifted into the frigid air. I wavered, tempted to get back in my bag and snooze until the others woke up, but I pushed the tantalizing urge away and packed, anxious to get on the Trail and generate some heat. "We'll eat breakfast just as soon as we get warmed up," I promised.

I walked past the lifeless Scout camp. Last night's revelry had been replaced with the acrid, dank smell of ashes, which lingered over the area like a giant whiff of halitosis. J.R. grouched, "This smells worse than Old Man Padgett's outhouse." (Old Man Padgett, Pap's neighbor back in the Kentucky knobs before Pap and Granny moved closer to the Bluegrass, thought "sanitation" was something you got at camp meeting when The Holy Ghost swept down through the tent top and cleansed your innards—which was another way of saying that he didn't believe in using lime in the poop hole!) I replied, "Different smell, same effect," and hurried up the Trail before the odor could become a permanent blight inside my nose.

The wind freshened in the hour it took me to reach Cooper Gap—a small dent between two mountains that was conspicuous only because of graveled USFS 42 (the same road that accessed Springer Mountain), which wound up the mountain and crossed over the "dent." "Okay, J.R., breakfast time. Grits or oatmeal?" "Anything but ramen, Alter-man!" I hunkered down behind a large oak tree near the edge of the road, out of the wind's bite, and cooked a double batch of instant grits—a winner, I figured, for we both liked grits.

Ahh! We gobbled the grits down, spoonful after wonderful spoonful, shutting out everything except the delicious taste caressing our taste buds. (Well, the taste buds really did belong to J.R . . . or did they? And how about the arms, legs and feet; what about the nose, eyes and ears, the finger-nails and the eyelashes? We had never really examined this muzzy part of our relationship and had always managed to sidestep the complicated matter; ever reluctant to wade into muddy water for fear we might founder in quicksand. Some things were better left in the closet of tacit avoidance! Still, I felt that being the Head Rooster in this henhouse did give me a certain legitimate claim to the real estate—sort of like leasing a car, except I was leasing a body for the trek up the Trail. Yep, using this logic I definitely had possession of the taste buds!)

Without warning, two camouflage-painted trucks bristling with anten-nas roared up into the gap and screeched to a halt beside the tree. Simulta-neously, the vehicles vomited out twelve mean-looking dudes who scared the pee-diddle out of me! Brandishing rifles nearly as wicked looking as the snarling teeth and fierce eyes that glared out of black and green face paint, they silently rushed my position, and my heart stalled out! The big brave Marine shrieked, "Run! Run for your life!" I dropped the half-empty pan of grits and jumped up, raising my arms (Yes! They were My arms!) high in the air, too paralyzed with fright to scream, and barely managed to squeak, "Don't shoot! I surrender!"

Jiminy H. Jasper! What had we wandered into? A homespun Georgia militia group? Or possibly a local skinhead outfit aching to have some early morning practice with a lonely hiker dude? "Damnation," J.R. croaked, "who did you piss off?" but I didn't have time to think about it. Without so much as a whisper, the assault force surrounded me. I screwed my eyes shut, hunched my shoulders and clenched my teeth, and waited for a gun to poke my ribs or handcuffs to be slapped on, or worse!

Nothing happened! After what seemed like a lifetime, I squinted through half-closed lids. My "captors" had flopped on their bellies and were spread out in a large circle that encompassed the trucks, the vehicles, and my tree. Their rifles pointed outward, threatening, defending against some invisible enemy. And we were right in the middle of their mischief!

Petrified, I whispered to J.R., "What in the name of scorched grits is going on? Are we captives or in protective custody, or what?" J.R.: "Darned if I know."

Suddenly, The Marine started to snicker, and then cracked up. "Neither, Chicken Man. We're caught smack in the middle of a training exercise. These are some of the Army's elite—a group of Ranger trainees. See, there's an instructor."

A tall, slim replica of John Wayne, without grease paint but wearing the black cloth insignia of a lieutenant and a dull yellow patch on his sleeve, stepped from the passenger seat of the nearest truck. Imperious and aloof, he gazed long and hard at the belly-down commoners who groveled at his feet. Then frowning, he drilled me with an icy stare, which raised the hair on my neck. The eyes—calculating steel-gray orbs—captured me in a penetrating shakedown that seemed to dig beneath my skin and stop time. Helpless as a mouse quivering beneath a viper's flicking tongue, I held my breath and wondered what the next few minutes held in store. His face changed like the seasons, reflecting in sequence, contempt, hostility, resentment, and finally pity.

Abruptly, possibly deciding I wasn't a spy (or more likely, he recognized me for what I was—just another grubby thru-hiker), he shifted the cold look back on the small haven of democracy he had created, now barricaded against all enemies, foreign and domestic. Apparently satisfied, he took a handset proffered by the driver and began to bark orders.

J.R. absorbed the instructor's every move. "See that guy? I was like that in my heyday. What a Marine that guy would make! Darn shame it's all wasted on the Army." However, I was more concerned with our predicament, though I breathed a lot easier now that the perceived threat had lessened. I whispered, "What are we supposed to do now? Get the heck outta

Dodge?" He chuckled, "Naw, at this moment, we're probably the most protected citizen in the US of A. Let's just sit here and enjoy the show." I lowered my arms slowly, not entirely convinced, and hunkered back down by
the tree, retrieved the pan of grits (fortunately, none had spilled on the
ground), and waited for the next act in the unfolding drama.

The defenders of democracy ignored me. Other than the instructor's
cryptic dialogue into the handset, no other words had been spoken, nor had
any of these trained killers made eye contact or cast furtive glances my
way—or otherwise acknowledged my presence. As far as the United States
Army was concerned, I didn't exist!

A dirty, mud-smeared boot pushed into the leaves about a foot from
mine, and I suppressed the urge to touch it—just to make sure I wasn't
back with Wahoola and Volunteer, still snuggled inside my sleeping bag
and trapped in some weird dream.

The god-like Ranger stopped talking and looked up at the sky, head
cocked as if waiting for God almighty Himself to sweep in and squash Evil
with a bold thrust of His terrible swift sword.

The picture caused me to giggle—only a puny, uncontrolled gurgle
from my belly—yet it blasted the eerie silence like a donkey's bray as the
ridiculousness of the scene suddenly hit me. J.R. growled, "What's your
problem? Can't you show a little respect, for cryin' out loud?"

But I had lost control of the giggle, and it swelled into a gut-twisting
spasm and gathered in a huge bubble at the back of my throat. Uh-oh! Desperately, I tried to head the bubble off with a spoonful of grits, but the gul-
leywopper backed up like a jammed sewer. Seeking the path of least
resistance, some of the grits spewed out my nose, mixed with a long yellow stream of snot. (The thought flashed through my mind that it closely
matched the instructor's patch.) The remaining grits shot out of my mouth
like a shotgun blast and shattered the "island of democracy" as muffled
sniggers pirouetted around the circle.

"John Wayne's" glare froze the air. Choked by the grits, I coughed and
hacked until the tears came. The instructor's face reversed his earlier
sequence, ending back with contempt, and it looked as if his lips formed
the words, "bug turd." However, The Marine said it must have been my
imagination, for no "officer and gentleman by Act of Congress" would
degrade himself with such language. The instructor stuck his nose in the air
and turned on his heel, effectively banishing me from his small empire.

On an unseen signal, the circle disintegrated in a flurry of movement
and the trainees dashed for the trucks. As he jumped to his feet, the owner
of the boot locked eyes with me. Then without breaking stride or disturbing
the granite set of his camouflage face, his right eyelid swept down and up in

a positive signal of acknowledgement. Ecstatic, I winked back, inwardly smiling at this tiny manifestation of human frailty even as I rejoiced at the tiny, fleeting bond of friendship that had briefly bridged two worlds.

The group tumbled into the trucks, and the defenders of Right and Truth and Mom's apple pie tore out of Cooper Gap amid grinding gears and spraying gravel—young fighting machines being engineered for flawless perfection, America's future rushing toward guts and glory and immortality.

Excited, I said, "Doggone! I can't wait to tell Wahoola and Volunteer what just happened!" J.R., still miffed, hissed, "You'd be wasting your breath. Nobody would ever believe this." He had a point. "Plus, if you hadn't been so all fired busy entertaining the troops with the 'snotty grits' act, you might have been able to unload that ramen." Darn!

The sun had sent the cold air hightailing it to higher elevations by the time I reached Justus Creek—odd name for the serene, burbling stream—and I paused on its narrow log-bridge crossing and looked down at the clear, inviting water. "Criminy, Ego, a bath would really feel good right now. Not that we need one yet, since this is only our second day on the Trail." To prove the point, I raised my arm and took a quick whiff. "Holy cow!" he groaned, "what're you waiting for!"

I sought out a sunny spot and filled the cut-down gallon plastic ice cream bucket, which did duty as my sink, with frigid water. Stripping to my shorts, I began to shampoo my hair and beard. That's the way Wahoola found me.

"Kinda cold to be doing that, isn't it," he remarked, observing the pimply texture of my arms. In spite of the sun, a hint of chill rode in on the slight breeze.

Poising the bucket above my head, I dumped the icy contents and rinsed the shampoo onto the ground. Dang, it was cold!

I gasped at the shock and muttered through clenched teeth, "Yeah, a little chilly, but not all that bad. You know how it is, 'Clean body; healthy mind'." (Not to mention, my beard was like concrete where the snot-grits had solidified from the little adventure earlier this morning, but that was my little secret!) I walked over to the stream and refilled the bucket. "Are you going to take a bath?"

"Naw, I think I'll wait a while longer, at least a couple of weeks. Got to let the thru-hiker odor grow to a respectable level or people might think we're fakers."

"If you wait two weeks to get a bath, even the thru-hikers are going to avoid you." In my mind's eye, I saw Wahoola sitting in a shelter by himself after having dosed a motley collection of thru-hikers with noxious body odor, sending them gasping into the forest. I chuckled.

"What's so funny?"

I told him, adding, "If you go two weeks without a bath, even tomato juice won't help. The hikers will probably give you a new trail name; something like 'Skunk Puke', or 'Vagabond Cesspool'!" I shook my finger at him, like a Baptist preacher pointing the way toward the fiery depths of Hell for the Unrepentant.

He mocked me back with his finger. "Naw, in a couple of weeks I'll be wallowing in the pigpen with all the other hogs, because all us thru-hikers are gonna smell the same." With that prophesy, he threw me a sloppy salute and crossed the bridge.

I flipped a "bird" at his back and yelled, "Just you wait and see!" Dang! I had forgotten to ask about Volunteer; but then, he couldn't be far behind. I peeled off my shorts, keeping a wary eye on the Trail, and finished my bath. "Yessiree, J.R., you and I are gonna be shining examples for all thru-hikers everywhere. We're gonna be spittin' clean all the way to Maine!" He thought about it and said, "Pap once told me about this traveling salesman who came through the community after a long, cold winter, peddling an elixir guaranteed to cure everything from hang nails to hemorrhoids. Pap said the man stunk so 'clean' that nobody could get close to him. We don't want to get *that* carried away." I replied, "But you've got to realize that rotten turnips probably 'stunk clean' by the time Pap and his friends got through their bathless winter."

About mid-afternoon, I found Wahoola basking in the sun on a large, flat rock atop Ramrock Mountain—a higher hump than most of the others—chewing a long blade of grass as he stared off into the distance of his memories. At my "hello," he scooted over and I sat down and removed my boots to let my feet air. Luckily, I was upwind, for I wanted to preserve my fresh smell as long as possible.

For several minutes, we delighted in the splendid panorama, speckled here and there with tiny hints of lush glens hidden in the recesses, its rippling swell of mountains seeming to spill off the southeastern horizon like a vast gray-brown sea. I gave a long sigh, as much for the beauty I beheld as for the relief to my feet, and asked, "How large is the pebble you picked up at Springer to carry to Katahdin?"

Wahoola slapped his thigh, exasperated, and groaned, "Oh, no! I forgot to get one."

"Hey, it's no big thing. Why don't you get one right now? We're only about twenty miles from Springer; almost in its back yard."

"Nope, it wouldn't be the same. I'd know." As if punishing Wahoola for his oversight, the sun momentarily disappeared behind a fluffy blob of white and sent a chill across the mountaintop.

Sorry that I had even launched the subject, I reached into my camera pouch and retrieved my pebbles, rolling them around in my palm like Mexican jumping beans. "I just happen to have an extra. Pick one." The cloud floated past, and the sun pulled the warmth back and sparkled the stones with a magical sheen.

Wahoola, ever weight conscious, selected the smaller of the two and simply said, "Thanks, Model-T." But his look said far more and warmed my heart. Plus, I had less weight to carry!

Wahoola and I hiked together the remainder of the afternoon, eventually descending into Woody Gap where Georgia Highway 60 crosses and, snake-like, winds down the mountain to the small town of Suches (pronounced "Such-as")—population about 600. Suches got its name, as the story goes, because the residents fondly tell outsiders, "Such as it is, it's all we've got." Named in honor of Arthur Woody, chief ranger and benevolent overseer for the Blue Ridge District of the Chattahoochee National Forest for some thirty years, Woody Gap is a small island of asphalt among the endless ocean of trees.

A man sat at a concrete picnic table in a parking area across the highway and waved his arms as he tried to get our attention. "Gee! What do you suppose he wants? That one's a suspicious-looking character," I whispered, taking in the stranger's looks: age somewhere between forty and sixty; neck-length scraggly, brownish-gray beard; frayed blue-denim jacket that failed to hide a huge beer belly, which hung suspended above scruffy, soiled denim jeans. An ancient camouflaged cap, tilted high, partially covered an unkempt mass of oily, salt-and-pepper hair that flared, Elvis-like, down against black, opaque sunglasses.

Wahoola murmured, "We'd better see what he wants."

"Whur you boys headed?" the man asked, punctuating the question with a well-aimed squirt of brownish liquid that erupted from a small hole between stained lips.

One of Pap's gems of wisdom, "You don't have to lie to strangers; just be stingy with the truth," seemed to apply to this situation. "A ways," I said guardedly. "We're hiking the Appalachian Trail." (Where we were really headed was a decent place to spend the night, for the sun was fast descending.)

"Are y'all thru-hikers?"

Wahoola shot me a warning look, the message clear, for we had heard stories about "locals" who hung around trail crossings to "have a little fun with them thru-hiker people." I glanced at the woods behind the parking area, fearful that even as I spoke, a gang of good ol' boys might be waiting for a signal from Ol' Jethro here to jump out and relieve us of our packs— even our clothes!

Wahoola said, "Well mister, right now we're headed for Neel's Gap." Not a lie; just a stingy crumb of truth!

Not convinced, he said, "Wal, y'all favor thru-hikers. Y'all got handles?" Without waiting for an answer he proudly announced, "Mine's Mountain Man. Wal," he chuckled, "it's not my real name, but I like Mountain Man." He fired another salvo of the brown stuff at the ground, narrowly missing his own scuffed boot. He motioned us closer, pointed at a rusty, beat-up, mongrel-red truck that stood nearby, and whispered, "Y'all need a ride down to Suches? I'll run ye down an' back up fer five dollars."

Wahoola and I glanced beyond the pickup at a sign well peppered with bullet holes: "Soliciting on Forest Service lands without a permit is a violation of Federal law," or some such. Mountain Man quickly glanced around to see if any Forest Rangers had sneaked up, and then continued in a conspiratorial whisper, "I gotta make myself a livin'. Them Smokies is always tryin' to keep us fellers from makin' a honest buck."

Wahoola spoke up, "Thanks anyway, but we've got everything we need to get us to Neels Gap. Maybe you might know of a place up the mountain where we could pitch our tents for the night. This old man here is pretty beat." I gave Wahoola a dirty look and then slumped my shoulders and put on a face of misery, throwing myself into the ruse.

Mountain Man nodded sympathetically. "God's truth, both of ye's lookin' kinda puny. Wal, if'n y'all was to go back through them bushes behind me, ye'd find a ol' loggin' road. Now they's a little flat spot 'bout a couple hunnert yards down, an a right good spring, too. Been coolin' m'suds in it fer years." He paused and licked his chops, momentarily fanning the embers of forgotten memories. Then the moment passed and he said, "I reckin you boys oughta find a place back thar to put up yer tents."

Wahoola glanced at me and I nodded. Not the best of places—too close to the highway, for one thing—but the path up the mountain looked steep. No telling how far we would have to go to find a suitable place to pitch tents, and Wahoola had spoken the truth: This old man *was* beat. We thanked the man, wished him well, and walked away.

J.R. piped up: "Well, Ace, that's pretty dumb." Too tired for caustic comments, I snarled, "What's so dumb about finding a good place to spend the night?" He said, "If we get ripped off, we're going to need evidence. He'd probably become the prime suspect." Well, if The Marine thought so . . . He was the "expert", having spent a couple of tours in military law enforcement during his Marine Corps days.

I hesitated, and then turned back. "Say Mountain Man, do you mind if I take your picture? You're the genuine thing."

"Why, I reckin it'd be jist fine." Grunting like an old hog, he pointed at the sign and said, "No charge." He visibly straightened and pushed his barrel-like belly out to its limit, and I snapped the shutter.

"Much obliged," I said, and we headed back toward the bushes.

He cackled after us, "Jist don't show it aroun' th' Post Office!"

Thirty minutes later, Volunteer, whistling a bouncy tune, came down the overgrown logging road, now little more than a scrubby path after years of disuse. "Jeepers, am I glad to see you guys! I didn't know if I'd catch you before dark. You won't believe this, but I just met the weirdest old coot back up at the road. He offered to take me into Suches to the motel for only four dollars, both ways, but I told him I wasn't interested. So he said that there were a couple of hikers back here, and I hoped it would be you." He shook his head. "Man! I wasn't about to go anywhere with him!"

Wahoola and I burst out laughing. The old goat had wanted to charge us five dollars! A last desperate push before day's end? J.R.: "Naw, it was Volunteer's boyish charm. Look what the old geezer was comparing him to. By the way, don't forget to sleep with the camera inside the sleeping bag."

I awoke at first light, filled with anticipation for Neels Gap and *real* food—not the usual trail fare, but ice cream and fresh fruit, maybe even hamburgers and fries—straddled the Trail just eleven miles away! A piece of cake to get there by mid-afternoon if I didn't lollygag too much, which I didn't plan on because my appetite had kicked into high gear overnight!

We didn't get ripped off during the night, and I felt ashamed of my suspicious behavior toward Mountain Man. But The Marine argued, "Nope, we headed off trouble by taking a picture." We'd never know.

Wahoola and Volunteer, acting like small kids waiting for Santa, got up when I did and joked their way through a quick breakfast. We broke camp together, but as we climbed out of Woody Gap, their eager bantering soon ebbed away with their footsteps, leaving me in the near-silence of the barren forest.

I climbed steadily but without rushing, fine-tuning my ears to Nature's sounds. Just ahead, leaves rustled and I caught a flash of brown as a chipmunk shot into a hollow log. A little later I glimpsed a blur of movement in a nearby oak tree, and a series of sharp, agitated "keek-keek's" punctured the silence as two gray squirrels skittered among the leafless branches and sent down a stream of invectives at the two-legged creature who had violated their sanctuary. Grinning, I took off my pack and left a peace offering—a small handful of ramen—but they refused to be pacified. J.R. said, "They might be happier with trail mix." I replied, "It's the thought that counts, and not the gift." He: "But that was no gift!"

Just as I gained the summit, a faint drumming sound floated up the mountainside—a slow thump-thump-thump that rapidly built in tempo and loudness, until it turned into a frenzied crescendo; and then it abruptly ceased, leaving its eerie echo in my mind. Startled, I waited for the noise to come again, but the only sounds came from overhead as small birds flitted among the sun-dappled branches. "Weird," I remarked, wondering briefly if what I had heard came from within. Replied The Marine, "I've not heard anything like it, not even in Nam, but it's not us."

The strange hollow drumbeat sounded twice more during the morning, the last time at Slaughter Gap, a lonely, foreboding place where a major battle had been fought between the Creek and Cherokee nations some four hundred years ago, the engagement so intense that the ground ran red with blood. The place steeped in eerie quietness; even the animals seemed to keep silent in respect for the dead. I could almost sense the ghosts of fallen warriors floating among the trees as they waited for release from their earth-chained bondage. Slaughter Gap! Blood Mountain! Violent names for a violent deed!

The sound of crackling twigs and disturbed leaves came from the shadowy depths and curdled my blood; then, relief washed over my prickled skin as two deer bounded across the Trail a dozen yards to my front. Ghostly reincarnation at work? I quickly replenished my water bottles beneath a skimpy dribble that seeped from a cleft in the rocks ("The mountain weeping," said The Ego.) and hurried from this abode of things not understood, leaving the spirits of history to their ageless wandering.

Close to noon, I reached Blood Mountain Shelter—at 4461 feet, the highest point on the Appalachian Trail in Georgia—just in time to hear Volunteer ask, "What kind of ice cream do you think they'll have?"

I laughed at the picture: Two grown men lounging on the steps of the old stone building, which was nearly as old as J.R. and in about the same condition, both having weathered many (but different) storms. Their voices sparkled with anticipation, and broad, little-boy smiles offset the grimy weariness. Evidently they had been discussing the gastronomical delights they hoped to find at Neels Gap, barely two miles down the mountain.

I slipped out of my pack, surprised that the mile-long climb up from Slaughter Gap hadn't exacted a stiffer toll; but then, the elevation change hadn't been all that drastic. Too, my pack was nearly fifteen pounds lighter than when I left Springer, courtesy of an almost empty food bag—except for all that ramen! A picture of the ramen-packed food box waiting at Neels Gap plagued my mind, but I quickly pushed the image away. That problem could wait another hour.

Volunteer almost choked on his drool. "Ohmigosh! What if they don't have ice cream! What if they're all out!" The words spilled out like a plea for mercy.

Wahoola said, "Naw, you know they're bound to have ice cream; probably Ben and Jerry's." (I'd never eaten any B&J's, but for some reason a quart of B&J in a thru-hiker's hand was considered a status symbol.)

Volunteer's eyes, partially out of focus, glazed over and his mouth moved as if he were actually eating ice cream. Without warning, he bellowed, "Spaghetti! That's what I want. *The Philosopher's Guide* promised it!" Indeed it had—bunkroom for thru-hikers, spaghetti dinner extra, at The Walasi-Yi Center. He jumped up, almost toppling Wahoola off the steps, and started prancing around like he had to pee really bad. "Spaghetti rules!" he shouted. "Spaghetti is king!" That boy had slipped his cork! But then food (or lack of), like a fickle woman, could do strange things to a body! The Marine probably knew that as well as anyone . . .

During J.R.'s early Marine Corps days, his class of Pensacola (Florida) flight school students had to endure a five-day Escape and Evasion course at nearby Eglin Air Force Base in the dead of winter. Students were to avoid capture; live off the land—a skimpy prospect at that time of year—and make their way to a final destination point twenty-five miles away. The students were divided into three-man groups, with each group receiving a parachute (to be used for shelter, bandages, toilet paper, etc.); an entrenching tool (to dig for rattlesnakes that supposedly over-wintered in the abundant gopher holes); a knife; one fishhook (no line); a single box of matches; a number ten can; and a map and compass (no pencil). Then the hapless trios were sent out into the wilderness with the warning, "If you get captured, it's the POW compound for half a day, and then you get to start all over. Now Sweeties, doesn't that sound like fun?"

J.R. and his companions quickly decided that "capture" was not an option. Rumors ran rampant about the POW compound: Locked in a three foot cube that sweltered in the hot sun; no water except for when the masochistic instructors decided to hose you down; no food or talking; discreet blows to private parts—to make the experience more realistic (at least according to the rumor mill). Nope, J.R. didn't plan to get captured!

His small band spent the first two days widening the distance from the infamous POW camp, stopping now and then to dig into a gopher hole in hopes of putting a little meat on the table, but the rattlesnakes must have moved further south to escape the winter's cold (as probably did the gophers), for all the holes were meatless. J.R. and company quickly turned to a diet of prickly pear cactus roots, which were all over the place (and seemed to be the only thing edible in the barren, winter doldrums). After all, in the classroom back at Pensacola the instructor had praised that wonderful plant, touting its tubers as manna for a downed pilot.

Pure bull crap! Boiling the roots to a slimy mess (without salt—not included in the inventory!) in the number ten can, the "Sweeties" yuked and gagged, grimaced and griped, and forced the concoction down, all the time keeping a wary eye out for their pursuers. They even added a couple of pine cones to one nasty batch, but the result reeked of turpentine, which found its way into their belches and caused voluminous, foul-smelling gas for the next few days, not to mention an attack of the runs. Said J.R., "It smells and tastes and poots just like the turpentine potion my Granny used to pour down my gullet when I was a young'un to get the stomach worms out of my gut." ("Poot" was the term invented by J.R.'s father to circumvent the crude alternative, for "fart" was a no-no in his house. The other bodily function was referred to as "grunt," a tidy word developed by J.R.'s maternal grandmother, Mam-maw, to keep her eleven kids from blabbing the "s" word in front of neighbors; however, this nicety sometimes caused confusion. Outsiders thought it a bit strange when one of the kids (or visiting grandkids) would announce to the world, "I've got to go grunt." Some of the neighbors even commented about how much attention her kids lavished on the hogs, going out as they frequently did to grunt with the swine. But in hindsight, both words served the purpose!)

Commented one of the afflicted companions, "Your Granny must have been a mean s.o.b.!" Fighting words under normal circumstances, but right then didn't seem the time or place, not with him and his buddies belching and pooting and trotting into the bushes all day long to grunt.

About noon on the third day, J.R. and company came to an isolated jeep trail, slightly overgrown but sporting fresh tracks in the sand. The road blocked their path like the Berlin Wall, lying as it did right across the ragged charcoal line drawn on the map, which ultimately led to the pickup point and salvation! There was no way around; the road had to be crossed.

The three "wannabe airdales" crouched in the high grass at the edge of the road, watching and listening, straining to detect the slightest off-key sound or movement, but the woods were deathly still. As one, they rushed across—right into a thundering barrage of blanks delivered from a skillfully prepared ambush in a small patch of scrub within spitting distance to the right. The "enemy" (for that's what they were!) yelled, "Stop! You're dead!" to which the panicked trio screamed, "No we're not!" Without breaking stride and ignoring the irate shouts, they fled into the forest, grateful that the Army prohibited instructors from firing live ammunition at students, which undoubtedly the cursing instructors wished they had.

In late afternoon the wary trio happened upon a small lake. They were on their last legs—weak from hunger and exhausted after an afternoon of hard hiking to put miles between the ambush site and themselves—and the lake seemed like a Godsend. One of the guys whispered, "Let's catch some fish," so they rigged a fishing line with cord from the parachute and started searching for something to use as bait. J.R. flipped over a rotted log and excitedly motioned the others over. A dazed, skinny two-foot garter snake slowly rotated its coils in the cold air—a meal in the making! "Supper!" J.R. hissed, and any thoughts of fishing vanished.

Skinned, gutted, cut into inch-long chunks not much thicker than a fair-sized night crawler, the serpent went into (unsalted) boiling water, along with prickly pear cactus roots, and soon became a stinking, slimy feast. In the semi-darkness of the parachute-tent, flames from the small, smokeless fire threw shadows across Neanderthal-like faces. Occasional guttural sounds came from the three scared, hungry fugitives as they swilled down Nature's provender. Said one sadly, "I thought snake was supposed to taste like chicken. This slop tastes like . . .", and he paused, struggling for a fitting superlative. The other guy quipped, "Like snake?"

J.R.: "Aw, c'mon guys. Garter snake soup is good for the soul,"—which in a way is proof that when a body gets hungry enough, anything is fair game!

So I could understand Volunteer's volatile behavior when he suddenly grabbed up his pack, said loudly, "See you guys later," and sprinted down the mountainside blathering about spaghetti and ice cream.

"Jeez, Wahoola, do you think he'll be okay?"

Wahoola, surprised at Volunteers sudden outbreak, said, "That boy's likely to break his neck because of spaghetti. I'd hate to have that hanging over me for the rest of my life. We'd better try to slow him down."

We chased after Volunteer, risking a nasty fall, but we never had a chance. That young'un was possessed by a dark power. "Spaghetti" had usurped his mind and soul!

Walasi-Yi (Cherokee for "Place of the Frogs") Center is a picturesque, sprawling stone building that sits beside busy US Highway 19 in Neels Gap, far beneath the broad summit of Blood Mountain. Owned and run by Jeff Hansen, a graduate of The National Outdoor Leadership School, and his wife, Dorothy, herself a thru-hiker (1979), Walasi-Yi Center houses a well-stocked outfitter store and small grocery. Just across a breezeway through which the Appalachian Trail passes, the Hiker Inn awaits weary hikers, who as guests also qualify for the acclaimed spaghetti dinner. (Author's note: In the late '90's, the Hansens, faced with a major renovation requirement, were forced to temporarily close The Hiker Inn and sadly the famed spaghetti dinners passed into Trail history.) Well qualified, the Hansen's have long been indispensable friends to hikers, helping them solve the myriad problems that inevitably develop during the thirty-mile trek from Springer Mountain.

Graciously, the Hansens also offer Walasi-Yi Center as a repository for mail drops. This was the first of my fourteen drops—planned stops where I would get mail and food boxes. For most, The Center is the first milepost on the trip north, an oasis of delight amidst a desert of deprivation.

Volunteer's pack leaned against the wall near the main entrance. "Well, I see he made it," Wahoola said as we went inside. An ice cream freezer near the door rallied our spirits and he sighed with relief.

Volunteer, sweated up like a racehorse at the finish line, stood next to the cash register, and his eyes were still slightly out of focus as he talked with an older lady. Her voice easily carried the short distance to where we stood.

"And do you want the spaghetti dinner, too?" she asked.

Volunteer's face ballooned into the biggest grin I'd ever seen. "Yes! Yes!" He danced a tiny jig in place—a pressure relief valve of sorts that kept him from bouncing around the room like a blown up balloon whose opening hadn't been tied off (either that, or he really did need to pee)! He saw us, and this time his grin almost swallowed his face. "I'm going to stay the night." Checking the wall clock above the counter he blurted, "Spaghetti in one hour and thirty-seven minutes!"

I whispered, "Dang, Wahoola, if he's this bad after only three days, what's he going to be like at the end of six months?"

Wahoola: "You're looking at disaster in the making." We shook our heads with mock sadness and left to seek our own pleasures.

A dilemma: Pick up the mail right now or eat? I turned to ask Wahoola's opinion but he had already ripped the top off a pint carton of B&J, which solved my problem. I grabbed a pint of something-chocolate and told the lady at the counter, "Ma'am, if it's okay I'll run a tab, because this is only the beginning." She gave me a nonchalant nod as if it were an everyday thing with thru-hikers, which it well might have been.

I polished off the ice cream, following it in quick succession with an apple, a banana, a peach, a cherry Coke, and I could have stuffed lots more down except J.R. reminded me as I picked up another pint of B&J's icy ambrosia, "A tab isn't like a credit card, Alter. You realize you're going to have to cough up the money before you go out that door." Jeez, what a spoilsport! Reluctantly, I put the ice cream back and went to settle the tab. The Marine, piqued, chastised me. "You're spoiled. What if all you had to eat was garter snake soup?" I scoffed. "Yeah, it's a hard world and you probably had to walk barefooted three miles to school each way, even in the snow." He: "How'd you know?" I answered him with a loud burp, which raised a few eyebrows among the dozen or so tourists who milled among the racks of clothes and backpacking equipment.

A younger lady now stood behind the counter. About thirty-five, slender and attractive, she pushed an errant strand of brown hair back into her straight, disciplined fold and adjusted her glasses as she rang up a sale. I waited until she finished with the customer, told her my name and said that I owed a tab. As she rang it up, I asked, "Are you Dorothy Hansen?"

"Sure am, and I believe we're holding a couple of packages for you, plus some mail. Come with me and I'll get it."

I followed her over to another section that did double duty as storeroom and unofficial mailroom. Stacks of boxes reached almost to the ceiling. Zoowie! Lots of hikers still to come!

She consulted a card file and cross-referenced a number, and then dug into one of the stacks and handed me two packages and a post card. "This large one is addressed to you (my food drop), but this small one says

'Model-T and David'. Is that your friend?" she asked, pointing at Wahoola, who licked at his fingers like they were Popsicles and seemed to be considering a third run on the ice cream freezer.

"Yeah, that's him, but he hasn't been housebroke yet." Being a thruhiker, she understood and laughed. "I'll take the small package, too, if that's okay."

I carried the packages outside to the pavilion—a concrete pad attached to the main building, with picnic tables where one could enjoy a spectacular view—and checked the smaller box again, noticing there was no return address. A mystery! I put it aside to wait until Wahoola came out of the store and began the drill of rearranging my pack so I could cram in the additional twenty pounds of food—enough to take me the eight days or so to Nantahala Outdoor Center at Wesser, 104 miles away.

It quickly became a drill in stupidity—or frustration—or both! There just wasn't enough room! "Dang it all, J.R.! The shut'n stuff won't fit!"

("Shut'n" was a byword I stole from J.R. and used when things got antsy or hectic—like now. The word was pure Kentucky knobs frying of the King's English, as J.R. learned when he discovered life beyond the "Knobs." But back in the dilapidated one-room school house of his early youth, the old schoolmarm, Miss Hessy, had conjugated verbs such as, "I sit; I set; I sut, like, 'I sut in the privy'." J.R. and his buddies took to conjugating like frogs to flies and soon were holding conjugating sessions out behind the coal shed during recess, giggling as they recited, "I shit; I shet; I shut, like, 'I shut in the privy'.")

I used "shut" mostly in its adjective form, although now and then as the situation called for, I would sometimes bellow, "Shut!" which frequently caused anyone nearby who hadn't attended Miss Hessy's class on verb conjugation to throw me a quirky look and ask, "Shut what?"

Thinking of Hippy Man, I dumped everything onto the concrete pad and made two piles—food and equipment. "Shut!" I growled at The Ego. The food pile was a monster, twice the size of the mound of equipment. "It's that blasted ramen!" I was inundated with the stuff! There were the five packs left out of the batch I'd started with. (I had cooked the partial package and three others and found it palatable fixed like that, but I'd sworn, "No more of the dry stuff!" Also, I had managed to palm three packs off on Volunteer). And now I had to deal with the additional twenty-four packs that came in my mail drop. Looking at the mess, it reminded me of a great big pile of cow manure.

"Shut! Shut! Shut!" I bellowed. A chubby, pimple-faced teenage boy going inside the Center shot me a panicked look as he darted into the store like a spooked deer, slamming the door behind him with a loud bang. J.R.

said, "Jeez, Alter-man, get a hold on yourself before they haul us off for child abuse!" I snarled, "Whaterwegonnado?" The dumpster down by the Hiker Inn was starting to look like a magic box. He thought for a moment and answered, "We can't afford to toss it, because we're going to need the calories to carry us to N.O.C., unless you want to go back inside and buy some other goodies." Bummer! What to do?

Wahoola came outside and shook his head at the large pile of ramen. "What're you going to do with it?"

"Heck, I don't know. Want some?"

"You crazy?"

"Jeez, Wahoola, I just don't know. Maybe I'll box it up and send it to Horseman."

He chuckled, "You'd better send it C.O.D." Giving me a sympathetic pat on the shoulder, he went back inside to get a soda. The ramen was my problem.

Reluctantly, mostly to assuage my feeling of guilt, I retrieved six packs from the pile for the journey on to N.O.C. and muttered to J.R., "Unless a miracle happens in the next few minutes, the rest is going in the dumpster. We'll just wing it."

The door slammed and the same chubby boy, now armed with a Snickers bar in each fat hand, walked outside. He saw me and blurted loudly, "I 'shut' it good Mister, just like you told me to."

At that moment the Trail goddess who keeps an eye on thru-hiker fools must have spiked me with a mental thunderbolt! I motioned for him to come over. "Say young feller, how you doing today? You look like a man who can hold his ramen. You *do* like ramen, don't you?"

He grinned and licked his chops. "Golly, Mister. Everybody likes ramen."

"Well rattle my mothballs, sonny. This is your lucky day, just happening along right before my Great Annual Ramen Blowout ends—in exactly five minutes! Yessiree! Right now the ramen's going at bargain basement prices. Talk about luck!"

He thought it was a swell trade—twenty-three packs of ramen for two Snickers bars! (So did I!) Laughing, J.R. said, "We'd best get out of here before his daddy comes looking for us." I replied, "Naw, you heard what the kid said: 'Everybody likes ramen.' Like father, like son." He asked, "Well, what're we going to replace the ramen with?" Struck by a flash of inspiration, I said, "Follow me."

I went inside and bought the Hansen's entire supply of Snickers— twenty-six bars—and mumbled apologetically to Dorothy, "I've got this awful sweet tooth . . ."

As I went out the door, J.R. asked, "What about all that other ramen at home waiting to be mailed?"

"Ohmigosh!" I practically ran to the pay phone down by the dumpster, shuffling impatiently as the phone rang and rang, praying, "Please let her be home! Pleeeease!" She finally answered and I said, "Uh, Honey, you like ramen, don't you . . ."

When I got back, Wahoola sat at a nearby table working with his pack. He glanced up and chuckled, "Saw you coming up from the dumpster. Got your little problem solved, huh?"

"Yeah. There's more than one way to skin a cat," I replied, not bothering to enlighten him. "Things are looking up."

And they were—to a point. I managed to cram everything into the pack, hefted it and groaned. With all the additional food and Snickers bars, the load seemed a lot heavier now, even without the six pounds of "absolutely essential" clothing and gear I had packaged up and posted with the Hansens to be sent home. Well, a body had to eat!

I asked Wahoola, "Are you about finished? Someone sent us a package together; no idea who from, because they didn't include a return address."

He sat down at my table and I opened the package. It held four chocolate Cadbury Easter eggs nestled in a handful of green artificial grass, along with a short note: "Happy Easter from the Easter Bunny." I recognized the writing and chuckled, "Now Judith's an Easter Bunny."

Easter was still two days away. "What do you think?" Wahoola asked. "Take them with us?"

"Might as well. If the Easter Bunny found out we ate them now, there'd be Hell to pay!" I handed two of the eggs to Wahoola, along with a handful of the grass. "For authenticity," I explained with a grin.

While we were trying to make room for the eggs, a woman, about thirty, wearing a blue tee shirt and toting an expensive-looking camcorder, walked up and offered her hand. "Hi fellas. My name's Lagunatic. I did a thru-hike last year and I'm back this year filming the thru-hikers, hoping to put together a documentary. Do you mind if I interview you?" The tee shirt was an eye-catcher with the logo "The Official A.T. Answer Shirt" in bold black letters, followed beneath by a numbered laundry list: "1. 15–20 miles; 2. yes, I've seen bears; 3. mac-n-cheese; 4. 50 lbs. or so; 5. in a tent; 6. 4–6 months, over 2,000 miles; 7. yes, I WALKED here."

"Neat shirt. My name's Wahoola. Where'd you get it?

"I'm also an entrepreneur. Want one?"

"Naw, I've got more stuff now than I can carry. Model-T here might be interested though." He blessed me a benevolent smile—the rat!

I laughed. "You're the first one he's admitted that to. Sorry, I'd better pass."

She interviewed Wahoola first, asking the usual "how goes it" questions, which he answered with shrugs and the usual inane malarkey.

She turned to me and I filled five minutes of tape with wise insight about the life of a thru-hiker, based on three whole days on the Trail, finishing the interview with the sage words, "If it's so hard, why am I having so much fun?"

Having sucked our brains dry, Lagunatic thanked us for our cooperation and sped away in her truck, looking for more willing subjects. "You ready to roll?" I asked, already regretting that I hadn't followed Volunteer's lead and stayed for the night—and the spaghetti dinner.

"Yeah, there's still daylight to burn. Let's go." I followed Wahoola through the breezeway, past the Hiker Inn, and we began the climb out of Neels Gap. The smell of spaghetti sauce wafted into my nostrils. That rapscallion, Volunteer, was probably stringing noodles out of his young mouth right now!

The next few days blurred together in a flux of ups and downs; misty dew-speckled sunrises and flaming, ocher-tinted sunsets; unlimited views of barren mountains that stretched as far as the imagination and, like magic, went "poof" at the horizon; road crossings down in the gaps, where faint tinges of green crept among the trees—Nature's recurring promise of joyous rejuvenation. Glossy green patches of galax relieved the boredom of the bleak slopes, and I anxiously watched for the first blossoms of spring. Fatigue, aching muscles, and sore feet, now constant companions, were mitigated by unrestrained excitement and anticipation. The desire to see what lay over the next ridge and beyond the next bend bolstered my steps and swept me along like a rudderless boat on turbulent waters, and the miles slipped past beneath my dusty boots.

We began to overtake other thru-hikers—ragtag vagabonds all: foot-sore, sweat-stained, stinking (like Wahoola and me!), most tottering beneath too-heavy packs (ditto!). We accepted them as family, regardless of how unkempt, beggarly, or bizarre they seemed. (The Marine did have a problem with one guy who had spiked his hair and dyed it orange and purple, and then for effect had added a nose ring to match his five earrings, but I didn't give it a second thought.) In turn, they accepted us, and bonds were forged.

Trail names, alien and absurd to outsiders, rippled across tongues like refreshing peppermints: Inward Bound; Mellow Man; Chopstick Nick and his girl companion, Sparrow; Shakespeare; Dog and Shug (whom I mistook for a young boy but turned out to be a saucy, bouncing red-head in her twenties); Duffle Bag Tim (who had no interest in doing a thru-hike but lived on the Trail).

Trail names were a barrel of fun. It usually went something like this: "Hey, how ya doin'? I'm Model-T."

A grin. "Doin' great! I'm Pookie." Pookie? This guy would make Popeye's archenemy, Bluto, look like Wimpy. Feeling like a Lilliputian, I try not to stare at the skull and crossbones tattoo on his right bicep (which dwarfs my legs), or the six earrings in his ear (six five-year pins to remind him of his age?), or the short, dirty-blond ponytail; but my eyes won't obey and fix on the skull and crossbones.

"Nice ta meetcha, Pookie." He pushes out a giant paw. Dang! It looks like a catcher's mitt! I hesitate, afraid I might be crippled for life; but then I grit my teeth and shake it, more afraid not to.

His hiking partner, a slim blond girl (who makes *me* look like Bluto!), flashes timid brown eyes and says, somewhat bashfully, "Hi. My name's Cryin' Susie." She looks about ten years younger than Pookie, maybe less, and her short brown hair has succumbed to tangles. She adds, "I cry easily," and I notice telltale tear streaks, still damp, on her cheeks. Pookie nods and his eyes soften.

I toss out a little encouragement. "Yeah, things are kinda tough early on, but it should get easier." I change the subject before Cryin' Susie cranks up the tear machine, "When did y'all leave Springer?"

"A week ago," Pookie says. "How 'bout you?"

"Four days ago." Suddenly, Pookie doesn't look so big!

Shuffling uncomfortably, looking embarrassed, he tries to save face in front of the gal. "Susie's had some foot problems; slowed us down a bit."

Susie's eyes start to water and I quickly shift gears. "Where you guys from?"

"Omaha," he answers. "You?"

"Virginia."

And that's it for now. We've covered the territory, sniffed each other out like strange dogs, and it's time to move on. It is too early in the hike to establish close ties, but from what Horseman had told me, this would come later, usually beyond Virginia—after over half the crowd have fallen by the wayside and fade away. Will Pookie and Cryin' Susie go the distance, or will this short interlude be a brief collision of kindred spirits, never to be repeated?

"See you guys up the Trail," I prattle, mimicking the standard Trail benediction. I haven't even gotten out of sight before I hear Cryin Susie wail, "Did you hear him, Pookie? Four days! Everybody's passing us." The wail becomes a blubbering sob. "We're never going to get to Maine!"

I: "Poor Susie." The Ego: "Charity begins at home."

Later, J.R. broke into my thoughts. "Do you think they have a chance?" I replied, "Who knows? We're on a strange highway without a road map. Those two may not get past N.O.C." He thought for a long moment. "True, but we've strung a rope across our different worlds, and if we do meet again it'll be a lot easier to get to the other side."

When I caught up with Wahoola, he was hunkered down against a huge oak a few feet from the Trail with his boots off. He had still been asleep when I shook the ice off my tent early this morning and started up the Trail, but he must not have lingered in the bag too long for he passed me a couple of hours later while I took a Snickers break. The day had finally warmed and I loafed along, taking my time and shooting the bull with The Ego, who happened to be in a good frame of mind for a change. Now, once again the tortoise (me) had caught the hare (Wahoola).

"Whatcha doin?" I asked. He might have been in a trance for all the attention he paid me, and his eyes were glazed, seemingly fixed on something way beyond the horizon. With his right hand, he picked at a blackish, corn-like mass on the bottom of his left big toe; while with his left hand he plucked bits of trail mix from a plastic bag.

I rephrased the question. "What's that?" A blister or callus obviously, but it favored a giant raisin. It could have been another piece of trail mix. "When did you get that?" Yuk! The thing was a gross-out!

He ignored my questions, asking me one instead as he pulled his eyes back into focus. "You know what today is?"

I noticed a foul odor—his socks, which dangled across a log, or the "raisin"? Or maybe he had sat down on a dead animal. Same difference! Ignoring his question, I told him, "Jeez Wahoola, you shoulda taken a bath when you had the chance back at Justus Creek. You're a menace to Planet Earth. If the EPA catches you, they're liable to lock you away!"

That drew a chuckle. "Aw, it's not that bad yet. You don't see any grass dying where I'm sitting, do you?"

"You're sitting on leaves, and it's too early in the season for grass. Why do you want to know what day it is? It's April 15th, our fifth day since leaving Amicalola Falls."

Wahoola continued to poke and prod the nasty thing, giving off unintelligible grunts between bites of trail mix. Without realizing what he'd done (at least I hoped it wasn't on purpose), he scratched his head with the poking hand, and then he stuck it in the trail mix bag and tossed a bite in his mouth.

J.R. said, "Sumabitch!" and I gasped aloud, "Shut fire in th' morning," which earned me a look from Wahoola like I was the one who ate trail crud.

"Naw, that's not what I meant. Today's Easter Sunday. We ought to stop early and celebrate; maybe cook an Easter dinner." I guess he meant we should add something extra to the mac-n-cheese.

"Okay by me. But you've got to do something about that smell. Right now you'd gag a maggot."

Wahoola treated his mouth to one last taste of trail mix with the poking hand and licked his fingers; then he prodded "The Thing" a final time and gave his diagnosis. "I think I got a blister." Like that explained everything.

About noon, we reached Tray Mountain Shelter. Coaxed by the warmth, we stopped and pulled water from the spring, bathed and washed our clothes, and discussed variations on a theme by mac-n-cheese—an interesting game with infinite possibilities for one-upmanship! Wahoola won hands down with his idea: "Macaroni ala sole of boot." I left him at the shelter playing with "The Thing," now washed and neatly covered with duck tape. Hallelujah!

Warming sunshine and gentle trail made for pleasant hiking, and whispering zephyrs carried strange earthy fragrances reminiscent of plowed fields and fertilized pastures up from the valleys. Near Addis Gap, a small splash of purple colored a brown slope near the Trail and I paused. A bed of wild iris defiantly pushed up through a blanket of dead leaves and shimmered in the sunlight, spreading beauty and joy to eager eyes. "Our first blossoms," I murmured. J.R. added, "Nature's gift on this special day," and we lingered for a few moments and gave silent thanks to The Creator as we counted our blessings.

That evening at Addis Gap, we decorated our "earth-table" with the four Cadberry eggs nestled in the artificial grass. Wahoola celebrated Easter with macaroni and cheese ala tuna (canned). I added a can of boned chicken to mine.

Lastly, after pots had been washed and food bags hung, we slowly ate the Cadberry eggs, savoring each bite as the flavor exploded our senses and mushed our minds. J.R. said, "Thanks, Easter Bunny, wherever you are." I added, "Double aah!"

Tray Mountain, Addis Gap; Kelly Knob, McClure Gap; Powell Mountain, Moreland Gap; up and down, do it again, repeat, over and over. The Trail had become an endless sequence of ascents and descents. Behind us, last week's mountains faded into the haze of the southern horizon; ahead, next week's travel stretched across the endless ridges to infinity.

Nature seemed to tap us with her magic wand, revealing sights seldom allowed mere mortals. We wandered across cloud-covered balds where time seemed to cease and spirits of the ancients mingled with the swirling mist. We pushed through maverick thunderstorms that roared and belched dragon's breath into the hail-laden downpour. Sometimes, we perched on lofty outcrops and for a short while reigned supreme over patchwork valley kingdoms of checker-boarded blacks, browns, and grays tinted with hues of green. Each day greeted us with the promise of more: new faces, new experiences, and a full measure of Nature's rich bounty.

The Trail seemed to speak to our hearts: "Come see what lies beyond the next range, the next bend. Come meet the challenges of this new day; put forth your best effort and purge your soul. Rise up and become one with the Earth, for wholeness and belonging are within your grasp."

Each step, each mile, each mountain conquered toughened us, and we endured.

Our muscles adapted to the rigors of the Trail and we increased our pace, easily averaging thirteen miles a day; some days, we reached down into our reserves and gutted out fifteen or even seventeen. Increased mileage meant more energy expended, and our appetites kicked into high gear! A box of mac-n-cheese or a noodle dinner just didn't hack it anymore, and Hunger moved in for the long haul, becoming a permanent resident along with its malevolent cousin, Pain. Of the two, Hunger was the greater aggravation, nagging all the time for me to eat now and not worry about tomorrow. Hunger spoke to my mind: "Empty your food bag! It's easier to carry in your belly than on your back! You can get more somewhere." But Hunger lied! The nearest food was at Rainbow Springs, still forty miles away. I thought about garter snake soup to take my mind off the food bag and told Hunger to take a hike. The wily demon replied, "That's what I'm doing."

Pain was more devious, a sly and cunning devil. Pain's M.O. was to lurk just out of sight and then pounce like a starved tiger when I least expected. Pain was also an adept planner: "Hmm, let's see. What's on tab for today? At six AM, wake Model-T up with a headache and back pain in the fourth lumbar. Eight AM, retain slight headache, but move back pain down into the small of his back and commence pain in left foot. Ten AM, increase pain in left foot to panic level; and then turn up the pain in his right heel. One PM, turn everything up four notches and throw in a few heat cramps. Five PM, full power on everything. Okay, now what did I leave out? Oh yes, before bedtime, a double whammy of tendonitis in right knee. Hmm, for tomorrow, a toothache might be some fun, and yeah, maybe even an earache and a few heart palpitations!" The Fiend! But I knew how to control him—as long as the ibuprofen held out!

So went the days.

"Rats! It didn't hold." The voice seemed to come right out of a big boulder a few feet off the Trail and stopped me in my tracks. Keeping to his schedule, Pain had cranked his torture machine up to full throttle, and my mind was down in the trenches slugging it out with the little bastard until the ibuprofen (Vitamin "I" in thru-hiker lingo) could stomp him into the dirt. I tried to push through the dim haze that frocked my brain—a barrier I'd thrown up to fend off Pain's assault—and wondered why the boulder was sharing this information with me, of all people. After all, rocks probably didn't carry on conversations with just everyone. I waited to see if the boulder intended to explain what wouldn't hold.

The rock spoke again, louder this time, almost a yell. "Darnit! I need some duck tape."

"Well now," I told J.R., "that is one smart rock. It knows exactly what it needs." Being a good ol' southern boy, The Ego knew that duck tape would fix just about anything, broken or not, and had insisted that I keep a copious amount rolled up on the hiking stick. I told the boulder, "Man, is this your lucky day! I've got duck tape!"

The rock kept silent for a long moment and finally asked, "Who is it?"

J.R. snickered, "There you go, Dummy, trying to milk horns again. The rock isn't doing the talking, for cryin' out loud. Somebody's back there." Feeling foolish, I walked around behind the boulder.

A slim, perky gal sat on a log and fiddled with her right foot. Seeing me, her wrinkled frown turned into a frustrated grin that showed off a mouthful of sparkling teeth. Like the rest of us, she looked trail-worn, and her dark shorts and yellow tee shirt already reflected the hard miles. Two long, plaited pigtails framed a face that qualified as "attractive," just missing "pretty" by scant inches. She said, "Hi my name's Moleskin Meg just take a look at these feet they're a real mess."

It was by far the worst case of blisters I'd ever seen, making Wahoola's "Thing" pale by comparison. "That's tough," I said, thinking of the hundreds of miles left to do. My feet were on fire, but at least I didn't have blisters! "I bet I know how you got your name."

Her brown eyes twinkled. "I've gone through two big packs of moleskin since I left Springer and I just opened the third but the darn stuff won't stick when it gets sweaty did I hear you say you had some duck tape?"

"Yep, right here on my hiking stick. Take what you need."

Meg tore off a long strip of duck tape, using it to hold the moleskin in place, talking all the time. She had the kind of voice that a Holy Roller hell-fire-and-brimstone, stump-kicking preacher would sin for—naturally loud, and it probably carried into the next county! "I have a partner named Lone Star he's from Texas he's somewhere ahead of me I'm from Hawaii this stuff is holding like super glue I've gotta start carryin' some." She paused and took a huge gulp of air, much to my relief for I realized my breathing had synchronized with her words and I needed a breath—badly!

"Are you sure I'm not using too much it's mighty nice of you to share . . ." She continued on for several minutes, pausing at long intervals to replenish the air supply.

"Holy cow! She's a walking TV talk show!" J.R gasped, to which I replied, "More like a walking shelter register," for we soon found out who was on the Trail as far as a hundred miles ahead; who was hip; who was a drag; all the latest Trail gossip. I felt lightheaded from lack of oxygen and tried to breathe normal, but I kept forgetting, caught up as I was in the verbal blizzard. When I did remember to go for a breath, I found myself concentrating on her mouth, marveling at how long it could go without air, and then I would lapse back into the no-breathing mode.

The words rattatattated past my ears and I almost missed it: ". . . take your pack off and have a seat . . ." I realized I was shuffling on red-hot feet and my pack felt like someone had slipped twenty pounds of rocks inside while I wasn't looking (an old hiker prank!). J.R. hissed, "Don't you dare. That's our ticket out of here!"

Moleskin Meg gulped air and the escape hatch briefly opened. I jumped through! "Gee, Moleskin, I hate to leave so soon but I've gotta catch up with my partner." I grabbed my hiking stick and blurted, "See you up the Trail," already running as the words tumbled out!

Her voice pursued me up the Trail. "By the way, what's your name what's your partner's name did I tell you how Lone Star and I met thanks for . . ."

"Jeez, Ego! My brain's fried." He: "Poor Lone Star!"

An hour later I met Lone Star, a skinny fellow with a morose look—like Winnie the Pooh's sad-sack donkey friend, Eeyore. In the ten minutes I was with him, he uttered two whole sentences: "I'm Lone Star from Texas," and, "You seen Moleskin Meg?" Everything else came out in one or two-word spurts, like a poorly tuned engine.

J.R.: "Opposites do attract!" I: "Yeah. Look at us!"

Late that afternoon Wahoola and I passed from Georgia into North Carolina. A faded brown pipe with "GA-NC" hand-painted in bold white letters had been screwed to a large white oak to mark the border. Wahoola whooped, "Only thirteen states left!"

My own whoop chased after his echo. We had come seventy-five miles in six days. I felt like a world-class hiker!

The next evening Wahoola and I pitched our tents in a small, level patch of new grass just north of Standing Indian Mountain. We had finished supper and were talking about the day's adventure, letting the dusk sweeten our words and mingle them with the night noises, now familiar welcome additions to our evenings.

A weak, garbled keening floated in on the slight breeze, more like a tinny prattling than a wail. The voice must have traveled at least a quarter mile—the nearest possible campsite. Wahoola glanced into the shadows. "That's a weird sound. Any idea what kind of an animal makes a noise like that?"

I shrugged, trying to stifle a grin. "All kinds of strange creatures in these mountains. By the way, how're you fixed for duck tape?"

J.R.: "Wrong question. You should have asked, 'How're you fixed for earplugs?'"

Wahoola solved the puzzle the next afternoon. I hadn't seen him since midmorning, when he roared past me with a full head of steam up—or maybe I was lollygagging too much, for the day reeked of springtime. I finally caught him at Mooney Gap, a wide spot in the Trail where a once-upon-a-time logging road crossed. He sat on a stump, staring up at the skyline as he munched on trail mix. "Well, there it is," he said, pointing up at a prominent summit. "Albert Mountain." The name opened up a valve deep in my innards and my strength flushed away as if I were a commode.

Albert Mountain had been our main topic of discussion for the past two days. Described as a mini-Kinsman (whatever that meant) in Horseman's notes, and as an "ass-over-teakettle scramble" in something I'd read later. But however the nouns and adjectives fitted together, it had to mean bad news! I had created the mountain in my mind as a rugged beast that flaunted sheer rock faces and narrow ledges, along with huge boulders spotted with small white rectangles that marked the path up through impossible places. In my mind's eye, I had already climbed Albert Mountain a dozen times, groping for finger holds, clinging to ledges barely wide enough to support a boot, inching up through the mammoth boulders and cursing the idiot who laid out the path. In one morbid scene, a body tumbled lazily through space (mine!). "Shut'n mountain!" I muttered to myself as I took off my pack and sat against a tree.

"By the way," Wahoola said, "a couple of hikers named Moleskin Meg and Lone Star left about fifteen minutes ago. She told me about this knight in shining armor who rescued her from a fate worse than—"

"Yeah, yeah," I cut in, "and she wanted to know if you carried duck tape, right?"

"How'd you know?" He grinned, giving away the game. "I told her the name of her 'knight'—when I managed to get a word in."

"Gee, thanks. I'll return the favor. How'd you like a case of ramen for Christmas?"

"Are you ready to go climb Ol' Albert?" Wahoola asked rising to his feet. "I'm going to get it over with."

"Not yet. I think I'll procrastinate a few minutes longer."

After Wahoola left, I ate a Snickers and studied the summit. From here, it looked rugged and high; the fire tower on top could have been a thin pencil in an artist's sketch. J.R. said, "Alter-man, if you sit here long enough, it'll all erode down around you and you won't have to climb it." I started in on another Snickers and growled, "Shut! Shut your mouth." He chuckled, "Which 'shut' do you mean?" I: "How'd you like to be paired up with Moleskin Meg?" That "shut" him up!

My imagination had run amok ("Again," gloated The Ego) and my fears proved groundless. True, the climb was hard, and I had to deal with a few boulders, ledges, and a couple of scrambles that might be described as difficult. But "ass-over-teakettle"? (Whatever that meant!) Hardly!

As I neared the summit, several voices carried down the slope. One (without question belonging to Moleskin Meg) overwhelmed the others. She said, "Okay guys, close it in. A little more to the left. And pucker'em up a little."

What the heck! I scrambled up the last ledge and stopped short. Beneath the old fire tower, six hikers with their shorts down below their knees leaned over a chain-link fence that had been built along the edge of a deep void. As they stared down into space, the six grungy butts wiggled back and forth in response to Moleskin's commands—like white pumpkins jiggling to a fairy godmother's wand—but I really didn't expect to see any magic performed. The Ego exclaimed, "Jesus, Alter, we're hallucinating!"

I blinked my eyes and rubbed away the sweat, but the image remained. Moleskin Meg stood near the base of the fire tower trying to focus a camera with one hand while she gestured with the other and bellowed out orders with the precision of a Marine gunnery sergeant. Several other cameras cluttered the ground at her feet.

"Dang, Moleskin, I read that this was an 'ass-over-teakettle' mountain. The asses are easy to spot, but darned if I see any teakettles!"

Sniggers erupted from the chorus line. One of the butts twitched and a voice yelled, "Hey, it's Model-T! Come on, you've got to get in on this!" I could have sworn it belonged to Wahoola, but the naked butts looked pretty much the same.

Moleskin Meg grinned mischievously and snapped out another order. "Over there's a spot, next to Lone Star. Get in line."

"What're we supposed to be doing?" I asked, dropping my pack and laying my camera by Meg's feet. I took my assigned place in the chorus line per the "Gunny's" orders and dropped my shorts.

"We're mooning Albert Mountain."

"Why?" I felt intimidated, for this was my debut at mooning. After all, mooning something as big as a whole mountain seemed like a giant leap for a first timer.

Someone in the lineup said, "We're rehearsing for Earth Day."

Well naïve me! So this was just a rehearsal! (According to the Trail "grapevine", some thru-hikers went in the buff on Earth Day.) Put that way, it didn't seem like such a big deal.

Not so with The Ego, who was having a cow. "Idiot! What we're really doing is mooning Moleskin Meg. Don't you feel exactly like what you're showing?" I got his drift. Put that way, it seemed like a very big deal! I reached for my shorts, but Meg, giggling, beat me to the draw and snapped the shutter. Feeling embarrassed, I smirked to J.R., "Too late, Butt-man. How does it feel to lose your virginity?" He scowled. "How does it feel to be a debauched nincompoop?" Jeez! Whatever happened to his sense of humor!

At the rear of the butt parade, Moleskin Meg orchestrated the cameras, clicking shutters and snickering and making snide comments about the poor material she had to work with. (She seemed to be taking a long time. Could she actually be enjoying this?) After an eternity, the clicking and whirring stopped, and we retrieved our cameras and our dignity—now slightly tarnished, as was Ol' Albert.

Wahoola declared, "We will ever after be known as the 'Lunar Seven'."

Snickered another, "Today, a 'full moon' rose over Albert Mountain."

Moleskin Meg said, "Gee, Model-T, I think your camera was out of film."

I told her, "Fortune smiled. I think that calls for a Snickers bar."

J.R.: "A hog is known by the mud hole he wallows in."

Another mountain conquered!

"You're a jinx," I accused Wahoola as another car whizzed by—one of only five in the twenty minutes we'd been standing here with our thumbs stuck out like Little Jack Horner practicing for the Christmas pie. "You're not smiling enough. Let'em see the old chompers."

Right now, Wallace Gap seemed the most isolated place in the fifty states, but then Old US 64 was a "has-been" since most of its traffic had been siphoned off by "New" US 64, a mile north, which did the same job but with fewer curves. I could almost smell the food at Rainbow Springs Campground (our destination), a mile down the mountain.

Another car zipped past, this one a silvery flash—possibly a Buick, although I couldn't be sure because the car's logo had been preempted by the young teen who stuck out his tongue and flipped us a "bird." "Did you see what that little bastard did?" I'd like to dangle him over that fence on Albert Mountain!"

Wahoola flashed a grin. The memory, less than three hours old, still tingled. He said, "Aw, it's not me. Have you looked at yourself lately?"

I laughed. "No, but Moleskin Meg has. And she saw you, too! When I get back to the real world, I'm going to get a tee shirt that says, 'I mooned Albert Mountain'." J.R., still in a huff, growled, "How about a bumper sticker that says, 'I bared my ass on Albert Mountain?' That's what you really did."

Wahoola mumbled, "It's all part of the total Trail experience."

Another vehicle—an old, dull-green pickup this time—hove into view. "Okay, here comes our ride!" I said. "Put on your Boy Scout smile." (Pickups, especially older ones, were usually good for a ride because the driver could motion you into the back without worrying about getting mugged or having the interior contaminated with some exotic disease.)

The pickup poked past at slow turtle speed and an elderly, gray-headed couple gave us a friendly smile, waved, and disappeared down the mountain just shy of rabbit speed.

"Rats!" I spat "I'm gonna walk. It's only a mile and it's all downhill. I coulda been there by now."

"Yeah, we might as well."

We took off walking. "I'm not even going to try to catch a ride," I grumbled. "I don't care how many cars go by, I'm not even going to stick my thumb out. Heck! I'm not going to accept a ride even if somebody stops."

Wahoola snorted at my tirade and then smiled wickedly as a vehicle approached from our rear. "Well, here comes a test case. Let's see how well you do."

Determined not to flunk, I tucked my thumb inside my waist belt (although Wahoola stuck his out without bothering to turn around). A mud-splattered blue minivan swung onto the shoulder in front of us and stopped. "If you fellows are headed down to the campground, we can make room." Looking from the outside in I didn't see how, for two women, six young girls, and a pile of gear were crammed into the vehicle. Wahoola smirked. "Thanks. I could use a ride but my partner here has taken a vow of abstinence."

I pushed in front of him. "Ladies, you are looking at a fallen angel. I just toppled off the wagon."

The driver, a frizzy-headed blonde, pointed at the three smallest girls and said, "Emily Jane, you, Jenny and Gertrude push that stuff around and find a hole." Half of the back seat opened up and we managed to fit in the small space by holding our packs in our laps.

As the minivan gathered speed, Wahoola whispered in my ear, "Sorry Model-T. You get an F' minus."

Gertrude wailed at the woman on the passenger side, "Mommy, Emily Jane's hurting me. She's got her knee in my side."

Emily Jane shouted at the driver, "No I'm not! It's that old man's stick that's poking her in the ribs! Mommy, something stinks in here. Pleeeease roll down the windows!"

Wahoola, whispering in my ear: "This defies the laws of physics—like a gallon of water in a quart jar."

I whispered back, "A ride's a ride!"

The small camp store had a decent selection of foodstuffs—much to Hunger's delight—though a little pricey (as most "Mom and Pop" ventures must be in order to survive in the jungle of High Volume). I bought enough food to supplement my food bag (and appease Hunger) for the next thirty miles and went outside to find Wahoola.

He stood in line behind five campers who waited to use the only phone. I told him, "You're going to be awhile. I'm going on, but I'll pick the first place I come to and pitch my tent. See you later." The sun was already a fiery reflection brushing the mountaintops.

I began the long trek back up the mountain with my thumb out of action, for I was convinced that the sure-fire way to catch a ride was to *not* try to catch a ride! It worked! About a hundred yards from the Trailhead, an old geezer in a rusted Chevy pickup stopped but I waved him on. No need to bankrupt my "luck account" on such a puny deal!

The climb out of Wallace Gap was steep and tedious, and dusk was thick when I finally came to a small clearing barely large enough to accommodate a tent on each side of the path. It was far from ideal, slanted and rocky, and the mountain fell off into a deep void just scant feet away from the site I picked (the leveler of the two—first come; first served) but it would have to do.

I pitched my tent in the lonely twilight. Feeling empty and isolated, sensing that the darkness had become an adversary, I realized this might well be my first night alone (not counting The Ego) on the Trail. I sorely missed Wahoola.

He arrived over an hour later, whistling disconnected warbles like a small lad trying to bolster courage as he passes a cemetery during a full moon. I hadn't been able to sleep—"Wahoola withdrawal," said J.R.—and immediately heard the whistling and footsteps. "Dang, I'll bet that's Wahoola!"

I unzipped the tent flap and looked out. The flashlight could have been a lightning bug from the way the feeble glow flickered on and off at erratic intervals.

"Wahoola? Is that you?"

"Is this home?" he asked, his voice flooded with relief. "I was afraid I might miss you in the dark. My batteries are about shot."

"Yeah man, this is home! Just wipe your feet before you come in." The night was friendly again! The wind began a soft lullaby and sleep quickly came.

I was awakened in the wee hours of morning by stout gusts, which snatched and clawed at the tent like a fierce beast. A jumbo puff yanked some pegs out of the shallow, rocky soil, and the fabric began to buffet and whip around like a thing alive, threatening to become a parasail and carry me out into the void.

I crawled outside and restaked the tent, this time piling some large rocks on all the pegs. I tied a safety line from the tent to a nearby tree for added insurance. J.R. commented about the maverick wind: "Nary a cloud in the sky. I don't know what we did to irk her, but I think Old Mother Nature is giving us THE LOOK." Indeed, stars littered the inky heaven like glitter tossed on a slab of black marble. At the bottom of the void, lights from a single, isolated village speckled the dark. I watched for a long moment, braving the chill and the gusts as I marveled at the immense, unfathomable canvas of the night sky. I whispered, "No, this isn't THE LOOK; this is *nirvana*! We've got to share this with Wahoola."

I crossed the path to his tent. "Wahoola, are you awake?" No answer. "Wahoola," I repeated, louder, but the only sound was the wind groaning through the trees. My hollow whisper mingled with the ghostly moaning. "Sleep well, my friend," I whispered. "There will be other nights." But would there?

I dropped off into an uneasy sleep, plagued by the feeling that I had somehow shortchanged Wahoola by not being more persistent.

I had lost Wahoola! Was he behind or ahead? I had no idea, although J.R. thought he was probably somewhere back of us. We had leapfrogged back and forth so much today that I had gotten confused. Furthermore, the four-mile climb up to the top of Wayah Bald had worn me out and I couldn't seem to muster the willpower to focus my mind clearly. Rivulets of sweat trickled down through my beard and became part of the mass exodus that soaked my shirt and shorts as it headed for points south. "Dammit J.R., I hurt more all over than anywhere else." That was a just bit of fluff though, because my feet felt like they were going to set my boots on fire. "I can't go another step right now," and that wasn't fluff. My legs felt like a spongy mass of jelled rubber. "Let's take a break." I took off my pack without waiting for his okay and plopped down against the south side of the stone observation tower, which faced the noonday sun, and removed my boots. The relief was immediate.

What a spectacular view! Toward the southern horizon, the fire tower on Albert Mountain appeared as a tiny mast on an ocean of mountainous waves. At the limit of my vision, where the waves became one with the sky, Tray Mountain—sixty trail-miles away in Georgia—appeared as a small nub. Had it only been five days since we had washed our clothes and bathed (our last time!) at Tray Mountain Shelter? Looking at the rugged ripple of mountains, it staggered my mind that I had *actually* come through that maze! How many others even now plodded through that wilderness, sweating beneath heavy loads as they struggled up and down the mountains like two-legged pack mules?

No need to torture myself with the view to the north; it would only be a mirrored image of what I now saw. My world had become a monotonous ocean of bleak mountains and I floated helplessly like a rotted piece of flotsam. My spirits felt lower than a gravedigger's boots and I told J.R., "I would cry if I could afford the tears, but I'm too dehydrated." The Marine wisecracked, "Look on the bright side. You won't have to waste any time watering the trees." I snorted, "I'm gonna eat a Snickers." I ate two and then tuned my obnoxious "insignificant other" out and closed my eyes.

"Do you think he's dead?" a gravelly voice asked.

"If he is, he died happy, 'cause he's got a smile on his face," a youthful voice offered.

"Naw, he's a thru-hiker by his looks. He must be dreamin' about food," a third voice guessed.

He got the trophy. I was just about to tangle with a plate-sized hamburger, loaded, and a huge platter of fries, when the voices made it all go "poof." I opened my eyes and chuckled. "You fellers owe me a meal."

The three could have passed for brothers: same athletic build, same height, all in their early twenties, same southern twang, all sporting thick shocks of medium-length, curly, brown hair (except for the oldest, whose hair was redder than Wahoola's). It came as no surprise when he told me his name was Red.

Red was evidently assigned the task of spokesman. He said, "We're The Mello Woodsmen. Hiking to Maine." His companions nodded proudly. "Sorry about cheatin' you outta your dream. How about we make it up with a couple of packs of ramen?"

"No thanks. I couldn't eat a bite right now," I lied. "Maybe another time."

"Well, if you're sure . . . C'mon guys, lets see what it looks like from the top of the tower," and they dashed up the stairway like Santa's reindeer headed out on Christmas Eve.

Before I could get up enough steam to uncross my legs, they dashed back down, looked at me like I had leprosy, waved, and disappeared up the Trail—wood sprites headed back out to surf the mountains!

"Dammitall, Ego, if those bucks can do it, by golly so can we." I pulled on my boots and struggled to my feet. Slowly, painfully, I forced one rubbery leg in front of the other and climbed the stairway. When I reached the top, I lifted my arms high and bellowed out an "OOOGA." "Well, I guess we showed them. Now, let's get back to that hamburger." I felt better. Said The Ego, "Humpf. Same view as down below."

I feasted on the illusive hamburger for two hours, but Wahoola never showed. "Gee, he must be ahead of us. Do you think we ought to go on? It's almost four o'clock." He: "You're the Greyhound bus. I'm only a passenger," to which I replied, "You're also *no* help." I peered back down the Trail but it was empty, so I slipped on my pack and quietly left.

When I reached Licklog Gap, dark and foreboding in the lengthening shadows, I spotted a cramped but level clearing close to the Trail and pulled in. Wahoola had vanished like late morning mist and I resigned myself to a lonely night, not hoping for a reprieve two evenings in a row.

As darkness came on, so did the jitters. Hidden eyes and alien things rustled my imagination, and my heart hammered the loud silence—much like the mysterious thump-thump drumming I had heard climbing out of Woody Gap (which turned out to be the mating sound of the male ruffed grouse). The trees turned into shadowy, spooky forms as the twilight deepened, and each night noise became a hungry bear—or worse, a restless ancient spirit seeking redress for grievous injustices.

I lit my stove and began supper, wanting to get it over with so I could pile inside the sleeping bag—a much safer place than out here exposed to the wily phantoms of the night. The Whisperlite's small flame played with the darkness, and its fluttery reflection caused the shadows to sway back and forth like emaciated Indian warriors in a bizarre ghost dance. Unable to suppress the urge, I cast frequent glances at the dim, wavering shades, dreading to look but more afraid not to. I tried to think of pleasant things; played the mac-n-cheese "a la" game; even tried whistling; but always my eyes strayed back to the shadows.

"J.R., it's gonna be a long night." He ragged me, "You can stand guard if you want, but it's early to bed for me. By the way, be sure to check under your sleeping bag for boogey men." Insolent scuz! Yep, it had the makings of a really long night!

I rinsed my cook pot, wiped it clean with my shirttail, and then tiptoed to a nearby tree (keeping a wary eye out for disembodied hants for the tree was in their territory!) to carry out the final chore of the evening, hoping that it would hold me until dawn. A movement at the edge of my peripheral vision! My heart skipped a dozen beats and my legs became as useless as flaccid celery stalks. "Sumabitch!" The Marine blurted. "We're being infiltrated!"

A ghostly form, faintly white against the ebony backdrop, detached from the trees and moved up the Trail toward us. I croaked, "What do we do now, hightail it out of here?" A pretty stupid question, considering my legs refused to work. "Naw, let's keep out of sight. Just wait and see if it's hostile."

"But ghosts know all, see all. They already *know* we're here!" Sweat popped out on my forehead.

"Aw, stop your blubbering," he said. There's no such things as—"

A whistle sliced the silence. "Jiminy! That's Wahoola! I'd know that whistle anywhere. It's Wahoola!"

I stepped from behind the tree and walked across the clearing. "Hey Wahoola, where the hell have you been?" My voice exploded into the night like an artillery barrage.

He jumped at least a foot. "Jeezzus! You scared the stuffin' right outta me!"

"One good turn deserves another. I'm so glad you decided to join me this evening," I said sarcastically, all of a sudden miffed because of my jittery evening—all his fault! "That's two nights in a row you've dragged in late." J.R. hissed, "Listen to you! You sound like a nagging wife. Next thing, you'll be trying to work him over with THE LOOK." My anger evaporated in a giggly spasm at the mental picture of me zapping Wahoola with a poor rendition of THE LOOK. I quickly changed the subject. "Why are you walking in the dark?"

"My batteries finally crashed. I didn't mean to be on the Trail after dark, but I took a little nap back at Wayah Bald and didn't wake up until the sun was going down. Heck, I didn't even know if you were in front of me or not." Déjà vu! "I figured you would be here at Licklog Gap if you were in front."

I grumbled, "We need Volunteer to keep our itinerary sorted out." (As far as we knew, he hadn't passed us.) "Say, if you haven't had supper yet, I could probably eat again!"

The next morning dawned cold and foggy. I quickly broke camp and shook Wahoola's tent, now limp and soggy from the mist. "Carpe diem, Wahoola. Are you gonna play today?" I heard a grunt (or was it a groan). "I'm outta here. I'll wait for you at the Jump-Up if I don't see you before. And, no naps today!" I detected a muffled sound—definitely a groan—as I headed into the pea-soup morning to seize the day.

By the time I reached the Jump-Up—a breathtaking overlook that seemed to hang an arm's reach below Heaven's door—the mid-afternoon sun had pushed the fog away. In the far off valley, the Nantahala River pushed through lakes of fog as it serpentined through the mountainous maze. Somewhere down in that labyrinth, N.O.C. (and *food!*) waited—a good thing, for I was almost out! Worse, I was out of Snickers bars!

Wahoola arrived within thirty minutes and we sat in silence, drinking in the view and refreshing our spirits. At last satiated, together we headed down a long spine that led toward civilization.

Said The Marine, "I'm hungry enough to eat garter snake soup." I swallowed my drool and chuckled. "I hope there's enough to go around!"

CHAPTER 3

A Fool and His Money Are Soon Parted

Snugly nestled against the bank of the Nantahala River like a tick on a dog's ear, the Nantahala Outdoor Center, or N.O.C., is a dream come true for rafters, kayak bugs, and canoeists. They flock to the popular mountain playground to frolic in frothy, icy swirling waters. Thru-hikers have a different kind of frolic in mind: They come to eat!

We might have been runners at a track meet as we sped down the mountain toward Rufus Morgan Shelter—a mistake, for by the time we reached the shelter Wahoola had developed a slight limp ("The 'Thing' had turned mean!"), and I had hot spots on the bottoms of both big toes. I asked him, "Why were you in such an all-fired hurry?"

"I was just trying to keep up with you."

"Well, I was just trying to not get run over."

Truth be known, I had succumbed to a tenderfoot trap—hightailing it down a long (in this case three and a half miles), easy downhill to "make" time. Just give the legs free rein and let'em rip! Easy hiking!

The trap? I never stopped to rest my knees or give the feet a chance to wiggle around in the boots—a surefire recipe for blisters or blown-out knees; instead, I just kept on barreling like a runaway train all the way to the bottom. Dumb! But then, thoughts of food and N.O.C. had skittered my brain!

It was nearly five o'clock by the time we reached the shelter. "What's the plan?" I asked. "Stay here and hit N.O.C. for breakfast, or go on in and pig out tonight?" The Center was only a scant mile away.

"We might be better off staying here. N.O.C. could be full up, and I don't think I want to shell out rent money when this is free."

What he said made sense. Money not spent on rent meant more for FOOD! But doggone—all that food so close! "Yeah, you're right," I reluctantly agreed, "but it's gonna be a long night!"

We pitched tents by a small stream fifty yards downhill from the shelter, cleaned up as best we could, ate the last of our food, and then settled into our sleeping bags to wait out the night.

Wahoola got up when I did—a rare occurrence—and for once actually beat me packing up. He already had his pack on, ready to head out as I crammed the last items in and fastened the pack shut. Stamping impatiently and sniffing the air like a hungry bear, he suddenly growled, "I smell food. Bacon and eggs and pancakes!"

"Aw, you're hallucinating. We're too far away." He had to be putting me on.

"Naw, I swear it's the honest truth. I can smell it!" His eyes did have a certain feverish—almost fanatical—gleam.

The power of suggestion? The brain playing tricks as it imagined a table laden with delicious eggs, bacon, sausage, grits, pancakes, donuts . . .? Suddenly my mind locked onto the image and the smells wafted into my senses. "Holy cow, I can smell it, too! And I can taste the bacon and grits!" Reason told me it was impossible, but I did!

"I can too!" Wahoola yelled. "Let's go!" and we hit the Trail running.

J.R. groaned, "Lord, deliver me from idiots who engage in Twaddle at six o'clock in the morning."

N.O.C. bustled with activity. Cars zoomed back and forth and the fumes and noise, removed from our lives these past few days, stifled our senses. Across the road in the churning, frothy Nantahala, three kayaks bobbed and pitched as they slalomed around pylons, mixing colorful reds, yellows, greens, and blues into blurred rainbows that flitting through the misted foam. The river, acting like a giant vaporizer, saturated the air with moisture, which refreshed and soothed our oxygen-hungry lungs. I inhaled deeply, greedily, again and again, nearly hyperventilating.

And there it was, unmistakable, this time for real! The delightful, tantalizing aroma of bacon and coffee mixed with the slight breeze, into my nose, my mouth, my soul! "C'mon!" I urged, and we rushed down the road like two bulls running from the business end of a cattle prod, chasing after the titillating smells until we followed them to the front door of the N.O.C. Restaurant. The overpowering aroma caused Wahoola to blurt, "Food orgy!" We propped our packs alongside several others near the door and hurried inside.

"Oh, man!" I gasped, almost too excited for words. A wave of almost forgotten sounds filled the air: dishes clanking, the excited hum of hungry diners, harried waitresses bustling trays piled high with food. And the smells!

We looked for a place to sit but the restaurant was jammed with tourists and river sprites. A sprinkling of rag-tag grubbies stood out in the crowd, easily recognizable as thru-hikers, all doing what they had come for—eating!

Lone Star and Moleskin Meg sat at a nearby booth with two other thru-hikers (later introduced as Dr. Doolittle and Robin Hood). She saw us and waved, and her eyes twinkled as she motioned at the high stack of pancakes that a harried waitress was placing in front of her. For the moment silence reigned at the booth; pancakes had triumphed over Moleskin Meg's awesome voice.

In a back corner Volunteer and Hippy Man (still attached to El Senor) wrestled with a large platter of breakfast delights. We tried to get their attention, but they were too busy eating. Wahoola said, "How about that! All this time I thought Volunteer was behind us." So had I. And Hippy Man—I thought he would be days ahead of us by now, the way he had breezed past when I left Springer. Hippy Man finally saw us and nudged Volunteer. They waved in unison like their arms were connected to the same camshaft, and then got back to eating.

This was torture at its worst—starving hikers (at least we thought we were) in a food paradise and no place to sit! We stood near the door and watched all the eating going on around us, drooling, feeling like the Little Match Girl standing outside looking in. At last, a man and woman left one of the booths and we rushed in—two predator piranhas on the prowl—and the feeding frenzy began.

Finally it was over, as fast as it had begun. We could hold no more. Wahoola gave me a doleful look. Burping loudly, he asked, "Do you think gluttony is a sin?"

I hurt too much to give a coherent answer. My body had become a big bloated belly, topped with an instinct-serving brain. I groaned, "Probably. According to the Good Book, the wages of sin is death and I feel like I'm gonna die."

Later, a bunch of us sat on a long bench beneath a skimpy overhang outside the N.O.C. Outfitter Store. Clean, shiny-faced tourists walked past—some gawking, most too wrapped up in their own small worlds to pay much attention to the ragged, unkempt mountain urchins who stared at them.

A weak drizzle started about mid-morning, but it didn't sap the festival mood. We swapped trail stories and went about the mundane (but necessary) chores that would enable us to continue on toward Katahdin. Rummaging through food parcels, we repacked food into plastic bags and ate or gave away what we couldn't carry or didn't want. (I only had nine packs of ramen to contend with from this food box, so I kept three and gave the rest away.) Eventually the drizzle turned into a light steady rain, though not hard enough to drive us inside. We sat, talked, and ate the afternoon away, but mostly we just rested.

Wahoola walked out of the Outfitter Store carrying a Therm-a-Rest mattress in one hand and a pint of B&J in the other. "Look what I just bought," he said with a satisfied smile. The pad was a replica of mine, only a different color. "Yours looked so comfortable that I decided to get me one." He had been scrutinizing mine for the past few days and I had felt sorry for the poor bloke. (Truth be known, I wouldn't have let a dog sleep on his old pad for fear of getting arrested for animal abuse!)

"About time. What're you going to do with your old pad?" I asked, eyeing the B&J, surprised that I felt hungry again after the humongous breakfast and all the snacking I'd done since then.

Wahoola saw my look and chuckled, "I found a little more room in my belly and it's not going to waste. I think I'll put the old pad under the Therm-a-Rest. That ought to make for some really good sleeping."

"From what I've seen, you've been pretty flush in the sleep department." Wahoola certainly wasn't sleep-deprived—food perhaps, but definitely not sleep. Jeez, the B&J looked good. I was more than hungry; I was starved—again!

(Actually, we were all experiencing the onset of "calorie deficit." Each day we expended the energy equivalent of running two marathons—according to some bean counter's math, between five and six thousand calories a day, which far exceeded our average "on-the-Trail" intake of about 3000 calories. Hence, simple math dictated that we would be in calorie deficit all the way to Katahdin. Big-time eating had to become a main priority, for once the body fat was gone the body would insatiably continue grabbing calories where it could, and muscles would atrophy as the body feasted. A scary proposition!)

I went inside and bought a pint of chocolate B&J (a concession to J.R.) to stymie the calorie deficit. Which brought on another thought: The food bag I now had just wasn't large enough, especially when I imagined the ol' body enjoying my muscles while I starved. I looked over the selection and finally settled on a vomit-green waterproof bag twice the size of the one I now had (almost as large as my pack). "What do you think, Ego? Large enough?" He said, "It's the largest one in the store." Chuckling, I said, "Then I guess it's large enough."

I went back outside and dumped the food from the smaller bag into the larger. "Much better," I mumbled, "but we've got a lot of room left." I said to the other hikers who sorted and packed and pitched, "Hey guys, if anyone has anything extra I'll take it. Anything but ramen, that is."

Soon the bag was filled to capacity: cans of sardines in assorted sauces, cans of Vienna sausages in assorted juices, five cans of Beenie-Weenies, crackers, three boxes of "classy" mac-n-cheese (Volunteer's contribution). "All right Marine! We've got it made," I said smugly. "Nothin's gonna eat our muscles. We're gonna *pamper* our fat!" I stood back and surveyed my creation, beaming like a new papa. "Yessiree! Our fat's going to *love* us!"

Wahoola watched the food bag expansion project with interest. "Model-T, are you going to carry all that or hire a Sherpa?" Volunteer and Hippy Man laughed.

"Aw, it's not all that heavy." To prove my point, I hoisted the bag up to my chest, not quite able to hide the grunt. The bag was *heavy!* "Well, I might need to lighten it up a tad," and I took out the three packs of ramen. Reconsidering, I pushed them back in and said, "I'll eat the heavy stuff first." Last night's hunger still lingered like a knife in my gut.

Wahoola and I went back to the restaurant to get in one final fling, for the day was fast winding down. It was decision time: Head on up the Trail in the light rain; crash at the N.O.C. hostel—seven dollars for a spot in a six-man bunkhouse (shower included, no linens); or go back to the Rufus Morgan Shelter. I asked Wahoola, "What do you want to do?"

"How about hanging around here tonight and splitting the cost of a cottage? Some of the others talked about hitching into Bryson City (12 miles away and the closest town) and getting some beer and goodies and partying down."

I thought about it: Ante up seven dollars for the cottage, plus my share for the beer and goodies. At the least, a twenty-dollar night, not to mention a sluggish start in the morning. But the six-mile climb from N.O.C. up to Swim Bald on a full belly in the rain, didn't hold much appeal either. On the other hand, a hot shower and a couple of cold beers, and then the camaraderie . . .

J.R. nudged me. "Think of all the Snickers twenty dollars will buy." That cinched it for me.

"I think I'll go back up to the shelter and stay the night, and then get an early start in the morning. You go on and join the others. We can meet up tomorrow afternoon."

He looked uncertain. "Are you sure?"

"Yeah, and maybe you can convince Hippy Man to send El Señor home before he blows his feet and legs out." (Hippy Man had developed a bad limp in both legs.) "How about we tent tomorrow night at Stecoah Gap? It's only a thirteen mile day."

"Okay, Stecoah Gap it is."

We finished our meal—scant by this morning's standard—and went outside. Wahoola watched as I shouldered my monstrous pack and laughing, shook his head. "I might catch up with you by early afternoon."

As I walked away, a twinge of guilt at deserting my partner rippled my conscience. But the solitude of the woods seemed more appealing than partying in some stuffy bunkhouse. Plus, all those Snickers . . .

When I walked past the N.O.C. Outfitter Store, Moleskin Meg was holding court at the bench where we had frittered away most of the afternoon. She lectured a small assemblage of scraggly thru-hikers on the many uses of peanut butter. Seeing me, she exclaimed, "Look guys, it's the Duck Tape Man!" and motioned for me to join the group.

"Damn!" I muttered to J.R. "Let's make a run for it! How'd you like to forever after be known as duck tape man? People saying, 'There goes, the Duck Tape Man. Hey, Duck Tape Man, quack for us! Say, he looks like a duck; yeah, he even walks like a duck. I bet he sounds like a duck, too. Hey, Duck Tape Man, give us a quack or two!'"

J.R. freaked. "No way! Let's get out of here!" I waved and bellowed two hearty "OOOGA's"—just to assert my true identity, and we fled!

At one time, the Stecoah Range between N.O.C. and Fontana Dam had the dubious reputation as the orneriest section of the entire AT, even exceeding the ruggedness of Maine. A faded, hand-painted sign on a guard rail where the Trail crosses paved Sweetwater Creek Road at Stecoah Gap warns: "Throo hikers beware—only 1 in 30 make it all the way. The test of staying power is here. The Smokies are vacation land."

Thankfully, the Stecoahs were tamed in the late 1980's, when dedicated members of the Smoky Mountains Hiking Club replaced many of the steep roller coaster sections of trail with winding switchbacks. Traces of the old trail are still visible today as they cut across the switchbacks, precipitously rising in heart-stopping straight shots to the summits.

Even with the switchbacks the going was tough! The monstrous food bag had become a Frankensteinian creation, which quickly turned on its master. And I hadn't even reached the halfway point in the long climb up to Swim Bald. I groaned, "Why? Why didn't I listen to Wahoola?" The Ego snarled, "Anyone dumb enough to show his rumpus to the world wouldn't have enough sense to listen to good advice." Jeez! Was he still hung up on *that?* I growled, "Well, we gotta keep ahead of calorie deficit." He muttered, "'Shut'!"

I stopped in the middle of the Trail and took off my pack. "I'm gonna do something about this right now." I dug into the food bag and began gorging on sardines and crackers, followed by two cans of Beenie-Weenies. "Gotta eat the heavier stuff first; get it outta th' pack." He said, "That flies like a lead balloon. All you are doing is transferring the load from your pack to your belly. You still have to carry it." (At least he admitted that the belly belonged to me.) I retorted, "Why do you have to make life so complicated?"

By the time I reached the top of Swim Bald, I had made half a dozen "transfer" stops and my stomach felt like it was going to explode. J.R. had retreated behind a thick curtain of silence, probably pouting at my obstinate refusal to ditch a lot of the stuff. No matter, for I had a more pressing problem. I dumped my pack against a tree and ran for a clump of nearby bushes, and then upchucked the contents of my stomach.

J.R. interrupted my interlude. "Well, Ace. That's *one* way to lighten your load." My head swam and my heart skipped like a drunken rabbit. I staggered over to my pack and crashed to the ground, rubbing my belly, which felt as if a crop of giant mushrooms had spawned in its dark recess. He derided me. "Pap always said that a fool and his money are soon parted." Struggling to my feet, I moaned, "It wasn't my money, and it wasn't his saying. Just leave me alone." He stomped off in a huff, and I slung the monster back on my shoulders and went on.

Late in the afternoon I reached the highway at Stecoah Gap, where Wahoola and I had agreed to meet for the night. We couldn't camp here. The only place to put up tents was the small roadside picnic area where I stood, and a concrete table took up most of the area. Cars whizzed past just out of arm's reach. Nothing to do but wait until Wahoola showed up, and then go on.

So I waited. I read the crude sign painted on the guardrail telling "Throo hikers to beware" again and again; counted the words (twenty-four); and the letters, (ninety, not counting numbers and punctuation); and the vowels (thirty-six); and lastly, the consonants. I watched the cars zip along the busy highway, returning the waves with feisty enthusiasm in hopes that someone would pull in and offer me a cold soda, for my water was gone and thirst thickened my mind. According to *The Philosopher's Guide*, a good spring was down a dirt road within a quarter-mile, but I was afraid of missing Wahoola if I left here. So I waited . . .

At last, voices drifted down the mountainside. Wahoola and Volunteer were caught up in a vigorous discussion as to whether Ben and Jerry's was really better than the less expensive brands. Volunteer declared his loyalty to B&J, but Wahoola disagreed. "It's all fat calories, and calories is calories. It just doesn't make any difference." Irrefutable logic, which ended the discussion.

They were soaked with sweat. "You guys are never going to get to Maine, partying all night and dragging your feet like seal tails."

Wahoola looked me up and down as if he were surprised. "I see you decided not to go nude today." I looked puzzled and he explained, "Did you forget? Today is April 22nd—Earth Day. Otherwise known as Nude Hiker Day. Remember?"

I laughed, my thirst momentarily forgotten. "Doggone, I forgot! And after spending all that time on Albert Mountain rehearsing! How about you guys?"

Wahoola, his mouth twitching with amusement, said, "Not entirely. The 'Kid' here and I decided to keep our boots on." He had to be teasing! Or was he?

Volunteer nodded and laughed. "Some of the hikers last night swore they *were* going to do it today, even if it was raining. By the way, we had a great time, lots of beer and pizza." He glared at Wahoola. "And B&J."

I terminated the discussion by pointing at the sun, which was already hugging the horizon. "It'll soon be dark and I don't want to spend the night here. It's asking for trouble."

They agreed. Wahoola's map showed a small flat area about a mile away at Sweetwater Gap, grossly misnamed because it had no water source. Everything between here and Sweetwater Gap looked steep, wooded, and dry.

"Well, it looks like Sweetwater Gap is our best bet," Wahoola said.

"Yeah, and we'd best get water here at the spring." We were all dehydrated and out of water. I said, "Let's toss to see who goes for the water."

Lady Luck frowned on Volunteer. He took off down the highway with six empty bottles bobbing up and down in rhythm to his stride, while Wahoola and I kept our fingers crossed that the spring would be where it was supposed to be, and that it would be running.

As we settled down to wait, Wahoola dug into his pack and pulled out his old sleeping pad. "Might as well get comfortable." He folded the pad into a seat and sat on the ground with his back against the picnic table. (I had been doing the same thing with my Therm-a-Rest, and each time I worried that a sharp rock might puncture it.)

I eyed his cushion with envy. "I wish I had something like that to sit on."

"What would you give for a part of this?" He said it blandly, like we were discussing the weather.

Idle talk, so I humored him. "I'd give a pack of ramen."

Wahoola grinned. "Naw, I don't eat that stuff. How about a Snickers?"

"No way! My butt's not worth that much."

"Got any bread?" he countered. He sounded serious!

I had half a loaf, squashed into a hard ball. "Yeah, I have bread." My interest blossomed. "And lots of peanut butter."

"How about four slices of bread and four spoonfuls of peanut butter for half my pad?"

"How about two slices of bread and two peanut butters for a third?"

Wahoola chuckled and stuck out his hand. "A done deal, but you have to carry it till lunch tomorrow."

Dang! I shook his hand and agreed, "Done deal, but I get the pad now," and I reached for my knife.

J.R., ever vigilant for a good thing, chortled, "Our fat's going to be pissed off, but our ass is going to adore us!" I: "Which should go a long way toward helping your headaches." Wise guy!

Volunteer returned with filled bottles. The spring flowed pure and cold from a pipe, and he bragged that he had drank a whole quart while there. Clutched by thirst, I told him, "Heck, that's nothing," and I chugalugged one of my quarts.

Wahoola sipped his sparingly. "I'm going to save mine for supper."

"I can get through the night okay with one quart," I said, "unless Volunteer wants to take pity on a poor old man and go get me a refill."

All he said was, "Ha!"

At Sweetwater Gap, I sat on my new pad staring at the dwindling water supply and tried to resist the temptation to gulp it all down in one euphoric rush. Instead, I barely wet my lips, wondering how small an amount of water I could get by with and still manage an edible Lipton Noodle dinner.

After carefully calculating, I poured a cup and a half into the pot, dumped in the noodles, and began cooking. That left slightly less than half a quart to get me through breakfast and to the next water source. (After I ate, the pot had to be cleaned, plus, it would be nice to brush my teeth!) I sneaked a glance at Wahoola's bottles—one full and the other still had a couple of healthy swigs left. Volunteer was in even better shape. J.R. chided me, "We're water paupers, just because you had to show off." Penitent, I said, "We can always suck on rocks."

Supper was a sad affair. The noodles quickly congealed into a large sticky glob, and each bite stuck in my parched throat and protested all the way down to my stomach—pure torture without water to wash it down. "Worse than dry ramen," The Ego complained. Finally done, I grimaced at the empty pot, its sides crusted with thick glue-like paste. I couldn't bring myself to waste the water to clean it.

Slowly, an idea began to form: Ed Garvey NEVER washed his cook pot—a fact he'd revealed in the book about his 1970 thru-hike, *Appalachian Hiker: Adventure of a Lifetime*—and he never got sick! If it worked for Ed, why not me (with a slight modification, of course)! J.R. groaned, "You're not thinking about doing what you're thinking about doing, I hope!" I snapped, "Shut up and let me think. I'm onto something big."

How to do this? A law of physics: Matter is neither created nor destroyed, just transformed, or some such hocus-pocus. It followed that the same holds true with water. "Okay, J.R. hold onto your hat. Here goes!" I filled my mouth with water (Ahh, it felt delicious!), swished it around, and then spit it into the pot. "Rubbadubdub, three men in a tub," I hummed happily as I scrubbed the pot with my toothbrush, dislodging the gooey food residue into the water. Good so far! Then I brushed my teeth and drank the Garvey brew down before J.R. knew what was happening. "How about that, Ol' Jobberknocker? Ed would be proud of us," I said, wiping the pot dry with the cleanest part of my shirt. "Done!"

J.R., making weird gagging sounds, groaned, "You oughta have to live in Old Padgett's out house. You're both full of crap." But his words rolled off my back; I was a happy camper and I crowed, "You should be proud. We're now physicists."

Volunteer broke into our silent drivel. "What in the world are you doing, Model-T?" Volunteer and Wahoola were watching me like a hawk flying over a chicken yard.

I threw them a smug look. "Cleaning my pot."

Wahoola said, "That looked pretty smart. I think I'll try it."

Wowie! I had suddenly been elevated from skuzzy thru-hiker to venerated guru, and Wahoola was my first convert! In my mind's eye I saw hordes of future thru-hikers practicing the water-saving "Model-T pot-cleaning process." I would send dedicated disciples out into the world to spread the word! With the help of all my "Model-T-mates," we would conserve millions of gallons of precious water each year and avert drought and famine. Through our efforts, all the springs would flow and the creeks would run. There would be water for all!

Volunteer shook his head and retorted, "You guys are worse than disgusting. You've became trail bums," to which J.R. added, "It had to happen sooner or later. I'm surprised it took this long."

Wahoola and I exchanged winks. We had crossed into new territory, had become charter members of a highly exclusive club. We had drunk our toothpaste water! We were scum brothers!

A freshening wind soothed our sweat-dried bodies as we talked, enjoying each other's company, while the dusk changed to ebony and the night breeze played in the trees. Far off down the side of the mountain, a solitary owl sent a forlorn hoot toward the thin sliver of moon rising above the trees; and before long, an answering call from a neighboring mountain mimicked the eerie sound. Conversation gradually diminished into yawns, and we took to our tents. I stashed the precious water bottle by my head and hoped I had the will power to resist its tempting nearness. Sleep came slow.

I awoke at first light swamped with thirst and drank the last of my water. Breakfast would have to wait until I found a spring or stream. Wahoola and Volunteer still slept, so I quietly packed and began the climb out of waterless Sweetwater Gap.

The climb was a real challenge—eight hundred feet of old Stecoah philosophy going straight up. Before I had gotten half way through the climb, I was sweating profusely; what little water I had hoarded through the night now dripped on the ground and there was nothing I could do about it. The Ego jeered, "Hey, ol' buddy, are you running on Garvey brew this morning?" Paying the jackass no heed, I gasped, "Shut'n hill. Where're the confounded switchbacks?" and shuddered to think how it must have been on the old Trail. Happily, the next few ascents were gentled by switchbacks, and I soon found water dripping from a rock ledge. Back in the game!

I reached Cable Gap Shelter around mid-afternoon. I hadn't seen Wahoola or Volunteer all day, but no matter. The sun beamed its rays into the clearing, warming the day, and I had plenty of time.

A small, clear stream sparkling with invitation flowed close by the front of the shelter. Slipping out of my pack, I knelt down and splashed the cold, fresh water on my face. Ambrosia! I gloated to The Ego, "The stream's all mine. I'm going to have a luxurious bath!" Life couldn't get much sweeter!

The stream (obviously female gender) seemed to sense my need and burbled, "Take me; use me; make me your own."

I gasped with excitement and J.R. wheezed, "What a lady! C'mon! Hurry, man! Time's awastin'!"

I quickly got my "tub" out of the pack and dipped it into the delicious, shimmering coolness. The sensuous liquid tendrils swirled with caressing smoothness over my hands. "Yeah, Ego, a real lady!" After a quick check to make sure I had the place to myself, I stripped and quickly washed my clothes, and then pulled the wet shorts back on and spread the tee shirt over a bush. The "Lady" flashed her silvery smile and seemed to murmur with a silky, sultry whisper, "There's more if you want it." Not satiated, I decided to linger in her embrace and shampoo my hair and beard.

Completely engrossed in the task at hand, head covered in suds, my orgy came to an abrupt halt as a loud voice behind me snarled, "Why are you washing your hair *here* when there's a perfectly good shower six miles up the trail?"

Startled, furiously wiping at shampoo and fighting the urge to flee into the nearby woods, I managed to get the soap out of my eyes and saw a tall, gangly, freckle-faced hiker. His hands were aggressively placed on his hips and a snarl twisted his lips. He wore full-length yellow gaiters, and red hair fought to escape the comical green beanie cap that sat squarely on his head.

"Huh?"

He glowered. "You know, the shower at Fontana Dam." (He must have meant the free showers available to thru-hikers at the TVA Visitor Center.) Before I could reply, he erupted, "Are these your boots?" (Of course they were. No one else was here.) "And that's your pack? Your gear is all screwed up. You'll never make it to Maine."

Holy cow! Who was this guy? Dumbfounded, I tried to think of something to say in my defense. Or better still, unleash the big, bad killer Marine. But then he never seemed to be around when I really needed him!

Wahoola and Volunteer walked into the clearing. The cavalry to the rescue! I prepared for battle—a duel, or maybe some saber-rattling and crusty name-calling. His call! Whichever way the action swung, I feared we were past a friendly handshake.

The stranger attacked in a different direction, immediately besmearing their gear and their chances of reaching Maine. Now, he faced three bristling (but speechless) antagonists.

Unperturbed, he asked, "When did you leave Springer Mountain?"

Wahoola found his voice. "April 10th."

"How many miles are you making a day?"

"We're averaging about fifteen," he replied with a smug look on his face. Fifteen was good!

The beanie guy, his voice harsh and accusing, snapped, "No you're not. You're averaging twelve point five. I left Harpers Ferry thirty-three days ago and I'm doing twenty-five miles or more a day. I'm going to Springer Mountain, then to Maine, and then back to Harpers Ferry. That makes two thru-hikes by fall." He hesitated, his eyes calculating, and then he slashed at our egos. "I'll catch you before you get to Roan Mountain."

J.R. finally crawled out of his hidey-hole. "Okay, Killer, it's your show," I told him. "Just leave enough to bury."

"Friend," The Marine said in a quiet, deadly voice that sent a chill down my spine, "you can catch us anytime you want. It doesn't mean a thing to us." Battle flags flying high, nose flared, J.R. was now in his element. I half expected him to sprout webbed feet and spit a "globe, anchor, and eagle" insignia out of his mouth, along with a wild, "Aarruuah!" as he leaped for the poor schmook's jugular. Instead, he assumed a threatening stance, hands on hips (Yes! They were *his* hands and hips right now!) and took one step forward. Wahoola and Volunteer, aware of J.R.'s Marine background, watched wide-eyed, anticipating swift vengeance.

The stranger abruptly turned, either figuring the odds were against him (or more likely not deeming us worthy of any further consideration). Insolently, he walked over to the shelter, picked up the register, wrote furiously for a moment, and then slammed the book to the floor. Without another glance our way, he stomped off down the Trail.

I told The Marine, "Darn, but I'm glad he wasn't in charge of the Rangers at Cooper Gap. He'd have ordered those guys to string us up and leave us for buzzard bait!"

The moment the stranger left the clearing, we rushed to the shelter and read what he had written: "4/23—Ward Leonard, Southbound."

Volunteer stammered, "Who in the heck is Ward Leonard?"

Wahoola replied, "I don't know, but if he's hiking twenty-five miles or more a day, we'll probably see him again. By the way, Model-T, I thought you were fixing to make mince meat out of that guy. You sure showed him."

I shrugged. "All in a day's work," and passed the compliment on to "Killer."

Sadly, when I returned to the stream the magic was gone. The "Lady" had departed.

Late in the afternoon, the three of us sat on a high perch north of Black Gum Gap and gazed down at Fontana Dam. A hawk drifted on an invisible current, riding the updraft with graceful ease until it suddenly swooped toward the monstrous slab of concrete far below. Rising nearly five hundred feet out of the Little Tennessee River gorge, Fontana Dam is the highest dam east of the Mississippi River. Yet, from our temporary aerie it looked like a small piece of cardboard holding back an inky-blue puddle. Beyond us, the mighty Smokies intimidated my imagination as they reared toward the sky in a display of magnificent grandeur. We had weathered the Stecoahs, but my pulse quickened as I thought of the challenge ahead.

Dusk was upon us by the time Wahoola and I stopped to pitch tents beside a small stream two miles from the highway that led to the small village of Fontana Dam, North Carolina (our next mail drop). Volunteer, brimming with excitement about taking a few days off to visit family and his fiancée, hurried on ahead to meet his father. Sadly, we watched him disappear into the twilight and wondered if we would ever see him again.

Later, Wahoola mused, "That Ward Leonard fellow sure won't get the 'Mister 1990 Trail Congeniality' award. I wonder why we haven't heard about him before?"

"Maybe it's because he's southbound and we're northbound. I haven't met any southbounders yet. Have you?"

He thought a moment and grinned. "Nope. Anyway, he goofed. I figured it out and we're averaging twelve point eight."

I chuckled and went to my tent. Tomorrow the Smokies!

Fontana Dam (the town)—really a hamlet set in a mountain cul-de-sac—buzzed with clean-smelling tourists who wandered in and out of small shops like bees gathering nectar from hollyhock blossoms. Raised eyebrows let us know we were not of their kind, which caused Wahoola to gloat, "We're getting there! Another few days without a bath and we'll truly smell like thru-hikers!"

"What do you mean 'we'? I took a bath yesterday at Cable Gap Shelter."

"Yeah, but it'll take a lot more than sponging off in a creek to get rid of this smell."

Instinctively, I whiffed my underarms, wrinkled my nose, and rolled my eyes. "It's gotta be the company I keep. Holy Sheemoli! Look at that!"

A large sign whacked my noggin as if I had been swatted by lightning. The big, bold letters glared provocatively, and the sign seemed to leer as it enticed me toward the beckoning door like a spidery seductress, whispering, "Come into my parlor . . ." Helpless, I grinned weakly at Wahoola and surrendered without a struggle. With saliva dribbling down my beard I told him, "See you at the Post Office. I'm about to commit gluttony," and I walked inside the soda fountain!

A sign in flowing green script, hand-painted on the yellow wall, read: "Chocolate sodas—$2.00". I gasped. Two whole dollars! (Dang it all! Damascus, my next money resupply, was almost 300 miles away. No matter. Caught up as I was in hedonistic passion, this seemed a minor detail.)

I told the gray-haired lady behind the counter, "One chocolate soda, please." Darn, I could already taste it! Unbidden, the words erupted through my drool, "And if you could add extra ice cream and double the chocolate syrup, I'd pay the difference." The Ego groaned, "You're a glutton for punishment. Haven't you learned by now that more isn't always better? Remember N.O.C.!" I: "Shaddup! I'm gonna do this thing up right." He retorted, "A fool and his money . . . Sad."

The woman smiled and gave me a sly wink, at the same time casting a furtive look around the shop (to see if her boss was watching?), and then nodded. She plied her trade like a master craftsman as she dipped, poured, whizzed and poured again. Entranced, I watched each move, silently applauding each step, and when she handed me the frothy brown treasure I accepted it with reverent awe as if it were the Holy Grail. She said with another conspiratorial wink, "That will be two dollars." What a wonderful lady!

I sat outside the shop and slurped it down in a noisy ecstatic glissade. Soon whopper burps began erupting from deep within my innards—awesome growls that mocked a pride of angry lions—and each rumbling burp became a winsome encore to the sublime experience.

A middle-aged couple walked past just in time to connect with one of the lustier encores. I heard the woman tell her husband in a barely audible voice, "George, did you hear that racket? That man is nothing but a beast in filthy clothing."

Unperturbed, I chortled to J.R., "A very observant lady, to recognize us as creatures of the forest." He, laughing: "She should see Wahoola!"

We picked up our food drops (thankfully, Judith had taken the ramen out). Wiser after the N.O.C. experience, I kept just enough food to get me to Hot Springs and placed the rest in a small "hiker's box" that sat in a corner of the Post Office. Even so, seven days of food added nearly twenty pounds to my pack. We got the food organized and went out to the main road to hitch back to the Trailhead, a good two miles away, hoping we would have better luck this time. (We had to walk it earlier.)

After ten minutes, an old rusty beat-up pickup pulled over in front of us. "You boys wantin' a ride?" The driver, thirty-ish, his pockmarked face peeking through a couple of week's accumulation of beard and grime, pointed toward the bed and said, "Just hop in back with Ol' Bud," which was the only place we could since the cab was crammed with an assortment of tools and trash, a collection probably started when he first got the old derelict.

We hesitated, and the man said, "Ol' Bud ain't gonna bite." We weren't as worried about Ol' Bud as we were the driver—he looked worse than us!

We crawled in the back and the dog immediately moved upwind. Said J.R., "That's a smart dog." Ol' Bud was definitely a mongrel—part golden retriever, part bird dog, with possibly some shepherd and collie mixed in. He hunkered into a corner of the bed, braced himself firmly against the side, and the truck sped off with a jerk, burning rubber and nearly tossing us out.

Tires squealed and odd grating noises came from underneath as the truck whipped around the sharp curves. We held on for our lives, but Ol'Bud sat in his corner, eyes closed, leaning in anticipation of each curve even before the truck careened into it, constantly weaving back and forth like a cobra swaying to the melodic sound of a flute. Said J.R., "That's one really smart dog!"

The curves finally gave way to a long flat stretch, and the dog immediately flopped down and went to sleep. Said J.R., "That dog's a lot smarter than some people I know!"

The truck whizzed past the Trail. Wahoola pounded on the cab roof and brakes screeched. The driver stuck his head out of the window. "This where you wanted off? I didn't recollect you saying."

Wahoola said, "Yep, this'll do fine. Thanks." We dropped our packs over the side and followed. (Ol Bud never opened an eye.) The driver took a swig from something wrapped in a paper sack, and then the truck lurched off with a jerk and a jarring clash of grinding metal.

We bent into our packs and began the one-mile stretch of several small but steep hills that stood between us and The Fontana Hilton (a rustic, large new shelter built on the edge of Fontana Lake, where we were required to self-register for a back country permit required by the National Park Service). The day had become unseasonably warm—approaching 90 degrees— and the lower elevation humidity was a killer.

Life quickly turned sour. The two dollar chocolate soda became a malicious ogre, scourging my bloated belly, clawing to be set free. A rank odor of old tires rose through the hiker stench as pure chocolate sweated from my pores. Worse, nausea rode the noisy belches like a demon on a tiger's back. With every other step came a loud burp and J.R.'s acid rancor:

Burrrrp . . . "Poot-head!" Step, step, burrrrp . . . "Diddy-butt!" Step, step, burrrrp . . . I was too sick to care.

One of the "burrrrp's" suddenly sounded like "baarrrff" and I shouted at Wahoola's back, a good ten yards ahead. "Wahoola, I've gotta take a break."

He waited until I staggered up. "Man, Model-T, you stink worse than I do." If my stink overpowered his, it must be bad! "And you're greener than a head of cabbage. What's wrong?" I was moved by his concern.

"Burrrrrrp. Baaarrrrfffff!" He moved back a step. "It's the soda," I moaned. "Too much chocolate. Go on ahead, and I'll meet you at the Hilton."

"Oh, is that all? I thought it was something big. Okay, I'll wait at the Hilton." So much for concern.

I watched him disappear, glad to be alone with my agony. I struggled over another steep crest, fighting off waves of nausea, and finally threw in the towel. Disgusted, dumping the pack on the ground, I went into the trees and spilled my misery onto the forest floor. Sometimes the lessons of life came hard! "Darn it! Two dollars down the drain," I fumed. The Ego guffawed, "You mean 'up' the drain, don't you, fool?" What could I say?

By the time I reached the "Hilton," I felt halfway human again. "You okay?" Wahoola asked.

"Yeah, just disgusted. Two whole dollars wasted."

Wahoola quipped, "Look at it as recycling the food chain. The worms will eat well for a couple of days." Yuk! "You want to stay here or go on?"

I looked at my watch—only 1:30. "Naw, let's go on to Birch Spring Shelter. It's only five miles. I want to sleep in the Smokies tonight."

With the backcountry permits attached to our packs and flapping in the breeze, we headed down to the Dam's Visitor Center. I grinned at Wahoola. "Do you think you stink bad enough by now? I could use a shower after sweating out all that chocolate."

"I guess it would be okay, since the next shower is at Hot Springs (105 miles away)."

We walked to the Visitor Center, excited, anticipating the hot water coursing down our sweated, filthy bodies. A small sign on the Men's Room door read, "Sorry for the inconvenience. Showers Out of Order."

I laughed. "Ward Leonard is a hot air balloon."

Wahoola chuckled, "At least we'll keep the skunks running for cover!"

Surrounded by concrete, water and noise, we started across the dam. Far below, on the downstream side, vehicles parked in a lot at the base

appeared as bright-colored insects; while beyond, the Great Smoky Mountains—ominous and mysterious—seemed to wait in brooding silence for
the two insignificant, puny mortals who were about to challenge their
supremacy.

With a surge of excitement, I tightened my pack straps and followed
Wahoola up the mountain.

It seemed as if I'd done nothing but climb since leaving Fontana Dam, but
the real culprit was today's fifteen rugged miles to Derrick Knob Shelter,
worsened by the food-heavy pack, the unseasonably warm spell, many
odorous reminders of yesterday's chocolate folly—and my newly acquired
bear-phobia! On the "up side," the views rocked my imagination.

Earlier today, I had perched on Rocky Top and basked in the sun,
snacking on peanut butter and cookies as I opened my soul to the immense
panorama. The fire tower atop Shuckstack Mountain, not far from Birch
Spring Shelter where I had begun the day, appeared as a tiny pencil stub on
the distant horizon, barely visible through the haze that gave the Smoky
Mountains its name. Could I have come so far in just five hours?

The earthly blanket, ruffled by the eons into a vast wrinkle of ridges
and hollows, seemed to rejoice as spring, in its ageless rite of rejuvenation,
splashed the bleak landscape with delicate shades of green. From my aerie,
Fontana Lake looked like a small blue mirror between two insignificant
mounds of forest, and the mighty Stecoahs, now shorn of their strength by
time and distance, faded into indifference. Said J.R., "I feel like a flyspeck
on life's window pane," and I had replied, "From where I sit, even a flyspeck seems pretty large."

"How many have you killed so far?" I asked, forcing the words
through a pain-grin as a cramp squeezed my right calf into a tight ball.
(Rough country, these Smokies!) I winced and massaged the pain away,
envious of the two section hikers who had been here when I arrived. Five-
mile days filled their short itinerary!

The Ranger thought for a moment. "About a dozen this trip, but I've
only been out for two days. I'd guess about a couple hundred this year."
(Today was only April 25th!) The man looked more like a kid—maybe
twenty-five, clean-shaven, his uniform spotless, but the twelve-gage shotgun (complete with night scope) cradled in his arm stripped away his youth
and his eyes had the serious sheen of total dedication. When he had sud-

denly appeared in the failing light a few minutes ago, a dark bear-like form against the white carpet of spring beauties that filled the large clearing, I was so startled that I nearly knocked over the pot of boiling mac-n-cheese, which was to be my supper.

"I go out for six days at a time. Hole up during the day and hunt for'em at night." He caressed the shotgun as if he were wooing a girl. "These hogs are really destroying the Park's ecology. They root up the forest floor and eat the young plants and acorns that the other animals need to survive. And they cause all kinds of erosion problems. We've got to get rid of'em." The Ranger gave the gun a fond pat, and I wondered if he had given it a name.

Tim, one of the section hikers, asked, "Where did the hogs come from? They're not an indigenous species, are they?"

The Ranger propped his shotgun against the chain link fence, which stretched across the front of the shelter as a foil against hungry bears, and slid out of his pack (about half the size of mine). "No. They're intruders. Someone brought them over from Europe years ago for boar hunting." He gave a wry chuckle. "The hunters didn't do as good as the hogs."

Wahoola and I had seen evidence of the hogs' destructive work shortly after entering the Park. Parts of the Trail were rutted and torn as though a small bulldozer had run amok. I turned off my stove and asked, "What do you do with'em? Do you ever eat them?" The vision of a giant wild boar being lovingly basted and slowly turned on a large spit, its aromatic juices sizzling and crackling in the glowing coals, flashed into my mind. Oh yes!

"No. We usually just let them lay where they fall, if it's not too close to the hiking trails. The bears love fresh pork." He chuckled, "And it helps keep the bears out of the hikers' packs." Lucky bears!

Twilight was descending like an octopus' inky squirt, masking the several deer that had filtered into the clearing to graze. I hadn't seen anything of Wahoola all day and twinges of worry nagged at my tired brain. A noise ruffled the woodsy shadows and anxiously I peered into the dusk. But the Trail was empty.

"Well, I need to get moving. The best hunting is at night." The Ranger pulled on his pack and picked up the "hog destructor." "Thanks for the company. You could be the only people I'll see until I come out of the woods." He cradled the shotgun, gave us a casual wave, and faded into the woods—a predator of another kind. I shuddered, picturing ravenous black bears stalking about in the pitch-blackness of the forest, ready to pounce on anything edible, even lonely hog killers and overdue hikers.

J.R. said, "What a wretched life Park Rangers must lead, roaming the backcountry for weeks at a time, shooting hogs, having little or no contact with people, with only bears, bugs, and snakes for companionship." I shoveled in a spoonful of mac-n-cheese and countered, "But when you think about it, isn't that pretty much what thru-hikers do? We roam the backcountry for six months with the same kind of companions. The only difference is, thru-hikers seek other game." He: "What do you mean?" I: "We hunt to snare our own elusive dreams." Suddenly, I felt a close kinship with the young Ranger!

Another spasm twisted my calf. I interrupted my meal and began kneading the afflicted muscle, and then jumped as a form shuffled toward the shelter. "Bear!" my mind screamed. Cramp forgotten, I lunged for the gate, slammed it closed, and struggled to snap the chain latch.

Wahoola limped up to the gate. "Now just hold on there. I've got a reservation."

Embarrassed, I tittered nervously, "Dang it, Wahoola. I thought you were a bear."

"Naw, I just smell like one." I didn't argue!

I had good reason for concern. Bears are a potential menace in the Park, and even the Park officials admit to the problem. It stood to reason: If they readily warn the public to beware and then put chain-link fences across the fronts of the shelters and advise hikers to keep the gates locked, then there is reason to worry—at least that's the conclusion J.R. and I had reached. Sort of like being put in jail for our own protection. A heck of a way to run a store!

In fact, the Great Smoky Mountains National Park had strict rules. Shelter use was mandatory on the Trail inside the Park, although use of tents was authorized if a shelter was full; in such cases, tents had to be set up next to the shelter. (So that when a hungry bear ripped through the flimsy fabric, the occupants could run screaming for the gate—at least that's what I read between the lines!)

So ever since leaving Fontana Dam I had visualized huge black bears stalking my behind, ready to snatch my pack (with me attached) and drag us both off into the deep forest. In my mind, I could see a lone Park Ranger a few years from now coming across some moldy shreds of cloth and scraps of tattered canvas, and maybe a few scattered bones. Scratching his head, he would wonder, "Hmm. Was it the hogs or the bears that did this poor fool in?" The day's imaginings had nibbled at my nervous system, and by the time I caught Wahoola at Birch Springs Shelter late yesterday afternoon I was jumpy.

Around midnight Maine Hiker (a young fellow from Maine, hiking home) had gone outside to pee. I awoke when he got up and, in the bright moonlight, watched him go out the gate. I must have drifted into a semiconscious stupor, for although I vaguely listened for the squeaks and clinks (which would reassure me that he was back inside and the gate secured), the noises never penetrated my sleep haze. An alarm went off, and panicked, I opened my eyes. Dang! I could see a black hole where the gate should be! "J.R., *the gate's open!*"

I tried to go close it, but my muscles seemed paralyzed. Struggling with all my might, I managed to sit up and to my horror saw a huge black bear standing right outside the shelter! Moonlight reflected off thick slobbering saliva as it oozed down long shreds of hog guts, which dangled from between wicked yellow fangs while the bear studied the food bags. The monstrous bruin nodded its head back and forth as though it were calculating which bag to rip open first. I struggled to get up, but my muscles had locked with fright and refused to move. Terror-stricken, I sobbed, "Ohmigodwe'redead!"

The bear shuffled through the gaping hole and bypassed the suspended food bags; instead, it came straight toward me and paused directly above my head. Its fetid breath overwhelmed my senses as hot saliva, mixed with bits of putrid guts, dripped onto my forehead. The beast bared its ugly fangs, grinned into my fear-crazed eyes, and grabbed . . . .

I awoke with a start and sat straight up inside the sleeping bag as my heart tried to burst through my chest. I cringed, staring into the darkness, straining for the smallest of sounds. The dream had been so real that I fancied I could actually smell the putrid odor of rotted hog flesh. Quickly, I crawled out of the sleeping bag and stumbled over to the gate. It was locked! I heaved a sigh of relief and got back into my bag.

As horrible as the dream had been, things became worse, then desperate. Checking the gate had awakened my bladder. I lay there and tried to go back to sleep—a futile waste of time, for the longer I delayed, the worse the urge to pee. I dreaded going through that gate but there was no putting it off. I had to go!

Vulnerable and exposed, I clung to a tree at the edge of the clearing, shivering as prickles played along my spine while I desperately struggled to unlock my panic-stricken bladder. Every bear within range must be scrambling through the forest to grab an easy meal! "Hurry, doggone it!" J.R. goaded. "I'm going as fast as I can," I grunted through clenched teeth, fighting a losing battle against the panic. I managed to stop the puny trickle and ran for the gate.

Pictures of monstrous, ravenous black bears had spoiled my sleep the rest of the night, even as rain began to fall on the tin roof. Said J.R., "Bear-phobia. You've given us bear-phobia." I: "Shut'n bears!" Yeah, last night had been bad!

This night promised to be a repeat. I tossed and turned, exhausted, my mind in turmoil from the images of hog-eating bears that danced right behind my eyes. At last, Wahoola's gentle, hypnotic snores soothed my fears and a cozy, lethargic drowsiness took hold.

Abruptly, the faint sounds of gunfire echoed across the ridges—small restless fingers that clutched at the threads of my consciousness. A final, lone shot, and then silence. I murmured, "Poor hogs. Looks like there'd be a better way." J.R. replied gently, "The Ranger's just earning his pay. Go to sleep."

Wahoola and I stopped for a mid-morning break at Silers Bald, an alpine slope covered with last year's calf-high growth—now brown and toppled, awaiting new life. He unwrapped a stick of jerky and said, "I don't know if you realize it but you've been walking all day with one foot in North Carolina and the other in Tennessee. That means we've technically crossed into our third state; only eleven to go."

Put that way, it sounded as if we were making good progress, although I wasn't sure if "technically" really counted because we would straddle the state line for nearly a hundred miles. I swallowed a mouthful of Snickers and chuckled, "Okay then, right now are you in North Carolina or Tennessee?"

"Technically, I'm in North Carolina and you're in Tennessee." He seemed to be hung up on "technically."

I grunted, "Yeah, and 'technically' I can stand in Tennessee and pee into North Carolina; or 'technically' I could put my spoon in my mac-n-cheese in North Carolina and stuff it into my mouth in Tennessee—"

Wahoola laughed and threw up his hands in surrender, cutting me off. "Okay, enough! Uh, could you hand me my water bottle?" I passed it to him. "Thanks. I just didn't feel like traveling all the way to Tennessee to get it."

Win a few; lose a few!

We stopped at Double Spring Gap Shelter for a pre-lunch snack and to check the register. The word "bear" leaped from an entry written four days ago by two thru-hikers we had yet to meet, Wild Bill and Dead Ahead, although we had followed their progress in the shelter registers. We knew from previous entries that they shared food and equipment: Wild Bill carried the stove and cooking gear, while Dead Ahead packed their large food bag. A summary of their entry:

"ALMOST stayed at this shelter. Got here in late afternoon; built fire outside in fire ring; went to spring to get water after hanging food bag from limb of a small tree close to the fire to keep bears away. Got sidetracked and forgot time. When we got back to the shelter, the fire was about out and a bear was in the tree, rocking back and forth. We yelled and waved our arms and threw rocks, but it didn't do any good. The food bag began to swing, and when it got close enough, the bear ripped the side of the bag and all the food got dumped on the ground and in the coals. The bear ate all our food, even the stuff that fell into the hot ashes—five days worth. But we got revenge. The last thing the bear chomped into was a can of pressurized cheese spread that was in the ashes, and it exploded and sprayed everything, including us, but it scared the heck out of the bear. We're out of here, headed to Clingman's Dome (three miles away) by flashlight. No supper till we hitch into Gatlinburg, except what cheese we can lick off each other and the rocks. Watch out for the bears!"

I chuckled to Wahoola, "I think they made up that story. Anyone would know to leave a food bag inside the shelter and lock the door."

Wahoola shrugged. "'Truth is stranger than fiction,' to quote an old cliche."

"Nope," I said, "I think they made it up, just trying to scare everyone."

Our break over, we headed for Clingman's Dome and lunch. I tagged along right behind Wahoola, keeping a wary eye out for bears—just in case!

At 6,643 feet, Clingman's Dome is the highest point on the entire AT, although a person would never suspect it. Looking at it from the south, the sprawling tree-blanketed summit seemed to rise only a little higher than its neighbors, unimpressive after the open view from Rocky Top and others of its kith. Without the observation tower, we would have had no view.

Tourists, somewhat resembling long columns of ants on an erratic mission, crowded the ramp walkway that led to the top of the tower. The tide of humanity swirled around the base, ignoring us, yet acknowledging our presence by giving us a wide berth. I hardly noticed until J.R. mentioned it. I passed the comment on to Wahoola, adding, "Jeepers, do we smell that bad? Maybe we should have used some deodorant. You have any?"

He said, "I don't carry the stuff. Too heavy." He pointed at the ramp. "You want to go up and check out the view?"

"Not now. I'm gonna yogi some food." I hadn't tried my hand at yogi-ing yet, but this seemed like a good place—lots of people. "You go on."

He threw me a deadpan possum look. "Maybe later. I think I'll sit here and see how it's done." His eyes twinkled mischievously.

"All right. Observe the 'Model-T technique'!" (Yogi-ing, named after The Master, Yogi Bear—whose life revolves around trying to separate tourists from their picnic baskets—is a technique developed by a

generation of hikers to help overcome ravenous appetites. According to
what I'd heard, the rules were simple: You never asked or begged for anything; instead, you simply set up a situation where someone might give
you something if they wanted to. Now, THAT didn't seem very difficult.)

I perched on a small wall beside the walkway that led to the ramp and
tried to look pathetic and malnourished. Dozens of people strolled past. A
few nodded but none stopped.

After about ten minutes Wahoola asked me, "When are you going to
start yogi-ing?"

I glared at him indignantly and growled, "It takes a few minutes to get
warmed up," and I drew up into what I hoped looked like a miserable hunk
of misplaced garbage. The tourists continued to come and go, but this
crowd must have been short on good Samaritans. The Ego said, "Maybe
you're going about it all wrong," to which I replied, "May be, but I haven't
seen any 'how-to' books on yogi-ing."

Wahoola: "Are you about warmed up yet? It's lunch time."

The Ego: "I think you need some bait. Yogi-ing couldn't be much different from fishing."

I told Wahoola, "Yeah, I'm ready to start now but I need some bait.
Yogi-ing's just another form of fishing." Reaching inside my pack, I dug
out the *A.T. Data Book* and said loudly, "Golly, Wahoola! We only have to
walk 1948 more miles to get to Maine!" A middle-aged couple passing by
glanced at us like we were a gob of chewing gum on the walkway and they
had just stepped in it. Smiling wryly, I said, "That's only the first cast. Fish
seldom bite on the first try."

A young couple with a pre-pubescent youngster in tow strolled by. I
blurted out the statistics again, so loud that a few people high up on the
ramp looked down at us. Amazingly, the young couple stopped and I gave
Wahoola a smug grin.

"Did you say you're walking to Maine?" the man asked. "You must be
hiking on the Appalachian Trail?"

I puffed up. "Yep, sure am. My partner here and I are going all the
way."

"That's always been a dream of mine but it'll have to keep a while, at
least until the kid here gets through college." A note of bitterness filtered
through, and his petite wife frowned.

The boy whined, "C'mon Daddy, let's go back to town. I'm hungry. I
want a hamburger."

An opening! "We hikers know all about hunger. We stay mighty hungry out here." Wahoola joined in, nodding vigorously.

The boy pulled on "Daddy's" arm and squawked, "I wanna go get something to eat. I'm really hungry!"

"Daddy" grimaced. "Yeah, it must be pretty tough on you fellas. Well we'd better go. Gotta feed Junior here." They slipped the hook and disappeared into the flow of tourists headed down toward the parking lot.

Wahoola smirked. "You scored *big*, Model-T. I don't think we can eat it all. Maybe we should save some for supper."

I shrugged and smiled wryly. "This is just a bad place to yogi because nobody has any food. You want to eat lunch right here?"

"We might as well. Maybe yogi-ing is like hitching a ride: The less you try, the more luck you have."

While we snacked, six thru-hikers (easy to categorize from their appearance) wandered down from the observation tower. The group returned our casual waves and went into a huddle across the walkway from where we sat. Shortly, one of the group—a pretty lass, about twenty, with short, brown hair and a healthy glow—left the huddle and came over.

"Hi, my name's Cupcake. You guys are thru-hikers?"

Wahoola laughed. "How'd you guess? I'm Wahoola, and this is my partner, Model-T."

Cupcake pointed at her friends and said, "We call ourselves the Brew and Pizza Group. E Z Strider has volunteered to hitch into Gatlinburg and get Big Macs and beer, and bring it on to Mt. Collins Shelter (3.4 miles away) for supper. Do you guys want to buy in?"

Wahoola flashed me a skeptical look, the unspoken message clear. We didn't know the Brew and Pizza Group; hadn't heard anything about them. But the clincher: Gatlinburg was a fifty-mile round trip from here and a hitch was hit or miss. Big Macs by suppertime at Mt. Collins Shelter seemed far-fetched.

"I think I'll pass," Wahoola said. "I've got a lot of food to eat up before I reach Hot Springs."

I said, "Me, too. And I don't want to carry any more than I have to. Thanks anyway." J.R. beamed with approval. "You're learning, Alter-man. Never throw good money after bad. Pap would be proud of you." Jeez! A compliment from the Marine!

We watched as the Brew and Pizza Group divvied up E Z Strider's gear and stuffed it into their packs. Topping six and a half feet (at least five feet had to be legs!), he could have been anywhere between twenty and forty years old. He had a giant stride and I wondered how the others stayed up with him. E Z Strider tossed the empty pack on his back and headed down toward the parking lot, whistling as he went, stepping out jauntily as if his chauffeured limo were waiting for him. We watched him disappear and I mentally congratulated myself for not getting sucked into a cocka-mamie scheme.

With E Z Strider successfully launched, the remainder of the group came over and introduced themselves: Pack Rat; whose youthful face belied an adult body; Capt. Sunshine, the acclaimed leader of the group, bogged down somewhere in his perennial thirties and, not surprisingly, from Florida; Chuck, (no trail name), a husky guy with big feet; and the patriarch, Hacker Hiker, a graying, retired school teacher fighting a late-six-ties paunch. Altogether, they seemed a friendly group, glued together by E Z Strider's easy humor (according to Cupcake, who obviously "had a thing" for him. We learned that E Z Strider was from New Zealand and had gotten a visa to hike the AT.)

A tiny seed of doubt clawed its way through the crust of my brain and I asked, "Do you think E Z Strider can get back with Big Macs by supper-time?"

Hacker Hiker looked surprised at the question. "Oh, yes, he's always come through for us before. He'll be there."

After the group left, the "seed" flourished and I remarked to Wahoola, "Maybe we should have sprung for a couple of Big Macs."

He dismissed the whole idea with a shake of his head. "Naw, he'll do good to get back by breakfast, if then." Reassured, I followed Wahoola to the top of the observation tower to see what I had been seeing for the past three weeks.

The climb over Mt. Collins was like all the other mountains—hard but necessary. "Just like paying taxes," J.R grumbled. Wahoola had pulled ahead and the solitude soon closed in, a peaceful, soothing balm until I entered a "dead zone" and witnessed heart-crushing devastation. All around, Frazier firs—recently mighty goliaths, now stricken caricatures felled by tiny balsam wooly adelgid beetles and acid rain—tilted at crazy angles or lay on the forest floor. Their naked bottoms were obscenely exposed in huge circular rounds of tangled earth, roots, and rock as they began their final journey back to the earth that had spawned them.

Sadly, I realized these magnificent trees, northern guests that had set-tled in an unfriendly land and existed only through their affinity for the Park's highest elevations, were doomed. Soon they would be nothing more than a monstrous entanglement through which only the smallest creatures could pass. The red spruce undergrowth would eventually replace the dying trees, but they could never equal the majestic beauty of these mighty Fraziers. I rubbed tears from my eyes and pushed on.

On Mt. Collins' tree-covered summit, I bellowed out two loud OOOGA'S: one to reward myself for the hard climb; the other as a memorial to the fallen Fraziers. J.R.: "What hath man wrought!" I: "What hasn't he!" "Sadness" had achieved a new dimension.

At Mt. Collins Shelter, the Brew and Pizza Group had already staked their claims on the floor, as had Wahoola. Hacker Hiker hadn't arrived yet and Capt. Sunshine seemed alarmed that I hadn't seen him—a mystery, since he had left Clingman's Dome well ahead of Wahoola and me. More intriguing, Wahoola had passed him near Mt. Collins' summit.

The Brew and Pizza Group's concern was infectious. If Hacker Hiker didn't show soon we would all backtrack and search for him. In the meantime, the B and PG'ers sat on a log in front of the shelter and talked about Big Macs and what brand of beer E Z Strider would bring, even placing bets on what time he would get here. I looked at my watch—a little after five.

I tuned them out, along with thoughts of delicious all-beef patties loaded with cheese, lettuce, tomato, onions, and special sauce on a sesame seed bun. Turning to Wahoola, I said, "It's suppertime. I'm cooking."

"Yeah, me, too," he replied, and we began the familiar routine.

Just then we heard a noise up the shelter path, and Hacker Hiker walked into the clearing.

"Cripes, Hacker Hiker, we were starting to get worried," Capt. Sunshine said.

Hacker Hiker looked vividly shaken—and embarrassed. Without even saying hello, he blurted, "Up on the summit I had to answer a call of nature. Some kind of wild animal roaming around up there nearly scared me to death. I've never heard anything like it in my life!" He looked back over his shoulder and shivered. "Whatever kind of varmint it was, it had the gosh-awfullest bellow. The thing did it twice!"

Alarmed, Cupcake asked, "What did it sound like?"

Hacker Hiker screwed up his face and belted out a couple of loud "AAARGA's." "Nothing like I've ever heard before," he repeated, shaking his head.

I turned three shades of red as Wahoola cast a wicked look my way and said, "I've heard that call before, too. It sounded more like an 'Oooga' to me, though."

"That's it!" Hacker Hiker exclaimed. "That's what I heard! What is it?"

I cut in. "Yeah, I've heard it, too. Legend has it that there's a tribe of 'Sasquatches' roaming these mountains. Could be that's what it was," and I stuck my face into the pot of mac-n-cheese, thankful my mouth was empty for I would surely have entertained my audience with "macaroni ala snot"!

By the time Wahoola and I finished supper, The B and PG'ers were wandering around aimlessly, alternating surreptitious glances at the sinking sun and their watches. Most nibbled at trail mix, and Chuck even threatened to cook a pre-supper, which drew traitorous looks from the others who still professed great faith in E Z Strider.

Wahoola and I cast smug looks at each other as we lounged against a tree, stomachs full, and watched the B and PG'ers' enthusiasm evaporate with the sun's descent.

"If these people think E Z Strider's going to cater their supper, then they probably believe in the Tooth Fairy," I gloated, just loud enough for them to hear. Even staid J.R. remarked how they resembled the "Peanuts" characters, Linus and Sally, on Halloween waiting for the Great Pumpkin to descend out of the black night.

Wahoola winked and replied, "Yeah, they're gonna be cooking in the dark." He looked at his watch, "Which will be in about thirty more minutes."

Chuck got out his pan and poured some water in it. Pack Rat caved in, muttering, "He must've run into trouble," and got out his cook kit. The wall of faith began to crumble as Capt. Sunshine followed suite.

Just then a whistling sound floated through the trees, shortly followed by the long-legged E Z Strider, his face plastered with an exuberant grin. We could smell Big Macs twenty feet away. The B and PG'ers jumped up and grouped around their hero, pounding him on the back and babbling congratulations. Cupcake rewarded him with a tender kiss on his cheek—a maiden's welcome for her returning hero!

E Z Strider removed his pack and set it gently on the ground, and then he and Cupcake removed two large bags crested with the "golden arch" and crammed with Big Macs. He pulled a six-pack of Budweiser from the bottom of his pack, wiggled it high in the air, and shouted, "Suppertime!"

Wahoola and I sat apart and drooled all the way down to our belly buttons, inhaling the wonderful smells and wistfully watching the Brew and Pizza Group revel in the miracle of Big Macs and beer.

Wahoola shook his head, growling something about "faith and mustard seeds."

I wiped a tear from my eye. "I'm gonna cry." Wisely, The Ego kept silent!

The wide-open space at Newfound Gap (where the Appalachian Trail and the over-mountain highway US 441 collide at the base of a spectacular memorial to the Park's great benefactor, John D. Rockefeller) dazzled my mind as I strode from the dark forest into the brilliant early morning sun.

Although it was only 8:30 AM, at least a dozen tour buses disgorged their human cargoes onto the pavement. Quickly, hundreds of tourists spread over Newfound Gap like a horde of hungry locusts. J.R. muttered, "Well, Alter-man, this really screws things up."

And it did! First out of Mt. Collins Shelter this morning, The Ego and I had decided to hike the four and a half miles to Newfound Gap for a leisurely breakfast, followed by the glorious extravagance of a sit-down commode. (Yes! According to *The Philosopher's Guide*, Newfound Gap had a Men's Room with running water!) Afterward, we anticipated a luxurious hair and body cleansing ritual in the Men's Room washbasin, assuming one was there. If not, we would "wing it."

As soon as I came out of the woods, a little girl in a flowered skirt pointed my way. "Mommy, is he homeless?" In other circumstances her innocence would have been refreshing, but not this morning.

"Shh! Don't point. It's not polite," the mother admonished, and then she grabbed her friend's arm and blurted, "Mabel, look over there! It's one of them homeless people."

I grumbled, "We can't eat here, not with people gawking and pointing. Let's find the Men's Room. Maybe we can salvage something out of this mess."

Making my way through the throngs of tourists (who parted before my busy hiking stick like the waters of the Red Sea did when Moses raised his staff), I found the sidewalk that led to the Men's Room. People crowded the edges, leaving the center to "that old wild-eyed coot," as I overheard someone whisper. I chuckled, "Say Ego, this could be fun! You want to stick around for a while and bug the tourists? It would give'em something to remember."

"Don't even think about it," he retorted. "The Park Rangers would haul us off in the loony wagon."

The Men's Room was jam-packed with men queued beside the commode stalls and washbasins. I crowded in, pack still on my back, making muffled excuses as I jarred a few unfortunates in my struggle to shed it. The room quickly emptied until only a couple of hardy souls remained in the small area, which took on the odor of a neglected sewer (according to one—a snotty, nattily-attired gent in wingtips; although the other man shook his head and ventured that something must have crawled in the wall and died). They didn't linger and suddenly I had the place to myself! Delighted, I headed for the "throne."

Afterwards, I turned the washbasin into a mini-bathtub, taking my time as I luxuriated in the cleanup chores. A couple of curiosity seekers came in, sniffed the air, gave me a dirty look, and quickly retreated. After that, word must have spread throughout the parking lot: "Beware the Men's Room! Troll in residence!" for no one else dared enter. Life was sweet!

Refreshed, sparkling like Mr. Clean, The Ego and I defiantly ignored the gawkers and pointers, spent a few minutes admiring the imposing Rockefeller Memorial, and began the climb out of the Gap. On impulse, I turned around and looked down on the busy parking area where ant-size humans had renewed their pilgrimage to the Men's Room. Feeling like a man purged by Ex-lax, I kicked up my heels, cranked out a supercharged "OOOGA," and was rewarded by dozens of people pointing my way.

The timing couldn't have been better! Wahoola stepped from the forest on the far side of the parking area and I sent another "OOOGA" down onto the crowd, shaking my hiking stick at the air like I was Moses chastising a balky Pharaoh. Wahoola saw me and waved, and then entered the swirling throng. I watched as the crowd opened before him and chuckled, "Enjoy the 'legacy,' Wahoola." The Ego growled, "Damnation! Did you have to make all that racket?" I snickered, "A little remembrance for the tourists. Let's find a breakfast nook."

Pecks Corner Shelter filled up fast. Last night's group from Mt. Collins came in soon after Wahoola and I arrived. Some hikers were already there: Tim from Derrick Knob Shelter two nights ago, now calling himself Myasis Dragon (and it was!); Trail Snails, husband and wife thru-hikers—traveling at a snail's pace; Charlie, an old geezer on a week-long outing; and a loose-knit group consisting of Mama Bear, Virginia Snake, and Cowboy Bob. Sharing the cramped space quickly removed barriers, and we soon became a gaggle of pulsating, symbiotic creatures tucked inside the shelter's small ecosystem, nurturing one another, giving encouragement, swapping food, and telling stories. How wonderful to be a part of this magnificent, wholesome experience!

When night shut us down, a symphony of discord began. Last night had been bad, but this was the worst I had ever experienced. As some snores ascended the unharmonious scale, others descended and a couple of loud zizzers got trapped in the odorous atmosphere. The old geezer, Charlie, lay next to me and pulsated my ears with loud, grating bullfrog sounds—the lead bass in the cacophony of grinding and sawing that polluted the night. I pushed my fingers in my ears, but the noise still filtered through. I tried thinking about some of the all-time great meals I'd had, but the raucous discord garbled the images into a distorted collage.

"Shut'n racket!" I snarled. "Dang it all, J.R., what're we gonna do? I can't sleep with all this going on." On my other side, Wahoola snored gently. Jealously, I poked him hard. (If I had to suffer, it was only fair to share the misery with my partner.)

"What'sitwhat'shappenin?" he mumbled.

"I can't sleep with all this racket going on. Besides, old Charlie's snoring right in my ear."

"Wha'dyahavetawakemeupforthat?"

"I gotta get some sleep," I fretted. "For cryin' out loud, I *can't* sleep!" My voice sounded hysterical.

"Whyn'tyoupokeCharlie'steadamehe'sthbadguyjeez." He slowly came fully awake. "Why don't you change ends? You don't have to snug up to Charlie's head, you know. Now how about letting me get some sleep? Jiminy!"

Why didn't I think of that! Sometimes Wahoola amazed me. I dutifully switched my sleeping bag and lay down between his and Charlie's feet. Immediately, a putrid stench like week-old fish assaulted my nostrils. J.R. groaned, "Oh man! Charlie's or Wahoola's?" I replied, "It doesn't matter. Anything is better than old Charlie's snoring." I stuffed my fingers in my ears and went to sleep.

Daybreak brought a heavy overcast and the moisture-laden air promised a dismal day. I procrastinated, dreading the coming rain, for after so many days of fair weather I had gotten spoiled. Eventually, an overfull bladder sent me hustling to the woods.

When I came back, everyone else still slept except Wahoola, who was sitting up in his bag watching Charlie saw away at invisible logs. He pointed at the old fellow's hairless pate, which stuck out of his sleeping bag like a giant peeled onion peeking from a sack of groceries. Wahoola shushed me and checked his watch. "Charlie hasn't breathed for thirty-five seconds," he whispered. I realized how quiet the shelter seemed.

"Gee, you don't think he's croaked right under our noses, do you?"

"This is the longest stretch I've noticed. Maybe you ought to punch him. You're really good at doing that."

I neutered his jibe with a contrite look and slightly nudged Charlie's shoulder. The giant onion stirred and suddenly shattered the silence with a humongous inhaling snore that caused us both to duck. "Dang, Wahoola! He's a time bomb waiting to explode! I'm putting miles between him and me today!" I scowled at the low-hanging clouds. "It's going to rain frogs and pitchforks."

Wahoola wiggled out of his sleeping bag and I gagged at the smell— definitely rotten fish! He shrugged as I held my nose and said, "No rain, no pain, no Maine."

"Yeah, I heard that one. I've got enough pain to get there without calling in the rain. By the way, you could stand to wash your feet."

He struggled into his boots. "Naw, the rain will do it for me. We're both gonna get our feet washed today." Right on cue, the first raindrops splattered the roof.

We ate and packed. Several of the others were now awake and watched our preparations with apathetic stares, but no one seemed in any hurry to rush today's adventure. Myasis Dragon asked, "You fellers going to hike in that?"

"Heck, yes," I said loudly to overcome Charlie's serenade and the rain, which had bypassed "frogs" altogether and now doused the earth as "pitchforks." I forced a grin. "No rain, no pain, no Maine." Trail Snails shook they heads and snuggled back inside their sleeping bags—not their kind of weather.

None of the others made any move to start packing. The rain drummed the roof and poured off the eaves like a miniature Niagara. I hesitated, watching Wahoola, hoping he would suggest that we wait awhile, but he put on his pack so I did the same. Hacker Hiker shouted, "You are two brave men to wrestle with this beast. My hat's off to you."

J.R.: "What he really means is we are dumber than mule balls, and if he's doffing his cap, it's in sympathy." I managed a weak smile and followed Wahoola into the storm.

We pushed through the cold downpour, shackled together by misery, sloshing along the Trail-turned-creek-that-washes-feet. Soggy misery developed underneath the Gortex rain suit—trapped sweat or sneaky rain, I couldn't tell; the effect was the same. The Ego grumbled, "I don't see any angels out in this mess." I asked, "What do you mean?" He snorted sarcastically, "You know, like the old saying: 'Only fools go where angels fear to tread.'" I was too miserable to reply.

The storm abated, but the temperature began to drop as the cold front ushered in an icy north wind. By the time we had covered the five miles to Tri-Corner Knob Shelter, my jawbone sounded like a rattler's button from the shivering onset of hypothermia, and Wahoola's face was distorted and drawn. I stammered, "We'd better get something hot down our gullets," and he nodded.

Inside, several hikers huddled around a fireplace built into a stone wall. Feeble flames, enslaved by the seesawing, clutching wind, belched smoke back into the shelter, forming a dense, gray pall. Oddly, the haze lightened and thickened at the wind's suctioning whimsy, and I had the inane thought that the shelter was breathing! A rash of coughing cut through the smoke.

The hikers stared with amazement as we pushed through the gate, and we saw the question written plainly on a few faces: "How could anyone be so stupid to be out in weather like this?" My sentiments exactly! Shedding our packs and dripping rain suits, we chattered a quick introduction and crowded toward the weak flames. The huddle split apart, accepted us, and closed again.

One of the group laughed, "You're either super-hikers or fools to be out today. Hi. My name's Wingfoot."

The famous Wingfoot! Wahoola and I had seen his register entries and wondered if we would meet him. (A renowned hiker on his sixth thru-hike, Wingfoot made part of his livelihood by testing backpacking gear, evaluating equipment, and making recommendations for improvement to the various companies he represented; in fact, he had helped develop the soggy Thor-lo socks I now wore.)

Wahoola answered with a wry chuckle, "We're definitely not super-hikers, so that should tell you something."

I braved the smoke and squeezed close to the fireplace, coughing and choking as downdrafts spewed smoke in my face, and heated some hot chocolate to go with a Snickers. It helped some, but I couldn't get a handle on the shivers; worse, my fingers were losing circulation. As soon as I finished the chocolate I told Wahoola, "I've got to get moving or pack it in here and get in my sleeping bag. These wet clothes are tearing me up."

J.R. immediately reminded me, "Think about it, Dufus. We can't afford the luxury of taking an extra day, or we'll run out of food before we get to Hot Springs. You really screwed up big time by not packing along some extra stuff." The Jerk! *He* was the one who had insisted I cut our pack weight to the bare bone. Dang! The thought of being without, even for a few hours, squeezed my gut with a steely grip. I mumbled to Wahoola, "I'm outta here. You coming?"

He didn't have the shakes yet. "Yeah, I'll be along pretty soon. I want to talk with Wingfoot a little while longer. See you at Cosby Knob (Shelter)."

With a puny show of bravado, I put the soggy rain gear back on and went out into the rain.

By the time I covered the three miles to Hell Ridge, my metabolism had cranked up again and I was sweating. The on-off rain had become a numbing, foggy drizzle, cold enough to let me blow smoke rings or spout curly white geysers of vapor—my choice. Exhaustion turned my legs into rubbery stilts, but stopping wasn't an option for movement meant warmth!

Near the side of the blue-blazed path that leads toward Snake Den Mountain, several hunks of jagged metal lay scattered along each side of the Trail. Curious, I took a close look. No doubt that these traumatized fragments came from an aircraft, though plane or helicopter, J.R. couldn't tell. An icy finger coursed down my spine—remnants from years or months ago, or could I be the first to happen on a tragic accident only hours or minutes old? Even now, did mangled, bleeding bodies lie just out of earshot, writhing in painful anguish, futilely screaming into the thick fog for help? I cupped my ears, straining to detect the slightest noise, any whimper or scream, which might resemble a plea for help. The wind moaned through the spruce and stirred the dense curtain, feeding my desolation, but that was all. J.R. muttered, "We're only wasting time. Let's move." I rubbed unfeeling fingers across a torn metal shard, pushed away the horrible mind-scene, and hurried on.

Cosby Knob Shelter was deserted. I had expected to find a bunch of hikers huddled around a smoky fireplace in a repeat of Tri-Corner Knob, but the fireplace was only a disconsolate hole in a dank, chilly shelter. A mouse scurried across a ceiling beam and I felt jealous. At least the little rascal had a warm nest to bed down in.

Dangerously close to going over the edge of rational thought as hypothermia spread through my limbs, I struggled to pull dry clothes from my pack. Bracing against the shock, I stripped off the wet stuff, hurriedly pulled on dry socks and long johns and, shaking uncontrollably, crawled into my sleeping bag to wait out the tremors.

The gloomy, fenced-in silence roared in my ears! Oh, for the snug coziness of my small tent and for the comforting solitude of forests where bears hadn't been conditioned by fawning, unknowing tourists to stalk the easy meal! I stuttered, "With any luck at all, this will be our last night in a jailhouse. Tomorrow, we'll be free as birds!" The Ego replied, "And tomorrow night we tent!"

As soon as my fingers thawed enough to hold a cup, I said, "Let's drink some hot chocolate. We may survive after all if—"

A noise outside the shelter stopped me cold. "Bear!" I gasped; I had forgotten to close the gate! Hurriedly, I struggled to get out of the bag— and jammed the zipper just below my neck. I worked frantically to get it unstuck, but the harder I tried, the more stubborn it became. Helpless as a possum up a gum stump, heart pounding, I stared at the opening.

Wahoola walked in, looking like a dunked donut. "How soon will the fire be going?" he asked, watching my futile attempt to get out of the trap. It's kinda early to be turning in, isn't it?"

I retorted, "I'm trying to get a head start on the snoring crowd, since I'll probably be awake all night. And the fire will be going just as soon as you get it started."

He laughed. "Need some help?" Bending down, he pulled the offending piece of fabric from the zipper teeth. "Easy if you know how."

I glared at the zipper. "Fabric doesn't like me; never has. That's why I turned to backpacking—you just stuff everything." I asked him about the aircraft pieces; he shared my concern but hadn't heard anything suspicious.

Before long, other drenched, shivering hikers straggled in—the B and PG'ers came first, soon followed by six hikers from Louisville, Kentucky, on their last night after a five-day trek along the Park's side trails. The Trail Snails, shamed into the wet ordeal by old Charlie, surprised us by coming in right before dusk. (Charlie had decided to call it a day at Tri-Corner Knob—hallelujah! Wingfoot and company were in for a real treat!)

Myasis Dragon and his pal, Lee, made a full house. Capt. Sunshine managed to get a decent fire blazing and soon the drab, dank dungeon became a cheerful plethora of dripping clothes, bags, packs—in a phrase, "stinking chaos," although The Ego called it "woodsy eclectic décor."

Spirits began to soar as the shelter warmed and cooking odors replaced the "essence of thru-hiker." Outside, a thunderstorm swept across the mountains. Chased by sheets of rain, gigantic flashes of lightning and ear-shattering thunder played tag all over the sky. We applauded the masterful performance from the safety of our small, cozy haven as we exchanged tidbits of food and trail gossip. Life couldn't have been sweeter!

Or so I thought! Between thunder boomers, one of the Louisville Six shouted, "Any of you guys want some goodies? This is our last night and we don't want to pack it out tomorrow."

That was like asking us if we wanted air to breathe! Simultaneously, a dozen pairs of hands reached out amid exclamations of, "Yeah, man!" and "Wow, whatcha got? Lay it on me!" Like magic, delightful treasures began to appear—Christmas in April! These guys had it all: sardines, crackers, candy bars, a small canned ham, cans of Spam, tuna, even deviled ham. Amazed, J.R. said, "If these are their throwaways, they must have been eating like Henry the Eighth! We oughta eat like this." I mumbled through a food-daze, my mouth stuffed with sardines and crackers, "Do you know of any Sherpas for hire?"

The eldest of the Louisville sextet (the most trustworthy?) retrieved two bottles of Asti Spumante from his pack and proclaimed loudly, "Celebration time. Would anyone care to join us?" Which proves once again that Trail Angels come in many disguises!

The mice also feasted during the night: The happy rodents turned Capt. Sunshine's boot strings into hors d'oeuvres and had a rip-snortin' party in Cupcake's food bag.

The next morning, Wahoola and I crossed over the northern boundary of the Great Smoky Mountain National Park, into the free, fresh air of the Pisgah National Forest! The sun beamed down from a cobalt sky—the solitary witness to our freedom—and blessed our passage with soul-nourishing warmth. I celebrated the event with my last Snickers and made an entry in my journal: "Sunday, 29 April—No more jails; no more bears; no more snores; very few cares." The Ego chuckled, "Not bad. Add this: 'No more rules for hiker fools; just jiggers of joy for this ol' boy.'"

We had been on the Trail a lifetime—nineteen days! Only 1900 miles left!

Two days later, I ran my finger around the inside of my peanut butter jar a final time and licked it clean—the last of the food—and began the long descent into Hot Springs, envying Wahoola's one-hour lead. He probably already had his nose stuck in a juicy hamburger. I began to run!

CHAPTER 4

Scratchin' in the Chicken Yard

"Perfect" trail towns are few and far between. In thru-hiker parlance, to be "perfect" a town needs cheap (or free) lodging, a post office, at least one "greasy spoon," a well-stocked grocery, and a laundromat (optional, at least for the guys). And if the Trail happens to go right through the middle of town—well hallelujah! According to the *PG*, Hot Springs had it all!

It was also "picture perfect." From my vantage point up on the mountainside, the buildings looked like tiny multicolored mushrooms that had sprouted in patchy profusion along the near bank of the French Broad River, a wide, silver ribbon that sparkled with sun-glints as it meandered through the narrow valley. An aura of friendliness rose upward with the clanks and bangs and shouts of a town going about the business of living. Before long I began to identify smells that accompany the awesome, albeit mundane, task of getting on with the day. Could one of the smells, tantalizingly fragrant with cooked onions, be pouring out the vent of a nearby greasy spoon? I picked up the pace!

Wahoola and I had agreed to meet at the Jesuit Hostel—$9 a night; work for stay if money is short—so I put the greasy spoon on hold and headed for two small brown buildings connected by a short breeze-way and identified by a large welcoming sign as the hostel. The place seemed deserted.

I looked inside the larger of the buildings, a combination kitchen/lounge. A short, stocky man stood at the sink washing dishes. Smiling, he wiped his hands on a stained dishtowel and shook my hand. "How you

101

doin? I'm Andy, the caretaker. You wouldn't happen to be Model-T, would you?"

"Yep, I'm guilty," I chuckled. "You must have met my partner, Wahoola."

"He said to tell you he was going to the Post Office and would meet you back here. He's already checked into the bunkroom. I can sign you in right now if you want." Pointing at a faded sign on the wall, he added, "There's a nine-dollar donation, but you can work it out if you're short."

All I could think about were food and shower. Digging into my belt pouch, I found a fiver and four wrinkled ones and handed them to Andy. "It's first come, first served for the bunks. Help yourself." He returned to the sink and I went into the bunkhouse to claim a bunk.

The bunkhouse was small but clean and neat. Five double bunks—ten berths—with bare mattresses (no pillows) crowded against three of the walls, leaving little room for lounging or working with equipment. J.R. grumbled, "I got better service than this in boot camp. For nine dollars, the shower had better be darned good." Other than two bottom bunks—Wahoola's and one other—the bunkhouse was empty.

A crude, handwritten sign taped to the wall by the door caught my attention: "If you need a FREE place to stay in Hot Springs, come to Club Geek past NOC on the French Broad River." The sign had been signed "Geek." "Hmm," I mused. "No date. No telling how long it's been there." The Ego said, "Too late anyway. We've already paid our money."

I picked one of the other bottom bunks and then propped my pack against the wall, suddenly feeling confused and a little overwhelmed by the closeness of civilization. What now? Food or shower? He cut into my thoughts. "Jeez, Alter, take a whiff of those armpits. We can't even get into a greasy spoon smelling like a week-old slop bucket." I took one whiff, gagged at the smell, which strongly resembled the fishy whang of Wahoola's feet, and headed for the shower without arguing.

All I had to put on was the same stinking clothes I'd just taken off. "Close enough," I said, staring at the fuzzy-bearded, hollow-eyed, stranger who watched me from the cracked mirror. The Ego remarked, "The odor goes well with your looks." I growled, "They're your looks, too. Let's go find something to eat. No telling where Wahoola's gotten off to."

Hypnotic, mouth-watering smells wafted up the street. Somewhat in a daze, I ignored J.R.'s impatient griping to get on to a real restaurant and turned in at the first place that had food—a small convenience store—"sushing" him with the promise that a greasy spoon would be our next stop.

As I came out of the store, Wahoola yelled from down the street. He struggled with an arm full of packages—at least six—and to see his grin, one would think he had struck gold!

I polished off a Snickers in two bites and said, "It looks like you hit a bonanza."

"I only expected to get a food box. Look at all this stuff! I didn't know I had so many friends."

"What're you going to do with it? You can't pack it out of town." The struggle out of N.O.C. up to Swim Bald still scorched my mind.

"Eat it." He shuffled the boxes for a better hold and frowned.

"Heavy, huh?"

"Yeah. I guess I've got a little problem on my hands."

I chuckled. "Not to worry. I'll help you solve it, no thanks necessary. After all, that's what friends are for." This had the makings of a great afternoon! "I'll go to the post office, and then meet you at the laundromat in a few minutes. We can get our clothes washed while we work on your problem."

Suddenly, a wispy breeze sneaked a whiff of Wahoola into my nostrils. Whew, did he stink! I asked him, "Jeez, Wahoola, when're you going to get a bath? You're gonna give us thru-hikers a bad name. In fact, you stink so bad the flies won't even come calling."

"Well, I don't see any flies on you either."

"Of course you don't," I crowed. "I'VE already had a shower. My momma didn't raise her son to become flybait." With that, I headed for the post office and he went in search of a laundromat. J.R., protesting about being put off again from a run on the greasy spoon, went "poof."

The laundromat was small, warmly humid, and filled with fat, middle-aged women and half a dozen runny-nosed pre-schoolers. I set my one package on the floor and took a seat next to Wahoola, who had already gotten a head start on solving his food problem, mostly by passing out goodies to the youngsters who flocked around him like he was Santa. They quickly demolished a box of crumbly chocolate chip cookies and then got sidetracked by a shouting match between a stringy-haired girl in a flour-sack smock and a ruddy-faced four year-old miniature Bluto, who screamed that she had taken one of his cookies. One of the fat women waddled over from the folding table, whacked both on the bottom and dragged them to separate corners. I laughed, "Welcome back to the real world."

Unperturbed, Wahoola handed some chewy caramels to the other four urchins and said, "You'd better go play. This man eats little kids." Wide eyed, they left to tease the two in "time out," except for one little fella who tugged on his momma's baggy shorts and whimpered in her ear, which caused her to fix me with a mean look.

"Jeez, Wahoola, you're gonna get us expelled from the laundromat!"

"No big loss. You want to share a washer?"

"Maybe, but only if we run the wash cycle twice. Your stuff's twice as dirty as mine. You got any soap powder?"

"Nope. I thought you might."

I saw a soap dispenser on the wall and pointed but Wahoola said, "Don't bother. It's broken."

"Dang, we've got to have soap." I went over to where a heavyset woman in a faded print dress pushed items into a dryer and asked, "Ma'am, where can we get some soap for the washers?"

She didn't look up. "Store down th' way."

"Is it far?"

"Rightly."

I wondered how far "rightly" was. "I don't know if I'm up to walking 'rightly', Ma'am. Maybe you could sell me enough powder to do up two loads of wash?"

"Nosuh." Shoot. We'd never get out of this laundry if one of us had to go all the way "rightly" to get soap—and it would probably be me, since Wahoola would claim he had to stay and take care of "his problem." I turned to go.

The woman looked at me and pushed untrimmed bangs out of her eyes. "I won't sell ye eny, but I'll give ye some if ye got a sack."

"I got a sack! Wahoola, give me one of your goodie bags!"

I thanked the woman, happy that I didn't have to go chasing after soap powder, yet a little disappointed that I hadn't a clue as to how far "rightly" meant here in Hot Springs.

Grinning, I dangled the bag in Wahoola's face. "I'm gonna have my own washer!"

Which led to the next problem. The only laundry either of us had was what we wore. Wahoola smirked. "Are you going to jump in with you clothes on?"

"It probably wouldn't hurt either of us. Maybe we can borrow something to put on while these things wash?" I didn't see any unclaimed clothes lying around.

Wahoola nixed that idea. "Just look at these women. Laundry is serious business to them. They'd laugh us right out onto the street." I had to agree.

"Okay," I said, "One of us is going to have to go back to the hostel and get our rain gear. We can change into that while our clothes wash. Let's flip a coin."

He flipped and I lost. Said J.R., now "unpoofed" as I went out the door, "I would guess that from here to the hostel and back is close to 'rightly.'" Idiot!

When I returned, two of the kids were crying, complaining that they had a bellyache (too many sweets?) but Wahoola seemed happy for he had managed to empty two of his packages. We took turns changing inside a small closet and cranked up the washers, and by the time the wash was done, we had emptied another package. The day had turned pleasantly warm so to save time (and get out of the stifling rain gear) we bypassed the dryer and put the damp clothing back on to body-dry. Then to J.R.'s delight, we headed up the street to the Smoky Mountain Diner to kick off a serious eating orgy.

When we got back, the hostel had come alive. All of the Brew and Pizza Group had filtered in, along with Trail Snails and the Mello Woodsmen (still grinning). As the afternoon wore on, the hostel quickly filled to capacity. Some we knew and several we hadn't met, but strangeness had no place in our small circle and camaraderie flourished. Tents began to pop up like mushrooms on the grassy lawn next to the hostel.

I found a man, about twenty-five and every bit as tall as E Z Strider, lying in the bunk above mine. "It looks like we're gonna be bunkmates," I said. "What's your name?"

"Sasquatch. Or Big Foot. It doesn't matter." I glanced at his boots—big—and he chuckled, "Yeah, I wear size thirteen." I soon learned that Sasquatch had only been married for four months, of which one had been spent out here. (It probably seemed like forever for this mid-twenties healthy male!) "I love being on the Trail, but I miss wife." He added that he was hiking home to upper New England as fast as his long legs would haul him. (Sasquatch had left Springer only a couple of days after us, so he hadn't kicked his butt into afterburner—yet—but he would though, one of these days. It all depended how strong the pheromone vibrations were that emanated from some small cottage in the far north.)

I told him, "Hiking home to your sweetie is about as good an incentive to keep on going that I've heard."

"Or the worst. I'm really tempted to hop a bus and go on home." His face clouded into discontent.

The source of his happiness lay far beyond my reach, so I wished him well and left him to his misery.

Some went seeking lodging elsewhere, the most popular place being The Inn at Hot Springs—a large Victorian frame house owned and operated by Elmer Hall, who thru-hiked the AT in 1975 and 1976. (Belatedly, Wahoola and I learned that although The Inn looked imposing and expensive, Elmer offered lodging to his fellow thru-hikers for ten dollars a night. Also, Elmer served up an awesome vegetarian dinner for his guests.)

Early the next morning Wahoola and I headed down to the Trail Café at the far end of town (yep, it was a "rightly" distance) to tackle the Traveler's Special: three eggs, two pancakes, two sausage patties, gravy or grits, and two biscuits, all for $4.29. After we had finished eating, Wahoola asked, "Do you want to hike out today?"

We hadn't discussed the possibility of staying two days in Hot Springs; in fact, it hadn't crossed my mind. I did feel tired and beat down, and my feet hurt with every step. I replied, "My feet could use another day's rest. How about you?"

"Yeah, mine, too. But I don't care about dishing out another nine bucks."

"I saw a sign on the wall at the hostel. Something about a place on the river called Club Geek. The sign said it was free but it may not even be there anymore. We could check it out."

He nodded. "Yep, I saw that. It might be the best deal in town."

We paid our bill and went in search of Club Geek.

We eventually found it. On the north side of the highway bridge that crossed the French Broad River, almost invisible as it leaned against a tree surrounded by tall weeds, was a crude cardboard sign with an arrow pointing to the right: "Club Geek this way." We followed a narrow, weed-choked, dew-drenched path past N.O.C.'s satellite compound and continued on along the riverbank until we came out on a small, slanted, sandy beach. The makeshift roof—a large green, slightly ripped nylon tarp—sagged to within a yard of the sand, and a rough sign tacked to a tree read: "Welcome hikers—Club Geek." Out on the gurgling river the rising mist softened the sun's rays, which reflected its rosy sheen over the sandy tract and mellowed the austere scene. A splendid little hideaway to fritter away the late afternoon!

Two men, wearing only dirty, frayed shorts, lay on the sand with their backs propped against a small log as they silently watched the current slip past. Both bore the jaded facade of weary thru-hikers. The larger of the two, short but burly, looked to be in his mid-thirties; oddly, he held a gray tabby cat with a stubbed tail in his lap, absently caressing its sleek coat, which caused it to purr with contentment. The cat jumped up at my "Howdy," arched its back, and hissed.

The man grinned. "Come on in. Ziggy's hell on mice, but he seldom attacks hikers. My name's Geek, and this lowlife is Mule."

Mule, as tall as Geek but fifty pounds lighter and perhaps ten years younger (though his heavy, black beard made it hard to tell), kicked at a pile of empty beer cans near his foot and said fuzzily, "Take th' load off an' grab a seat, soon's I move my breakfast dishes outta th' way." I supposed he meant the beer cans, and he confirmed my guess, adding, "I don't usually have beer for breakfast, but it's th' cheapest calories I could find." Mule's eyes were hidden behind dark sunglasses, but I'd have bet a box of Snickers bars they were as red as the morning sun.

We gave our names and shook hands. I joked, "We saw your chic advertisement at the hostel and wondered if we could make reservations for the night."

Geek said, "Mule, check our guest list." Mule grinned and puffed up like he'd been awarded the Pulitzer Prize for Idiocy. Ziggy, deciding we were not giant two-legged mice, settled back into Geek's lap and hummed noisily like a well-oiled machine, loud enough to be heard above the river's swish. "Yeah, we got room, but th' room service sucks. Bring your own bottle."

Wahoola chuckled, "As long as the rent's right, we can live with that."

Curious, I asked, "Is Ziggy a thru-hiker, too?"

"Sort of. Actually, he's a thru-rider."

Wahoola asked, "What's a 'thru-rider'? That's a new one."

Geek explained. "I got the little tyke from a farmer when I was canoeing the Mississippi last year. A couple of days after we got on the Trail, I threw him on top of my pack when I tried to beat a thunderstorm to a shelter, and he's refused to walk ever since—haven't you Ziggy?" and he affectionately tickled the cat's belly. Ziggy exploded into a flash of fur, grabbing Geek's hand in his claws and clamping a finger with razor-sharp teeth. Geek relaxed his hand until Ziggy let go and then held it up. "He never draws blood on me, but he'll wipe out a shelter's mouse population in nothing flat. Got thirteen confirmed kills one night at Blood Mountain Shelter!"

Geek's eyes twinkled, and the smooth, loving strokes resumed. Beyond his small eccentricity, I detected a spirit as untainted as the first green blush of spring and as free as a frolicking cloud. "By the way, I'm leaving in about an hour on an overnight rafting trip, but Mule and Ziggy will keep the Club open. Just come on down when you're ready."

Wahoola said, "Sounds good. If it's okay with Model-T we'll be back before suppertime," and I nodded. We thanked our hosts and headed for the

Smoky Mountain Diner for a pre-lunch. Said The Ego, "Lucky cat!" I: "Lucky Geek," and we were both right.

We spent the rest of the day arranging food for the next stretch to Erwin, Tennessee, writing letters, and jawing with the other hikers. J.R/I called home and spoke with Judith, who said that Kelly, their eldest son doing a resident program in family practice medicine at Roanoke Memorial Hospital, hoped to get a few days off to join J.R. at Damascus, Virginia, and hike with his dad for thirty or forty miles. J.R. was ecstatic.

Chores finished, we wandered over to The Inn for a look-see. Elmer answered our knock and interrupted his preparations for the vegetarian supper to give us a tour of the old mansion. In the kitchen, the basics for a monstrous tossed salad covered a table, which reminded me that I hadn't eaten anything for an hour!

We thanked him and went back to the hostel to get our packs and head for Club Geek. On the way, Wahoola mentioned, "Boy, a salad sure would taste good. How about we have a salad for supper? A *big* salad, with onions, tomatoes, cucumbers; the works!" He clawed at the air like he was plucking the veggies from an invisible garden, and his eyes came unglued, just like they did going into N.O.C.! "We could buy the fixin's and take it down to the river and eat it. Yeah! A *big salad!*"

"Okay, let's do it." Thinking about it, a salad would be a nice change from all the greasy stuff we had been eating.

We got our packs, said farewells, and headed for the nearest of the town's two grocery stores, which happened to be on our way to Club Geek. Filled with expectation, we propped our packs beside the door and went in.

"Sorry, we ain't got no lettuce today," said a chubby, moon-faced girl behind the cash register, giving us an apathetic look. "Should be gettin' some in a coupla days." She chewed vigorously on a wad of chewing gum, daring us to dispute her prediction.

Wahoola glowered at the girl and I thought he was going to throttle her. "We can't *wait* a couple of days! We gotta have lettuce *today!*"

I pulled him away before he went off the deep end and gave the girl an apologetic roll of the eyes (which bounced off her stone glare like a B-B fired at a bank vault). "C'mon, let's try the other place," I coaxed, easing my muttering, disappointed partner out the door.

After a "rightly" walk, we entered the other store, headed for the small produce section, and stared in dismay at several bare or nearly depleted bins. "Slim pickin's," I muttered. "Don't get your hopes up."

Wahoola poked me in the ribs. "Look over there!" Beyond the well-stocked bin of potatoes, I glimpsed a single, pathetic, greenish globe. He hissed, "That may be the last head of lettuce in Hot Springs. C'mon, let's grab it!"

It didn't look so hot—in fact, it looked pretty gross. The outer leaves, in the advanced stage of a slime-mold blitz, oozed a yellowish-green, foul-smelling pus. "Jeez, Wahoola, even thru-hikers can't stomach this. How about we just get the other fixin's and pretend the lettuce is there."

"Naw, it's not the same. The only head of lettuce in Hot Springs, and it's fly food," he said bitterly.

As we turned to go, Wahoola impulsively (or vindictively?) poked his finger into the slimed crust and jiggled it around. I wouldn't have touched that obscenity for a dozen boxes of Snickers, but then Wahoola's trail-crud at times sort of resembled the lettuce. Maybe it wasn't such a big deal for him! "Wait a minute, Model-T. This may be a diamond in the rough."

He opened up a small gap in the rotting leaves. Amazingly, down beneath the fungal blitzkrieg, the lettuce showed crisp and green. Delighted, we gathered up the other veggies—still categorized as "slim pickin's": two reddish-green tomatoes, which had all the appeal of cardboard; an onion with a top sprout that jutted out like a green, spiked hairdo (as did all the other onions); the least shriveled of two cucumbers; and a scrawny, flaccid carrot. Today was *not* a "good salad day" in Hot Springs, North Carolina.

On the way to the checkout with our vegetable rabble, I grabbed a large bottle of Thousand Island dressing. "Plenty of dressing for our big salad, Wahoola!" He grinned like he had won the lottery!

A heavy-set woman with short frizzy hair and streaked mascara stood at the cash register. She immediately reminded J.R. of Ma Kettle, the frazzled mother of a dozen offspring in the old Ma and Pa Kettle movies from his younger days. She gave us a condescending smile, which quickly turned into a frown when Wahoola placed the slimy lettuce on the counter.

"Lordee! I told that worthless man to throw that out!" She punctuated "out" with a violent toss of her arms that ended with a hostile jab toward a skinny, bald clerk at the far end of the store. He shot her a guilty glance and continued to stock a shelf. I wondered if the worthless man was some hapless employee or her husband—the latter, I guessed as THE LOOK (normally reserved for tormented husbands) briefly flashed. Her attention switched from the poor man back to the lettuce.

"This belongs in the dumpster. I can't sell anything like this."

Wahoola said stubbornly, "It's the only head of lettuce in Hot Springs. We've got to have it!"

She hesitated, looking us over good, probably trying to decide whether she could be held liable if we got food poisoning from the lettuce and took her to court. We must have seemed like two kids begging candy for she suddenly giggled and said, "I wouldn't want to stand between you boys and the only head of lettuce in town, but I ain't gonna charge you for it." She reached under the counter, pulled out a large paper bag, and told Wahoola, "Here, sonny, drop it in this since you already dirtied your hands."

She rang up the other items, apologizing for their poor condition, but charity only extended to the lettuce because she charged us full price for the rest. Before we got to the door she was spraying Lysol all over the checkout counter and her hands and anyplace else that might have been contaminated.

Outside, Wahoola broke into a laughing fit, struggling to breathe as he gasped, "Did you get a look at her face? She must have decided we're too crud-bound to be laid low by rotten lettuce."

I joined his fit. Tears streaming, I wheezed, "Yeah, she probably thinks thru-hikers eat stuff like this all the time out in the mountains!"

As soon as we regained control, we headed for Club Geek, with Wahoola clutching the bag with our big salad fixin's close to his chest. Charity hadn't quite extended to two paper bags but we didn't mind. We had just experienced every thru-hiker's dream—free food!

Mule still sat in the same spot. The thought crossed my mind that maybe he hadn't moved all the time we'd been gone, until I noticed a new supply of "cheap" calories in the form of a twelve-pack. (Supper?) This morning's empties were gone, as was Geek. Ziggy jumped over Mule's leg and pounced on an imaginary mouse.

Mule popped the tab on a can and took a long swallow, burped loudly, and swiped his arm across the dribbling residue on his beard. He removed the dark glasses and dug a dirty thumb into bleary eyes, as if that would make the redness go away. "Pick any room in th' house. Geek's gone an' they's only Ziggy 'n me. I'm gonna work on my cal'rie decifut while he's gone an' babysit ol' Zig here." He giggled and scratched his head. "Or would that be cat-sittin'? Anyway, Geek said tell you he'd see you up the Trail." He burped again, tossed the empty at his feet, and reached for more "cal'ries."

Mule drained the can in a couple of gulps and ushered up a humongous belch. "We might have more comin'," he announced blandly. "Tall feller with big feet named Sackwatch came down earlier an' said he n' couple others might be back." He must have meant Sasquatch. Mule's speech had begun to slur, but he definitely had "cal'rie decifut" on the run.

We unpacked and decided it was close enough to suppertime to prepare the salad. I told Wahoola, "I'll cut up the onion and other stuff if you'll do the lettuce." I mimicked the lady back at the grocery, "Since you already dirtied your hands, Sonny." Grinning, he went to the water's edge and soon returned with a small ball that glistened like a small orb of light-green jade in the late afternoon sun.

He said, "I washed the lettuce in river water. It has to be cleaner than what came off of it."

Mule twisted his face into a fuzzy frown. "Tha' ain't gonna g'it. Lemme me haf' it," and Wahoola handed him the small head. Mule held it in one hand and poured beer over it, saying with a solemn voice, "I ba'tize you, lettuce, in th' name of . . . ." He stopped and stared foolishly at Wahoola. "Now thas dumb. I shoulda put a pan unner th' lettuce. Lookee all th' cal'ries I just wasted."

Mule was losing it, fast. I chuckled to Wahoola, "I think Mule got it wrong. Ziggy's going to be 'mule-sitting' tonight."

I barely grabbed the lettuce before Mule toppled back into the sand and began to snore.

We went to work on the salad. I drained the rest of Mule's opened beer over the lettuce, cut it into halves, and handed one to Wahoola. He ripped his into chunks and dropped them in his coffee pot, which did double duty as his cook pot. (I nearly gagged, just thinking about the pestilence thriving on Wahoola's slime-infected fingers!) We split the veggies, and then I poured half of the large bottle of Thousand Island dressing over my creation before handing the bottle to Wahoola. He looked at the large puddle of dressing on my little pile of salad and then did likewise, saying complacently, "This oughta kill any little critters in there."

"Yeah, if the acid doesn't get'em, they'll smother to death." A thought: "You ever eat salad with a spoon before?"

"Nope, new experience—like everything else out here." Put that way, it didn't seem so unusual.

J.R. waxed philosophical. "Every time a hen scratches in the chicken yard, it's a new experience. Life is just one big chicken yard, and we're scratchin' in it every second of every day, uncovering new experiences. The more you scratch, the more you enjoy life." Cool way to put it!

Mule must have gotten hungry again, for he roused out of his doldrums shortly after we finished cleaning our cookware, dumping Ziggy off his chest as he sat up. He reached for another entree from his twelve-course dinner, changed his mind, and tottered off into the woods just as Sasquatch arrived carrying a large brown paper bag.

After hellos, he dumped his pack on the sand and began unloading the bag. Out came two sixteen-ounce cans of pork and beans; a large loaf of bread; a whopper bag of ruffled potato chips; and the clincher—a package of "el-cheapo" foot-long hot dogs. He managed to slide the words around long strings of slobbering drool which dribbled down his chin: "Man, I'm gonna pig-out!"

Wahoola leaned over and whispered in my ear, "It looks more like a 'dog-out.'"

"You mean a 'fart-out,'" I whispered.

Uh-oh! Sasquatch had unrolled his sleeping bag alongside my Therm-a-Rest. Sleeping arrangements taken care of, he opened both cans of beans with a tiny opener, and then the bread, chips, and lastly, the foot-longs. Picking up a dog (which looked like an obscene, dangling organ as he held it gingerly by one end), he blanketed it between two slices of bread and wolfed it down. Fascinated, Wahoola and I watched as Sasquatch put away two more of the flaccid danglers in exactly six bites. Then he started on one of the cans of beans, gobbling it up like we were a pack of wolves circling to rob him of his prey. It was *not* a pretty sight! Brownish-orange liquid oozed down his whiskerless chin, marking its passage on his dirty gray tee shirt before pooling on stained shorts, but he didn't seem to notice. (Neither did Mule, who had returned from the woods and resumed working on his own version of supper.)

In a flash, I realized that Sasquatch planned to devour the entire pile of food at a single sitting! J.R. groaned, "Heaven help us! Major gas attack on the way." I added, "Yeah, Club Geek's fixing to become Chez Fart in short order!" J.R. bridled at my use of "fart" and I retorted, "Chez Fart or Chez Poot, it doesn't matter. Killer farts are on the way!"

I managed to catch Wahoola's eye, jerked my head at the lethal mess, and mouthed the "F" word. He nodded and winked, and then said, "You know Model-T, there's enough daylight left to make another couple of miles if we wanted to. It would be kinda nice to get Lover's Leap (a rocky lookout high above Hot Springs) out of the way today and not have it facing us in the morning."

As he spoke, a faint rumble came from over the mountain at our back. The sun, low against the horizon beyond the river, suddenly took on a brackish sheen as a black cloud moved over the summit and scurried toward us like a mouse hustling after cheese.

I considered the new complication: a night exposed to Sasquatch's gastro-syncopated fanfare, or leave now and hope to find a level spot to pitch tents before the storm hit. Sasquatch let go with a long, noisy fart, and J.R. exclaimed, "Holy cow! That one woulda made Ol' Beck proud!" (Ol' Beck was a mule that had belonged to Pap when J.R. was a kid. The large cantankerous animal had a special affection for J.R., often expressing it in a most unusual way. Without fail, when he would bend down by Ol' Beck's stringy tail to hook the traces to the singletree, the mule would fire a couple of loud, odorous salvos with clockwork precision. And each time, like a stuck record, J.R. would jerk on the traces and yell, "Quit pootin' in my face, you peckerheaded sumabitch!" (He picked up *that* term from Old Man Padgett, which earned him a five-minute face-to-face encounter with Pap's lusty razor strop, after which he started to use Pap's by-word, "sonofagun.")

Sasquatch fouled the air again, worse this time, grinning it away as he finished off the second can of pork and beans. J.R. muttered, "Peckerheaded pootin' sonofagun. He's worse than Ol' Beck!" That settled it for me. "Let's get on up the Trail."

As we put our packs on, the three Mello Woodsmen came in. Red, looking haggard and wobbling like a seasick Marine, flopped down on the sand, looked pathetically at Wahoola, and groaned, "I got the cruddin' runs. Th' Doc says I got giardia an' I'm gonna hafta stick around here for a few days till the medicine knocks it out." Sweat beaded his pallid skin and he gave off an odor that reminded me of a badly managed compost pile. "Is it okay if we hang out here?"

Wahoola said, "Model-T and I were just leaving. Fine with me, but you'd better ask Mule. He's the resident caretaker."

Mule patted the sand and his voice chased after Red, who staggered off into the bushes for another confrontation with the nasty parasite. "Plen'y room. Me'n Ziggy love company, don't we Ziggy-Wiggy?" But Ziggy could have cared less. Purring, he rubbed up against his newfound friend, Sasquatch, who shared tiny bites of the last "dangler" with the feisty feline.

The thunder rumbled louder. "We're outta here," I said. "Enjoy the beach, fellas, and take care of Red." In reply, Sasquatch "sang" again, which caused Ziggy to arch his back and hiss like he had been slobbered by a dog. The two Mello Woodsmen rolled their eyes and fanned the air, while Mule, smiling happily, continued to swig at his supper.

After we left, Wahoola remarked, "Poor Mule. Between Red and Sasquatch . . ." The words tapered off, but the meaning was clear.

I replied, "It's Ziggy I feel sorry for."

The Ego: "Maybe we should have stayed. It's going to be an evening of riparian entertainment at Club Geek." Riparian?

A half-mile up the Trail, we came on a tiny clearing and pitched tents in semi-darkness as the first raindrops fell. I snuggled into my sleeping bag and listened to the patter of rain and the muffled sound of thunder. Close by, Wahoola already snored softly. In the morning, replenished with strength, calories, and resolve, we would struggle back to the mountaintops and continue north. Hot Springs, population 678, had been good to us.

The storm passed and for a while I listened to the hypnotic, staccato dripping from the overhead limbs. Slowly, I let go of the world outside and retreated into a place of dreams and carefree release.

"You want to call home?" Wahoola asked, the smirk on his face belying any sincerity as he lifted the phone from its cradle on the wall. The unconnected end of the useless cord dangled in the cold, damp air—a mocking reminder of civilization.

"Sure," I chuckled, pointing at a wireless switch box tacked to the wall. "Turn the light on so I can see how to dial." Of course nothing happened—no wire; no electricity; no workee—yet the ridiculous incongruity made us laugh. A special touch by Sam Waddle, the volunteer maintainer, or his dry wit creeping through? (Several years back, Sam, who owns a farm at the base of Cold Spring Mountain, had adopted Jerry Cabin Shelter—then known as the dirtiest, most rundown shelter on the entire AT. Now, Jerry Cabin enjoyed the reputation of being among the cleanest and best kept.) Nearby, an American flag proudly fluttered, typifying Sam's steadfast love for the shelter and, I suspected, his country.

Wahoola flicked the switch a few times for effect. "I guess Sam forgot to pay the electric bill." Joke over, we hastily began munching a quick lunch of snack stuff, for the day masqueraded as a flimsy caricature of winter, bringing with it a chilling fog that seeped through our clothes and sucked away our warmth.

Wahoola picked up the register and began to thumb through it—a ritual as important to thru-hikers as eating (well, almost). "Lagunatic was here yesterday with Sam. Says here she and Sam brought goodies for the thru-hikers."

I glanced around the shelter, hoping to see a stack of goodies in a dark corner, but yesterday's passing thru-hikers had cleaned the leavings like sharks. "Always our luck—day late and a dollar short," I complained, wondering what kind of goodies we'd missed as my tongue massaged a mouthful of pasty peanut butter, trying to thin it with saliva so I could get it down.

"Yeah, I reckon so. It's no big deal."

"Free goodies is always a big deal." Quickly licking my spoon clean, I put my stuff away and stood, alarmed that my fingers and toes had started to become numb. "Jeez, Wahoola, this cold is chewing at my bones. I've got to get moving while I can still walk."

He lifted an eyebrow. "You didn't take a very long break."

"Old age affliction," I growled, flipping the light switch one last time, and then I took off up the Trail with legs pumping at Ward Leonard speed. I paused for a last glimpse at the edge of the clearing, but Jerry Cabin had already disappeared in the dense mist.

The sun eventually routed the fog, which retreated in sullen defeat; the day quickly warmed and life again became tolerable, a lot better than yesterday. Yesterday had been a miserable day . . .

It had started out nice enough. The rain had stopped sometime before dawn, and the sun peeked shyly through scudding high-floaters, bringing a promise of fair weather. Anxious to be on our way, we hurriedly packed our wet gear, ate a couple of breakfast bars, and began the steep climb out of Hot Springs.

My day immediately began to sour. I followed Wahoola, trying to match him step for step, but he soon left me behind. For some reason I felt drained and lethargic, as if invisible leeches had attached their slimy bodies onto my life force and sucked me dry. Worse, the pack, always a weighty presence, this morning had turned into a wretchedly heavy torment. I carped, "If this is payback for rootin' around civilization, keep me in the hog lot next time." The Ego disagreed. "Blame it on too many trips to the greasy spoons." Whatever the reason, I couldn't seem to get my butt into gear.

In the valley snuggled beneath Lover's Leap (a desolate precipice perfect for such a purpose), Hot Springs stretched and yawned and got on with the morning's routine business as the tinny clanging of a bell called children to school. The French Broad, looking like a poorly thrown lasso—almost roping the town, except that the top of the loop had collapsed—gave off tufts of swirling mist that rose lazily toward three circling turkey vultures. Downstream, barely visible, ruins of the old spa at the large, bubbling mineral springs that gave the town its name sullied a broad, green expanse of riverbank. (Yesterday, a couple of hikers had bragged about sneaking in and soaking the trail tarnish away in the soothing water. The way I now ached, I wished I'd gone!) I kicked a rock into the void—a token sacrifice—and went on.

Things had not improved by the time I reached Hurricane Gap, where the Trail crosses a graveled forest service road. At the edge of the Trail, a small patch of bluets encircled a low-set granite stone, which simply read: "In Memory REX PULFORD Sept. 22, 1920—April 21, 1983." (At Walasyi-Yi Center, Dorothy Hansen had told me about this man, her father, who died here during his 1983 thru-hike—victim of a massive heart attack. She and Jeff had erected the memorial to his memory.) The spirit of this hiker, unknown but nonetheless family, seemed to linger over the spot, gently caressing the tiny, glistening blue petals with soft tendrils of breeze. J.R. and I stood in reverent silence and paid our respects before moving on.

About mid-afternoon, storm clouds began to gather in the western sky. "Gonna be a biggun, Ego," I muttered. "Maybe we'd best take a break while we can," and I pulled off the Trail at a convenient stump. I had just finished a Snickers when Sasquatch blew past, his legs pumping up and down like long piston rods. He slowed but didn't stop, instead calling out that he'd see me at the store in Allen Gap. Said J.R., "Methinks that young lad got a whiff of pheromones on the North wind this morning and has finally got his butt in gear." I chuckled, "It sure wouldn't have been last night, unless his schnozzle mistook the 'riparian entertainment' for a message from home." Another thought—"But then, if there's a store at Allen Gap, there's bound to be food. We'd better start hoofing it off this mountain before the storm breaks."

By now, I well knew the "storm overture" of Nature's orchestra: First, distant kettledrums sounding a hollow tattoo, quickly building into a thunderous crescendo as the percussion section shatters the heavens with inane cacophony. Then comes the hushed reedy flutings of the woodwinds, playing on the ears with a dull whisper that sharply rises to a harsh, discordant groan as stringed instruments agitated by maniacal fiddlers rent the air. Without warning, the brass section shrieks with lusty abandon, and the wild performance, now fully joined, impales the spirit with frightening fury and turns hot sweat to cold shivers.

So I braced as the Storm Demon raised its baton and the curtain rose to the first dissonant sounds. The "overture" quickly increased in tempo; quaking, I bent into the onslaught of flailing limbs and stinging hail and the inevitable drenching, and made my way off the mountain.

The store gradually appeared through the opaque curtain lowered by the driving rain. Shivering, I hurriedly propped my pack outside the door of the small, concrete block, no-frills building and went inside. One small ceiling light barely lifted the gloomy darkness to minimum visibility, creating an eerie glow that pushed my eyes to the limit as they tried to adjust. Once my eyes focused, the blurred figure behind the counter transformed into a skinny woman in a faded flower-print dress. She glowered at me like an angry momma bear.

At first I thought it was her God-given, born-with look but as soon as she spoke, I knew different. "Jist lookit what you brung in with you. I might's well of left the door open an' invited the storm in." Most of her anger seemed directed at my feet—at least that's where THE LOOK seemed to settle.

I glanced down at the widening pool on the floor, fed by the drenched clothes, and then back at the path of muddy footprints leading to the door—undeniably mine. Withered by THE LOOK, I stammered an apology, which was so distorted by my shivering that it sounded as if I had a speech impediment. In more friendly surroundings it might have been comical, but at the moment I felt an overpowering urge to run back out into the storm where THE LOOK couldn't follow.

I must have cut a pretty picture because she mellowed some and packed THE LOOK away. "Well, you might's well stay since th' damage is done. Just try not to track up more'n you have to."

Wrapping my arms tightly around my chest to control the shaking, I smiled weakly and rattled, "I thank you k-k-kindly, Mam. I c-c-could sure use a c-cup of coffee or ch-ch-chocolate. Anything h-h-hot, for that m-matter." The shivers began to subside, giving me control of my mouth again, and I realized with dismay that neither Wahoola nor Sasquatch were here. J.R., quailed by the unexpected appearance of THE LOOK, tiptoed into my thoughts like he thought the woman could hear him. "Maybe she ran them off." I asked, "Have you seen any more in the last hour or so that looks like me?"

The woman cackled, "Thank the Good Lord no! One of ye's enough." She reflected. "They's a hiker did come through bout a half-hour or so ago. A tall'un, with big hocks." Sasquatch! "He was hungrier'n a pot-bellied porker. Ate a bunch of snack'n stuff." She frowned. "He tracked up m' floor, too, an' I'd a run him off if'n he didn't kept on throwin' business at me."

Her message was plain: Buy something or hit the road. "Coffee?" I reminded her.

"Naw, we ain't got nuthin' hot this time a day. Had coffee first thing this mornin. Only makeit up oncet in th' mornin.'" She cackled again—a stinging rebuke for the muddy floor?

The door swung open and her attention was diverted to two heavy, middle-aged women who hurried inside to escape the downpour, trailing water in their path. "Sisters?" I wondered, for they favored one another and each had brassy-blonde, neck-length hair and a prominent dimpled chin.

The woman at the register flashed a disapproving look at the dripping duo—more mopping up for the old crone—and as her eyes narrowed and her lips pursed into a closed vise, a deeper hostility, more like a smoldering anger, emerged. J.R. said, "These two have been here before and something has soured their welcome. Let's get out of the line of fire."

Shivering again from the chilly gust that had followed the women inside, I considered leaving since the rain seemed to be slackening. But I still held onto the idea of something hot. He said, "Let's stick around until these gals leave. Maybe we can talk 'Miss Bones' into cranking up the coffee pot." I tiptoed over to a dark corner to watch the proceedings and muttered, "Worth a try."

I took a closer look at the merchandise. Cigarettes were everywhere. Large cardboard boxes filled with cartons of cigarettes reached to the ceiling, hiding the back wall. Loose cartons covered two large tables and a large rack above the cash register was crammed to capacity with single packs. A smudged sign taped to a wall read, "Cigarettes—All brands. Lowest prices anywhere."

The two women scurried back and forth from the tables to the cash register until they had laid up a small mountain of cartons and then signaled with a nod that they were ready to pay. "Miss Bones," still frowning like she had a severe case of the seven-year itch, began punching keys on the old register, filling the room with whirs and clanks as the gears spun, until a delicate ding ended the sequence. Finished, she glared at the women and pointed at the total, which jumped out in big white numbers—$301.79. Without a word, one of the ladies pulled a roll of bills from her purse and peeled off several, took her change, and then both began loading the cartons into two heavy black garbage bags the other lady pulled from her coat pocket.

Remarked J.R., "Strange," and it was. Not a word had been spoken since the women had entered the store.

I eased over to the front window, glad to see that the storm had been replaced by a heavy drizzle, and watched as the women pushed their stash into the trunk of a rusted-out, faded green Chevy. Mission accomplished, the woman with the money cranked the engine, which spewed a cloud of foul-smelling, dark-gray smoke into the drizzle, and the car lurched down the mountain into North Carolina.

Hoping to break the ice, I chuckled to the grim-faced lady, "Those two sure have a bad cigarette habit."

She snarled, "Them two got worst habits than cigarettes," and she dismissed them with a slap on the counter. "Now, whatcha gonna have?"

A small table next to the tables laden with cigarette cartons held a puny supply of snack cakes. Nothing looked appealing. Doing my best "Boy Scout" impression, I said, "If I could talk you into making a pot of coffee, I'll buy the whole pot." (At that moment, ten cups seemed a realistic goal!)

Turning the frown on again (she switched it off and on like an outside light), she spit the words out slowly and deliberately, "I done tole ya, I only makit up oncet in th' mornin.'" Pointing at an antiquated cooler, she said, "They's some ice cream in thar if you're so inclined."

"Yes'm." Fearful of making more muddy tracks, I tiptoed to the cooler. Inside, small "nickel" cups (except a crude sign priced these at thirty-five cents each) of chocolate, strawberry, and vanilla formed a single frosted layer on the cooler's bottom. J.R. growled, "The irony of life. We're drowning in a sea of cigarettes and clutching at overpriced ice cream. I don't smoke and today isn't exactly an ice cream day." I: "We'd better buy something before that lady gets her dander up. She's liable to pull a forty-five caliber from under the counter and send us hightailin' it down the road."

Closing my eyes, I picked one at random—strawberry—tiptoed to the counter, and gave her two quarters. Silently, she worked the cash register and handed me the change, along with a tiny wooden spoon. "Sorry about the mud and water," I apologized as I pussyfooted toward the door.

She called as I went out, "I only makeit oncet a day." Guilty pang, or her way of accepting my apology? Maybe she had a heart after all! Smiling, I struggled into my soggy pack and headed back to the muddy Trail, eating ice cream and humming sketches of "In the Good Old Summer Time" in a hoarse, off-key baritone as I walked through the gentle rain. The Ego laughed. "When you go scratchin' in the chicken yard, you turn up the darndest things." I, shivering: "Yeah. Everything but coffee." So much for yesterday!

By the time I reached the top of Big Butt, still part of Cold Spring Mountain, the sun had come out and the disappointment of missing the goodies at Jerry Cabin Shelter had been sucked into the giant whirlpool of life's maladies, along with yesterday's misery. I paused at the edge of a cliff and gave myself an attitude adjustment as I gazed out on a magnificent, sunny vista that stretched to the hazy horizon—a wide, rolling chessboard of browns and greens, which sported a strange collection of shadowy pieces that moved across the board in unison with passing clouds. Rejuvenation came easy!

Nearby, a small marker ringed by stones and displaying a miniature American flag (more of Sam Waddle's handiwork?) nestled beside the Trail. According to the marker, here reposed the ashes of Howard Basset, who thru-hiked the AT in 1968 (one of the first fifty daring souls to do so). Reflecting, I said, "Two markers; two men; two hikes so different. Howard Bassett's journey led him to Katahdin and beyond, while Rex Pulford's was tragically cut short; yet, both are forever etched in the permanence of the Trail." J.R. murmured, "There are far less rewards in life."

After a few miles the Trail left the forest and entered a broad, alpine clearing. I'd been following an old mountain road for the past hour, and my mind filled with thoughts about the people who might have lived in this high wilderness a hundred, even two hundred years ago. What stories this old road could have told!

The Trail eventually left the road and soon came to a clearing. Off the path to the right, two waist-high tombstones faced each other like oversized bookends, about six feet apart. Oddly, the writing pointed inward on both stones, as if the undertaker had gotten confused about which was head and foot and had covered both possibilities by planting a marker at each end; but I knew that wasn't the case. "The Sheltons' grave," I said solemnly, trying to recall what I'd read: Two relatives, David and his nephew, William, both Union soldiers who were part of a nine-man recruiting mission to their home at nearby Shelton Laurel—a bastion of Union fervor in the midst of Southern defiance—hiding out in an old cabin here atop Cold Spring Mountain. The party ambushed by Confederate cavalry and captured, except for William, David, and thirteen year-old Millard, David's great-nephew, who had come to join up. The three had been shot and dumped into this common grave.

J.R. mused, "Violence becomes a way of life in troubled times, and men's consciences atrophy as rage and indifference take root. History books couldn't begin to hold the accounts of atrocities committed in the name of patriotism." I stared at the granite sentinels, pitted and corroded by generations of mountain storms; posted to stand eternal watch above their charges; stark reminders of a tragic day when honor and glory and youthful innocence were sacrificed to the god of War (or Waste?). In the center of the grave, a small bouquet of dried, faded flowers softened the somber scene and seemed to cry out, "Why?" I murmured, "Yes indeed, why?" but the ghosts of history remained silent. A cloud covered the sun and I hastened from the clearing.

Thirty minutes later, a fiery spasm suddenly racked my intestines. Like a searing knife, the pain stopped me in my tracks, doubling me into a hunchback. More spasms quickly came, each building on the other's pain, leaving me weak and covered with cold sweat, and I groaned, "Jesus! I'm gonna die!" I sagged against a tree, hoping the raging pain would pass before I dissolved into a soggy pool of putrid DNA. "God A'mighty! Don't let it be giardia!"

Gradually the spasms subsided into fledgling cramps and, like a poorly designed robot, I teetered up the Trail on rubbery legs, praying I could make it to Flint Mountain Shelter, a long two miles away. I counted my blessings—nausea and diarrhea hadn't yet struck!

A premature fancy! The next spasm attacked without warning, harshly giving way to sudden volcanic pressure. "Diarrhea!" I shrieked. "We're gonna explode!"

Frantic, I searched the woods. An impenetrable thicket of mountain laurel crowded the Trail to my right, while on my left, the mountainside dropped off sharply. Jesus! Racked by diarrhea and no place to go except the two-foot wide sacred national treasure. Sacrilege! I began to run.

And pray: "Please, Lord," I gasped, "give me a place. Any place but the Appalachian Trail." The "volcano" convulsed, threatening to erupt!

A small opening in the mountain laurel! Possibly a deer trail—barely large enough. It didn't matter for my prayer had been answered! Without breaking stride I lunged into the tangle and managed to get ten feet before the thick growth trapped me. No time for niceties, such as taking off the pack and searching for the toilet paper. Time had run out!

After two more stops, these under more favorable circumstances, I reached Flint Mountain Shelter just as rain clouds began to darken the sky. A new structure, it had been built in memory of Matt Sperling by his parents and the Carolina Mountain Club, but I didn't dally to read the dedication plate or to smell the fresh logs—more pressure was building!

Wahoola stood outside the shelter, fiddling with a piece of gear. I hadn't seen him since he had breezed past me on the old logging road south of the Shelton gravesite. He stared hard. "Where you been, Model-T? You look like—"

I cut through his words. "Where's the privy? Is there a privy?"

"Yeah, there's one behind the shelter, but it's only half-finished. Why?"

I threw off my pack and shoved past him, grunting, "Privy. Gotta get to the privy!" I began to run—again.

The privy wasn't much: a seat (with lid) set over a deep hole in the ground; no sides or roof—still to be built. No matter. After a laurel-choked deer path, this was luxury; plus, dignity and diarrhea mixed like oil and water.

When I returned to the shelter, I was surprised to find Sasquatch and another thru-hiker, Bill (in his mid-twenties, but no trail name to go with his short auburn jaw-line beard). I hadn't noticed them in my rush for the privy. Sasquatch seemed to have suffered no ill effects from his night at Club Geek—more than I could say for myself.

Wahoola asked again, "Where've you been? Feeding the bears?"

"Busy supporting the local ecology."

"Got the trots, huh?"

"Yeah," I admitted wryly. "I sure hope it's not giardia." Another cramp twisted my gut but I gritted my teeth, hoping to put off the trip outside, and began making my nest. Then, just as rain began to pummel the roof another harsh cramp convulsed my abdomen, bringing unyielding pressure, and I grabbed my rain jacket and dashed into the downpour. Perched on the unstable seat like some prehistoric fowl, I turned my face up to let the rain wash the tears and pain-sweat away. The Ego complained, "Diarrhea on a rainy afternoon in a roofless privy. The 'King of Crud' sits on his throne and surveys his cruddy kingdom. Somehow, I fail to see any 'adventure' in this." I blinked the water out of my eyes and reached for the plastic bag that held my dwindling supply of toilet paper. "The adversities of the Trail are wondrous to behold," I replied. "All part of searching for 'nirvana.'" He: "What you mean is, 'Shit happens.'" I: "At least the toilet paper is dry." It had the makings of a long night!

Drenched and shivering, I hastened back to the shelter. Bill had brewed some tea and he offered me some, saying, "Hot tea's good for lots of things, including diarrhea." Grateful, I sipped the fragrant brew and felt better as the warmth soothed my intestines.

I made two more trips to the privy before the cramps subsided into dull gastric twinges and I was able to sleep. I still hadn't been attacked by nausea, a definite symptom of giardia. Could the polluted lettuce have been the culprit? Or, like J.R. suggested, just too much of the "greasy spoon"? I'd know soon enough.

I awakened as pale gray light filtered through the front of the shelter. Outside, the wind blustered with noisy gusts, pushing through the trees and causing the branches to groan in protest before spiraling upward toward distant mountaintops. The rain had departed, leaving in its stead a chilling dampness, and I was sorely tempted to turn over and go back to sleep.

Then my fogged mind congealed into rational thought. I wasn't cramping! No diarrhea since midnight! No nausea! I had been saved from "The Big G"! I closed my eyes in relief and whispered, "Thank you, Lord, and whap me with a tobacco stick if I ever put rotten lettuce between my lips again." (I couldn't bring myself to blame the wonderful "greasy spoon"!) From J.R. came a fervent "Ditto!" Recharged and ready to tackle the world again, I quickly packed and hit the Trail, leaving the others to their dreams.

Wahoola overtook me in mid-afternoon as I sat beside busy US Highway 23 at Sam's Gap munching a Snickers and absently watching the traffic struggle up the long grade out of North Carolina. *The Philosophers Guide* dangled from my non-eating hand, but my mind was three miles down the bottom of the mountain at the Little Creek Café where, according to the *PG*, Grannie Boone's delicious homemade pies awaited. I mumbled aloud, "To go or not to go; that is the question." Cars whipped past, probably heading down toward that very place. How easy it would be to just stand up and stick my thumb out. But getting back might prove harder than going down, and a three-mile hike up a busy winding mountain highway held the appeal of a dose of castor oil. Still, I could get a whole pie and eat it there, and then get another for supper. But, three miles . . . Dang! I could almost smell those pies all the way up here!

Wahoola halted in front of me, and his voice cut into my mental tug of war as he asked, "Are you going down?" I grinned guiltily, realizing he had read my mind.

"I'm contemplating the idea while I eat a Snickers." I polished the bar off and stuffed the wrapper in a plastic bag with several others—the day's accumulation.

Wahoola eyed my little trash bag. "You've got quite a pile of those wrappers. How many have you had today?"

Only half-listening, I answered, "I don't know. Two, maybe three." I had more important things on my mind—like Grannie Boone' pies. "If it's important, I can count'em," I said, dumping them between my legs. Sheepishly, I met his eyes and announced, "Six."

"You know you've got a little problem, don't you? You've become a Snickers addict."

"Naw. Some of these are probably from yesterday. Let me count," and I began recounting today's journey, ticking them off on my fingers like I was driving home an important point: "Let's see now. One before I left Flint Mountain Shelter this morning; one at the bottom of Frozen Knob, then another about half-way up. Yep, had another at the top." He raised an eyebrow. "A long climb. Had to get some energy going." I thought for a moment. "Oh yeah, I had one for lunch and then the one just now. That makes five."

"You've got six fingers up." He shook his head sadly. "You need a support group. Bad!"

The accusing pile of wrappers seemed to mock me. Jeez, it hadn't seemed like that many, spread out over the day. Six! I bridled, "I only ate two yesterday."

"Yesterday, you had the trots."

The evidence lay in plain sight. I didn't know if he was teasing, but he had struck a sensitive nerve. My craving for Snickers bars had grown from one or two a day to four or five. And it looked as if today might be a seven-bar day, if I had another for supper. By simple math, I was consuming a pound of Snickers a day! And to support my "habit," assuming resupply every five days or so, I'd have to carry five pounds of Snickers! (This small detail had nagged the edge of my mind for several days, but I had managed to ignore it.)

Reality was ugly! I rationalized, "Snickers have lots of calories n' quick energy. Anyway, five pounds isn't all that big a deal. If I send my tent home and take a chance on staying in shelters; that's three pounds right there! Maybe I can do without my rain jacket . . ." Hearing myself speak the words aloud, I groaned, "Jesus, Wahoola! I've got a Snickers habit! What am I gonna do?"

"You're going to have to hop on the wagon, but it doesn't have to be 'cold turkey'. I'll help you. Why don't you just give me all of your Snickers and I'll dish them out when the withdrawal gets too bad." Was he serious?

His eyes gave him away. "Sure. That's like putting a piranha in a bowl of gold fish. Gimme me a break!" He grinned as I moved closer to my open pack and its dwindling cache of Snickers. "I'll taper off." He gave me a skeptical look, shaking his head like he didn't believe I could do it.

No longer in the mood for Grannie Boone's delicious homemade pies, I put my pack on and followed Wahoola across the busy highway and up the mountain toward Big Bald, five miles away. The northwest horizon was beginning to change from lead-gray to an ominous tinge of dark purple, and the acrid smell of "storm" rode in on the freshening wind.

Big Bald is a sprawling tundra-like barren, which, at a little over 5,500 feet, seemed on this day to actually kiss the clouds that scurried past in wispy blobs just beyond arm's reach. The bald's sheer immensity and command of the surrounding mountains created the illusion that the world emanated from this precise spot, flowing out from our feet toward infinity in a fruitless quest to mate with the heavens. Off to the east, Mt. Mitchell rose in defiance at the angry, purplish-black sky. Although Mt. Mitchell stands 1100 feet higher than Big Bald, and at 6684 feet is the highest point east of the Mississippi River, to my eyes it seemed diminished by Big Bald's regal vastness.

We pushed against the stout, frigid wind that swept the bald, following a narrow deep-rutted path toward a distant solitary post that marked the summit. The broad expanse of knee-length golden grass churned and rippled like waves on an angry sea, and our human frailty seemed magnified a hundred fold by the exposed vastness of this swirling ocean of amber.

We finally reached the post, a tottering, storm-beaten relic that slammed back and forth against the turbulence—now close to gale strength—as it clung precariously to the mountain. (Earlier, we had talked about tenting on the summit, hoping we might glimpse the peregrine falcons that had been reestablished in the area in recent years, but the approaching storm had transformed the beautiful barren into an ominous landscape—not a place to be caught in the open!)

Even standing had become difficult, and the temperature, dropping fast, cut through my polypro long johns and skimpy gloves with insolence. Wahoola yelled, "Let's head for the shelter!" I nodded and we pushed into the howling wind, hoping that the trail would soon lead down into the tree line. Bald Mountain Shelter was only a mile away but already my fingers had lost feeling. Shuffling my walking stick from hand-to-hand, I tried to grab what warmth I could by alternating my hands beneath my armpits. It wasn't much.

"Oh for a Snickers!" I moaned to The Ego, thinking of the three remaining Snickers just out of reach inside my pack, my earlier resolve weakened by the moment. "Suck it up," he growled. "We can't stop in this. If you've got to have a 'fix,' you're just going to have to wait." I held the picture of the Snickers in my mind (small comfort) and stuck close to Wahoola.

I couldn't believe my eyes! The shelter, a double-decker, was packed, and sleeping bags—most occupied—covered the floor like a frumpy blanket. A couple of hikers, stoic dim apparitions, watched as I rechecked the interior. Even in the thick dusk I could tell that no amount of revamping would create additional room, and my body sagged as bitter disappointment joined the shivering weariness. Wahoola must have felt the same, for his face was drawn, almost surreal, as if a makeup artist had rearranged his features for the part of monster in a grade B horror flick. Briefly, I wondered what my face looked like.

A strong, clear voice came from the upper deck. "Sorry fellas, it's a full house. I wish we could work you in, but . . ." His unfinished sentence,

filled with sympathy and apology (a cleansing of conscience for the fortunate few?) suffocated my spirit like a hangman's noose being drawn tight.

Wahoola looked at me for a long moment and shrugged. "Don't worry
about it," he said, his voice betraying none of the emotion his eyes revealed.
"According to the *Data Book*, there's a campsite a half mile or so on up the
Trail. We'll be fine. You ready to go, Model-T?"

"In a moment," I mumbled, digging into my pack and ripping the
wrapper off of Snickers number seven. I bridled at his smirk. "What? Popeye has to have his spinach when a crisis comes up. I gotta have my Snickers!" He managed what passed for a grin, although in the near dark it might
have been a sneer. I hurriedly finished my "fix," slung my pack on, and followed Wahoola into the woods.

Almost immediately fog engulfed us—whitish-black bleakness that
swirled in cadence to the frigid wind and cut straight to the bone—soon
bringing with it a light rain laced with sleety pellets. Rushing across Big
Bald, neither of us had stopped to put on rain gear, nor did we take the time
during the brief stop at the shelter, harboring the vague notion that we
would be able to set up camp before the storm hit. Now we paid for our
folly as the rain increased, drenching us to the skin. Shivering uncontrollably, I stumbled along behind Wahoola, trying to match his pace, fighting
off the onset of apathetic sluggishness as hypothermia began its snakelike
coiling around my mind. My fingers and toes began to go numb, and for
the first time I seriously considered tossing my hiking stick into the undergrowth so I could put both hands beneath my armpits to delay the deaden-
ing, but I couldn't bring myself to part with this old friend.

Wahoola stopped abruptly, pointing his flashlight's weak beam into
the foggy downpour; then attempting to overcome the storm's roar, he
yelled, "That campsite's got to be close by. How long's it been since we
left the shelter?"

I pushed my arm in front of the light. "Fifteen minutes." We strained
to see through the darkness but the wind and fog trapped the feeble light.
"It'll be easy to miss in this mess," I shouted.

We pushed on, carefully watching for a worn path, a blue blaze, anything
that might be interpreted as a side path; but as the minutes passed, it soon
became obvious that we had missed the campsite. Now really concerned, we
began to look for any place to pitch tents. Trees and jagged, up-thrusting rock
crowded both sides of the Trail, which had started rising steadily toward Little
Bald—a mile and a half from the shelter and higher than Big Bald. I checked
my watch and was dimly aware that forty minutes had passed since we
walked away from the shelter. Would this night never end?

Stubbornly, I glued my eyes to Wahoola's boots—shadowy, muddy pendulums in the faint glow of my flashlight—and matched my pace to his, fighting away the urge to lie down and go to sleep. The wily serpent tightened its steely bands as it hummed a hypnotic, mellifluous requiem: "Sleep; sleep; the earth is your bed. Just close your eyes; peace comes with sleep." The slippery words gnawed at my will power, "So easy to escape this shivering misery; to elude this numbness that seeks to shrivel your spirit and push your soul into a dark pit. 'Sleep' can take you away from all this." My mind responded, "Yes, so easy to flop down on the muddy path; pull my tent over me; just surrender to the warm release of sleep and get away from the misery and quit trying to scratch in a chicken yard covered with concrete and give up . . ."

I bumped into Wahoola, who suddenly halted and swung the thin thread of light in an arc. He shouted a single word, but it was enough to jolt me out of my trance as, dazed, I attempted to focus on the message. Laughing, I loudly echoed, "Home!" as my brain accepted the image: two small alcoves, one on each side of the Trail, each just large enough for a small one-person tent. Breathing a sigh of relief, I turned in at the tiny clearing to the right and murmured, "Thank you, God, for showing mercy to two fools." Said J.R., "Make that three."

Inside my sleeping bag, still in wet clothes, the numbness gradually departed and the shivering, replaced by damp warmth, finally ceased. When I was able, I slithered half out of the bag and sprawled in the tent opening, barely sheltered by the small rain flap, and cooked the last of the supper provisions—mac-n-cheese. The stove's tiny flame danced and fluttered, playing constant tag with the blustering wind as it flared and ebbed, threatening to retreat back into its stove womb, then surging again to a brilliant orb as the wind momentarily relinquished its hold. J.R. reflected, "That flame's like life: lots of ups and downs, ins and outs." I answered, "Like tonight," feeling my life force balloon in response to the first spoonfuls of mac-n-cheese and the warmth of my snug microcosm.

Wahoola yelled from his tent, "Are you gonna hang your food bag?"

It took me a moment to answer, for my mouth was crammed with searing mac-n-cheese. Noisily, I sucked in air like a ruptured bellows, trying to cool the food before it cooked my esophagus, and yelled back, "Are you kidding? If the bears are willing to come out tonight to get what little I have left, they can have it." Reconsidering, I added, "Except for the Snickers!"

I balked at cleanup for the first time since leaving Springer Mountain. Ignoring the twinge of guilt, I pushed the pot, along with any tidbits of mac-n-cheese I might have missed, outside into the rainy darkness. "Let the bears be happy with that!" I growled, opening up the wrapper of Snickers number eight. "Here's one they're not gonna get!"

The nor'easter bore down, shrieking like a multitude of Hell's denizens frenziedly seeking to escape Satan's wrath, clutching at the flimsy tents and trying its best to toss us off the mountain. Finally admitting failure, the beastly tempest relinquished its frantic grasp and roared away to seek easier prey, leaving behind a gentler offspring that calmed the forest with tendrils of soothing massage. I felt sleep creeping into my body and gave myself up to the warm, damp womb I called "home" this night.

J. R. broke into the cozy twilight of near-sleep. "Jeez, wake up, Alterman. Kelly (his and Judith's eldest son) is 29 today. We've got to celebrate." Indeed, today was May 5th. "No problem," I said, shaking the cobwebs away and reaching inside the depleted food bag beneath my head. Slowly savoring the last Snickers bar (number nine for today, but what the heck? We didn't have a birthday cake!), J.R. and I whispered in unison, "Happy birthday, Kelly. This one's for you!"

Satisfied, I snuggled deeper inside the bag and closed my eyes. Immediately Wahoola's accusing face wavered before me. "Nine Snickers today, Model-T?" the apparition whispered, giving a sad shake before it faded into the darkness. Fighting off panic, I muttered to myself, "Well, the Snickers are all gone now. Tomorrow I'll *have* to go 'cold turkey'."

During the night, I had a troubled dream about a giant puppeteer who looked down on earth's vacillating stage and pulled at the tangled strings that manipulated the events of my life. His face was twisted into a diabolical grin as he plucked the strings at random and merrily hummed an off-key rendition of "Night on Bald Mountain."

Dawn. I struggled back to consciousness, tuning my ears to the outside. All seemed unnaturally still, except for the sporadic dripping of water from the trees. Unzipping the flap, I was taken aback by a scene of eerie beauty. While I slept, Nature had quietly repainted the landscape gray with freezing mist, adding a delicate layer of cottony ice to the trees before finishing the mural with a netherworld pall of dense fog.

Climbing out of the tent, I rubbed my eyes in disbelief. Just five feet away from where I had pitched my tent in the rain last night, a drop-off plunged at least a hundred feet into a ravine. I shuddered as the strange dream rushed to the front of my memory, bringing the realization that my trip had almost come to an untimely end at this forlorn spot!

I packed with numb fingers and kicked Wahoola's tent. "Nature left us a 'calling card.' Enjoy!" A muffled grunt reached my ears, telling me that he had survived the night. I hit the Trail running.

The numbness had disappeared by the time I crossed Little Bald—far different from its sprawling "older sibling," imprisoned as it was by a cadre of silent, gray monoliths that jutted up from the thick forest floor and dashed any hopes of a decent view, even on a clear day. The dense freezing mist infected me with a perverse feeling of gladness—I hadn't *expected* a view so I eluded disappointment! Quickly working through the desolate boulder field, I began to descend.

Before long I stepped out of the fog and into a jeweled, glittering world where the sun's rays danced across ice-coated foliage. Looking upward, it seemed as if Nature had drawn a precise line around the mountain, dooming the summit heights to perpetually exist as a frozen, bleak land, while decreeing that the kingdom below should live forever in joy, harmony, and sunshine. Reveling in my newly found utopia and suddenly ravenous, I stopped at a sun-warmed rock, which offered a birds-eye view of a wide, patchwork valley—the view I had been denied from the summit. Far below the quilted pattern of woods and fields played hide and seek with wispy sheets of mist that floated up from the valley floor. Nature had set a magnificent table for us! A shame I couldn't do it justice.

Dumping the contents of the food bag onto the rock, I took stock: a skimpy tablespoon of peanut butter if I did some serious scraping; a squashed piece of bread embedded with enough cookie crumbs to possibly equal half a cookie; and a bouillon cube, type unknown. I mentally kicked myself for squandering all the Snickers on a single day of Snicker-binging, but then gave a wry chuckle at the meager pile. "Well, Ego-man, Mister Bear would have had mighty slim pickings last night." Replied The Ego, "Maybe Wahoola can help us out, if he drags his lazy butt this far before we leave." Grateful that he hadn't chided me for running out of food, I said, "It's no big deal. We're not going to starve between here and Erwin (fourteen miles away)." He grumbled, "True. Maybe you can imagine us up a good lunch."

I wolfed down the food, except for the bouillon cube (deciding to save it for lunch), drank all of my water, and went off into a fantasy daydream about a food bag that magically produced Snickers overnight to replace those eaten the previous day. The fantasy slowly switched over to food possibilities in Erwin, and a quantum leap carried me to a greasy spoon with a pie case stacked with Grannie Boone's delicious homemade pies.

My mouth slathered with drool as I mentally gorged on thick, creamy chocolate topped with two-inch golden meringue—

Wahoola broke into my thoughts. "Nice view."

"Yeah. You had breakfast yet?" I asked, hoping he hadn't. He always carried gobs of food.

He took off his pack and gazed down into the valley, where thin wisps of smoke, now visible in the thinning mist, rose from houses tucked away in groves of forest. "Not yet. Too cold to stop back up on the top." Expectantly, I waited for him to take a seat and open his food bag, but he continued to focus on some distant point and the silence grew.

"A good place right here to eat," I finally ventured, trying to hide any hint of eagerness as I covertly studied his face.

"It would be, except I don't have any food left. You got any?"

Drat! "Naw. I just finished off the last of my crumbs. I'm hungry enough to eat ramen."

He grinned. "You wouldn't eat ramen if you were starving." He took a seat beside me, opened his pack, pulled out a sad-looking plastic bag with the remains of picked-over trail mix—a few peanuts and a half-dozen M &M's—and began to munch.

He had just finished "breakfast" when a large black Lab toting red saddlebags trotted up and sniffed our boots; then panting rapidly and wagging his tail, he plopped down on the rock, unrolled his long tongue several inches, and unleashed a long string of slobber. I scratched him behind the ear. "Hello boy. What's your name?"

The dog's master, a tall lanky man with long, stringy hair and a scraggily beard that hid most of his face, came up and thrust out his hand. "I see you've met Woton. My name's Cruise Control." He looked to be in his early thirties. "Say, aren't you the hikers who came by the shelter last night? That was some kind of storm! We sure hated to see you go on."

Wahoola and I exchanged knowing glances, recognizing the voice— the same that had apologized as we shivered in the dark outside the shelter. I harbored no animosity; the shelter had been crammed.

We soon learned that Cruise Control was a disk jockey from Richmond, Virginia, and that he was justifying his thru-hike by interviewing hikers and sending audio tapes back weekly (or when he could get to a post office) to the station he worked for. "So far, the tapes have been well received by the folks at Richmond," he said.

"If you guys are going on to the next shelter (No Business Knob Shelter, two miles away) and don't mind, I'll interview you while we eat lunch."

"Sure," we answered at the same time.

"Okay, see you there. C'mon Woton," and without a backward glance, the twosome took off.

Wahoola's face was utterly guiless. "Are you thinking what I'm thinking?"

"You know it! Cruise Control's got *food!* It's *yogi time!*" We hightailed it after Cruise Control.

"Do you smell smoke?" Wahoola asked, pausing in mid-step and sniffing the air.

I nodded, catching a definite whiff. "Someone must have a fire going at the shelter." I checked the time—11:45. No Business Knob Shelter (strange name!) couldn't be much further. The smell wafting toward us reminded me of a Halloween hot dog roast and I sucked at the drool that threatened to dribble down my beard. "Dang, Model-T, I hope Cruise Control's got lunch ready, or else I'm gonna have to fight that big Lab for some dog food!" Rolling his eyes, Wahoola sniffed his way up the path like a beagle scenting a rabbit, except this rabbit was Cruise Control's food bag! I ran after him.

Wispy gray smoke lazily rose from a smoldering fire in front of the shelter. Woton, lying just beyond the reach of the smoke, gnawed at something nasty looking between his paws. Content for the moment, he paid no attention to his master, who lounged against the shelter's front with a can of beer in one hand and a large paper plate piled high with food in the other. Nor did the four scruffy characters who surrounded his master seem to bother him—perhaps because Cruise Control wore an enormous grin that almost swallowed his face.

One of the "scruffies" saw us and shouted, "Hey! You fellas come on in here. Grab a stick and cook some dogs. We got beans; we got chili! And there's beer 'n pop in that cooler over there." He seemed excited to see us. Heck! I was excited to see him! But, who were these people?

They definitely weren't hikers. Two wore ragged camouflage trousers, while the other two had on torn, dirty jeans. They looked to be in their late twenties, except for the one who had shouted the invitation; he might have already sneaked past the thirty mark. A young, thin-faced woman sat inside against the shelter's back wall, running slim fingers through long, stringy hair as she watched the happenings with vacant eyes. Off to the side of the shelter, a small boy fought an imaginary enemy with a stick sword and his high-pitched yells left little doubt that he had sent his foes into retreat.

Wahoola barely nodded toward a large half-full bottle of bourbon, which sat in plain view just inside the shelter. Trouble? Cruise Control obviously didn't think so, for his arm hoisted food from the plate to his mouth like a well-honed machine. A pro at timing, with remarkable precision he chewed and swallowed and spluttered out bits of food with smooth words about his fame as a disk jockey and his mission to enlighten the public about life on the Appalachian Trail through the wonderful medium of radio. "Gee, you could take lessons from this guy," J.R. said with admiration.

Without breaking stride, Cruise Control set the beer can on the floor beside the bourbon and yanked a small radio from his jacket pocket. All eyes followed the small black case as if it held the power of life and death. And when he flipped the "on" switch and thrust the device inches from the nearest spectator's mouth—a bald fellow with a huge beer belly that protruded over his dirty denims—and began snapping out questions, the poor man jumped back a foot like he had been smitten by a plague.

"Don't look a gift horse in the mouth," I muttered at Wahoola, and we headed for the food.

Cruise Control finally lost interest and, followed by his fan club, came over to refill his plate. In between mouthfuls of beans and hot dogs we discovered that our "hosts" were a small group of romping, stomping, happy-go-lucky "good ol' boys"—most from nearby Johnson City—who referred to themselves as the RAT Patrol (taken from the initials of their leader, Randy Allen Tarpley, the fellow who had invited us to join in the festivities). Randy, who told us to call him the Head Rat, was short and stocky, about 5' 7", and had friendly eyes and an infectious smile, which was totally at odds with his ragged, dirty tee shirt and oily, shoulder-length pony tail. Surprisingly, Head Rat talked more like a college graduate than a high school dropout (something to do with teenage rebellion against his university professor dad). I immediately took a liking to Head Rat— nothing to do with the fact that he owned the half-full bottle of bourbon!

Head Rat said, "I'm glad you guys showed up. We didn't get any hikers at all yesterday and it was starting to look like the whole weekend was going to be a bust." (I'd forgotten that today was Sunday.) Scratching his crotch, he added, "And we've got all this food left. I guess we can take it home and try another shelter next weekend."

Determined to reduce his logistical problem, I picked another dog out of the plastic bag, wallowed it around in some chili, and crammed the whole dripping affair in my mouth. "Do the RAT's do this kind of thing often?"

"Actually, this is only the second shelter we've been to." He chuckled at a fleeting memory and continued, "We hit it lucky at the other one last weekend. Had about six or eight hikers." He glanced at the bourbon bottle. "And we were kicking our heels up; had too much to drink. I think we scared some of'em. So we're watching it this weekend because we RAT's gotta protect our reputation." I must have looked skeptical for he added, "We voted to leave the hard stuff at home—after this is gone."

Which caused me to whisper, so Wahoola couldn't hear, "Say, Head Rat, you wouldn't happen to have a couple of Snickers, would you?" No such luck!

Randy went on to explain that his little group had taken on the self-assigned mission of cleaning up some of the area shelters, doing trail maintenance, and feeding the hikers when they could afford to buy food. He looked affectionately at his RAT Patrol. "And we plan to have a good time while we're at it." Then pointing at Cruise Control, who had again activated his little black box, he said, "I'd better get over there and make sure these guys don't sully our reputation. You fellers eat all you can hold, 'cause we have plenty."

Wahoola said softly, "Gosh Model-T, I'm ashamed. I thought we'd stumbled on a bunch of trail bums and here they are treating us like royalty. And look at the good they're doing."

"Me, too," I admitted. "I feel lower than a bullfrog's pecker." The confession somehow made me feel better. I looked Wahoola straight in the eyes. "As a penance, I'm only going to eat three more hotdogs," I said, stuffing more food into my remorseful mouth.

Cruise Control sidled up and said in a low voice, "The Head Rat wants to take me home with him. Says he's going to feed me and wash my clothes and bring me back here in the morning and put me on the Trail. The curse of being a celebrity, you know. They all want to get on the radio. Hey, they'll probably even want to feed me steak!" He rolled his eyes with feigned boredom as if to say, "Not again! Why do my fans demand so much of me?" Then unable to hide the anticipation of a shower, bed, and real food, he smirked. "Well, men, it's my cross to bear. I'll catch you somewhere up the Trail."

We wondered if he would. But such is the price of fame!

In spite of our guilt feelings, Wahoola and I stuffed our bellies until at last, unable to hold another bite, we expressed our heartfelt thanks to the RAT Patrol, whom we now viewed with great respect as true Trail Angels. Flipping a friendly "bird" at Cruise Control, along with a mocking grin, we staggered up the Trail toward Erwin, hardly believing our good fortune, yet cursing our gluttony with each step as we pampered bloated bellies. Said The Ego about the RAT Patrol, "Pap always said that the best fishing worms came from a pile of rotten manure." I suppose he was paying them a compliment!

We stared at the open hole where a bridge had recently stood—the Trail's passage over the mighty Nolichucky—now a watery chasm. The Head Rat had warned us about this place and had given us two options: We could follow the narrow paved road where we now stood, which paralleled the river, a half-mile to the right and walk across on a trestle railroad bridge (no walkway!); or we could follow the road to the left for three miles and cross on a highway bridge, and then follow a series of roads back to the Trail. (The old bridge had been demolished as part of a highway renovation project, and work on the new bridge hadn't yet started.) The dark, swirling water seemed to mock us as we tried to decide.

"How brave do you feel?" Wahoola asked.

"Not brave enough to jump in and swim if a train comes by." The thought of bobbing up and down like a piece of waterlogged flotsam in this current gave me the willies!

"Me neither. I'd rather face the dogs." (Head Rat had also warned us about a couple of vicious dogs that lived in a house close to this road, having said that he personally knew of three thru-hikers who had been bitten.)

"Good choice," I growled, cocking my head toward the distant toot of a train and digging the canister of pepper spray out my belt pouch. "Real good choice!"

The afternoon had turned into a stifling oven—no breeze—and the sun beat down on the scorching pavement, building up enough heat to almost fry an egg. Worse, I had slipped on slick pine needles coming down the steep descent—no switchbacks—and as a result had developed a sharp pain in my right ankle. It began to throb as we walked side by side through the sweltering heat.

He pointed at a group of small houses ahead to our left. "Keep an eye out for dogs," he reminded me. As if cued in, two small dogs, one a dirty, two-toned brown, the other black with large patches of white on its chest and legs, dashed out from behind a hedge. They looked too cute to be the attackers. I whistled and called, "How ya doin', fellas?" and bent down to scratch the brown dog's ear.

In a flash, he turned from cute little dog to vicious mutt, intent on making a meal of my hand! I jerked it away, at the same time jumping backwards as he dashed inside my hiking stick for a quick taste of ankle, and barely averted a canine tattoo by giving him a taste of my stick. He backed off, snarling and growling, fangs snapping like a trick set of false teeth, and then he and his black partner began a coordinated attack, which also included Wahoola.

J.R. gasped, "Darn, these little bastards are good! Their daddy must've been a Marine!" True. Their strategy could have been taken right out of the Marine Corps' manual on battle doctrine: While one charged in on a frontal assault, absorbing the victim's attention, the other sneaked in on the flank or rear and attacked. These mutts were smart, and what they lacked in size, they made up with persistence and uncanny coordination. They must have had a vendetta against hikers (or else, as The Marine later suggested, they were bored to death and hikers provided their sole form of entertainment)!

"Get out of here! Get on home!" Wahoola yelled. We swung our hiking sticks, whacking the pavement to let them know what waited on the business end of our weapons if they came within range, and kicked and shouted like we had bees in our shorts. I tried for a close-in shot with the pepper spray and almost lost the canister and a finger as the brown dog darted beneath my swinging stick. I scored a lucky poke, somehow managing to shove the psychotic kamikaze away, and then shelved the pepper spray idea—an invitation for hand-to-hand combat.

We fought our way down the lane, back-to-back, thrusting and parrying, yelling and whacking, trying to guard each other's flank and rear. Wahoola suddenly connected with a solid whack, which brought sharp yelps from the black dog and sent him squealing like a stuck pig back up the lane. The brown dog tried one more halfhearted thrust, which I easily parried, and then scampered after his partner, yelping and having a hissy fit like it was us who had attacked them!

I gasped with relief, chest heaving from the exertion. "I guess we showed them!" My leg pain had temporarily dissolved in the adrenalin rush and I felt great.

"Yeah, a piece of cake," Wahoola chuckled, shaking his hiking stick high in the air, declaring victory. "Maybe they'll think twice before attacking anymore thru-hikers!"

Impulsively (J.R.'s doing?), I yelled, "Semper Fi; Do or Die! Marines Number One! Aaarah!" Wahoola got a kick out from that and asked me to repeat it. J.R. was in high heaven!

As we crossed the Nolichucky, making our victorious entry into Erwin (without fanfare), I prattled, "Jeez Wahoola, just think! Today we conquered two man-eating predator canines. We could become knights-errant on a quest to make the trails of America free from ravaging animals. I might even change my trail name—Model-T sounds so blah. How do you like Ninja Hiker?" Another flash of inspiration struck. "Or how about Samurai Strider? Gee! We could travel America's back country and make the trails safe for all people of all races, young and old!" I glanced at Wahoola, expecting to see a fervent gleam denoting agreement and dedication to this noble purpose shining from his eyes. He wasn't even listening.

Instead, he pointed at a large building at the end of a parking lot. "Doesn't that sign say White's Supermarket?" Sure enough it did! Excited, I pushed aside grandiose plans of future conquest and hurried after Wahoola. "Ice cream!" he croaked as we dumped our packs by the door and rushed inside, oblivious to the stares of the customers.

We edged through the after-church crowd, which gave us decent leeway, toward the rear of the store in search of the freezer. I hissed, "I'm gonna have a float. A chocolate float!" It was all I could do to keep from whooping.

"A what?" He twisted in mid-stride and gave me a perplexed look.

"A float! You know, ice cream and cola." He still had a quizzical look. "If you want one, get what I get." I took the lead—a knight-errant on a different kind of quest.

We each bought a quart of ice cream—vanilla for Wahoola—and Cherry Cokes, and then sat on the sidewalk near our packs with our backs against the building. I smiled at a well-dressed older couple (coming from dinner at a nearby restaurant after church?). Their glance took in our ragged, filthy clothes and spread-out legs, still sweaty, and the dark wet imprints on the sidewalk. The woman bent toward the man's ear, whispered a few words, and went inside. The old fellow paused, pulled out a small handful of change, and gently placed it on the walkway, grunting gruffly over his shoulder as he opened the door, "I've been in hard times m'self, young fellers."

"Sunday Christian charity," I laughed.

Wahoola blushed. "They think we're homeless!"

"We are." I dug my spoon out of the pack and opened the container. "Okay. You do whatever you want to, but I'm making a float." I began to eat the chocolate ice cream as fast as I could.

"Why're you doing that?"

"You've got to eat out a space so you can start pouring in the Coke." I demonstrated, rolling my eyes with sheer delight as the chilled sweetness flowed across my tongue. "The more space you make, the quicker you can add the Coke."

His interest peaked. "Man, that does look good. I'm gonna make a vanilla float!" and he began to spoon ice cream into his mouth.

Sighing with ecstasy, I murmured an impromptu thought: "This little delicacy is what I call 'Float Down the Throat.'" I worked at it—ice cream out; more soda in, until the sinkhole took all the Cherry Coke and I held a magnificent creation in my dirty hands. Beaming at Wahoola, I toasted his work in progress by swallowing a big gulp of the bubbly-brown liquid, wiped the fizzy overflow on the front of my tee shirt, and rent the air with a loud belch—just as a man and his pretty teenage daughter went past. (Honest injun! I couldn't suppress it.)

The girl jumped at the sudden noise, like she had been cold-nosed by man's best friend, and she fixed pretty brown eyes on the source. I shrugged, trying to appear contrite, but the expression turned into an embarrassed grin as she flushed bright red. Looking her straight in the eye I motioned toward Wahoola. "His," I grunted. "He's intestinally challenged." The damsel came dangerously close to self-immolation and hurried after her dad.

Wahoola had easily mastered the technique and now had all the Coke inside his container. He slurped and groaned with delight as the soda fizzed down his throat, reminding J.R. of his great-uncle Fred's old, flea-bitten coon dog when it got a good backscratching. "Ahh! Model-T, this is great! You're a genius."

Without warning, he shrieked and jumped to his feet, trying to dodge the stream of dingy coke/ice cream slurry that poured from the bottom of his carton. He tried to staunch the flow with his finger, and then his hand, but even duck tape couldn't have cured this dilemma. Growling a string of obscenities, he watched the thick liquid ooze down his arm, onto his boots, and form a puddle on the pavement. "Now what do I do, Mr. Expert?"

"No problem. Make it into a wineskin." He caught my drift and positioned the carton above his mouth, holding it so that the liquid streamed down into his maw. Grinning, I chuckled, "By the way, when you do 'Float Down the Throat' get an ice cream carton that has a solid bottom, not a flap."

The girl and her dad came out of the store while Wahoola guzzled the steady stream, tilting his head far back like a turkey trying to see where rain comes from. I nodded at the strange performance and said solemnly, "He's also socially challenged." The lass tittered; the father glowered; Wahoola choked; and I caught the stream in my empty carton. Mortified, The Ego grumbled, "Pap also said that when manure gets above the boot tops, it's time to clean out the barn." I guess he meant it was time to get out of Erwin.

We braved the Sunday crowd one more time, buying enough groceries to get us on to Damascus, Virginia, 115 miles and eight days away. (While

Wahoola wasn't looking, I sneaked three six-packs of Snickers into my basket—after The Ego reminded me that going cold turkey could do great psychological damage to one's psyche!)

That night we camped a stone's throw beyond the N.O.C. Camp—a whitewater rafting satellite of the main camp—about a mile upriver from the demolished bridge. A few yards away, the river glided noiselessly past a large sandy beach, its benign waters a stark contrast to the angry current on the far side. Down river, the railroad bridge, barely visible in the thickening twilight, spanned the banks like a giant sleeping dragon that threatened to awaken at any moment and consume us in a hideous, loathsome rush. My thoughts wandered further downstream to the two wily nippers. Had they scored against any hapless hikers since our pitched battle?

I munched on Snickers number one in the privacy of my tent (thus circumventing possible damage to my psyche!) and remarked to The Ego, "A bizarre afternoon." He: "It all goes with the scratchin'."

Train sounds echoed across the river—a forlorn rumbling that rode the night breeze and penetrated the deepest reaches of my soul. Somewhere in the twilight of my imaginings the master puppeteer glowered down at his useless strings—now hanging in tangled disarray. I replied sleepily, "Scratchin' does turn up the dangedest things."

CHAPTER 5

Horse Piss and the Indignant Nose

We got an early start on the climb out of the Nolichucky valley and managed to put nine miles beneath our boots before stopping for lunch on a lovely bald (aptly named Beauty Spot). Sasquatch greeted us with a handshake and introduced his dining companions, Carbuncle Kate and Left Handed Communist, young ladies with strange names and the frayed appearance of thru-hikers. They smiled but didn't speak. Surprised to see Sasquatch, I said, "I expected you to be miles ahead by now, the way you blew past the other day." (A couple of miles before Sams Gap, he had shot past me like an angry rhino, legs pumping, hardly slowing his stride to say hello.)

"I kinda got hung up in Erwin." (J.R. snickered, "His nose done got stopped up, or else the pheromones got overpowered by B.O., cause that boy done run outta steam again.")

Curious, I turned to Carbuncle Kate, a short, stocky lass in her mid-twenties, with a pert smile that struggled to flourish from behind thick glasses. "How'd you get a name like that?"

She gave me a wry look, saucily tossing her long, brown pigtail that hung from beneath a blue-gray bandanna onto a faded tie-dyed tee shirt with crazy striped patterns. "When I left Springer Mountain, my pack rubbed a large sore on my hip and people started calling me Carbuncle Kate. Now I'm stuck with it."

"Well, that's a terrible name for someone with such a pretty smile." I thought for a moment. "How about Smiling Kate—Skate for short?"

Wahoola nodded his approval. "Just sign the registers as Skate from now on and it'll soon catch on."

She beamed a smile of gratitude. "I like it!" and another trail name was born!

I asked Left Handed Communist, who seemed shy, almost sullen, so opposite from Skate, "How about you? Need a name change?"

She stuffed a stray wisp of short, dark hair beneath her red and white bandana, which, like Skate's, covered her hair in peasant style (both girls could have stepped directly from a picture of a Russian commune). All she said was, "I really am not a Communist," and went back to writing in her journal. An enigma!

The others soon left, and Wahoola and I idled away a couple of hours, lazily enjoying the gentle, sun-warmed breeze. Finally, we reluctantly headed toward the massive silhouette of Unaka Mountain (a two-Snickers affair, with its endless series of switchbacks that stair-stepped toward the heavens), and ended a grueling afternoon at Cherry Gap Shelter by four o'clock.

The shelter was full—old faces: Skate, LHC (sounded more patriotic than Left Handed Communist!), Sasquatch; and new: Peter the Ent. a youthful twenty-something, tall and gangly; Felix the Cat, also in his twenties, who had a phobia about dirt (he constantly brushed at the floor and complained that there was no broom); and the Yoopers, a husband and wife team in their middle thirties from upper Michigan (hence the name). After introductions, Wahoola and I picked a small clearing across the Trail and pitched tents, and then I went to the spring to fill my water bottles.

J.R. (possibly influenced by Felix the Cat) started in on me. "Plenty of sun left and lots of water. Be a good time to wash up." I (definitely corrupted by close contact with Wahoola) replied, "Jeez, we had a bath at Hot Springs just six days ago." Sniffing my armpit, I said, "We're not that bad yet." He persisted. "So, Ace, when do you plan to take the next bath?" (I wished he wouldn't call me Ace! It reeked of contempt and insult.) Gritting my teeth, I did a quick calculation and realized the next opportunity might not come before we reached Damascus, still seven days away. He replied stubbornly, "In seven days, even Wahoola's going to be avoiding us."

I glanced at the sun—at least two hours of daylight left—and the air felt warm. "Yeah, this might be a good time to take a bath and wash the outfit. Will that make you happy, Jarhead?" (Two could play the same game! Most Marines hated "Jarhead," considering it a smirch on their impeccable reputation. Another was "Sea-going Bellhop," but I planned to save that for bigger game!) No reply. He'd had his little victory and gone off to gloat. Dang, I hated when he gloated, especially when he was right. The beginning of a migraine began to nag as I went back to the tent to get my ice cream bucket.

I hid behind some rhododendrons beside the tent and washed my tee shirt and shorts, leaving them draped across a branch while I shampooed and bathed in the remaining water. (The spring was at least a couple of hundred yards away, and my feet hurt. I wasn't going back for more water if I could help it.) Wahoola walked over from the shelter, where he had been gabbing, and caught me naked.

"What're you doing, Model T?" he asked, knowing perfectly well that I was bathing. Even a blind man could have figured it out.

"Washing," I growled. "Something you would greatly benefit from."

He shook his head and gestured at the sun, which seemed to hang by a flimsy invisible thread just above the mountain, ready to crash into the trees. It seemed to diminish before my eyes, as if some alien power were sucking its life-giving energy into another solar system, and I felt a quick twinge of panic at the falling temperature. How could I have miscalculated so badly?

"Bad timing huh?" I grunted sheepishly.

"Only if you don't mind sleeping in wet clothes." He flashed the "owl look" at me. Dang him, too! I hated that look! He shook his head with disbelief and began working on supper—probably smirking.

I dumped the coffee-colored water on the ground and pulled on my wet clothes—the long-range plan being to let them body-dry before the day lost its warmth. I now realized how flawed the strategy had been as the sun quickly sank and goose bumps popped out. "Face it, Model-T," I told myself, "you're the 'Jarhead' for listening to that 'Sea-going Bellhop.'" As if on cue, a band of high cirrus clouds moved across the shrinking sun and a westerly wind began to stir the leaves. Shivering, I hastened to my tent, dug out my rain jacket and trousers, and put them on over the wet garments. Suddenly the day had turned into a stranger.

We sat in front of our tents, facing one another across a small patch of ground, and cooked supper. The WISE, reeking Wahoola, comfortable in his dry clothes, cooked mac-n-cheese; while I, shivering in clean damp clothes, huddled close to my pot of noodles and fought the breeze for any extra heat while attempting to avoid his mocking eyes. As soon as the noodles were done, I jumped into my sleeping bag, damp clothes and all, and ate supper in dejected silence as I berated myself for listening to the Jarhead. At least he had enough sense to vacate the premises for the evening!

Marvel of marvels! I woke up *dry!* The Jarhead, back seeking forgiveness (or breakfast) grunted, "Osmosis." Not willing to let him off the hook so easily, I snarled, "What's that got to do with anything?" He explained, "That's what got us dry—osmosis," and he downloaded a graphic visual via the cranial synapses:

A picture of J.R. sitting in a high school freshman science class appeared. The teacher, wizened, gray-haired Miz Rowe, who wore thick rimless glasses, was attempting to explain the process of osmosis to the thickheaded group. She stood at the blackboard with her back to the class, writing as she enunciated each word clearly, "Osmosis, the passing of molecules through a semi-permeable membrane." Bored to death, J.R. pulled a long, crusty booger out of his left nostril, and amid chortling from the guys and gasps of disgust from the gals, he flicked it at Miz Rowe's back—a serious lapse in judgment on his part, for what young J.R. didn't realize, she had eyes in the back of her head. Belatedly, he discovered that the edges of her glasses acted as tiny mirrors, giving her a miniature picture of what went on behind her back!

But Miz Rowe had a kind heart. She "allowed" J.R. to demonstrate his handwriting (in lieu of visiting the principal's office) by writing over and over, five hundred times, "Osmosis is the passing of molecules through a semi-permeable membrane. Flicking a booger is NOT osmosis."

"Yeah," I admitted, mellowing, "it must've been osmosis." Who could stay mad at such a schmook!

About mid-morning, Wahoola and I took a break (a guilt-laden Snickers for me; trail mix for him) and stared at the night's destination—Roan Mountain—which dominated the distant horizon. He said, "Today's the day."

"You bet! Tonight we're going to sleep in rare air." Roan High Knob Shelter, an old fire warden's cabin located just below the summit, is billed as the highest shelter on the Trail (at 6,285 feet, it barely lags beneath Clingmans Dome's 6,643 feet—the highest place on the Trail). I gave him a playful slap on the shoulder. "Enjoy it, because this is our last 6000-footer until we climb Mt. Washington in the Whites."

He shook his head. "Naw, that's not what I meant. Today is Ward's last chance to make good on his promise."

"What do you mean?"

"You don't remember? He said he'd catch us before we got to Roan Mountain."

I'd forgotten about our run-in with Ward Leonard at Cable Gap Shelter. Now his boast rushed back into my mind. I said, "Well, it looks like ol' Ward was full of hot air. He'll never catch us now," and then hesitated. "Will he?"

We jumped up and got moving!

Wahoola soon pulled out of sight, determined that Ward wasn't going to beat him to Roan Mountain! I didn't see any real need to hurry; if he hadn't caught us by now, it wasn't going to happen. I took my time, enjoying a particularly charming section of trail and dallying in a daydream where, by conjuring up a mental image of any food item I could cause it to materialize right in my hands! Sunlight filtered through the leaves, which fluttered at the playful tickling of a frivolous breeze. Feeling good, I hummed a bouncy tune while I walked—music to fantasize with. What a morning!

A noise at my back ruptured my fantasy. I turned around and jumped off the path—just in time to avoid getting trampled by Ward! Long, yellow-gaitered legs cranked up and down like locomotive pistons (I could almost swear that steam hissed from his ears!) as the hiking machine zipped past. His face was frozen in a scowling mask, a surreal expression against the thick crop of freckles and green beanie that sat square atop reddish hair.

No words, no acknowledgement of his passing, except for a faint rush of—pizzazz? As he disappeared around a bend, The Ego said, "Ward came, Ward conquered, but Ward didn't see." I: "Dang! I hope Wahoola's got quick reflexes."

"Just look at this mess." Wahoola stood in the doorway of the old fire warden's cabin-turned-shelter and glared at the trash that littered the rough plank floor. "This sucks!"

I echoed his sentiments with a strong epithet. After the hot, grueling climb up Roan Mountain—plus being "one-upped" by Ward (He had graced Wahoola with a syrupy smirk as he throttled past, which Wahoola answered with a "fowl" gesture!)—all I wanted to do was get my bed made, eat supper, and crash.

Frustrated, I aimed a swift kick at a filthy, stain-splotched mattress, which competed with several empty beer cans and food wrappers for floor space. A large mouse dashed from its interior and scampered between Wahoola's legs, causing him to jump a foot and squawk like a scared hen. He scowled at the mattress and at me, and then he waved the whole mess away with a sweep of his arm. "Well, I'm not sleeping in that filth. Let's go on up to the top and see if we can find a tent site."

"Okay by me, although it might be worth waiting until Felix the Cat shows up and watch him have a nervous breakdown." If there had ever been a broom here, it was long gone.

We followed a narrow footpath upward and soon reached the broad, tree-covered summit—no view, but as a tradeoff Nature gave us a soft carpet of spruce and fir needles and plenty of tent spots between widely spaced trees. Three thru-hikers huddled around a small fire cooking supper. Two, who wore a patina of streetwise hubris, introduced themselves as Dead Ahead and Wild Bill (Yes, the owners of the food bag that had been "killed" by the bear back at Double Springs Shelter!). The other fellow, Indiana Dan, wore an elegant buckskin jacket, cooked his meals in a large aluminum wash pan on a wood fire, and slept in a net hammock. (We soon discovered he had just gotten out of the Marine Corps—a possible explanation for his unusual approach to backpacking?)

Wild Bill proudly displayed the infamous food bag, which had a long rip up one side that had been sewn closed in a crude zigzag pattern, giving it a weird, "frankensteinian" touch. Dead Ahead boasted, "This is our good luck piece. We're gonna carry it all the way to Katahdin!" to which Wild Bill added, frowning, "If another bear doesn't get hold of it."

Indiana Dan had dug a bunch of ramps—a plant that resembled green onions on the bottom and leeks on the top part, and smelled like onion, garlic, and Wahoola's feet—earlier in the day, and he gave us a few to add to our mac-n-cheese. His eyes twinkled as he said, "They can also be eaten raw, but I'd be much obliged if you'd wait until I'm a couple of miles upwind." (A secret weapon to counter the after effects of Sasquatch's "el cheapo" hot dogs?)

Supper was deliciously spicy. The dancing flames warmed our hearts and loosened our talk, until at last the embers dwindled into tiny red orbs and the deepening chill sent us to our tents. I snuggled in my sleeping bag, listening as an owl sent its incessant question through the night, thinking that Nature should have tasked this symbol of wise philosophy to ask "Why" instead of "Who"—a far more significant query.

My thoughts floated past the day's events and settled on Ward Leonard. I felt a twinge of sadness for the human hiking machine, who at this very moment was probably pushing through the haunting darkness, grinding out endless miles, alone with his misery and sadly estranged from the Trail family. As I drifted off, The Ego grunted, "I wonder if he's ever eaten a ramp?"

During the next two days, I sampled an unusual slice of life's tangy pie.

Knowing what to look for now, soon after leaving Roan Mountain I dug my first ramps ever. I peeled and ate one raw on the spot (it tasted pretty much like it smelled, except for some scent that DID remind me of Wahoola's feet—though I wasn't about to stick my tongue between his toes to do a comparison check!) I carried a dozen stripped-down (earless) specimens to have for supper.

Then came Hump Mountain. Even from five miles away, the mighty bald had intimidated my mind as it hunched its back like a sleeping behemoth, so huge that it's spine touched the heavy overcast. Weak-kneed, I traced the thin thread of the Trail, clearly visible against the dead grass, straight up the monster's back. J.R. growled, "Clearly a beast to let lie!" Alas! On the way up, I must have tickled the monster's ribs, for it awoke and gave me a good thrashing with near hurricane-force winds; scrubbed my skin raw with lashing sleet; and for spite, hid its nefarious pawing behind a curtain of absolute whiteout. I finally escaped the beast's clutches, exhausted but exhilarated to get beyond its lair, and crowded in with eleven others at Apple House Shelter—once an explosives shack for a nearby mine in days of yore—so cramped we had to form two rows, feet-to-feet, with a small walkway in between.

When I got there, Sasquatch had just returned from a store two miles away, carrying a sack filled with junk food and (yep! "el cheapo's"), and was starting another "pigout." Wahoola, showing total disregard for his own wellbeing, had placed his Therm-a-Rest next to Sasquatch and, like a small puppy, greedily wolfed down what tidbits Sasquatch deigned to toss his way. I took the last small spot across the aisle from the two gluttons and ate six raw ramps, blowing my breath their way as payback for not sharing (much to the discomfort of the other nine). There was even talk of evicting me from the shelter! Unwilling to push my luck, I added the remaining ramps to my mac-n-cheese, ate, and then covered up my head and went to sleep. (The other hikers would forget about the nasty smell of ramps when Sasquatch and Wahoola—he'd managed to finagle a couple of "el cheapo's"—got down to business.)

No one got evicted, though the smell was so rank when I got up to make a midnight pee-call that I was tempted to lead a hiker's revolt. The Ego squashed that urge when he said, "It smells more like ramps than 'el cheapo' perfume. Better let a sleeping dog lie." So I meekly crawled back into my bag and hoped no one else woke up!

Tension filled the air as we ate breakfast the next morning, when some of the group began to talk about the upcoming fourteen miles of Trail—from US Highway 19E to Moreland Gap. Some local landowners, angered by ATC's use of "eminent domain" to acquire protected right-of-way through their properties, were openly hostile to hikers. The Don Nelan Shelter had been burned days before (fact), and reports of fishhooks strung on near-invisible monofilament at eye level across the Trail (rumor) surged among the hiker community. I reread the cautionary notice tacked to the shelter wall, which in effect warned hikers to hike through the hostile section in pairs or groups and not to stop overnight until reaching Moreland Gap Shelter.

I packed and asked Wahoola, who still lollygagged in his sleeping bag, if he wanted to pair up. He chuckled, "Naw, I figure the danger's over since Ol' Ward went through. He probably threw the fear of God into the landowners and tore hell out of the hook lines. Heck! He's probably going lickety-split up the Trail right now with a head full of fishhooks and doesn't even know it!" He "perfumed" the air with last night's leavings, which caused Sasquatch to arch his eyebrows in wonder that a "novice" could come so close to emulating The Master. (I was sorry I had no ramps left!) Wahoola grinned, adding, "Anything Ward missed, the Marines can mop up. I'll catch you later." I rolled my eyes and headed into the early morning mist.

After three or so miles, the Trail came out on a narrow paved road that paralleled a small stream. Up ahead, a small community of ramshackle, clapboard houses in dire need of paint transfusions squatted along both sides of the highway. Nothing stirred—no sign of life, no wood smoke from cook stoves, no noises of children at play, no metal-on-metal sounds of a community gearing up for another day. It appeared to be a bleak oasis of human endeavor on a dreary overcast morning.

Eerie! As I hastened along the road, my eyes nervously searched the dark interiors of dilapidated screened-in porches and collapsing, weed-choked outbuildings for any movement. Nothing! Absolutely nada! In my mind's eye, I re-read the warning back at the shelter, and my heart skipped a beat as everything suddenly became crystal clear: In the manner of good mountain folk, these people had a stubborn loyalty to kin and neighbors, and here was a lone hiker on which they could prove their leanings and send a warning to intruders—"Leave us be!"

Reaching for my pepper spray, I strained to detect the ambush that had to wait somewhere close by. "Jeez, Marine, you're the trained killer. What the heck are we gonna do? Is this a trap?" He muttered with scary grimness, "It could be. Just keep your cool."

A few yards ahead, the road passed between a decrepit gray barn and the stream's bank, which dropped sharply down to the water. J.R. warned, "Okay, this could be the place. It's ideal for an ambush." I could smell my fear—a vile stench akin to rotten potatoes, which oozed out with the cold sweat, suddenly forming a beaded film across my forehead. Reasoning fled and my imagination blossomed into an unruly monster—good ol' bubba-boys dressed in camouflage britches and brandishing ancient double-barreled shotguns and axe handles rushing out of the barn, yelling, "We got ye now, hiker trash. We's agonna cut off yer balls an stuff'em in yer mouth an watch ye choke t' death." I could almost hear the women's curses as they flung rotten eggs and stinking, slimy tomatoes at my trussed-up body, while scrawny barefoot boys in ragged overalls and gingham-clad pudgy girls dodged in and out, whipping my legs with birch switches and spitting as they drenched me with night soil from stinking chamber pots and peppered my skull with walnut-sized rocks launched with dead-eye accuracy from lethal sling shots and—

The Marine whapped me. "Quit your blubbering and get a grip on it. Jeez! We haven't even *seen* anybody yet, for cryin' out loud!"

We were almost to the barn and I felt so weak I thought I was going to faint. Each step became an effort and my heart raced on a runaway course. Impulsively, I reached down and picked up two large rocks, each about the size of a baseball—a small comfort—suddenly determined that I wouldn't go down without taking at least two of them with me!

And then I was past the barn. Nothing! Not a movement of any kind, and I almost passed out with relief. J.R. kicked me in the butt and I got going again, but I held onto the rocks—just in case—for I had another a hundred yards to go before I cleared the buildings. Getting past the barn had reduced the odds, but it could still happen!

Warily, rocks at the ready, I reached a rickety old outbuilding and then relaxed my guard as I noticed a neat white house at the end of a graveled driveway that left the paved road just before the building. Not a very likely place for an ambush. Relieved, I walked on past.

Without warning, the sound of gunfire erupted from behind the outbuilding. "Pow! Pow!" A series of shots in rapid succession, followed by a high-pitched yell! The Marine screamed, "Ambush! Kill the bastards before they kill us!"

I dropped the rocks and ran for my life! These people weren't going to get *my* balls! Without breaking stride, I glanced over my shoulder to check the "how's"—how many and how close—just as a small boy peddling a rusty bicycle with wobbly training wheels came from behind the building. The tow-headed tyke wore a faded, black cowboy hat, which was too small to cover his unruly tangle of reddish-brown hair. He halted on the pavement, blowing smoke from the barrel of his six-shooter and then fired off another string of caps. Waving, he yelled, "Hey, mister, you wanna play with me? Cops and robbers?"

My heart did its best to burst out of its heaving cage. I managed to put the brakes on my panic and returned the young renegade's wave, shouting, "I don't think so, Sonny. Right now I'm busy having a heart attack!" Blushing, I got the heck away!

Chagrined (for being denied the opportunity to exhibit his mighty prowess as a warrior—or mortified at being spooked by a five year old?), The Marine grumbled, "Some ambush, Rambo. That little tiger almost had our balls. I'm so glad you were able to overcome the enemy in such an aggressive manner."

"Shaddup, Jarhead. You're the one who yelled ambush. Wise-ass Marine . . ."

"Now, now, Model-T, don't become coarse. Remember, you're in the presence of an officer and a gentleman. Besides, if you can't stand the flak, get off the battlefield." What the heck did that mean? The Dorkhead!

The Trail undulated over a series of steep ridges—leg killers—that slowly stair-stepped toward Moreland Gap, still many miles away. In late morning I got a shocker on top of a ridge: Tied to trees on either side of the Trail, remains of monofilament with short droppers tied to fishhooks dangled in limp spirals. Even in the booby trap's benign state, the wicked little barbs sent chills of apprehension up my spine. Warily, I looked around but the woods were empty. (Within the next mile, I spotted three more similar ambush sites, all now defused—ominous symbols of spent defiance.)

Later, as I took a Snickers break well beyond the "combat zone," Wahoola joined me. Grim-faced, he scowled, "Can you believe anyone would stoop so low as to put fishhooks across the Trail? And torching the Nelan Shelter! What kind of lowlife . . ." He struggled for more words but was too ticked off. I knew just how he felt!

We decided to stay together the rest of the way to Moreland Gap—in case Ol' Ward might have fallen short of our expectations. Soon, the overcast turned to steady rain and footing quickly became treacherous, causing our anger to be converted to misery as we plodded along the muddy path.

Although we kept a wary eye out for more booby traps, we failed to see anything out of the ordinary. The rain finally retreated back into the heavy overcast, but the misery remained.

Wood smoke! I saw Moreland Gap Shelter through the trees! "Jeez, Wahoola. I don't know about you but I'm happy to get this little section of Trail behind us!" Weary, anxious to get the wet stuff off and something hot in my belly, I briskly strode to the front of the shelter, only to feel my spirit sink like a concrete block in muddy water. The shelter's dingy cinder block interior was filled with a thick cloud of noxious smoke, which rose steadily out of a feeble fire that fed off of wet wood. The lone occupant (from his looks a "local," since he was dressed for the occasion in camouflage britches and a WWII Army jacket) coughed and gagged as he furiously tried to push the smoke back outside toward the fire with a dirty, green blanket. Almost contemptuously, the smoke lazily split apart and then whirled and rejoined itself on the backside of the blanket before settling back around the frustrated fellow.

He screamed, "Crud-mamma'n smoke! Can't keep it outa th' crud-mamma'n shelter. Whatta crud-mamma friggin way to spend a weekend." He peered at us through watery eyes—suspicious orbs in a sallow, pock-marked face. Almost as if he were attempting to explain his presence on the National Treasure, he barked, "Damn guys better git here soon wit sum beer an take over this here crud-mamma'n 'far'. Else I'm headin' back down whar ye kin breathe real 'are'." He jumped out of the shelter and kicked at the fire. "Crud-mamma friggin far!"

Wahoola didn't miss a beat. "Yeah, life can be a real crud-mamma'n pisser at times." He grinned at me. "Especially on this crud-mamma'n Trail."

"Crud-mamma"—a new epithet even for The Marine—seemed to be the mainstay of this guy's vocabulary. Quirky English, for sure! Unwilling to let Wahoola hog all the fun, I jumped in. "Yeah man. This crud-mamma'n pack's agivin' me a friggin, crud-mamma'n backache an my friggin boots's agivin' me big crud-mamma'n blisters. An' that ain't all! My belly's fixin' to eat my friggin backbone, I'm so starved. Buddy, I'm so crud-mamma'n miserably happy out here I'm about to go ballistic."

"Bubba"—that's what I decided to call him (though not to his face)—stared at me like I had just walked out of the crazy house. Wahoola looked at Bubba and, pointing at me, twirled his finger close to his temple in the universal gesture that meant, "He isn't all here."

Bubba nodded hesitantly and then grunted, "You guys got arey smokes? I done run outta th' crud-mamma'n thangs."

We shook our heads. Anticipating his next question, Wahoola said, "Ain't got no crud-mamma friggin beer neither." With that revelation, Bubba went back to his blanket-fanning, shutting us out of his world.

We moved away from the smoke and huddled. "I think we should go on a ways," Wahoola said. "No telling what kind of show this guy and his buddies will put on tonight. Okay with you?" I eagerly agreed.

We threw Bubba a casual wave and walked off as he began another round of cussing: "Crud-mamma friggin guys. No friggin smokes. Crud, Crud! Jeazers friggin crud-mamma!" Smoke and coals scattered as Bubba kicked the 'far' again.

I nudged Wahoola. "Ain't this the crud-mamma'n life!" So much for Moreland Gap Shelter . . .

Thirty minutes later we walked into a nasty hailstorm, which pummeled us with peas and marbles and quickly covered the ground with a layer of white, creating a Currier and Ives winter landscape—harsh beauty, yet a deadly trap for the unprotected. The rapidly falling temperature marred the scene and sent us hightailing it down the Trail seeking a tent site.

As I drifted off to sleep that night, an image of Bubba kicking the "far" diddybopped into my mind. Was he still choking in the smoky shelter? Had his friends showed up with smokes and beer? A picture of his buddies sitting around a beat-up, dirty table in a dim, rundown bar down in the valley replaced Bubba. I could see them clearly as they sat with battered ball caps pushed way back, toothpicks stuck in tobacco-stained teeth, butt cracks peeking above low-hanging britches as they straddled wobbly chairs and farted and guzzled draft beer while they guffawed about the joke they were playing on poor old Bubba—who was way up on that "sumabitch ofa mountain waitin' for us, only we's not 'bout to go up there when we kin be down here whar it's warm and they's lotsa suds. Thet ol' bubba-boy's gotta be dumber'n hog turds."

I nearly choked trying to hold the laughter inside, but it finally erupted in loud guffaws that left tears and snot running down my face. Wahoola called from his tent, "What kinda fit are you havin' now?"

"You'd never believe it. Go to sleep."

Yep, a most unusual slice of life on the Appalachian Trail these past two days!

A sad event occurred the next day—a month exactly since we had walked up the Approach Trail to begin our adventure. As we lingered at the foot of Laurel Fork Falls, a beautiful, cascading rush of roaring, frothy energy set against a cobalt sky, Wahoola announced, "I've been thinking about doing two twenty-five mile days to reach Damascus and take a few days off to visit my parents (at Beckley, West Virginia). But I don't want it to be a problem for you."

A shocker! I felt my gut tighten at the thought of going it alone. But we *had* agreed that we wouldn't be tied to one another. Too, I had a slight problem of my own—one that I'd been mulling over and hadn't figured out how to handle: I had promised J.R. that we would take a few days off when we got near Roanoke to celebrate Judith's birthday and their anniversary. I said, "It won't be a problem. I've got to take some time off at Roanoke. We can meet up somewhere north of there."

We agreed to make the split at Watauga Lake after sharing one last meal together (hopefully a hamburger with all the trimmings) at the Rat Branch Store and Grill across the road from the lake.

By the time we conquered Pond Mountain (a 2000 foot climb with few switchbacks) and crossed its four knobs, we were ready for a hamburger. Ed Green, the owner, knew what it took to please thru-hikers, but the food seemed to clog my throat as the dreaded moment of parting drew closer.

Back outside, I fumbled with my pack straps, searching for words to bridge the gap that suddenly widened between us, but nothing came. Memories of the past few weeks flooded my mind and my eyes started to mist. Damn, I hoped I wasn't about to bawl! Wahoola broke the silence. "Watch yourself, Model-T. I'll see you somewhere beyond Roanoke," and he quickly walked away. I thought his eyes looked misty, too.

"Yeah. See you up the Trail," I echoed hollowly, wondering if I really would, already regretting words not spoken, watching silently until he disappeared. "Well J.R., it's you and me now." Feeling an empty pit deep within my innards that a dozen hamburgers couldn't fill, I dabbed at my eyes and slowly followed after Wahoola.

Sadly, the anticipation and excitement rapidly dwindled to smoldering stubbornness—get over the next mountain; make it to the next shelter; hang in for another day. Every effort, each movement, seemed mechanical, as if I had been stripped of nerves and rewired into a robotic clone. My enthusiasm dwelled at about worm level, and for the first time I thought about chucking it all and going home. J.R. wisely kept his own counsel, giving me space to work through my doldrums.

Then came Skate!

Late the next afternoon, exhausted and depressed after fighting a section of overgrown trail all day—I'd only made thirteen miles—I lounged on the floor of Iron Mountain Shelter and vacantly stared at the magnificent oaks that filled the clearing as I tried to muster enough energy to cook supper, dreading another lonely evening (when the pit seemed emptiest). A shout came from the woods: "Model-Teee!" and Skate, Left-Handed Commie, and a young hiker, Eco-Warrior, came striding toward me. (I quickly learned that Eco-Warrior, eighteen, short and stocky with a thick mass of long, reddish-brown hair that almost obscured his round face, had graduated from high school the previous summer, and that this thru-hike was his graduation present. He had a quick smile and a quicker wit, and I took an immediate liking to the young man.)

Skate asked, "Where's Wahoola?"

"Gone on ahead. He wanted to visit his folks in West Virginia."

Astutely, she picked up on my emptiness. "Is everything okay between you two?"

"Yeah." I explained our separate plans for the next few weeks, confessing, "It's like losing a brother, though. I sure do miss him." There went the misty eyes again!

"I'm sure you'll be back together in no time at all," she said, nodding sympathetically. Somehow, I felt better having talked about my loss.

Peter the Ent and Felix the Cat arrived a little later. Felix dropped his pack, grabbed a broom from a corner, and began to sweep the floor while he hummed a wordless tune in rhythm with the strokes—a happy little feline in a litter box of joy! Watching him indulge his mysophobia in such a cheerful manner even made me feel better!

The next morning I was surprised to see Skate packed and ready to hit the Trail when I left, for seldom did anyone get out before me. She put on her pack and said, "If you don't mind some company, I'll tag along for a couple of miles."

"Fine with me."

I quickly realized to my amazement that this gal was a worthy competitor for Ward Leonard! After a couple of miles—for her, a warm up; for me a mini-marathon, because I had to run at times just to keep up with those piston-pumping legs—we passed a rock monument in a small clearing just off the Trail to our left. Saved just in time to avert a coronary! Gasping for breath, I wheezed at the lady hiking-machine's back, several steps ahead, "Lookee there. Let's see whazzat."

Once a chimney but now filled with concrete, the odd marker served as a gravestone at the head of a concrete slab. Letters had been inscribed in a large oval of concrete set into the chimney: "Uncle Nick Grindstaff . . . Born Dec. 26, 1851 . . . Died July 22, 1923." Below the stats, etched in small letters, the sad epitaph read, "Lived alone; suffered alone; died alone."

The questions worked through my mind as we silently gazed at the grave: Who was he? How did he end up in an isolated cabin-turned-grave on this lonely mountaintop? What had his life been like? Curious, I made a mental note to find out more about Uncle Nick Grindstaff.

When we left, Skate took off in high gear. I inhaled the dust from her hiking boots and groaned to The Ego, "Jeez! I shoulda named her 'Swifty'!" He, admiringly: "Or 'The Streak'!"

Her two miles became eight, and we reached Double Springs Shelter by 9 AM. I convinced Skate to stop for a late breakfast, which to her meant filling water bottles and eating a breakfast bar, and before I could unwrap a second Snickers, she was rearing to move out. We streaked another eight miles (I half-expected to blow past Wahoola!) and got to Abingdon Gap Shelter—only eight miles from Damascus—by early afternoon. I flopped on the ground, panting like a winded beagle. "Holy Cow, Skate, you gotta show some respect (mercy!) for your elders! Criminy! Sixteen miles by two o'clock! What's your hurry, for cryin' out loud?"

Her eyes twinkled mischievously as she answered, "Pizza."

"A twenty-six mile day for a pizza? You're kidding!"

She wasn't! She rested for a few minutes, until Eco-Warrior showed up. Then the pair bounced off down the Trail like youngsters heading for a birthday party; busily chatting as if they hadn't a care in the world; heedless of the exhaustion, which would be waiting for them at the end of twenty-six miles; their brains consumed by pizza! I watched them disappear and got a box of mac-n-cheese out of my food bag. "Crazy kids!"

As the sun went down, the night sky slowly filled with brilliant diamonds, some so shiny-close they could have been fireflies sending out mating flashes just beyond finger's reach. The view was too wondrous to sacrifice for the flimsy safety of a stuffy tent, so I pulled my sleeping bag outside onto the dew-dampened grass where I could gaze on The Creator's endless universe. A shooting star arced across the heavens, disappearing faster than my eye could follow. I realized with a start that I hadn't thought of Wahoola all day; nor did the empty pit seem so vast. I murmured, "That Skate is one smart cookie," and J.R. agreed, paying her his ultimate compliment, "She'd make one heck of a Marine." Intuitively or not, she had pulled me out of the quagmire of the previous two days and put a band-aid on my tattered spirit. I: "It's gonna be okay." J.R.: "Yeah, we owe her big!"

I came down off the mountain early the next afternoon and entered the small town of Damascus, Virginia. Passing a store, I happened to glance at the reflection in the plate glass window and was shocked by the stranger who stared back at me—a lean, grizzled, mountain man with wild-looking eyes and a bushy, white beard. Startled, I realized I was the stranger! What had I become? Worse, what would I be like by the time I reached Katahdin?

I had come 451 miles; only 1692 left. Hoisting my hiking stick at the reflection, I gave a devilish grin and went looking for The Place.

The people of Damascus, population just shy of 1000, bill theirs as the "friendliest town on the trail" and it very well may be, for the city fathers allow the white blazes to go right up Laurel Avenue, the town's main business street. Right away, I noticed that these people are different. They look you right in the eye and give you a smile when you ask a question. No mumbling of quick answers or moving across the street to avoid having to share the same air. "Another 'perfect' trail town," I thought as I walked up the sidewalk, nodding to the people and enjoying the friendly "hello's".

Emboldened by the cordial atmosphere, I stopped a grizzled old farmer coming out of the small hardware store with a tray of tomato plants. He had a whopper of a belly (which had likely gained its prominence from decades of fried catfish and pinto beans)—so huge that his faded, patched coveralls acted more like a giant girdle than clothing. Doing my best not to stare, I asked, "Excuse me, Sir, but would you happen to know where The Place is?"

He studied me for a long moment and then spat a glob of brownish liquid across the plants, barely missing my boot, and drawled, "Why young feller, I reckon ever'body round here knows th' whereabouts of Th' Place." He sent another squirt of tobacco juice through the air, finessing this one against the tire of an ancient, rust-brown pickup at the curb. I waited patiently as he struggled with the battered door of the old derelict and pushed a pile of junk into the floorboard to make a place for the plants.

That done, he pulled his sagging belly back into position and motioned toward the bed of the truck, which was cluttered with junk and, oddly, an old rocking chair that had somehow escaped the trash pile and sat upright like a mountain throne. "Git a seat on that rocker. I kin haul you thar quicker'n I kin tell ye."

Ah! Damascus! This town was like a fizzy chocolate soda on a hot August afternoon. I climbed up into the bed and sat on the "throne," gloating to The Ego, "The Model-T is going to arrive at The Place in style!" He asked, "Do you realize how stupid you look?" Unperturbed, I answered, "Yeah, but only from the knees up." I knocked on the top of the cab. "Whenever you're ready, kind Sir!" The starter wheezed; the motor gasped, belching a gray-black cloud of noxious smoke into the still air; and we lurched away from the curb with the speed of cold honey.

Before I had time to get settled, the old truck pulled into a narrow side street and jerked to an abrupt stop in front of a large two-story frame house, toppling me off my "throne" onto the pile of rusty junk. The engine sputtered, backfired with an ear-splitting bang, and died.

"It's the Model-Teee!" a voice yelled. I stood, grinning sheepishly at several hikers sitting around two wooden picnic tables under the canopy of a large cherry tree, and gave them a jubilant bow as if it had all been for their entertainment. Someone shouted, "Nope, it's Granny Clampett!" (of TV's "Beverly Hillbillies"). Another voice snickered, "Looks more like Jethro to me." I raised my arms, hoping to salvage some dignity, and spread my fingers in "victory." Then I cautiously picked my way through the rusty metal and climbed down.

The old geezer squinted with what passed as a wrinkled smile, showing gaped, yellowed teeth. "Good luck to ye, young feller, an' watch out fer them rat'lers. The mountain's full of'em." I nodded and thanked him for the lift, jumping aside as he replied with a long squirt of amber spit. He coaxed the truck back to life and it bucked away amid spasms of grinding metal, pooting a black smokescreen as it moved up the street.

The house was colorful, to say the least; and with its yellow clapboard siding and bright orange roof, it looked like a mansion to my trail-weary eyes. A white plywood sign tacked by the door that opened onto a screened-in porch told me that this was indeed "The Place." I suppressed an atavistic urge to roll in the lush greenness of the yard and carried my pack over to the tables to accept the inevitable ribbing that my "grand entrance" had generated.

Before they could get it launched, a loud voice—as familiar as my dusty boots—blasted the droning small talk. "Well, Model-T, that was one hell of an entrance. What do you have planned for an encore?" Wahoola! He came through the screen door and we grabbed each other in bear hugs like we hadn't seen each other for months.

"What're you doing here? You're supposed to be in West Virginia."

His eyes twinkled beneath that unruly shock of red hair. "I thought I'd better hang around till you showed up—just to make sure you hadn't been kidnapped by sex-starved women." Quickly pushing me away, he wrinkled his nose. "I needn't have worried, though. They wouldn't be able to get past the smell."

He had that right! The difference in our body odors caused a ripple of discomfort. He chuckled, "Oh yeah, I'm also waiting for my ride home. A friend is coming to get me tomorrow afternoon. You want to go to Quincy's (the town's popular pizza place)?" He frowned, taking a step backwards. "After you take a shower, of course. Hurry up and I'll wait. By the way, I'm in the room at the top of the stairs."

I still couldn't believe that Wahoola was actually here! "Yeah, wait for me. I won't be long."

Inside, I passed through large, high-ceiling rooms that reminded J.R. of his grandparents' old farm homes, and followed a narrow stairway up to the second floor. I quickly found Wahoola's spread, dumped my pack on one of the thick foam pads—no-frills beds—that lay on the floor, and headed for the larger of the two upstairs bathrooms.

"Okay Ego, we've gotta make a fast job of this. Don't want to keep Wahoola waiting." I took off my boots and removed my socks—I'd wash them later—and turned the shower on in one of the two stalls. Hot water! This was going to be *great!* I stepped in, fully clothed (let the shower do double duty and save a trip to the laundry to boot!) and The Ego immediately grated on my pleasure. "Say Ace, what do you plan to use for soap? Or have you gotten so depraved that you don't need it anymore?" Darn it, I wished he wouldn't call me that! But he had a point—I didn't have any soap.

I felt along the top edges of both stalls and found three small remnants. "Okay, Smarty, we now have soap. Satisfied?" No response, which was fine with me.

One piece of soap, solely dedicated to the under arms of my tee shirt, quickly disintegrated into scum-like yellow. I grabbed another piece and began working on the shorts, humming the melody from "Singing in the Rain"; the shorts lathered up good and I began to bellow words to go with the tune: "I'm showering in the rain; as the dirt flows down the drain; What a glorious feeling to be baaathing again . . ." The last piece of soap magically disappeared into my hair and beard and The Ego, deciding he was missing out on a good thing, joined in as I tackled another chorus: "The waaaater is hot; and stiiiink, we do not; cause we're showering, showering—"

Fierce pounding on the door put a stop to our serenade. Wahoola yelled, "For gosh sake, hold the racket down. The old lady next door wanted to know if she should call the Law—thought somebody was being throttled! You ready to go?"

"I thought it sounded pretty darned good. Yeah, be right out." The Ego snickered, "Gee Mountain Man, I'm glad to be acquainted with somebody who's so bodaciously tough he doesn't even need to dry off after a shower." Oh hell! I didn't have anything to dry off on. I growled at The Ego, "Don't blame me. I'm really out of practice when it comes to bathing."

I shook myself like a dog, put my socks and boots on, and walked out of the bathroom, ignoring Wahoola's pained look of resignation as I dripped the remnants of my delicious shower down the steps and out onto the sunny sidewalk. Casting a sidewise glance at my partner, I asked, "Did that old woman *really* say that?" He just laughed and shrugged—typical Wahoola! I felt warm all over, in spite of the damp chill.

Later, a few of us sat around the picnic table in the shade of the cherry tree, just hanging out and killing time until supper. Gentle talk vacillated like a wobbly top, switching from one subject to the next, but without fail always coming back to food. I had drip-dried, my belly was full (for the moment), and I was among friends; life was jim-dandy! I burped loudly—evidence of a whole pizza I'd put away a couple of hours ago. None of the other hikers paid to any attention to the crude noise; after all, it was a respectable trail sound.

Hobbit, a thru-hiker who played a mean guitar and had a sterling voice to go with it, pointed down the side alley, which led to a nearby grocery store. "I'll be . . . Will you look at that!"

I knew that tie-dyed tee shirt—Skate! She cradled a large striped watermelon in her arms as if it were a newborn lamb. (It probably weighed as much!) Butterfly Lady, Hobbit's wife and trail partner, shook her husband's shoulder. "Hobbit, she's going to hurt herself. Go help that girl."

"No need," I said. "She's strong as an ox. Stronger even." How well I knew—I had hiked behind those powerful legs. "She'll make it." Cosmic Charlie and Flyin' Ryan began to shout encouragement, and soon we all joined in.

Skate wobbled up to the nearest table and dumped her load with a loud thump, which might have cracked a smaller melon, and Wahoola chuckled, "Are you going to eat all of that by yourself?"

Panting, her face red as a beet, she gasped, "Everybody looked so pathetic sitting around like little children that I felt sorry for you. Dig in." We did!

Naturally a seed-spitting contest evolved. Wahoola, being from West Virginia (the home of long distance tobacco juice spitters), was disqualified and given the role of referee. It became obvious after several undecided rounds (a little brown mutt kept grabbing the seeds before the "ref" could render his decision) that there could be no clear-cut winner so Wahoola wisely declared the contest null and void. Undeterred, we finished off the watermelon and spit the seeds at each other. We (and the dog) had a great time!

The afternoon slipped toward dusk until the sinking sun cast long, thin shadows across the yard, spurring a few to start supper on the picnic tables. Someone called our attention to a group of girls, ages six to nine, accompanied by two ladies, who were coming across the street toward us. The girls, wearing shorts or pedal pushers, giggled nervously as the chaperones herded them our way like mother hens with a contrary brood of chicks. We waited, wondering what they could possibly want from a bunch of grungy thru-hikers.

One of the women said, "Hi. We're a local Brownie troop and the girls have made friendship necklaces for you." Sure enough, each little girl clasped a colorful circle of twisted yarn. The Brownies clung to each other in a long line—thirteen in all—connected by arms around shoulders or waists, with their eyes pointing in every direction except at us. Since there were only four of us cooking, I went inside and rousted out what hikers I could find.

One by one, the Brownies stepped forward and ceremoniously bequeathed the gift of friendship, until only I remained. I asked, "Now who's going to make me a friend?" No takers—not hard to understand, remembering the grizzly, wild-eyed reflection I had cast in the store window. Then after an uneasy silence, one of the older girls timidly stepped forward, her eyes glued to the ground, and said in a quiet voice, "I'll give you mine."

Delighted, I bent down while she gently lifted the yarn over my head, and then she hurried back to the brood. Only then, after she was safe inside the brood, did she look me full in the face and bless the gesture with a shy, toothy grin. I returned her smile with misty eyes and said, "Thank you. It's so nice to have a friend in Damascus."

What a wonderful sight! A group of jaded hikers "oohing" and "aahing," making over the circlets of yarn like each had been given the key to the town—which in a way we had; and standing apart from us, the gaggle of lassies blushing with embarrassment and giggling as they did little twisty, shy movements and counted the blades of grass. Soon the two lead-ers gathered their brood and led them away from the surreal existence of hikers and back to the reality of homes and families, but the warm joy of acceptance lingered.

After supper I went to Cowboy's (a nearby convenience store with one of the few pay phones in Damascus) and called home—actually J.R. did the talking, becoming maudlin and gushy when Judith confirmed that she and Kelly would be arriving about four o'clock the following day. After he hung up he said, "I can hardly wait! It will be so nice having someone to talk to besides you." I replied, "Great! I'm glad you feel that way because it's your show while Kelly's here. I'm on vacation as of now!" Without warning, I went "poof"—one of the perks of being an alter ego—and left him gawking at the phone. Let him worry about things for a few days; he had been getting pretty uppity of late—calling me "Ace" and complaining about every little thing. Yeah, an attitude adjustment would do the Dufus good.

Judith and Kelly arrived at 4:30, shortly after Wahoola left—an easier parting this time for we had both undergone a subtle weaning (or possibly Kelly's coming diminished the loneliness). Kelly fit right in with the thru-hiker community. Other than standing a hand's width higher than his dad, he was a younger copy of the pre-Trail J.R., including a beard, except Kelly had a thick growth of short, curly hair. His infectious grin and ready wit quickly tore down barriers and he was jokingly dubbed "Edsel" by one wag.

J.R. was like a kid with a new toy, leading Judith and Kelly all over town and showing them off to every hiker they met. I crouched barely out of sight—just in case he started to screw up things—but he did okay. They ate supper at the Dairy King (the only place open because Damascus rolled the sidewalks up early!) Then Judith headed back for Roanoke while J.R. and "Edsel," anticipating an early start the next morning, made an early night of it.

I hated to miss out on Trail Days, an annual festival begun three years earlier to celebrate the thru-hiker migration through the area, but the main hiker events were scheduled for Friday through Sunday, three days hence. Unfortunately, Kelly only had Wednesday through Saturday to hike since he had to be back at Roanoke on Sunday. So I bit the bullet and watched enviously as the town mushroomed overnight with myriad tents of all makes and colors. Looking toward the greater reward, I pushed aside the anticipation of seeing old friends, reminding myself that this was J.R.'s time and that I had to keep the Jarhead halfway happy if I/we were going to make it to Katahdin.

Early the next morning we turned our backs on Damascus (and the excitement of Trail Days) and headed north.

Surprisingly, J.R. did a decent job. Preoccupied with showing off his backpacking skills (thanks to me!) and dedicated to helping Kelly have a good time, thoughts of his mentor and guru never crossed his mind— which was fine with me. I idled the miles away from a fine vantage point high up on the mezzanine deck of J.R.'s cerebrum, half listening to the tiresome prattle of my two-legged jackass and Kelly's automatic "yeah's" and "uh-huh's." What the heck! As long as *they* thought they were having fun . . . At least the views were great!

Thank goodness for that! On the second morning out we began the long climb along numerous switchbacks toward the summit of Whitetop Mountain—a broad, treeless expanse only two hundred feet lower than its neighbor, Mount Rogers (at 5729 feet, Virginia's highest peak). Blustering rain and pea-soup fog plagued the ascent and J.R. grumbled apologetically to Kelly, "It's not all sunshine and roses out here. We may be in for a thrashing up on top." Hump Mountain lingered fresh in (our) mind! But as we reached Buzzard Rock, a lofty perch on the edge of the open summit, the opaque blanket split apart and graciously gave us a sneak preview of the Alleghenies across a wide valley.

Miraculously, the wind slackened and the sun pushed through, drawing the clouds higher to reveal the grandeur of the Almighty's handiwork. Spellbound, unable to take his eyes from the peaks and valleys laid out before him, Kelly murmured, "I had no idea that such beauty existed!"

J.R., smiling at the amazement on his son's face, said, "God tickles our souls in many different ways." A cameo moment—father and son forging an unbreakable bond cemented with paradisiacal glue! Even Trail Days couldn't match this!

Abruptly the wind roared back in, feisty and pushy, trouncing us and breaking the spell, and we hurried on. The sad thought occurred to me, "Too bad some people are not very ticklish."

Nor could Trail Days hold a candle to the stunning landscape of Grayson Highlands State Park with its unfettered, breathtaking views from Rhododendron Gap and Wilburn Ridge. We passed a small herd of wild horses, which stood with their backs to the strong gusts while they nuzzled tufts of grass. A few feet off the Trail, lying in the shelter of some trees, a small brown bundle with curious eyes raised its head and posed for a picture. Deciding we were no threat, the newborn foal jiggled its small tail to acknowledge our passing and then laid its head back into the grass. Another tickling of the soul!

Saturday—the last day and only ten miles from Kelly's pickup point at Dickey Gap where the Trail crosses VA 16. (We were to meet Judith and Brenda, Kelly's wife, and their daughters, Lauren (5) and Jesalyn (2), at ten o'clock the next morning.) To tell the truth I could hardly wait! Although I had enjoyed my short vacation, Kelly and J.R. were about as much fun as eating chitlins. Oh, they *thought* they were having a great time; but an "almost" doctor and a stuffy Jarhead? Nope, these two guys didn't know how to have *fun*. I was getting soooo bored!

The only real fun had happened yesterday morning, although I wasn't a player. J.R. and Kelly had camped in a thicket a couple of miles from Old Orchard Shelter, and J.R. had suggested they wait and cook breakfast "in style" (his nebulous term) at the shelter, which seemed like a good idea to me. Maybe we would run into a few thru-hikers and I could nudge J.R. into some sort of interesting dialog. (I was starved for hiker talk, but all the hikers had disappeared—probably partying back at Damascus!)

Old Orchard Shelter, complete with picnic table, was unoccupied. Crestfallen, I resigned myself to another blasé day and morosely waited for the grits to come to a boil. At least grits were able to stir my juices.

The grits were almost ready when a group of young adults—maybe two dozen, equally split between males and females—came into the clearing. Youthful faces shone with anticipation and excitement (or cleanliness, for as they drew closer the smell of "clean" permeated the air). All of them carried crisply new backpacks and wore clean apparel, which made our lot look like dirty, faded castoffs dug from the depths of a dumpster behind a Goodwill Store. Against the group's pristine image, we looked like something dredged out of a sludge pit of societal pestilence—at least J.R. did, for Kelly hadn't been corrupted by Wahoola and still applied the washcloth at every opportunity.

J.R. squeezed his arms against his armpits, trying to minimize the earthy odor that threatened to overwhelm the "clean," and said to the group (which stopped a safe distance away), "You all are out early. Where're you from?"

A tall man, older and exuding an air of authority, detached from the others and walked over. He had prominent cheekbones and a neatly trimmed goatee, which gave him an Abe Lincoln appearance. His piercing blue eyes quickly frisked us from behind gold-rimmed glasses. Then possibly deciding we weren't crackpots bent on doing bodily harm, he gave Kelly a firm handshake. Hesitating (as if he were about to squeeze a slimy night crawler), he quickly shook J.R.'s outstretched hand and unconsciously wiped the greeting on his trousers before gesturing at the group, which stood in a loose huddle and looked expectantly at their mentor like trained poodles in a circus act. "We hail from Washington and Lee University (Lexington, Virginia)," he answered (somewhat haughtily I thought). "I teach a course on outdoor skills and my students are out here doing their practicum."

A professor! The voice, cast from the same mold as J.R.'s professor in Chemistry 101, opened a long locked closet and sent J.R. into a flashback tailspin. I caught a flicker of the skinny freshman slunk deep in his seat trying unsuccessfully to stifle a loud yawn, which earned him an icy stare from old Doc Chadwick who was scribbling chemical formulas on the blackboard with his left hand like the end of the world was moments away, while at the same time clearing a path with the busy eraser in his right. The voice came strong and vindictive, asking "Mr. Tate" to "please explain to the class why water requires two hydrogen atoms for each oxygen atom." The unlucky "Mr. Tate" squirmed and hem-hawed and finally opined that oxygen must be twice as big as hydrogen, which filled the air with snickers from those who had been paying attention. The white-headed professor shook his head with amazement, baffled that his well-prepared explanation, reduced to simple terms so that even monkeys could grasp the concept of water, had failed to make a dent in the brain of this cotton-headed *homo sapiens*. Doc Chadwick then opined with scathing sarcasm that perhaps "Mr. Tate" might be more comfortable pursuing a career in home economics or PE. Mortified, J.R. had turned beet-red, nearly self-immolating as he mumbled a barely audible "Sorry" at his only friend that day—his dirty sneakers. Yep, this professor's voice chewed at his psyche just like old Doc Chadwick's.

J.R. shivered and fought the urge to hide beneath the picnic table. After an awkward moment, he got a grip on his run-away imagination and said in his most authoritative Marine Corps voice, "I'm J.R. Tate and this is my son, Kelly. He's a *doctor* at Roanoke Memorial Hospital." There! Let him digest that little gem—a doctor against a college professor! That should level the playing field! (J.R. was so excited by the thought that he missed the professor's name and had to call him "Professor" the rest of the time—short as it was.) "I'm doing a thru-hike of the Appalachian Trail and Kelly has joined me for a few days."

"Professor's" eyes brightened with interest at that revelation. "Class, this is Mr. Tate and he's hiking from Georgia to Maine. I have explained to you about so-called 'through hikers.'" He turned back to J.R. and said, "I was hoping we would meet some 'through hikers' so the students can see what it's like living in the outdoors and having to rely on the very skills that they are learning. Would you mind talking to them for a few minutes, prehaps answer a few questions? Let them find out first hand how a *real* outdoorsman functions?"

He stressed *"real,"* which caused J.R. swell with pride, like he was on the receiving end of a decoration for gallantry in battle. Before he could accept the challenge, "Professor" lowered his voice and said, "Confidentially, I've always wanted to do a 'through hike' but could never find the time. Maybe you can teach *all* of us something." He stressed *"all,"* and ol' J.R. puffed up like a peacock strutting before a harem of peahens!

The group gathered around and The Marine, trying to emulate the Professor, began to lecture the students on the fine points of long distance backpacking, asking them to interrupt if a question arose. Right off the bat a pretty lass with nary a hair out of place and makeup done to perfection asked, "What's that weird odor?"

Without missing a beat he replied, "We call it 'trail smell.'" Smiling benignly, he raised his right arm high and offered the stinking armpit to the class, explaining, "The full effect can only be experienced by close olfactory observation, if anyone is interested." (A male voice came from the back of the group, barely breaking through the "yuks," "I'd compare it to fresh dog poop." Another muttered, "Too mild. Try a week-old dead cow.") An old pro at sidestepping confrontation (gratis THE LOOK), J.R. quipped, "I see we have some pre-veterinarians in the group," and plunged on.

Another girl asked, "How do you take a bath on the trail?" J.R.'s reply: "Nature's showers are very refreshing." Another question, this one from a nattily dressed boy who could have made his living as a male model: "Do you carry deodorant?" J.R.'s response to that delicate inquiry: "My deodorant is 'trail smell.'"

A "Barbie doll" cutie at the front looked him full in the face, batted her big blue eyes, and said innocently, "Shakespeare must have been a hiker, too." J.R. arched a skeptical eyebrow, waiting for her to explain. "In *The Temptest* he wrote, 'I do smell all horse piss, at which my nose is in great indignation.'"

The group dissolved into laughter—except for "Professor," who didn't look happy, but J.R. was too charged up to notice. A question from a petite brunette: "What do you eat out here?" J.R. jumped on that. "We're just having a breakfast of grits, followed by coffee. Let me demonstrate." He quickly finished off the grits and explained the clean up routine as he poured an inch of water in the pot, added a spoonful of instant coffee, and scrubbed the dregs from the side of the pot with his toothbrush while he waited for the water to heat. Then, with a show of bravado that hadn't been included in *my* clean up checklist, he brushed his teeth in the coffee and drank it with a loud sucking noise. "There! That's the way we do it out here," he proudly brayed, wiping the pot clean with the inside edge of his tee shirt. I could hardly contain my glee! Wahoola and I had done a bang up job of teaching him our version of "outdoor skills"!

He paused, as if he expected cheers and applause for his stunning performance, and wiped a dribble of brown, sudsy grit-water off his beard with his arm. "Any more questions?"

The "male model" gagged, as did some of the gals who had pushed to the forefront in hopes of impressing "Professor" with their sincere dedication to the "Great Outdoors." A male voice grunted, "Holy shit!" and one "lulu" chirped, "I'll take an 'F' before I do *that!*" "Professor" fixed J.R. with an icy stare, which translated into "flunked," while Kelly visibly withered and tried to sink into his boot tops.

But J.R. hadn't quite finished. Grinning foolishly at the unexpected class reaction, he farted once (a gunshot in the silence) and then belched loudly—both of the gross emanations as much a surprise to him as to his audience—and abruptly school was over. Unable to keep quiet any longer, I chortled, "Dang, Ego, you gotta watch about mixing toothpaste with coffee."

"Professor" herded his collection of would-be backpackers over to a far edge of the clearing, where they huddled and listened attentively as their mentor tried to do damage control, emphasizing his lecture with vigorous finger jabs at the "through hiker."

Crushed, J.R. slumped at the picnic table. Kelly recovered quickly and chuckled, "Gosh, Dad, did you learn *that* in the Marines?"

"It's a long story," he groaned. "A long, *sad* story. Let's get out of here."

Sunday morning—Dickey Gap: A picnic lunch of KY Fried that Judith and Brenda had brought; a short "hike" with granddaughters Lauren, Jesalyn, and daughter Alyson; a finalization of plans to meet Judith at Pearisburg on May 27th, one week hence; and finally the conversation dwindled into maudlin snatches of procrastination. It was time to go.

Last minute hugs and a cameo moment—J.R. and Kelly posing for an "end of the hike" photo with Lauren and Jesalyn beside a brown, wooden marker with large yellow letters that read "APPALACHIAN TRAIL." Then after a tender kiss from Judith and a final wave, they were gone.

J.R. watched until they disappeared around a bend. Mist warped his vision as he heaved the heavy pack onto his shoulders and plodded up the Trail.

"Dammit, Ego. Sometimes you're dumber than moose patties." This was the second time today he had missed a white blaze and mistakenly followed a deer path off through the woods. He stared at the thick grove of mountain laurel that blocked our way—impenetrable to humans (though the deer must have squeezed through somehow)—and growled, "Oh hell. How'd that happen?"

Yesterday's parting must have affected him worse than I'd thought, for since Judith and the others had left he had been in a fog, trudging through the forest like a mechanical moron, bumping into trees and losing the Trail. I'd hoped that letting him run things for a couple of more days would clear his mind but we were getting nowhere fast. Worse, he seemed to have lost what little motivation I'd pushed into him since leaving Springer. Worrisome! A three-day-old corpse had more pizzazz! For the first time I began to dread the upcoming days off-trail at Roanoke. What if he balked at continuing the trip—although common sense told me that after a few days at home, as soon as THE LOOK showed up (as it surely must) he would be more than happy to hit the Trail running!

I itched to get back into the old familiar stride, so I loaded my voice with concern and told him, "It's okay Marine. So you got off the Trail a couple of times, but what the heck! It coulda happened to anybody. You've had a lot on you these past few days. A short rest and you'll be chewing nails and spitting out tacks!" I gave his bankrupt psyche a friendly pat. "You just settle back and don't worry about a thing 'cause the ol' Model-T is gonna haul us to Pearisburg." No response, so I sweetened the pot. "Yeah, Judith's gonna be there waitin' for her big brave Marine to walk out of the woods and into her yearning arms. Just six more days and you'll be squeezin' your little love-toy like a rubber ducky. Yessiree!"

It was as easy as stealing nickels from a blind man! J.R. sighed, "Yeah, a little rest . . ." and he wandered off into a dark crevasse.

I put the boots into high gear and reached the day's destination, Chatfield Shelter (an older six-person type that sat at the edge of a lonely clearing ringed with thick rhododendron and mountain laurel) by five o'clock—a seventeen-mile day in spite of The Ego's bungling! Other than a couple of youthful hikers who sped past a mile back, I hadn't seen another soul all day, which was a real disappointment because I was starved for thru-hiker companionship.

I grouched, "Here we go again; another lonely night." Said J.R., rising out of his funk, "This place looks like a setting for 'Twilight Zone.' Why don't we go on a way and pitch the tent?" I thought about it, but the day's push had sapped me. "My legs are shot. Spooky or not, this is home for the night."

Automatically, I scanned the register. The latest entry, written this morning, read in big bold letters: "This place sucks! Mice were all over everything last night—the worst I've encountered in forty years of hiking!" Thumbing back, entry after entry depicted hordes of hungry mice descending on hikers and gear at the first sign of dusk, chewing holes in boots, bags, and packs without fear. Bad news! No wonder I had it to myself!

I stuffed a cookie in my mouth and leaned back against the wall, eyes closed as I chewed. My mind immediately filled with the remnants of an old "Twilight Zone" episode where hordes of mice swept over a hapless, unsuspecting victim and cleaned his bones. I sensed movement and opened my eyes in time to see a mouse grab a cookie crumb near my leg. "Crud-mamma'n mouse!" I yelled, kicking as it scurried out of harm's way. "Crud-mamma'n shelter! Shut'n, crud-mamma'n mice!" Frustrated, I kicked the floor. "Let's get outta this mouse hell!" J.R. actually snickered—a big improvement in his attitude—and said, "Settle down, Bubba-boy. If you go around 'crud-mamma'n' everything, you'll soon be kickin' at 'fars.'" I had to chuckle. "Well, I'm not about to let these busters make Swiss cheese out of everything tonight. Let's get on out of mouse range and pitch the tent." He grumbled, "That's what I said in the first place. Why can't you listen?" But I was already flying up the Trail on rejuvenated legs!

After four miles I still hadn't found a decent place to put up the tent. Finally I came out on a high ridge and had a clear view of Groseclose (a small hamlet of buildings anchored by a motel and a truck stop) snuggled beside busy I-81 far below. A constant stream of vehicles, most with lights glowing in the early dusk, flowed up and down the narrow valley that separated the Blue Ridge from the Alleghenies. I absorbed the picture for a few seconds and then climbed a rickety stile, which spanned a dilapidated fence, and started down a broad hillside meadow toward the glimmering neon lights. The tiny tip of the sun's orb hovered at horizon's edge, ready to plunge the earth into darkness. Anxious, I checked my watch—6:30—and grimly pushed on down the narrow, winding path. "Gotta find a spot *fast.*"

"Not in this field, unless you want to sleep with bovines tonight," The Ego retorted. A soft grunt (or was it a snort?) off to my right rattled my spine and my eyes locked on a big black bull and his harem of eight cows not ten feet away.

J.R.'s words were urgent. "Talk to them. Softly, so they know we're not a threat." I stammered, "It's okay Mr. Bull. That's a nice looking nose ring you've got." The bull eyed me warily and pawed the grass with a mean-looking hoof. "Dang, Ego, I don't like the way he's eyeballing us." He growled, "Just keep on talking, and keep on walking."

I inched forward. "Nice Mr. Bull, I'm a chicken eater. Haven't touched beef in days. Some of my best friends are bulls, at least they're filled with bull." The big Angus took a step toward me and snorted loudly, pawing like he meant business, while the cows gazed at me with bored curiosity as if this were a silly game of "Bull-Chase-the-Hiker" and they already knew what the outcome would be. J.R. snarled, "Holy cow, Alter, get that red bandana out of sight before it turns us into a bullfighter!" I grabbed the sweaty rag, which hung from my shoulder strap (I constantly used it to wipe the sweat from my eyes and face) and crumpled it in my fist.

I eased past the herd, mumbling nice nothings, all the while keeping a wary eye on the bovines. "Almost there, Alter," he whispered. "Keep on—"

"Aaah!" I yelled as my boots slipped on something slick in the middle of the narrow path and my legs shot out from under me. Down I went, right on my skinny butt—into a gooey mess.

Disgusted, I sat in the huge pile of cow (or was it bull?) manure and watched as Mr. Bull raised his head toward the darkening sky, twisted his upper lip into a hideous smile, and shattered the soft dusk with an earsplitting bellow. "Damn, J.R., that bull's sniggering at us." He retorted, "Yeah, we're probably sitting in his pile of shit."

The huge animal tossed his head and pawed the ground, and then switched his tail a couple of times as if to say, "Don't mess with me or my cuties." Then seeming to lose interest (game over?) he went back to grazing. I flipped the bull a concise gesture of my opinion of his little game and shifted my bottom into the grass beside the path, scooting around like a grotesque crab as I attempted to wipe the stinky stuff away. J.R., still raw over his "*tete-a-tete*" with the Washington and Lee group, mimicked the "Barbie" gal, "Well Model-T, you do smell all bull piss, at which my nose is in great indignation." I didn't bother to reply; after all, who could argue with that indisputable fact!

By the time I reached the truck stop, wobbling like a drunken elephant with exhaustion, dusk had fallen. And I still hadn't found a place to pitch the tent! Hopefully something would turn up after I crossed under I-81. I peered at my watch, the face barely readable in the dim light—almost 8 o'clock! Night was nipping at my heels!

Timidly, very conscious of the manure stink (which refused to go away even after I had squatted in a small mud puddle and tried to mask the odor with mucky water), I hesitated in the shadows outside the door of the brightly lit truck stop. To go inside or not? J.R. said, "We've got to have something sweet. Our blood sugar has to be zilch, the way you've pushed us today." He was right, but the smell . . . "Shut-fire, they'd throw us right out on our bony tush. Jesus Ego, we stink worse than Wahoola ever did!"

The door opened and a gray-haired man walked out just as a giddy, lightheaded feeling struck without warning, causing me to reel against the side of the building. He stopped in front of me and asked with a clipped Yankee accent, "Say fella, are you okay?" Alarm changed to revulsion as he whiffed the air and looked down at his shoes. "Bejesus! I must've stepped in some crap."

I shook my head, trying to clear the dizziness away. "Yeah, I'm okay. It's been a long day." Suspiciously, his eyes zeroed in on my dim shadow and he sniffed again, aggressively this time. I growled and pointed vaguely at a couple of trucks across the parking lot. "Awful stink, isn't it? Doggone cattle trucks. They oughta make 'em park behind the building."

The man stared into the murky dusk. Unconvinced, he muttered, "Nasty", gave me a contemptuous glare, and hastened to his car. J.R. snickered, "Cattle truck? Jeez, Dum-dum, couldn't you do better than that?" Incensed, I retorted, "Aw, he probably didn't know a cattle truck from a house trailer. What're we gonna do?" I felt the "woozies" coming on again.

I sensed movement at my back and pressed against the wall, as if by doing so I could contain the fetid odor. A man's deep voice called my name. "Model-T? Is that you?"

Hacker Hiker! I hadn't seen the retired teacher (or any others of the Brew and Pizza gang) since we had spent the night together at Mt. Collins Shelter back in the Smokies. He started to hug me—like hikers usually do when they haven't seen one another for a long while—but instead he sniffed the air and looked down at the concrete. Seeing nothing suspicious, he drew back and gave me a questioning look.

"Boy, Hacker Hiker, am I glad to see you!" I couldn't believe my good fortune! "Yeah, it's me that stinks," I admitted with an embarrassed grin. "I slipped and landed in a big pile of bull crap coming through that cow pasture just now."

He chuckled, "How can you tell cow manure from bull manure? I thought it all smelled the same."

"The bull claimed ownership," I explained perfunctorily, wanting to get on to more urgent matters.

Thankfully he didn't press for an explanation. "You're hiking late. Where are you headed tonight?"

"Somewhere to pitch my tent; on the other side of I-81, I guess."

He shook his head. "Some bad weather moving in. Storms, heavy rain, flash flood warning, the works. Supposed to hit tonight and last through tomorrow."

Bad news! "Then I'd better find a hole and climb in. Where're you staying?"

He pointed down the road toward a flickering neon sign. "My gang and a couple of others got the last motel room. We're going to hang out here until the worst is over." He hesitated, struggling with his olfactory judgment. "We're wall-to-wall but we could probably squeeze you in."

At least eight hikers and gear in a room not larger than a six-person shelter—I couldn't add to their misery. "Thanks anyway, but I'll find something soon. You could do me a big favor, though, considering my current condition. I need a quart of ice cream—chocolate if they have it—and a Coke." (I could eat ice cream on the run.) I pulled some stray bills from my belt pouch and handed them to Hacker Hiker, adding, "Much obliged, and see if you can find a Snickers, too."

I stood in the shadows and watched through the window as my benefactor bent over the ice cream freezer. On the wall above his head a clock's hands unceasingly measured time—each sweep of the minute hand a glaring reminder of time forever gone—and it's silent admonition cut through my fatigue. It was 8:27!

I followed a narrow paved road through an underpass beneath I-81, digging chunks of rock-hard ice cream out of the cardboard carton and spooning them into my mouth as fast as I could, flinching at the odd-clanking noises the vehicles made when they passed over the expansion joints. A wave of loneliness descended as the friendly lights of Groseclose gave way to the dark. Garnering strength, I picked up the pace, determined to go on to Davis Path Shelter still nearly three miles away—especially in light of the predicted storm.

The Trail soon left the road, making a sharp swing into another cow pasture—and more manure! Cow patties, nearly invisible in the deep dusk, heralded my passage with foul odors as my boots squished the thin-crusted plops; however, I didn't see any cows. Then came a series of dilapidated stiles—twenty-four by my count—obviously built by the farmer-owner years previously to aid in traversing his many fences. I struggled over several before realizing that a short section of fence had been cut away from the stiles' sides—a detail obscured by the dark—and kicked myself for squandering time and energy when I was in such short supply of both!

At last I came to a large pasture free from the disgusting cow patties—a tradeoff of sorts, for this field was rank with chest-high orchard grass that choked the Trail. This would become a tangled mess as soon as it started raining, and for the first time since leaving Chatfield Shelter I was glad I had come this far—especially since the air had now become heavy with moisture. Rain was definitely on the way! I wiped the sweat out of my eyes and pushed ahead.

After what seemed like an eternity the path left the high grass and began a gentle ascent through a thick forest, a stifling dungeon in the breezeless humidity and tomb-like blackness. Flashlight time! Almost as if it were in cahoots with the feeble beam, the rain began; first as a diminutive rattle on the overhead canopy; and then gathering strength, water began to drip through the leafy ceiling like a leaky faucet.

The Trail, climbing steeply now, began to take its toll as sweat poured into my eyes, stinging and blurring the thin thread of light so that I could hardly see the well-worn track. How much further? If only it would rain harder and wash away the sweat and stench and bring me some relief and take away my pain and exhaustion and give me back my youth and send in the clowns and . . .

I was standing in front of the shelter. How long had I been here? At first glimpse, the shelter seemed deserted. I moved closer and waved the weak beam over several covered mounds, which seemed to fill the floor, and then jumped backwards as a muffled voice drifted out of the darkness. "Who's there?"

"It's Model-T. Is any room left?"

A soft hiss came back—"Model-Teee!" Skate's smiling face, distorted in the dim glow, lit my flagging spirit like a Roman candle! "Where have you been? We were hoping you'd catch us!" She punched the bag next to her. "Scoot over Eco-Warrior. Model-T's here." After several elbow jabs, the bag grunted and wiggled over a few inches, opening up a narrow berth before returning to its dormant state.

What a surprise! (I thought Skate and Eco-Warrior were a day or two behind me.) "Jeez, I'm glad to see you guys! I'll be inside in a minute. Gotta catch my breath."

Taking advantage of the shelter's large overhang, I stripped off the dung-stained shorts and sweaty tee shirt and dashed naked through the rain (modesty seemed so superfluous at this stage!), and draped the garments over a bush. Maybe Mother Nature would give them a good cleansing by morning!

I pulled on dry long johns and then lounged beneath the overhang, mulling over the day's unusual events as I slowly drank the Coke, reveling in the delightful fizzy burn as it coursed down my parched throat. "We did twenty-five miles today, Ego," I murmured. "Our longest day yet." A long pause and then he replied, "Not shabby at all."

I sat for some time just listening to the rain, my mind as hollow as the black void around me. Without warning, a picture floated into the haze of near oblivion: A manure-splotched marionette dressed in hiker attire lay in an obscene heap on a small stage, while an enraged puppeteer sought to unravel hopelessly entangled strings. Giving up, he wrinkled his nose with disgust and threw his arms toward the heavens, shrieking with frustration, "My stage smells all horse piss, at which my nose is in great indignation!" Said J.R. drowsily, "I think he meant bull piss."

My face relaxed into a weak smile, which seemed to soften the pain and exhaustion. Quietly, I crawled along the floor and made my nest in the narrow space between Skate and Eco-Warrior.

CHAPTER 6

Another Way to Take a Bath

I dreamed I was a melting vanilla ice cream cone, and I was clasped firmly in the hand of a huge creature that favored the Jolly Green Giant. It licked at my dripping face with its greedy pink tongue, all the while making noisy, slobbering sounds while it slurped away my nose and mouth. Horrified, I watched the tongue leap from its lair, searching and probing for my eyes as I desperately wriggled to escape. My vision dimmed as the tongue flicked lightly across the eyelids, and then all became black oblivion as the tongue came again, this time digging hard and taking away my eyes. I cringed as the creature's voracious tongue sought my dripping flesh and stripped it away with gluttonous frenzy. Hysterically, I screamed and screamed . . .

I awoke shaken and trembling with the rough drag of the tongue still vivid. Lying motionless with my eyes closed, I let the image slowly dissipate and listened to the soothing patter of rain on the tin roof. No need to be in any rush this morning, not with this weather. I slowly relaxed and retreated back into an opaque void, hoping I could go back to sleep—without the dream.

Uninvited, the scene slowly began to replay in my mind, this time with me playing the role of detached onlooker rather than victim. Once again the giant creature opened its mouth and the tongue emerged like a fat, venomous serpent, stretching out, out, until it traced a sticky path across my face, leaving a trail of hot mucous in its wake.

Jesus! Not again! The tongue flicked across my nose and I wiped at the slobber with my hand, at the same time struggling out of the stupor. Enough tonguing for one night! Might as well get on with the day. I opened my eyes and barely had time to duck as the purplish-pink tongue made another pass. The culprit, a large black Lab, stood beside my head with its eyes fixed on my mouth, where undoubtedly the next lick was aimed.

"Sorry fella, I don't believe in kissing on the first date," I grunted, scratching him behind the ears and letting him nuzzle my neck as a consolation prize. Apparently satisfied, the Lab wagged his tail and gingerly threaded his way between the slumbering hikers, back to his place between two sleeping bags by the far wall. Curious! Why had I been singled out for a licking wakeup call?

I started breakfast—a domino effect, for the smell of cooking food is more effective than an alarm clock for ravenous hikers. New faces and sleepy introductions: First out (after Skate) were the Green Mountain Trio (consisting of Tom, a ski instructor at a resort in Vermont, with the build to go with the job; his wife Susie, a nurse, pretty and pert; and their face-washing Lab, Lincoln)—to be downsized and become the "Duo" in early July when Tom left to resume his job.

Next to wake up: The Yoopers, the middle-aged, married couple from Michigan's Upper Peninsula. Although our paths had briefly touched before, they now quickly let me know that they hiked as the "spirit" moved them. They studied the rainy dawn for a few moments, made an inaudible comment, and snuggled back into their comfy bags. It didn't appear that the "spirit" was going to do much moving this day!

Then came Mississippi Tripper, a mild-mannered, soft-spoken enigma. Tripp, as he asked to be called, could have been twenty or forty—hard to tell, for his boyish face was overlaid with a handsomely raffish look that hinted of fallen innocence. Clashing with his good looks, his speech suffered an impediment—as if he struggled to create a new pathway each time he spoke so that the words could get from his brain to his mouth. (I later learned that Tripp had been in an automobile accident, which damaged the area of his brain that controls speech.) Yet his rich Mississippi accent offset the halting speech and floated into my ears like a refreshing breeze.

We enjoyed a leisurely breakfast, trying to carry on a conversation above the rattle of the rain, which seemed to intensify as the morning progressed. Procrastinating, we squandered time in idle chatter and hoped for a break in the weather, but the storm showed no sign of letting up. By ten o'clock I was fidgeting like a dog with fleas, for the day was fast slipping away and I hadn't yet put a yard of Trail beneath my boots. Said The Marine, "It's time to consider options." I asked sluggishly, "What options?" It sounded like a typical Marine "no-brainer." He: "Lollygag around here all day or suck it up and make some miles." He had to be crazy! "Jiminy! You mean go out in *that?*"

The wind blasted the rain across the mountain in thick sheets, making it nearly impossible to see to the edge of the clearing. Just thinking about slogging through that maelstrom for eleven miles to Knot Maul Shelter gave me the willies! But then if I hung around here, J.R. would bitch and gripe and drive me crazy. I considered the *true* options: chancing a broken leg (or worse), or putting up with The Jarhead's drivel for the next twenty-odd hours. Put that way, my course was clear. I growled, "Shut 'far', we can only get so wet." As I began to pack, he tried to smooth my ruffled feathers. "Heck, Alter, the storm can't hang around forever. Just look on it as another way to excel." Another "no-brainer"!

Skate gave me an incredulous look. "Surely you're not going to hike in this weather!"

I postured with a macho shrug. "It's just another way to take a bath!"

"Model-T, you're totally insane!"

I finished packing and then, gritting my teeth, dashed through the rain, yanked my shorts and tee shirt off the bush, and crouched beneath the narrow overhang behind the shelter to exchange dry for wet—a chilly trade-off! I took a tentative whiff of yesterday's manure pile, now a permanent ugly imprint on the seat of the shorts; not too bad, considering. The Ego chuckled, "What we have here is an olfactory souvenir of our longest day." I pulled the nasty garment on. "What we have here is not fit for mixed company," I retorted, mentally resolving to ditch them at the first opportunity. Shivering, I went around to the front, stuffed the long johns inside the pack, and then snugged the rain cover tight.

The rain intensified, drumming an ear-splitting roar on the tin roof and rolling a wall of water down across the shelter's front, causing me to wonder if maybe I'd made a rash decision in going along with The Marine. My peers watched silently, waiting for my next move—entranced spectators waiting for the gladiator to choose the Lady or the Tiger. Still I hesitated, fiddling with a pack strap, and then a boot string. Said The Marine, "Well, Ace, let's pee or get off the pot. What's it going to be?" I replied grittily, "Let's pee." Struck with the uncomfortable suspicion that my peers were staring at a fool, I heaved the pack onto my back and, bellowing a loud "OOOGA," stepped through the waterfall and into the Tiger's lair.

Oblivious, blissfully wrapped in the arms of Morpheus, Eco-Warrior snored the morning away. How I envied him!

One thing to be said for a drenching, chilly day: It keeps a body moving just to stay warm. The miles passed in tedious misery as I slogged through the drowning Virginia landscape, boots filled with water, feet and fingers prune-shriveled, wet to the bone. As I waded through the muddy torrent that passed for the Trail, I tried to think up new cuss words to lambaste the Marine; however, sensing mutiny, he barricaded himself in a hidey-hole and stayed out of sight. I had to hand it to him though, for the hotshot weather predictor knew what he was talking about: The storm didn't hang around "forever"; instead, it escorted us until we were within a half-mile of Knot Maul Shelter and then scooted away. "Good call, Weather Quack," I grumbled, but he refused to come out and accept the "accolade."

Knot Maul Shelter was dry and unoccupied. I changed out of the wet clothing and snuggled inside my sleeping bag until the shivers subsided. Within the hour, my companions from Davis Path Shelter began to straggle in (except for the Yoopers, who hadn't been moved by the "spirit")—all looking like drowned rats but unwilling to be shown up by an old gray-bearded geezer.

After they had changed into dry clothes (the guys discreetly turning the other way to give the gals a little privacy, and they returning the favor—an accepted trail custom during bad weather; otherwise, the rear of the shelter would have done duty as the dressing room), Skate asked in a matter of fact tone, "Anyone for hors d'oeuvres?" Unable to believe our eyes, we watched as she pulled a container of Pringles from her food bag, followed by a can of smoked oysters and a can of cheese spread—as easily as a magician lifting a floppy white rabbit out of his hat. Hors d'oeuvres to go with mac-n-cheese! Things were looking up!

Just before bedtime, J.R. emerged from his hideout and apologized for being so pushy. Warm and dry now, I graciously accepted his apology—mainly because my mind was on tomorrow and Levi Long's Corner Diner in Bastian, home of the monster "Trailburger" and giant "Hiker Shake" (at least according to *The Philosopher's Guide*). I could afford to be forgiving!

An hour before dawn a whip-o-will perched on a tree just outside the shelter and cranked up its motor with nonstop "whip-o-will's", whistling incessantly for at least twenty minutes. The persistent bird repeated its routine again and again—tiny fingernails of sound rasping through the gray softness—causing me to cringe as each new round of torture began. Suddenly the sleeping bag by my side erupted in a spasm of oaths, followed by several loud thuds as Mississippi Tripper beat his boots together in an effort to scare the pest away.

The bird responded with a rapid stream of calls. Tripp crawled out of his sleeping bag, leaped from the shelter, and shook his fist at the offending fowl, shouting, "Begone! Begone you scoundrel!" For good measure, he launched a couple of rocks toward the tree to show the bird he meant business. Blessed quiet followed Tripp back to his sleeping bag—except for a few muffled sniggers, including mine, and a giggly, inquisitive "Begone?" from Skate.

The whip-o-will waited a few minutes, lulling us into a false sense of tranquility, and then renewed its grating serenade from the rear of the shelter, beyond range of Tripp's lethal barrage of "Begones." Tripp muttered, "I'd like to pluck that bird and stew him in with some grits." The speech impediment drew the sentence out to infinity, but I resisted the urge to prompt him.

I whispered, "It would probably beat the gazoomus outta garter snake stew."

"What? I thought we ate everything in Mississippi but I never had snake stew. Have you?"

"Yeah, but it's a long story. Jeez, I'm hungry. You got any extra grits?"

"Some. I'd cook up a batch right now if it still wasn't nighttime."

I peered into the clearing. The foliage was just becoming visible as the ebony began to change over to a washed-out gray. "Heck, it's practically daylight. I've got some Squeeze Parkay."

Trying not to disturb the others, we huddled in a corner and pressed a pot into service. As the grits started to bubble, Tripp grunted, "Grits is good."

"Anytime and Amen." I could get to like this Mississippi boy!

The roar got louder with each step, causing a twinge of doubt to nip at my innards. Of course it had to be the creek. I had already crossed Little Wolf Creek ten times this morning, each time managing to rock-hop across without getting my feet wet. Obligingly, until the last quarter-mile the stream had only purred like a playful kitten. However, this roar filled the air with an angry insolence and sent a shiver up my spine.

The group from last night's roost, Jenkins Shelter (including The Yoopers, who had lit a fire under their butts to catch up), had passed me earlier while I cooked breakfast in a tiny sunlit clearing at the side of the Trail, which made me "Tail-End Charlie." So whatever danger the roar portended, they should have already faced it and gone on. As a feeling of utter desolation crowded in, J.R. growled, "We should have taken the bypass."

(Earlier, against The Jarhead's counsel, I had disregarded the small sign tacked on a tree way back up on the mountain, which pointed toward an overgrown blue-blazed trail and warned hikers to take the fair weather route in case of high water. He had cautioned, "A lot of water's rolling off these mountains right now, after all the rain we've had the past three days. That creek's gonna be a bear." He wasn't telling me anything I didn't know—I had hiked through the mess! "I don't think so," I countered. "This blue-blaze will add at least a mile to our day, and look how grown up it is. Anyway, it doesn't take long for a small stream to run off and this *is* a creek, not a river." Then I laid the clincher on him. "Besides, how are *you* going to explain to the others that *you* were too chicken to follow the white blazes?" Reluctantly he threw in the towel, grumbling, "Sometimes it's better to be a dry chicken than a drowned lemming.")

I soon met the roar face to face—Little Wolf Creek had grown into a full-fledged river that coursed at near flood as it flung it's wrathful tentacles at the skinny log on which Tripp precariously balanced. He fed a log to Tom, who stood on a partly submerged boulder and tried to maneuver the end onto another rock—the next in a series of zigzag boulders that protruded from the swollen stream like hippo heads. Susie and The Yoopers stood on the bank, ready with another log, while Skate and Eco Warrior scoured the nearby woods for suitable "building material" and Lincoln barked encouragement.

"Gosh A'mighty, Ego, they're trying to build a bridge!" I watched for a few seconds, wondering how people who had been perfectly sane just hours ago could have gone bonkers so fast—and all at the same time! I had to ask anyway. "Hey Susie, what're you guys doing?"

"Building a bridge." She looked at me like I had asked the dumbest question in the world, which I probably had. The Yoopers seemed a little more tolerant. Skeptics?

I estimated the distance to the other side—at least fifty yards. "A far stretch," I remarked (tuning out J.R.'s smirking, "I told you we shoulda taken the bypass"). "You're gonna be here awhile."

Susie rolled her eyes at Tom, who now inched his way along the second span toward the next abutment. "It's his baby. But it's the only way across, unless we backtrack and take the bypass." (The Ego snorted, "See!")

Eco and Skate pulled a partly rotted, scrawny log to water's edge. Seeing me, they smiled and Eco shouted, "Hey Model-T! You come to give us a hand?"

I shrugged noncommittally, not ready to squander the next few hours on bridge building, especially when Levi Long's monster "Trail Burger" was so close. I studied the turbulent water. It couldn't be too deep. After all, it was deep waters that ran smooth, and this stuff bucked and romped like a mad steer. Knee-deep at most, I guessed! "Okay Killer, you guys are always bragging about how the Marines are experts at making amphibious landings. Well, Ol' Buddy, this is your chance to shine." He wimped out. "Darn, Alter, that was a long time ago. And this current looks mean—" I interrupted, "If I may quote you, 'Once a Marine, Always a Marine; Semper Fi,

Do or Die; Pee or get off the Pot.' Hell's bells, man, we're gonna be heroes!" That stung him and he asked, "Live or dead?"

I told Eco, "Got no time for such foolery. Watch how the Marines do it."

Rousing cheers—Tom had made it to the third rock and now hoisted his arms in victory. Simultaneously, like a long, disembodied worm, Tripp inched his way to the rock just vacated by Tom, and Susie (brave gal) took Tripp's place on the wobbly log, ready to receive the next "span" from The Yoopers. I shook my head at Skate and Eco. "Crazy! I'll see you two tonight—if you ever get across."

Oddly, they also shook their heads at me and Skate echoed, "Crazy," but I don't think she referred to the bridge!

I walked a few yards downstream until I spotted a place where the water seemed to churn with most frenzy (by my logic, the shallowest crossing place) and went to the water's edge. Sneaking a glance at the "construction crew," I was gratified to see that bridge building had taken back seat to the real life drama about to unfold. "C'mon Killer, let's show'em what an old farty Marine can do!" Bellowing a long, loud "OOOGA," I gave the gawkers a thumbs-up and tromped into the water.

The swift current immediately rose to my knees, clutching greedily as it tried to upend me onto the bottom—a tricky affair, blanketed with round rocks of all sizes and made ice-slick by a slime-like goop. Two wavering steps, and a boot got trapped in a small crevice between two large rocks. Bracing against the strong flow with my hiking stick, I managed to back it out. Two more steps, more careful now, exploring with my foot before anchoring the boot on the bottom, only then easing into the next step to repeat the process. The water crept up toward my crotch, but I kept inching toward the far bank.

Almost halfway! All things considered, it was going better than I expected, but the current was taxing my strength. Pausing to catch my breath, I glanced at the builders and was faintly annoyed to see that their attention had been refocused on trying to negotiate another span into place. The frigid water swirled around the bottom of my pack, numbing my legs and butt—nothing that The Marine and I couldn't handle though.

"Heck, Killer, this is a piece of cake!" Full of piss and vinegar and strangely exhilarated, I shouted "OOOGA" at the top of my lungs. The others paused in their collective effort and looked at me. The gals cheered, while the guys made ape-like noises peculiar to the male species when they exhort one of their own to do an incredible feat. I managed a small bow, and then with a show of bravado I stepped off again—into a deep hole.

The water closed over my head and I sank like a rock! Weighed down by the pack, I didn't have a chance. The current catapulted me onto my back and suddenly I was thrashing around on the rocky bottom, anchored by my pack like a helpless turtle as I flailed at the water and futilely tried to upright myself. Somehow I had managed to hang onto my hiking stick, and I jabbed one end into the bottom and pushed hard, managing to roll onto my stomach. Planting my feet and bracing against the current with the stick, I reared up out of the hole like a submarine on emergency blow.

Air! I had to have air! Gagging and coughing, trying to squeeze air into starved lungs, I gulped in long draughts even as water spewed out of my mouth (along with God only knew what else—sand and small pebbles, maybe even a tooth or two!). As soon as the spasm subsided I ran my tongue over my teeth, relieved to find everything intact, and then rubbed the water out of my eyes and took stock.

The current had dragged me several yards to the lower end of the deep hole. Still facing downstream, I grappled with the torrent and fought to hold my position in the chest-high water. Then slowly, keeping my boots glued to the bottom, I inched up the slanting side.

I became aware of screams piercing the roar and carefully glanced backwards to see what catastrophe had befallen the bridge builders. The gals pointed at me, screaming and carrying on like they were standing in a tub of mice. (Was Skate crying? Impossible to tell since my vision was still blurred.) The guys stared wordlessly from their wobbly sanctuary (waiting to see if they would have to jump in and save my skinny butt?). When they realized I was safe and they wouldn't have to get wet, they started to applaud, making those "male exhortation" noises again, reminding me of a group of chimpanzees in an old *Tarzan* movie. Tom yelled, "Hey, Model-T, I missed the part where you went under! Would you mind doing it again?" Fat chance! Another shout, this time from Eco. "So that's how the Marines do it!" I flicked a "finger" at the guffawing buffoons in reply.

Susie shouted, "You almost drowned!" Jesus! Had I? It had all happened so fast.

Humiliated, I yelled back, "Naw, it's just another way to take a bath!" J.R. snapped, "It's also the end of your Marine Corps 'career,' ACE." Determined to get in the last word, I retorted, "It was a chicken outfit anyway." He wouldn't let it rest, snarling, "Dumb bastard."

Slowly making my way toward the bank, I snapped, "You want to see a really 'dumb bastard,' look in a mirror sometime," and he sniggered, "I rest my case." Confused, I wondered if I had been tripped up and decided to let well enough alone.

Soaked and exhausted, I slithered up onto the grassy bank, slipped out of the waterlogged pack, and lay on my back, gasping, staring at the sky. After a while I began to giggle, and then raucous laughter racked my ribs. The Grouch barked, "I don't see anything funny about a near-drowning." Wheezing, I spluttered, "J.R., you are no longer a Methodist, for you have been immersed in the pure, icy waters of Little Wolf Creek. You are now a Baptist!" He shot back, "I'm also afflicted with an idiot for an alter ego." Jeez! Where was his sense of humor? "Well, you did get a bath out of it," I countered, but he was so ticked off he refused to answer. Family spat . . .

I sat on the bank and watched as the others, one by one, lost their footing on the shaky, half-rotted logs and slipped (accompanied by screams and jeers) into the cold, turbulent waters of Little Wolf Creek—all that is except Tom, who somehow made it all the way across without getting his feet wet.

The final tally: Baptists—eight; Methodists—one. (Lincoln didn't count.)

Levi Long's Corner Diner, an old one-story building with a long narrow porch, lies nestled in the small valley community of Bastian, Virginia—population about 400. Levi looked almost as weathered as his store. The short-sleeved white shirt he wore also did double duty as a corset, stretching paper-thin over a midriff that had seen years of his wife's honest mountain cooking. A worn wide-leather belt fastened with a large brass buckle held up his jeans, pulling in his belly barely enough to keep the shirt buttons from popping off. Outside in the graveled parking lot Levi's Ford truck stood at the ready, waiting to haul him up the mountain to the Trail crossing—a thrice daily ritual that Levi religiously performed during the hiking season—to carry hikers down the winding highway to Bastian and back to the Trail when they were ready—all for free.

Skate and I were not so lucky. We had reached the highway ahead of Tripp and Eco (The Green Mountain Trio and The Yoopers had decided to bypass Bastian) and immediately stuck our thumbs out. After waiting fifteen minutes for a vehicle to come by (none did!), we began the two-mile trek down the mountain. We had already stepped off a good third of the distance when a woman in a rust-spotted, green clunker stopped and offered to take us the rest of the way—if I didn't mind sitting in the back seat with four fifty-pound sacks of grass seed. Patting her frizzy peroxide-blond hair (the inch-long black roots tattled!), she said to Skate, "Sweetie, jist put yer pack in th' back with yer pappy an' squeeze on in." Skate looked dubious, a normal reaction considering the two young children and large, dull-eyed dog that filled the rest of the front seat.

I said sweetly, "Yes, 'Sweetie,' let me get in and then give 'Daddy' your pack."

She gave me a withering glare as I clambered onto a bag of seed and pulled my pack in, totally filling the back seat area. "Gee, 'Pappy,' I don't believe there's any room left," she said glibly. "I'll just walk on down."

"Don't be silly, Darlin'," the woman said. "You kids scoot yer butts over an' let th' lady in." Struggling, Skate finally maneuvered her way onto the seat and, holding her pack in her lap, managed to close the door. The big mutt, which looked like it carried the genes of the entire mountain canine population, eyed Skate warily, and then climbed over the children and flopped down in the floorboard under the woman's feet. She kicked at it a couple of times and snarled, "Git yer ass outta th' way, Gilbert. I gotta git to th' gas pedal." Reluctantly, Ol' Gilbert bellied under the children's legs and pushed into the small space beneath Skate's legs; then heaving a loud, slobbery sigh, he settled down.

One of the kids, a pretty flaxen-haired girl about five years old, wearing a faded dress with pink and white flowers, was sandwiched between Skate and her runny-nosed younger brother. She elbowed him and screeched in a high-pitched voice, "Git over Melvin Jodine (rhymed with 'dime'). You done squeezed th' lights outta me." Melvin Jodine stuck his tongue out and slapped at her. "Ain't not," he screamed in her face, which sent thick yellow snotty bubbles dribbling out of his nose. Ol' Gilbert, long since conditioned to such brother and sister bickering, didn't even perk up his ears.

The mother half-heartedly whacked at the two and snapped, "Both o' you younguns is gonna git a whuppin' soon's we git home." She managed to squeeze the stick shift past the boy's wiggly body and get it into the right gear, and we headed on down the mountain.

Little Melvin Jodine stuck his tongue out to catch the yellow ooze. I tapped Skate's shoulder. "'Sweetie,' Melvin Jodine needs to borrow your bandanna." If looks could kill . . .

The whopper Trail Burger and giant Hiker Shake were worth the ride!

Skate decided to linger and play "mother" to Tripp and Eco, who had just arrived as I was settling my bill, so I accepted Levi's offer of a ride back to the trailhead. His firm handshake and "Godspeed" were still fresh in my mind when I reached Kimberling Creek, a six-foot wide benign stream that lazily wound beside a narrow gravel road at the base of the mountain. I rock-hopped across to a battered mailbox atop a weatherworn post, pulled out a soiled spiral notebook, and recorded my passing, letting the world know that the Model-T was still headed for Maine. Flipping through the latest three pages for any earth-shaking news, I noticed that Felix the Cat had passed through yesterday. Remembering his previous antics, The Ego said, "Do you suppose he now carries his own broom?" I chuckled, "If he does, we should have some clean shelters up the way."

A few yards downstream, lying in a shallow hole just beneath the surface of the water, the outline of an old bathtub was barely visible. The famous Warren Doyle Bathtub! (According to rumor the tub had been placed there in the mid-eighties by young Warren, who lived close by at the time.) Word was, hikers occasionally found sodas and beer in the tub, courtesy of local anonymous donors. Could this be my lucky day?

I went over and looked into the murky depths of the old tub—now half-filled with silt—and felt a stab of sorrow for this stained, discarded relic from the carefree, frolicking days of another age. Impulsively I jabbed my hiking stick into the silt on the off-chance that a bottle of beer just might have sunk to the bottom, just waiting for some curious hiker to resurrect it from its watery grave. Pushing the stick to the bottom, I stirred vigorously and watched as the silt turned into a large amoeba-like cloud that seemed to come alive as it swelled upwards into the slight current and began to ooze over the top.

My stick struck something! Excited, I got on my belly and reached down into the muddy depths to retrieve my prize. Pay dirt! My hand closed over a bottle and my mouth watered at the thought of the cool liquid that was about to roll over my tongue.

Something bumped against my hand! I yelped and let go, jerking my arm out of the water. "Dammit, J.R., there's something alive down there! A snake just skittered across my hand!" Shuddering, I checked for telltale puncture marks. He wanted the beer as much as me and snorted impatiently, "Snakes don't skitter; they slither. You only spooked a crawdad."

I thought about it, trying to recreate the feeling. "Really, I think it was more like a 'skittering slither.'" In my mind I could see a huge water moccasin lying deep in its murky lair, curled around the precious bottle as it patiently waited, ready to sink its deadly fangs into the hand of anyone dumb enough to invade its kingdom. "Nope, it slithered."

"C'mon," he chided. "Get the bottle and let's go. We don't have all day." When I refused budge, he changed tactics. "Just think about it. Water moccasins are cold-blooded creatures. They don't live in cold mountain streams."

Well, that made sense—sort of. Half expecting a large, evil head to rear up out of the silting cloud, I worked the stick until I managed to pin the bottle against the side of the tub. To be on the safe side I waited a couple of minutes, but nothing happened. "Okay, here goes nothing. I hope you know what you're talking about." Gritting my teeth, I plunged my arm to the bottom, grabbed the bottleneck, and hoisted the prize up into the light of day. "*Yes!*"

The topless, slime-covered, mud-filled bottle seemed to leer at me. J.R. snickered, "It's all yours, Bubba. I just went on the wagon." Foolishly, I stared at the deteriorated, unreadable label. "Damn! All that trouble for *this?*" Disgusted, I flung the bottle back into its muddy grave. "A curse on you, you filthy crud-mamma'n obscenity! May your days be filled with darkness and despair." J.R. said, "You can't lay a curse on that poor bottle. Warren Doyle himself might have popped the top on that orphan." Tantrum finished, I backpedaled. "Yeah, you're right. How about this: 'May you rest in peace—until some other dumb hiker resurrects you?'" His solemn "Amen" gave closure. Then we both cracked up at the absurdity of the situation.

Still choked with laughter, I began to remove my boots. "Now what's the matter?" he asked. I slowly lowered my feet into the dingy water, being careful to keep them near the surface (just in case!), and replied, "I'm gonna get something outta this old tub, even if it's only a foot wash." J.R. lampooned the situation. "Well, when you think about it, it's just another way to take a bath!" We broke up again.

That's how Felix the Cat found me—with my feet dangling in Warren Doyle's Bathtub. Perplexed, I asked him, "What're you doing here, Felix? I saw your entry, where you had gone through here yesterday."

He looked like he was about to cry. "Model-T, I don't know what's wrong. I've had bad diarrhea and cramps ever since leaving Damascus. I can't get rid of it." Poor Felix did look terrible—sunken eyes, sallow face and emaciated appearance, all outward manifestations of misery endured for the past 120 miles. "Last night at Helvey's Mill Shelter (one and a half miles from here and my destination for tonight) was the last straw. I just can't take another day of this."

Remembering my bout with a similar malady after leaving Hot Springs, I could almost feel his pain. If it was giardia, he needed medical help. Felix, his face doleful, added in a timorous voice, "I'm headed back to Levi's to call my sister. I'm finished with the Trail." Words of doom!

I felt diminished by his broken spirit. For in spite of his obsessive/compulsive behavior with the broom, he was part of the Trail family. I suggested, "Maybe you can go home and get well, and then get back on the Trail." Somehow the thought made me feel better.

"Yeah maybe," he muttered, but dejection lay like a massive weight on his troubled spirit and deep down I sensed that he would not return.

A flashbulb went off in my head and I smiled encouragingly. "Well, if you can spare the time why don't you sit here and soak your tired feet in Warren Doyle's Bathtub. He wouldn't mind." I scooted over to make room and coaxed him again. "Aah, this silt is like a magic potion."

Felix sat beside me and took off his boots. I told him, "Get'em down as far as you can; the further, the better. Push'em down into the thick stuff. Yeah, now doesn't that feel better?"

What the heck! He was going home anyway. I waited, eyes fixed on the dirty water, to see what denizen would latch onto his marble-white toes. After several minutes, half disappointed that nothing happened, I swung my feet out of the tub and washed away the scummy silt in the clear upstream flow, sighing contentedly as I put my socks and boots back on. "Well fella, I need to move. Good luck and get well." We shook hands and I walked up the Trail, out of Felix's life.

For several yards I kept my ears tuned for a yelp that would indicate a "skittery-slithery" creature had pumped some life back into Felix the Cat's sagging soul. The Ego grumbled, "You're incorrigible." Looking back through the trees at the forlorn, disheartened figure that sat on the bank, dangling his legs into the mysterious depths of Warren Doyle's Bathtub, I shook my head. "If I am, it's because of the debauched company I keep." Suddenly I felt a migraine coming on.

A small battered sign tacked to a scrubby pine beside the dirt road read, "Woodshole—½ mile". I hesitated, calculating time and distance as I studied the stubby arrow that pointed to the right. Go or no go? From here, it was ten miles on to Shumate Bridge on the outskirts of Pearisburg, where Judith would be waiting at noon tomorrow.

The distance lay like a wet blanket on my soul. According to hiker reports (and the *PG*) Woodshole, complete with privy, shower, and a refrigerator stocked with drinks and candy bars, was an absolute must! The urge to turn right singed my brain like a hot iron. J.R. scowled, "It's only four o'clock. We can get another four miles in by supper, easy." He brought out

the heavy artillery, adding, "And if we're late to meet Judith, THE LOOK .
. ." He didn't need to finish the sentence! "Yeah, you're right," I said,
adding, "in the morning, we'll be glad we did the extra miles."

Disappointed but resolute, I squared my shoulders and briskly strode
across the road toward the small opening where the Trail continued on the
other side, only to swing to the right and head down the middle of the
road—much to my amazement and J.R.'s vexation. "Just where the heck
do you think you're going?" he asked, blistering the silence. "Aw, J.R., we
just *can't* miss Woodshole, not being this close. We may never come this
way again." Really miffed, he snarled, "Not on *my* legs, we won't." I tossed
him a carrot. "Don't worry, Worry-wart, we'll get away by six in the morning, or earlier," to which he replied bitterly, "We'd better. And that shower
had better be working, 'or else' . . ." His "or else" carried about as much
threat as a three-legged Chihuahua so I tuned him out and turned my
thoughts to the cold sodas and candy bars that waited just down the road.

The two-story restored log cabin that serves as Tillie Wood's summer
home sat like a stately patriarch in the wide, green clearing. Clearly she
loved this place because her affection showed in the care and attention that
had been lavished on the well-kept buildings and grounds. A long, recessed
porch with several inviting rockers bespoke of pleasant evenings spent in
soft conversation as twilight moves down from the mountaintop to slowly
ease the earth into night. The newly-painted tin roof, its orange-red coat
glowing against the green treetops, seemed to proclaim a message of
spring and rejuvenation as Woodshole joyously welcomed a new season of
flowers and leafy branches—and yes, hikers!

A smaller building set apart from the house also had a porch that
sported an eclectic assortment of seats—now occupied by Skate, Eco, and
The Yoopers. I was surprised to see them and had mistakenly thought they
were hours behind me. (We had leapfrogged one another all day yesterday
and had tented last night near Dismal Creek Falls. They must have passed
me earlier while I ate lunch and grabbed a quick snooze at Wapiti Shelter—scene of murder and mayhem back in the '80's.)

Skate saw me first and squealed, "Model-Teee! It's about time you got
here. Tillie said for us to make ourselves at home and that she would be
down in a little while to say hello." She motioned at the corner of the building. "There's a solar shower around on the side. It even has warm water;
that is, if Eco Warrior didn't use it all." Eco chuckled but didn't rise to the
bait. She pointed at a large white refrigerator in the breezeway. "And
there's sodas and candy, all on the honor system—if Eco hasn't eaten
everything."

Eco laughed. "Naw, I saved some for *you*, Model-T." A true friend!

Following Skate's directions, I climbed a short ladder to the loft, which served as hikers' sleeping quarters (ribbing The Ego with a few choice "I told you so" phrases as I went), shoved my pack against the wall, and made a beeline for the shower.

The sun, already brushing the treetops, was too weak to rejuvenate the solar-heated water, which had been depleted by Eco. (Skate had nailed his guilty hide to the wall of truth!) I quickly soaped and rinsed, shivering under the icy stream, all the time thinking unkind things about Eco. Using my sweaty tee shirt as a towel, I dried off as best I could, pulled my filthy clothes back on, and headed for the refrigerator, giving Eco a recriminating look as I opened the door and got a Coke. I muttered, "Darn, my money is still in my pack," and I put the drink back.

"It's on me, Model-T. I already put the money in the kitty." His face read like a road map of Guilt City. I hoisted the soda, toasting his "generosity" and (after a wicked grin) gave him "absolution." Asked The Ego, "You going to let him off the hook so easy?" I replied, "Are you kidding? A cold shower for a *free* soda! That's the best offer I've had all day!" I popped the tab and took a long, satisfying swallow and he growled, "Well, you don't have to drink it so fast." I, smirking: "Or else . . .?"

A little later, when Tillie and two other ladies came outside to enjoy the evening breeze and soft dusk, as a group we strolled over to the porch. She introduced us to her friends, Juanita Mitchell and Dorothy Mauldin. Juanita (who like Tillie hailed from Roswell, Georgia) accompanied her to Woodshole each season, giving companionship and helping out, especially with the real "southern" breakfast, served in style in Tillie's ornate dining room for the first eight hikers to sign up—all for the ridiculously low price of $3.50.

Dorothy, also known as Ankle Express to her trail friends, had stopped by for a brief visit. A talented poet, she makes the Trail and its hikers come alive in descriptive prose, and then etches the words onto paper in beautiful calligraphy!

Three true "southern" ladies! Immediately, they made us feel like family instead of passing strangers. Skate and the others signed up for the magnificent breakfast. Reluctantly, I declined because the breakfast "bell" would ring at seven sharp, and The Ego and I had better be eating up the miles to Pearisburg by then, or face a real "or else" . . .

True to my word, I silently packed in the dim light of dawn's gray beginning and gobbled a breakfast bar. Skate's sleepy whisper startled me. "Model-T, you and Mrs. 'T' have a good time. Just watch yourself." I patted her shoulder and went down the ladder into the soft morning stillness. Already I felt an emptiness, for Skate is one of those rare individuals who seems to bring out the best in people. Would our paths converge again?

As I walked through the dewy grass, I mentally thanked Tillie Wood for her unselfish generosity and kindness—an angel without a halo. One backward look at the clearing to forever etch it on my mind, and then I began the half-mile walk up Sugar Run Road to the Trail crossing, grinning as I casually glanced at my watch—5:45!

It had rained during the night, although I hadn't awakened. As the dawn brightened, the forest glistened with regenerated promise. Chirping, twittering birds buoyed my spirit as they searched for breakfast amid the dripping leaves, giving voice to the silent music of the universe—a wonderful day in the making! Even the pack felt light and I seemed to walk on springs. J.R. put a spin on things. "Today's the day! Just think, Alter! Real food and clean clothes, and tonight sleeping between clean sheets on a *bed*. And *Judith!*"

Poor Schmook! He could hardly contain himself! Well, let him have his fun—I could afford to be magnanimous for nine days (the compromise we had reached after a heated argument, for he wanted to take two weeks off). "Yeah, Ego, we're gonna have a great time." (That is, until THE LOOK made its debut, but why rain on his parade.) Together, we mocked the birds with off-key chirps and bounced along the Trail like a larger-than-life caricature of Tigger.

Smoke drifted through the trees around Doc's Knob Shelter. Curious, I turned down the blue-blazed path to see who was there; maybe eat a bite, for even though I'd only come a little over two miles since leaving Woodshole, the snack cake was long gone and hunger pains had started to knot my belly. The Ego said, "Keep it short. We still have eight miles left."

A lone hiker sat at a warped picnic table in front of the shelter, trying to coax the last smidgen of peanut butter from an empty jar by running his finger around the inside. Clearly a case of "empty food bag."

I cleared my throat and Mississippi Tripper turned around with a startled look. Relieved to see a friendly schmooz, he pulled his finger from the jar and, smiling wryly, stuck the finger in his mouth and sucked vigorously—a wasted effort for it looked more barren than Old Mother Hubbard's cupboard. I chuckled. "Breakfast?"

Removing his finger, he examined the wet skin. "Yep. It's mighty slim pickin's but this heah's it." His stammered words, embellished by his rich Mississippi accent, evoked scenes of cotton fields and old mansions; of chivalrous gentlemen and beautiful, gowned Southern belles. Licking one last time, he said, "My belly's just 'bout gnawed through mah backbone. Reckon I'd best take myself on to Pearisburg while I can still walk."

I grinned wickedly and blurted, "Dang, some grits would really taste good right now." Tripp looked at me like I was trying to rub salt into his ravaged backbone. J.R. prodded me, "We don't have time to do any cooking," to which I countered, "Not exactly what I had in mind. Just watch."

I took off my pack and dumped its meager contents on the plank surface in front of Tripp. Two packages of instant grits and a crushed fried pie (smashed beyond recognition, although the wrapper was intact) fell out. Not exactly a windfall.

Tripp eyed the grits with a raw, covetous look. Quickly recovering, he flushed with embarrassment and returned his attention to the empty jar—a true southern gentleman! Nonchalantly, I tossed the grits to him and said, "I'd really like to visit but I've got to be at Pearisburg by noon." Then cramming the fried pie into my mouth, I followed with water and then automatically licked the wrapper before tossing it into the fire. "Watch out for whip-o-wills, Tripp. Catch you later," and with a casual wave I headed back to the Trail, smiling to myself at the grateful gleam in his eyes, which told me I had made a friend for life!

He called after me, "Much appreciated, Model-T. Keep on trucking." I turned and replied with a loud "OOOGA!" but Tripp was already cooking grits.

Angels Rest—the northern anchor of Pearis Mountain's fifteen-mile spine! "Aptly named," I told J.R. as I took a badly needed five-minute break before beginning the two-mile descent to Shumate Bridge. The jumble of large boulders overlooked a narrow valley where, two thousand feet below, New River weaved through like a long, wiggly serpent. Miniature cars crawled along a ribbon-like road that wound alongside the silvery flow, sending up faint sounds, which mixed with the manmade odors that rode the up-currents. On the far side of the valley—six miles away, yet seemingly more like an arm's reach—Peter Mountain continued the spine that had fallen beneath the river's onslaught during the rising of the Alleghenies. Everywhere flame azaleas spotted the woods, their orange blossoms beautifully brilliant against the emerald green. Definitely a place for angels to rest on their heavenly sojourns!

Reluctant to leave such beauty, I lingered, turning five minutes into ten as I savored the view, until the minute hand began to gnaw a hole into the serenity as time ran out. Pushing aside the pain and exhaustion, I wobbled to my feet and said, "Okay Ego, let's do it." Energized with excitement, he shouted at some buzzards lazily circling at eyelevel to our front, "Yippie! Get outta my way, you flop-headed turkeys. I'm in afterburner!" Then in his most authoritative Marine-like voice he ordered, "Okay, my man, drive on." Naturally, the buzzards ignored him; and naturally, so did I.

Looking down from the last small hump, we had a good view of Shumate Bridge; but my eyes were automatically drawn to the parking lot at Wade's Grocery, near the east end of the bridge. Crunch time. Would anyone be here to meet us? J.R. bounced around inside my skull like flubber. "Hell's bells, Alter, where is she? Do you see her anywhere? Oh damn! I knew she wouldn't be here. Something has happened!" I don't know where *his* eyes were looking, but *mine* were staring straight at Kelly's champagne-colored Honda mini-van—and the tiny figures that were waving like crazy!

J.R. spotted Judith, Lauren, and Kelly's younger brother, Chris. "Damn, Alter! A real reception! I knew she'd be here." The hypocrite.

I glanced at my watch—11:55 AM, Sunday, 27 May. Returning their waves, we hurried toward the parking lot. I told him, "Have a good time, Ego. See you in nine days," and like the magic genie, I went "poof"!

All the poor Schmook wanted to do was eat and sleep. Ordinarily this wouldn't have caused much of a problem, except that Judith had big plans. For starters, she wanted to go to a gala performance of the Roanoke Symphony, but none of his clothes fit anymore. Trousers that had strained against his belly just eight weeks ago now gathered in folds around his skinny waist, held up by a belt cinched to its last hole. Worse, his size fifteen shirt hung from his wasted frame like it had been mistakenly lifted from the hefty men's rack at Goodwill. (Taking stock in the mirror, he had grumbled about the cruel prank "someone" was playing and had tromped into Kelly's bathroom and jumped on the scales. Then unable to accept that he had lost thirteen pounds, he bounced up and down on the lying machine, trying to loosen up its sluggish internal works. But the scales flipped back to the same reading each time and the Dufus stomped back to the bedroom, loudly complaining that Kelly's scales were broken and if he had his own scales he could *prove* it was all a cruel joke.) Which led to the second problem . . .

He and Judith were practically homeless. Alyson had rented a small apartment across town so she could "get a life." Seizing on the opportunity, Judith closed down their townhouse apartment (the lease having expired), put all of the household goods in temporary storage, and moved in with Kelly and family, since she planned to accompany them to Kentucky in early June to help set up their new home and his office. (When J.R. finished the Trail in September, he and Judith planned to relocate near them.) In the meantime, she had set up a temporary bedroom in their basement—which in itself was not the problem. But, continuously raiding the refrigerator was!

J.R. would tiptoe into the kitchen and ease the refrigerator door open. Then drooling with anticipation (but hoping to escape detection), he would hastily slap together a whopper sandwich out of whatever goodies remained from the previous sneak attack—his favorite: a double slice of bread slathered with mayonnaise, lettuce, four slices of assorted luncheon meat, four slices of cheese, a healthy covering of strawberry jam, three big blobs of peanut butter, more mayonnaise, more lettuce, all topped with two more slices of bread. Masterpiece finished, he would scurry to the bathroom to gorge in private.

Aggravatingly, these four-inch marvels only dulled his appetite for about an hour, at which time and burning with guilt he would traipse back to the kitchen, first making a perfunctory excuse about how thirsty he was since coming off the Trail. A whirlwind creation; a dash for the bathroom; and then more gustatory guilt!

One afternoon Lauren caught him in the act as he piled the makings high and then squashed the giant sandwich to make it look smaller. Busted, J.R. gave her a guilty grin and proceeded to wolf it down, whereupon Lauren, having never seen such a humongous sandwich (not to mention watching one being eaten), had hurried away to find her mother. With her large innocent brown eyes clouded with concern, she asked, "Mommy, is Pap-pa hollow inside?"

Brenda, frustrated at the dwindling food supply, struggled for an answer. "I think he may be, Dear."

That evening at supper, long after the others had finished and departed the table, J.R. (as usual) remained behind to finish off the last morsels, even swabbing the bowls clean with bread. Watching the performance from the sidelines (also a nightly ritual), Lauren explained to sister Jesalyn with the authority of a five year old to a two year old, "Mommy says Pap-pa is hollow inside."

Giggling, Jesalyn toddled over and touched Pap-pa's skinny legs to see if she could feel any peas or other food under the skin. Pap-pa burped a couple of times and asked, "Did you hear those frogs 'ribbit'? There's a bunch of 'em in my belly and they're hungry—especially for little girls!" Chased by a couple of really loud belches, the girls fled squealing, heading for safe haven in Mam-ma's lap and chattering excitedly that she'd better watch out "'cause Pap-pa has man-eating frogs in his belly!"

Listening to the exchange in the next room, J.R. smiled with satisfaction, rubbing his distended belly as the "frogs" serenaded, trying to ignore the nagging reminder that preyed at the fringes of his mind—soon his food-starved brain would send his conscience-stricken body sneaking back to the refrigerator.

Kelly and Brenda both worked, so by necessity Judith had assumed the role of chef—which led to the third problem: J.R.'s voracious appetite kept Judith shackled in the kitchen. If she wasn't running to the supermarket, she was slaving over the hot stove—not one of her favorite pastimes—which meant that between all the cooking and cleaning, her grandiose plans were quickly going down the drain.

On the afternoon of the sixth day, while Judith hurried through preparations for another supper, J.R. sat at the dining table and watched her rush about the kitchen while he neatly polished off a full quart of chocolate ice cream in record time. "Say, Honey, that smells good. What's for supper?"

Judith turned just in time to see him upend the carton and slurp at the tiny stream that dribbled into his open mouth. She scolded him with the tone she used on two-year-old Jesalyn. "I wish you wouldn't do that. You're *not* on the Trail right now." J.R. was busy guiding his tongue into crazy contortions as he tried to coax the last small bit from the carton so her caustic remark passed right over his head. He finished with a loud, satisfied burp and wiped his mouth with his tee shirt, which made Judith frown. Shaking her head, she went to the sink and began to skin chicken breasts without answering his question, but he didn't seem to notice—or care.

I did! Afraid to sink far beneath the patina of the Schmook's consciousness for fear he might commit a *faux pas* that could do irreparable damage and get him (us) pulled off the Trail permanently, I shuddered as THE LOOK briefly surfaced—a dark, ominous shadow flashing across her face like a killer shark flitting over a reef—and then silently disappeared. Blissfully ignorant, The Schmook missed it, but there was no doubt in my mind. Storm clouds were gathering on the horizon! I resolved to remain especially vigilant.

Tossing the empty carton into the trashcan, he asked, "Honey, can you get some more ice cream when you go to the grocery? There's only two more quarts in the fridge." Judith's knife whacked the chicken breast so hard I almost jumped out of his skull. Terrified, I half expected THE LOOK to leap out and spear J.R. through the gozzle, but it stayed put—which told me THE LOOK was saving itself for bigger things!

The Schmook was having a ball (he thought); he had even rationalized his frequent trips to the refrigerator—a necessary embarrassment, for he had to gain back lots of weight, else by the time he reached Katahdin he would be a scrawny skeleton. So the days cloned themselves, one after the next, as he squandered the hours with his drone-like existence. Even the couch had started to develop a permanent depression that exactly matched his skinny butt.

I cringed the moment the first doubts assailed his lethargic reasoning and he started thinking about *not* continuing our journey. Why trade a comfortable bed, air conditioning, all the food he could eat, a real bathroom, and lots more, for the austere rigors of the Trail? Worse, Duty began to yank his chain, and Duty was a strong adversary. It forced him to put on a suit and attend Lauren's first dance recital (where he quickly became a doting grandfather, applauding and beaming with pride as she twirled and pirouetted across the stage in a frilly tutu). Duty sent him outside to mow the lawn—never mind feet and muscles still in turmoil after 600 miles of abuse. And like a scratched record, over and over the wily usurper urged him to remain and help Judith close out the townhouse.

With horror, I suddenly realized that Duty had been replaced by *fun!* J.R. was actually enjoying himself! Like a runaway train careening down a steep track, his mind leapt into the revitalized role of husband and grandfather, tossing all thoughts of returning to the Trail onto the trash pile of deserted dreams. Katahdin had never seemed so far away, and I sunk into despair.

Oddly, an unwilling ally came to my rescue. For although J.R. relished his reentry into "Shangri La," there were still thorns among the roses. One prickly moment had surfaced on day five:

Judith: "I don't see any of your underwear in the wash." An accusation; not a comment.

J.R.: "That's because these are still fresh. I've only worn them for three days." With pride, he adds, "On the Trail, I've worn my shorts for two weeks at a time without washing them."

She, shaking her head angrily: "Well, you're not on the Trail now. You go right this minute and change." THE LOOK leaps to the surface.

He: "Aw heck!" Grumbling, head down, he heads for the bedroom, missing THE LOOK's smirk.

Another instance; day six:

Judith (glaring at J.R. as they sit in a restaurant): "Why do you insist on eating with a spoon. You DO have a fork." THE LOOK springs from her eyes, piercing his brain.

The Schmook, wilting: "But a spoon is so much easier to use. I don't even carry a fork on the Trail."

She, wapishly: "Well, you're not on the Trail now." THE LOOK glowers at him to emphasize the point.

J.R., reaching for his fork (remembering how simple and easy the meals were on the Trail): "Yes, Dear."

The final straw, as they eat breakfast the next morning with the girls (Kelly and Brenda have already left for work):

Judith: "Must you make those annoying noises while you eat?"

J.R. (oblivious, focused on the next bite): "What noises, Dear?" unaware that he has been sucking in air to cool his food before it slides down his throat, or for that matter, that he has been slurping and uttering little sounds of ecstasy with each bite.

Judith: "Those loud slurping noises, like a hog eating slop from a trough." She imitates a couple of exaggerated slurps to make her point. "And all those little 'ooh' and 'aah' and 'hmm' sounds you make while you eat. If you're going to live with me, you'd better shape up."

J.R. (mumbling into his plate, eyes downcast as he flashes back to Chemistry 101): "Yes Ma'am."

Lauren to Jesalyn, giggling: "Pap-pa is a hollow hog. Go 'oink' Pap-pa."

Jesalyn, wondering: "If he's a hog, can he still have frogs in his belly?"

THE LOOK, fixing the poor old coot with a malevolent glare, gloats!

The peccadilloes, of minor consequence taken singly, kept piling up into a large mound of trepidation until J.R. found himself dangling from a limb of indecision—a person wavering between Duty and Fun, or the free, simple life of the Trail, whose memories (resurrected by THE LOOK's damning recriminations) now wafted through his mind like honeysuckled perfume.

Suddenly it was June fourth—their thirtieth anniversary and the last day of playtime, if J.R. honored his pact with me. (We had agreed to get back on the Trail on Tuesday, June fifth, but that was before he got doused with Duty.) This morning, we spoke for the first time since coming off the Trail—a sure sign of his desperation! "Jeez, Alter, what am I going to do?" I replied, "Your call, but Wahoola and Skate and a lot of others will be terribly disappointed if we don't come back." He groaned, "Man! I just don't know." Feeling like a selfish cur I added, "And of course, we can have fifteen hundred more miles of the simple life—without THE LOOK . . ." I let the words dangle and pushed away the stab of shame, reminding myself that Katahdin was at stake! "Jiminy Pete! I just don't know . . ."

I did!

Kelly and Brenda had given him and Judith a gift certificate to a nice, upscale restaurant for their anniversary dinner. The candlelight evening went well. J.R. did his best not to be a trail slob, and Judith was careful not to jump on him for small transgressions. During the meal he postured like a strutting peacock, regaling her with stories of life on the Trail—the hikers, funny incidents, the grandeur. She pretended to hang onto his prattle like they came from the mouth of a venerable soothsayer.

And then the words just slipped out (with a little push from me), becoming a maverick thought crashing into the intimate conversation. "And when you pick me up in Maine, maybe you'll get a chance to meet some of my friends." As soon as the words were spoken, an immense weight fell from his shoulders, although he held his breath and waited for THE LOOK to come.

If it did, it was camouflaged in the cloud that floated across her face. "So you're still going?" The bright mood vanished, casting a pall throughout the room. "I thought you might have had enough." Her face softened as she continued. "But then you wouldn't be happy, not finishing what you set out to do, so it's better you just go on and get it out of your system."

J.R. said earnestly, almost pleading like a small child, "I really want to finish this. Thanks."

Judith smiled, her eyes misty. "It will cost you dessert," but the evening had been sullied by the imminent separation.

Ecstatic, I whispered, "Good call, Ego! Another day or two, and THE LOOK would have eaten you alive. Just think, fifteen hundred more miles . . ." Manipulating the Schmook was as easy as feeding a hungry piranha!

At eight o'clock the next morning, J.R. and Judith stood at the end of Shumate Bridge, heedless of the shaking span as heavy trucks rumbled past as they groped for words of farewell. THE LOOK, locked in its cage for the time being, had been replaced by sad resignation—a heart-wrenching look J.R. was all too familiar with from their many separations during his career as a Marine. After all these years it still cut like a hot knife into his soul.

She gave him a tender, sustaining kiss. "You'd better be going. It'll be hot today."

J.R., gazing through blurred eyes at the large, red ball trying to push through the early morning mist, attempted to control the lump in his throat and said gruffly, "Yeah, it'll be a scorcher." A last hug and he pushed away. "I'll see you in Maine."

He reached the middle of the long span and turned to see if she had left, but she still lingered, anchored to the pavement like a desolate statue. He waved a final time but got no response. I said softly, "C'mon, Marine, let's make some miles. Just think how sweet the 'homecoming' will be." He shrugged, a faint smile chasing away the frown. "It always is." Bolstered by excitement I told him, "I relieve you, Sir. I have the conn." (He liked naval terminology.) Then squaring *my* shoulders, I turned toward the shrouded sun and headed for Katahdin.

Things quickly went to hell in a hand basket. Without warning, summer pounced like a hot tiger, encumbering our progress with hot, sticky days. Short climbs became miserable; long ones almost impossible. Belatedly, I realized the reservoir of stamina that I had developed during these six hundred miles had seeped into the cushions of Kelly's couch, leaving me a weak, rubbery shell. So fighting the heat and gravity and gasping for breath, I plodded over the mountains on trembling, balky legs. The routine: Walk fifty steps; stop and count to fifty; repeat again and again, the steps becoming less and the breaks longer, until I finally gain the summit—another mountain "conquered"—and then try to wallow out of the dull fatigue-haze and marshal enough strength to hike to the bottom and tackle another beast.

Thankfully, the springs and small streams were running, and I drank until my belly sloshed like a large water bag. Sweat poured, sopping my shorts and running down my legs and into my boots, leaving them wet and stained white with salt residue. Every few steps I wiped at my hair and face with my bandanna—wasted effort, for the salty liquid stung my eyes and blurred my vision. Soon my ankles became chaffed, and then bleeding-raw from the constant rubbing of wet, salt-impregnated socks against skin. Mile after mile, day after day, I prayed for rain, but the cloudless sky mocked me and misery rode on my shoulders.

J.R. took to cussing a lot—about anything and everything—bloodsucking bugs, waist-high poison ivy, constant thirst—you name it and he had a fitting epithet. I reminded him, "Which would you rather have, this or THE LOOK? Besides, as long as we can pee we're not going to dry up."

He, grumbling: "THE LOOK doesn't seem so bad right now." How fast mortals tend to forget!

Worst of all, we seemed to be in a hiker vacuum for we hadn't encountered any others of our kind since getting back on the Trail. According to the shelter registers, Moleskin Meg and Doctor Doolittle were a scant half-day ahead. In one register, an entry from Wahoola exhorted me to "partner up" again, but the entry was dated five days ago, and sadly I realized I would probably not see him again. Also Skate and Eco, now a week ahead, had left messages urging me to put my legs in high gear and catch up. So The Ego and I hiked the rippled landscape of southwest Virginia in lonely silence, fighting for each step and wishing for company with which to share our misery.

The days wearily dragged past like a befouled net; landmarks hove into view and then disappeared in summer's sultry haze: A stifling, airless evening at War Spur Shelter (an old friend, where two brash, excited "wannabe's" penned a joint entry in the register, "3/17/90—Planning and preparing for a through hike beginning April 11. Wet and chilly (40-50 degrees) today. Ready to go for it! J.R. Tate and David Jones."). Only three months ago, but it seemed a lifetime! A long break in the welcome shade of the mighty Keffer Oak—already a leafy adolescent when La Salle paddled down the Mississippi—now a venerated patriarch and reportedly the largest oak on the Trail south of the Mason-Dixon line. Passing through sun-drenched alpine meadows dappled with wild daisies—thick quiescent carpets of whites and yellows that danced in the shimmering heat waves—only giving the beauty a cursory glance as I hastened toward the far tree line to escape the searing sun.

Came Sinking Creek Mountain with its broad panorama of earthy colors—a valley landscape so full of God's handiwork that it overwhelmed the fragile fabric of imagination. Came a lonely stone memorial atop Brush Mountain to mark the spot where America's most decorated World War Two veteran met an untimely end in a fiery plane crash in 1971. The Marine and I rendered a solemn, sweaty salute to Audie Leon Murphy, Medal of Honor recipient. Said J.R., "Damn shame he wasn't a Marine." (The words sounded familiar!)

And then came God (or so The Ego thought).

"Gads! This is murder!" I wheezed, gasping for breath, groaning out a gravelly "OOOGA" to celebrate reaching Cove Mountain's summit—the reward for three hours of dogged perseverance on a humid, hundred-degree afternoon. Suddenly dizzy, my legs went spongy so I sank to the ground beside a shaded rock and closed my eyes, too tired to lift my arms and wipe the sweat out of my eyes. "Water; need a drink." The words croaked in my ears (Mine? Spoken out loud?). Wearily, I slipped out of my pack and reached for my water bottle, amazed that less than a cup remained. What had happened to the remainder? "We drank it an hour ago, Dummy." The raspy words again—The Ego's? Greedily gulping half of what was left, I resisted the urge to drain the bottle, quickly replaced the cap, and then shoved the bottle out of reach.

I leaned my head back against the rock and again closed my eyes to escape the sun's powerful thrust, rubbing my temples to ease the mounting headache, but it seemed to pound worse with the world blocked from view. My eyes wandered to nearby Dragon's Tooth—a massive rock that had long ago convulsed out of the summit until it resembled a giant molar nibbling at the hazy blue sky. Immediately, the image pushed some of the throbbing away and my vision, blurred by the onset of heat exhaustion, cleared enough so that I could barely see the top shimmering in the rising heat waves. The Ego cut through the lethargic focusing. "We might as well die here as later on. Another mile in this furnace and heatstroke's gonna kill us anyway." Surely he exaggerated—or did he? I sneaked a quick glance at the midday sun, which did it's best to punch through the scrawny pine branch and sizzle me into a crisp strip. Fanning my face with the soggy bandanna, I vainly tried to stir the air, for the breeze had beat a humiliating retreat from the sun's relentless onslaught hours ago. He was right; heatstroke did indeed hover overhead, ready to pounce.

Thoughts of cool, refreshing Trout Creek tantalized my mind. Before beginning the climb up the long, crescent sweep of Cove Mountain, I had eaten lunch beneath a stately sycamore and dangled my feet in the stream's burbling current while I watched tiny trout minnows dart at cracker crumbs that fell into the water. The picture vanished as another wave of dizziness attacked. Scared that I was about to slip over the edge of consciousness, I decided to risk another small taste of water.

As I reached for the water bottle, a voice came down from the heavens, faint but clear: "Model-T." I looked up but the sky was empty, except for the shimmering heat-haze. Then the voice floated through the stillness once more, a faint, insistent sound: "Model-T." Again I scanned the heavens, but to no avail.

J.R. whispered weakly, "Jesus, Alter! I think we're dead. That must be God Almighty Himself calling us home." A clammy shiver passed down my spine. "Downright weird," I said, and it was! I hadn't felt any stabbing pain, no convulsions; but then again, maybe that's the way it happened—here one second, on the other side the next. Resigned, J.R. muttered, "Yeah, we've croaked."

Not ready to chuck the trip so easily, I told him, "Maybe we're hallucinating; maybe the heat's playing tricks, causing us to hear things." Then the call came again, clear as shattering ice, too real to be a figment of our imagination. Convinced that we *had* expired, I said wearily, "Well hell, there goes Katahdin," and briefly wondered if I might be able to strike some sort of deal with The Almighty to get back on the Trail. J.R. hissed, "Say something for gosh sake. We can't keep God waiting."

Then muddled reasoning prompted me to say, "Hold on now. As busy as The Almighty is, He's not going to waste time doing his own calling. More likely it's Saint Peter, or even Gabriel." J.R. replied haltingly, "You may be right." Thinking back to his childhood Sunday school days, he tried to remember who was supposed to greet arriving souls but drew a blank. I told him, "Well, we can't talk to thin air," so resigned to our fate we quietly waited for the "Greeter" to show himself.

The voice, becoming harsh with impatience, shouted, "Model-T! Up here. On the 'Tooth'!"

Straining to see through the haze, I finally made out a miniature figure waving from the tip of Dragon's Tooth, some three hundred yards distant. "Danged funny way to run an operation," I muttered to J.R. "Why doesn't the front man just swoop on down so we can talk without having to scream our lungs out?" He replied testily, "*We* didn't write the greeting protocol. Maybe we're supposed to fly up there and meet him." Maybe we were! I felt my shoulders—nothing but wet tee shirt. "We're not going to get off the ground without wings. I'm going to find out what's going on." Cupping my hands, I yelled, "Who is it? Are you Saint Peter or Gabriel come to take us up to the Pearly Gate?"

The "Greeter" shouted back, "Naw, it's Indiana Dan. How ya doin?"

I almost peed in J.R.'s shorts! "Much better now, thank you! What th' heck are you doing up there?"

"Just hangin' out. I just got back on the Trail. Been up to Nags Head (North Carolina) for the last week hang-glidin' and havin' fun." His arms seemed to be flapping as he squawked, "How about you?"

The Marine and I held our breath, waiting to see if Indiana Dan was going to swoop off the tip in a hang glider; worse, maybe his mind had gotten addled by the heat and he thought he could fly! But he stayed anchored to the rock, so I yelled back, "Nothing exciting. Just hikin' the Trail."

The last I saw of Indiana Dan, he was standing on top of Dragon's Tooth, flapping his wings like a rooster and crowing into the haze. Said

J.R. as we began the hazardous descent to Lost Spectacles Gap, "Damnation! I really thought he was gonna jump." He sounded disappointed. Sucking on a couple of pebbles to keep my mouth from drying out, I mumbled disgustedly, "The Almighty calling . . . Jeez! You wouldn't know a burp from a jackass's bray."

The next few days flew past in a blur of monotonous drudgery: up at dawn, stagger onto the Trail, get as far as the heat and humidity permitted, then collapse in a puddle of sweaty DNA as the sun sank into the trees. Beautiful country, this Virginia countryside, spotted with lush green fields and staggering views from high cliffs—though little appreciated in the struggle to make another mile or climb another mountain. Adding to the woe, the Trail paralleled the Blue Ridge Parkway for miles, a monotonous mating that ground into the will to persevere. The only salvation: Occasionally the Trail crossed the Parkway at scenic overlooks with magnificent views, where often tourists, ripe for yogi-ing, pulled in for a quick gaze. Curious about the sweltering, bedraggled person foolish enough to be hiking in such heat, they eagerly plied me with cold sodas or water and I gratefully accepted their acts of kindness.

Nearly as bad as the torrid weather was the loneliness. Other than tourists and an infrequent day hiker, the Trail was empty; my peers had simply disappeared. "Holed up in air-conditioned motels—like we should be doing," The Ego grumbled. A red film of jealousy assaulted my senses and I snapped, "Well, I'd better not find out about it. I'll make their lives miserable!" Down deep though, as names disappeared from shelter entries I feared that many, exhausted and discouraged, might have gone home.

At least a few hardy souls still battled the heat. According to the registers, Dead Ahead, now traveling alone (No entries from Wild Bill! Who had the food bag?), was a couple of days ahead; and Wahoola, no longer leaving me messages, had opened the distance to over a week. The Brew and Pizza Group had split up—Captain Sunshine gone home to Florida; Hacker Hiker now a solo act; E Z Strider cruising in high gear, now three weeks ahead; Cup Cake, spurred on by Cupid, barely managing to match his pace.

Flipping back through the pages, old names leaped out like memory mileposts: The Green Mountain Trio; Mississippi Tripper; Geek and Ziggy; The Total Rec's. In one register, an entry from early March: "Ward Leonard; Southbound." An inch of pages later—same register—"Ward Leonard; Northbound."

Concerned, I realized Skate and Eco Warrior had not written any entries in days—disturbing, for they had been ahead of me a week ago. I felt as if I were a castaway drifting alone in this vast mountainous ocean. "Well, Ego," I muttered, resigned to another lonely, stifling night with the mosquitoes and crickets, "maybe tomorrow . . ."

At last the rain came—timidly at first like a scared virgin, then gushing from the sky as if a gigantic plug had been pulled. Soaked (with real water for a change!), I slogged through the downpour and made my way up the short blue-blazed path to Cornelius Creek Shelter. Two men in their mid-twenties, both wearing black Spandex shorts and identical blue windbreakers pulled over white mesh tee shirts, lounged on sleeping bags. Flashy racing helmets hung on the wall, making it easy to guess that these two were bicyclists—especially since two shiny red bikes leaned against the shelter beneath the wide overhang.

I claimed the other end of the shelter and began the familiar ritual or getting out of wet garb and into dry. That job done, I struck up a conversation and quickly learned that they were brothers (Chuck, eldest by two years and firmly entrenched in a corporate job; and Stan, getting ready to grind through a graduate program), and that they were on day three of a two-week bicycle tour of the Blue Ridge Parkway. Stan said, "The Parkway's not far from the shelter. In fact, we brought our bikes down that narrow path." He pointed at the edge of the clearing but I couldn't make the path out in the rainy dusk.

They seemed in no hurry to cook. Ravenous, I had finished by the time they got started. Sprawled on my poncho liner against the far wall, I watched their preparations with weary indifference. Chuck obviously had taken on the role of chief cook, while Stan was saddled with clean up.

Chuck turned to me, bragging, "We just bought this stove. It's the new MSR International model. Burns anything." Grinning with the confidence of a pro, he licked the small gasket on the needle and plugged it into the fuel bottle connector, and then pumped air into the fuel bottle with a few vigorous strokes. Opening the valve, he let a small amount of fuel run into the small cup beneath the generator and confidently intoned, "Four, three . . . Uh, we have a 'hold.'"

The Marine said, "Dang, Alter, he sounds like a rocket scientist."

Apparently not satisfied that he had enough fuel in the cup to go for "lift off," Chuck let in more gas until it nearly overflowed the rim. Then the count resumed. "Two, one, ignition aaand, blast off!" He lit a match and touched it to the fuel.

I watched with amusement as flame shot to the rafters—a common mistake among novices. Chuck told Stan in a voice laced with older brother authority, "Always run in lots of fuel. It makes the generator heat up faster." Impressed, Stan watched as the flame settled back down, flickered a few moments, and then died. Chuck opened the valve again and lit the misty vapor that spewed from the heated generator, and then trimmed the flame into a steady, blue orb. Not a bad job so far—except for scorching the rafters. "Okay, I'm ready to cook," he announced.

Stan handed him a small pan filled with water but Chuck said, "Hold on a minute. I forgot the heat shield." (Two pliable aluminum shields come with most MSR stoves: The circular one, put in place first, acts as a barrier between the flame and the fuel hose to reflect heat upward and keep the fuel hose from catching fire. The other shield forms a cylinder around the stove to trap the heat and fend off the wind, which can steal the heat and extend cooking time considerably. For safety's sake, the cylinder should never be used without the circle, for then there's nothing to shield the flame from the fuel hose.)

Chuck grabbed the cylindrical outer shield, snugged it tightly around the stove, and braced the overlapping ends with his sneaker. "There. That oughta take care of it. Okay, hand me the pan."

My indifference melted away as I watched the pot begin to steam and then come to a roiling boil. As Chuck poured some kind of grain cereal into the pan, The Ego said, "Maybe we should say something." I thought about it. "Naw, experience is the best teacher. Besides, it might not happen." He: "And then again it might."

Reconsidering, I asked, "Uh, Chuck, do you guys always cook without the base shield? A lot of heat can build up under that pan."

He considered the question. "It'll be okay. Most of the heat goes into the pan's bottom."

He spoke with confidence, like he knew what he was talking about. Maybe he really was a rocket scientist! "Okay Ego, I tried."

Moments later, we watched with fascination as the intense heat melted the fuel hose and fire engulfed the stove, their supper, and once again roasted the rafters. Chuck kicked the fiery mess to the ground outside, narrowly missing one of the shiny bikes, while Stan beat at the flames which, fed by the leaking fuel, greedily licked at the floor.

Helpless to do anything else, they watched until the blaze finally died and darkness softly returned to the forest. "Damn!" Chuck muttered. (A pretty trite oath, I thought, after *those* fireworks. "Crud-mamma'n far" would have worked well, but that probably wasn't in his epithet inventory.)

Generously, I asked, "You fellas want to borrow my stove? I'll be glad to set it up for you."

Stan gazed at the tarnished image of his incensed brother, who was attempting to salvage what was left of his smoldering sneaker, and said, "Thanks, but I think I'll eat some crackers and peanut butter and call it a day."

Undaunted, I told them, "Well, there's an outfitter at Roanoke. It's only about fifty or sixty miles by road." They didn't say anything. "And there's another outfitter at Waynesboro, but that's a good hundred miles north."

Chuck pitched his ruined shoe out into the rain and grunted, "Thanks, but we'll be okay. Say, Bro, when you get done pass the peanut butter."

I crawled inside my poncho liner, my conscience only slightly muddied, and drifted off listening to the "rocket scientist" compete with the rain pelting the roof as he attempted to explain to his younger brother about how "we could repair the stove if only we could find the right kind of tubing and a clamp and a certain tool and . . ."

Fat chance! A final comment from J.R. about the evening's excitement: "Now *that's* what I call entertainment." I replied groggily, "Free, too. Go to sleep."

Two days later, as I ate a late lunch at Johns Hollow Shelter, two hikers emerged from the trees. "Model-Teeee!" Even before I saw the faces, I recognized that high-pitched screech.

"Where the heck have you two been?" I asked, more relieved than curious, for I hadn't seen Skate or Eco since Woodshole.

After giant bear hugs, she answered, "Eco broke his foot."

I glanced at his feet but saw no cast—only heavy new all-leather boots—and raised an eyebrow. He mumbled something about having a stupid accident that somehow involved a bed, but I couldn't follow what he said and asked him to repeat it.

He shuffled like a tot being scolded for not eating his veggies. Giving me a wry, embarrassed look, he blurted, "I broke it against a bed."

"A what? Did you say 'bed'?"

"Yes, a daggone bed!"

I waited for an explanation but he closed the subject by taking off his pack and lying down on the floor with his eyes shut. Skate said, "Drug time," and fished a plastic bag filled with white tablets from her pack. "Here, Eco," she said, handing him two pills. "Make it last." He swallowed them and lay back down.

"Hurting, huh?" I asked Skate. "What really happened?"

"Just like he said, a 'bed'. When we reached Cloverdale (a thriving community just off of I-81, through which the Trail passes after skirting Roanoke), we decided to take a rest day and agreed to split the cost of a motel room." (This is an accepted practice among the trail community, especially when dollars are in short supply, as happens most of the time. Sharing a room with a member(s) of the opposite sex is strictly a unisex convenience—no impropriety implied.)

"When Eco got up in the middle of the night to use the bathroom, he stubbed his foot against a bedpost."

Unable to hike the next morning, he and Skate had hitched a ride to Roanoke. An X-ray revealed a stress fracture, which prompted the young doctor to shake his head sadly and tell Eco that his trip had come to an end. Eco responded to this dire prediction by snapping, "Bull! I'm going to Maine if I have to crawl!" whereupon the doctor, being a hiker of sorts himself, shrugged his shoulders and said, "Yes, you might have to do that," and gave Eco a handful of Tylenol III tablets. He also told Eco to go an outfitter and buy the stiffest-soled boots he could find, which he did.

Since then, Skate had stuck with him, indulging her "mothering instinct" and parceling out Tylenol III when Eco's pain outdistanced his machismo. My respect for Skate, already high, went through the troposphere. As for Eco Warrior, he had "the right stuff", but hiking with a broken foot? Not too bright. (However, I did know a skew-brained Marine who had carried out dumber stunts!) "You've got guts, Eco," I said. "Dang! It's good to see you both again!" Skate's smile reminded me of a momma sow whose piglets had come home after a day of carousing in the hog lot.

Ottie Cline Powell might have been awed to know that the little piece of Bluff Mountain summit where he died would one day be enshrined to his memory. Little Ottie, as he is affectionately known by generations of hikers, was sent outside by his teacher one cold winter day to get an armful of firewood to keep the old wood stove going at Tower Hill Schoolhouse. He wandered away and was found five months later, on April 5, 1891, some seven miles and several mountains from the school. Little Ottie was just shy of his fifth birthday when he disappeared.

I shielded my eyes from the late afternoon sun, which cast an odd, elongated shadow from the small stone that had been placed in the middle of the Trail to mark the exact spot where Little Ottie's body had been found, and watched as Skate doled out more tablets to Eco—his first since leaving Johns Hollow five hours ago. Clashing with the isolated mountaintop were coins, odd-shaped stones, small bouquets of wild flowers, and similar items placed at the base of the marker by passersby as tokens of memorial.

We sat in silence, each with our own thoughts. Mine turned inward to the fragileness of our existence, accented by a moment frozen in time: A small face smiling with pride at the important mission entrusted to him;

walking through the schoolhouse door into the cold Virginia countryside, never again to be seen until found atop this high mountain; his small crumpled body an incongruous mound among the summit's rocks. How had he gotten this far? How long had he sat here, a scared little boy looking off into the haze-filled valleys, whimpering for his family until, finally anesthetized by helplessness and despair, he just lay down and went to sleep? Where was he now buried?

A ripple of sadness coursed through my mind and my eyes misted. Blinking back tears, I dug into my belt pouch, found a coin, and gently placed it by the other tokens as I offered up a silent salutation, "Rest in peace, Little Ottie." Gruffly, I told my companions, "See you down at the Punchbowl."

That night at Punchbowl Shelter—aptly named for the nearby pond, which shimmered like a large flat mirror as it reflected moonbeams back toward the glittering stars—I lay beneath my mosquito net, listening to mosquitoes hum and enjoying the deep, croaky "ribbit" of an old bullfrog. I had the night to myself, for Skate and Eco had quickly gone to sleep as darkness descended. The waxing moon cast an eerie, yellow glow into the woods, creating a spectral display that teased my eyes and played tricks with my mind. Here and there, tiny pockets of phosphorescence illuminated the forest floor like frozen fireflies, then faded into the dark.

Suddenly, one of the shadows moved and my heart leaped against my chest! Startled, The Ego hissed, "Little Ottie!" (According to trail gossip, his ghost had *actually been seen here* on moonlit nights—his slight form walking at the edge of the clearing, his arms reaching out for help toward bewildered hikers, his small face streaked with tears.) I stared at the shadow, spellbound, unable to breathe. Could it actually be!

The shadow took form and a doe cautiously walked into the clearing, quietly nuzzling the grass. Relieved, I exhaled loudly, causing the deer to freeze and gaze at the shelter. Satisfied there was no threat, it resumed grazing.

I stared into the phantom shadows for a long time, listening to the old bullfrog, wondering if perhaps it might be Little Ottie reincarnated. Eventually I slept.

Breakfast at Pedlar Dam the next morning was a hoot!

The dam, which backs up water into a beautiful reservoir that serves as the main water supply for the people of Lynchburg, Virginia, formed a "postcard" picture. Water spilled over the top, sliding down the entire width of the dam's steep concrete slope in a continuous thin, sparkling sheet, infusing the air with refreshing, oxygenated vapor. I inhaled deeply several times and sat down on the steps of the sturdy footbridge that crossed the runoff stream. A perfect place for breakfast—and I had it all to myself!

Except for three curious horses and one persistent mule, that is. One of the horses immediately ambled over and got right in my face, nuzzling my beard for a crumb. What intimacy! I gave it a nibble of cookie—a mistake—for the other two decided they wanted in on the action. The mule, determined to hog the show by eliminating the competition, charged in, biting and braying, ears laid back, heels kicking. That mule wasn't satisfied until he had chased the three horses a half-mile to the far end of the field. Excited, The Jarhead yelled, "Son of an ass! That critter's got Marine blood in his veins. Yee-haa! Go get'em, Chesty!"

By the time the mule trotted back, I was already headed across the footbridge. But I did leave him half a cookie (at The Jarhead's insistence).

Realizing that Eco wouldn't be able to make many miles a day until his foot healed (if it did), I had said goodbye last evening at Punchbowl Shelter—a sad parting, for we realized we might not see each other again. So now determined to pick up the pace, I sank back into the hiker vacuum.

I "dined" at the small picnic area beside busy US Highway 60, all the time desperately wishing that some lucky tourists would pull in and let me liberate them from whatever food they had stashed inside their air-conditioned cars (in exchange for a few Trail stories, of course—always "quid pro quo")! Instead, the cars whizzed past while I gagged on dry ramen noodles mixed with tang and peanut butter. The minutes stretched into an hour and still no one stopped. I gave it another frustrating twenty minutes, then tossed a few "crud-mamma'n" insults at the unheeding motorists and reluctantly began the long, hot climb up Bald Knob.

And spotted a cougar!

After two hours of strenuous climbing I reached the top and had just started walking along the relatively flat, broad spine when J.R. asked, "What's that big tomcat doing up here?" About thirty yards ahead, a large cat padded up the Trail. Startled, I stopped in mid-stride and gasped, "Darn! That's no tomcat. It's a cougar!"

The cat must have heard us for it stopped and swung its head around, eyeing me curiously while the tail, so long that it almost dragged the ground, twitched ever so lightly. "Sonofagun J.R., it *is* a cougar! I've got to get a picture!" Ever so slowly, I moved my hand down to the belt pouch, removed the camera, and brought it up to my eye. "Please," I silently prayed, "just one shot."

It never occurred to me that the cougar might attack, for I was too taken with the moment. I was going to bag me a cougar! It stood like a statue, ears laid back as if it were posing. Excited, I pushed the wrong button (the one that opens the lens for a wide panoramic view but makes the subject smaller). The faint click galvanized the cougar into action; cursing, I slipped my finger a fraction to the right and snapped the shutter just as the cougar leaped into the underbrush.

Trembling, I stared through the viewfinder at the empty Trail. "Damn! I can't believe I screwed that up. All I got was a tail shot. Damn! Damn! Damn!" Disgusted, I kicked at a rotted log beside the pathway, stomping mushy wood into pulp. The Ego tried to console me. "Heck Alter, so what if we didn't get a perfect shot. We have the real picture tucked away in our brain." Rankled with disappointment, I growled, "Yeah, but try to make a negative out of *that!*" He countered, "Look on the bright side: 'Stolen water is sweet, and bread eaten in secret is pleasant.'" Unable to help it, I asked, "One of Pap's sayings?" Chuckling, he replied, "Nope, Proverbs." Sometimes The Marine amazed me!

I stood on The Priest—a gigantic mountain that was birthed eons ago by a massive upheaval of the bedrock on which Pedlar Dam rests, some twenty-five miles back down the Trail—and stared down at the Tye River, nearly three thousand feet below. Joining hands with Time, the rolling stream had sliced through the magnificent chain of mountains like a liquid sword carving a snow bank in halves. Beyond the cut, Three Ridges (tomorrow's challenge) simmered in the heat-haze, just waiting.

"Too late to tackle a four-mile knee buster today," I told J.R., turning in at the blue-blazed path to the shelter. "Tyro can wait until tomorrow." (We had a mail drop at the tiny hamlet a mile off the Trail.)

Capt. Noah, a former high school teacher in his late twenties, now at a career crossroads, was the lone occupant. Lithe and muscular, he resembled a hockey player more than a teacher, although he hoped to continue as an educator after finishing the Trail in mid-August—a month and a half before my expected date to finish! We enjoyed a quiet evening together, but with him moving in the fast lane, it was only a random brush of two souls on the road to Katahdin.

The next morning, by the time I had packed and started down the torturous descent, Capt. Noah was long gone. I hadn't gotten far when food possibilities at Tyro began to prey on my mind, and suddenly the glorious image of a bologna sandwich appeared in Technicolor! It grew with each step, until it assumed monstrous proportions, with great gobs of mustard dripping from huge slices of bread. And by the time I reached the highway at the bottom of the mountain, drool oozed down my beard like a long, shiny, transparent worm.

I heard a vehicle coming—bad timing, for the road was still several yards away—but I decided to try for it anyway. Dashing across a dirt-packed parking area, I stuck out my thumb just as a pickup whizzed past. Brake lights flashed and wheels screeched, and I ran toward the truck.

"Tyro?" I panted. One of the two men in trout fishing garb nodded his head and motioned toward the bed. Grateful, I climbed in and we sped away. "Hot dang, J.R.! Bologna sandwich, here we come!"

Tyro was only a narrow swelling beside the pavement—mainly a peeling, white-frame building with a wobbly porch. I was surprised to see Capt. Noah, who lounged against a post eating a snack cake and drinking a soda, and acknowledged his gustatory grin with a perfunctory greeting as I rushed inside. That bologna sandwich still burned my mind!

Storeowner and postmaster Byron Bradley, a kindly gentleman of sixty or so with friendly eyes, greeted me from behind a counter reminiscent of the 1940's. Next to the counter a glass-enclosed case displayed several kinds of luncheon meat, and I quickly spotted what I wanted!

"Can I get a bologna sandwich?"

"Why sure. I can make you any kind you want. How many slices?" Mr. Bradley wiped his hands on a stained apron that covered matching dark gray cotton-twill shirt and trousers—a practical man. And he sure knew his thru-hikers!

Overcome with anticipation, I blurted, "I want a big one. How thick are the slices?"

He lifted a large roll of bologna from the case and asked, "Just how thick a slice do you want?" Resting a big butcher knife against the roll, he measured off a half inch. "About like this?"

Slobbering like a rabid dog, I spluttered, "Maybe a little thicker. About this big," and I opened the space between my thumb and finger about two inches wide.

He chuckled, "I never cut one *that* big, but I'll sure do it if that's what you want." I liked this man!

Just to be on the safe side, I increased the distance another half-inch. Mr. Bradley eyeballed my hand, adjusting the knife until I nodded my approval, and then whacked off the large slab. Expertly catching it with a piece of waxed paper, he laid it on an ancient scale and said, "One pound, four ounces. Now how do you want it, on bread or with crackers?"

"Bread is fine—four slices, please; two on each side and don't spare the mustard." I thought for a second. And how about a thick slice of onion, too?"

Mr. Bradley knew how to make a thru-hiker sandwich! I got a large soda, paid him, and took the masterpiece outside to make a fantasy come true!

Leaning back against the porch wall, I tried to wash the last bite down with a second soda. Already I could feel the sandwich congeal into a brick-like lump in my stomach as I fought a twinge of bloated nausea and did my best to squeeze the picture of Pap's wagging finger from my mind. Just the thought of putting on my pack and climbing Three Ridges made me cringe.

Amused by my gluttony, Capt. Noah said, "I didn't think you could do it, Model-T. Impressive performance." I burped loudly, acknowledging the compliment (hoping I wasn't going to have to dash to the rear of the store and upchuck my fantasy), but his attention had shifted to a lone figure walking down the highway from whence we had come. In the shimmering heat waves, the person resembled a dancing apparition.

"You know him?" I asked.

"It looks like Warren Doyle."

Great! One of the three people I really wanted to meet during this thru-hike. (Ed Garvey and the blind hiker, Bill Irwin, were still somewhere back down the Trail—as far as I knew.)

When the hiker strode up to the porch, I stuck out my hand. "Dr. Doyle, I presume. I'm Model-T."

He gave my hand a perfunctory shake and said, "Warren, if you please."

No pretentious airs here: Stocky; a few pounds on the heavy side; filthy sneakers; a long, sweat-stained, blue tee shirt that hung so far down it covered his shorts; a blue ball cap with an A.T. patch on the front—Warren Doyle looked anything but a distinguished Professor for Appalachian Studies at George Mason University. The face behind dark-rimmed glasses didn't look a day older than forty, although a short jaw-line beard may have masked his true age. But there was something about the eyes that reminded me of The Marine—an impenetrable barrier built from years of distancing himself from underlings in order to preserve the dignity of leadership and sidestep the pitfalls of familiarity.

I immediately decided it would be difficult to breach that barrier. In spite of the commonality of the Trail family, Warren Doyle would be a hard man to get to know.

But he didn't mind talking. Warren was on his ninth thru-hike, and he was leading a "Circle" of thirteen hikers from Georgia to Maine. (Actually, as I gleaned from his explanation, the "Circle" was a ceremony wherein the participants committed themselves to completing the hike.) Warren told me he had twelve such ceremonies planned at predetermined locations on the journey. So far, all but three had joined the "Circle," a serious decision, Warren explained, for ". . . if someone joins and then drops out, the 'Circle' will be broken."

Also, he and others of his group had undertaken the task of pushing a measuring wheel the entire length of the AT in order to compare mileages with ATC's official length of 2142.8 miles. (I also found out the group had a support vehicle, which carried their food and equipment and met them at agreed-on road crossings at day's end. Thus, the group could get by with daypacks and cover a lot more miles.)

"Where's your group?" I asked.

Smiling faintly, he said, "They're swimming up at the Trailhead. I came down to buy drinks and ice cream for them."

Warren chuckled when I told him about dangling my feet in his old bathtub at Kimberling Creek (though I didn't mention the empty beer bottle or my overactive imagination).

He sighed, a faraway look creeping into his eyes. "Yes, I had some fine times in that old tub." The look turned sad. "Now, it's only an eyesore." Shrugging, he went into the store.

But the mood he invoked lingered like a foul odor. I imagined a young Warren and his friends splashing and playing, yelling at each other's antics as they jumped in and out of the stained tub. Rusty memories; remnants of days forever gone. Fun times; sad times . . .

Suddenly I felt nauseated. "Dammit J.R., we've got to swear off of bologna." I went back inside, prepared to endure Mr. Bradley's sympathetic "I-told-you-so" grin with appropriate humility, and meekly asked for an Alka Seltzer.

Back at the Trailhead, courtesy of Mr. Bradley arranging a ride with one of his customers, I said goodbye to Capt. Noah (who took off like a bullet) and Warren, and then set out across the beautiful, bouncy suspension footbridge that spanned the river. A short distance downstream, the "Circle" romped and splashed in the water, young and old alike. Someone spied Warren, and the group made a mad dash for the bank, squealing like starved pigs as he began to unload cartons of ice cream and sodas from a large sack.

Amused, I stood in mid-bridge and watched the antics. Someone yelled my name. "Model-Teee! Down here." Skate, her long pigtails streaming water down onto her bright tie-dye shirt, waved frantically to get my attention. "Warren's going to slack pack Eco and me until Eco's foot gets better. See you in Waynesboro!"

I gave her a "thumbs-up" and passed on across the bridge. Unbidden, a burp erupted, long and loud, and essence of oniony bologna flooded the damp air, causing me to gag and grimace. I gave a sigh of desperation and began the long 3000-foot climb up Three Ridges. Without warning a cloud of face gnats—tiny black instruments of torture—swarmed down, each determined to get inside my head by any means possible. Frustrated, I slapped and waved my arms like a wild man, but the gyrations only made the gnats more determined and added to their fun.

"Crud-mamma'n gnats; crud-mamma'n pack; friggin' crud-mamma'n Trail. Crud! Crud! Crud!"

The tantrum made me feel better and I blurted, "Jeez, Ego, maybe Ol' Bubba was on to something after all!" I tromped on up the Trail, thrashing, swearing, burping, calling down curses on the little, bologna-frenzied, black bastards that tried to drive me insane! J.R. soon joined my tirade.

Model-T (left) and Wahoola ready to head for Maine

Wahoola and Volunteer (far right) make camp

Snickers time!

Cupcake, E Z Strider, and Big Macs at Mt. Collins Shelter

Mule (left) takes a break from cheap "cal'ries" at Club Geek

Breakfast, Model-T style

Ice cream at 3-B's. From left: Skate, Eco Warrior, Model-T, and The Orient Express

Under the water tower at Greymoor Monastery

Halfway!

Telephone Pioneers Shelter—after water! Back row: Shug, Journeyman, Journalist, Mule, Model-T. Front: Melanie and Tim of Thatcher's Children, Tripp, and Dog

A sad farewell to Jan and Bruno at The Inn at Long Trail

Model-T and Tripp in the "pit" on Mt. Moosilauke

Walkin' on the Happy Side of Misery—Franconia Ridge with Mt. Lafayette in the background

Moleskin Meg and Wahoola crossing the Kennebec, with a helpful shove by Pennsylvania Creeper

The "legend" and Model-T's mentor, Ed Garvey, who never cleaned his cook pot

Mahoosuc Notch—"virtual" Trail

Bridging West Branch of Pleasant River—Maine style

Mainlining!

Paying homage to "the greatest mountain' from the placid bank of Daicey Pond

Katahdin!

CHAPTER 7

A Windless Sea
Sails no Ships

The gnat-horde dogged my steps for a couple of miles, buzzing in a thick, black cloud around my head, trying to crawl into my mouth, darting into my eyes and up my nose in crazy kamikaze attacks, vying with each other for a sweaty drink. Every gnat within three miles must have gotten the news: "Hey! Didya hear th' latest? Another human-thingy's headin' up th' mountain! Free booze for all! Hurry!" Snorting to dislodge the interlopers while grinding my fingers into my eyes, I screeched with sadistic glee, "Two more of th' little bastards down; only a gazillion left! Crudmamma'n little freakin' bastards!"

But no amount of slapping, screaming, or cussing, seemed to discourage their assault. I squished them between my sweaty fingers, watching with fanatical delight as they dissolved into sweaty black scum. With every breath, I sucked gnats into my mouth, gagging as they stuck to the back of my throat. I tried to dislodge them by spitting my way up the Trail but always seemed to end up forcing them down into my belly with a mouthful of saliva. In spite of my best efforts, hundreds must have ended up in my stomach. The Marine complained, "Jeez! It wasn't *this* bad in the jungles of 'Nam." Frustrated, I snapped, "Quit your bitchin'. Gnat goulash can't be any worse than snake soup. Besides, look at all the protein we're gettin', and free at that."

The one bright spot in my misery: The gnats had to travel a lot further than I did as they continuously swarmed around my head.

Eventually the gnats thinned out to a tolerable plague, and the climb up Three Ridges became an ordeal of guts and persistence. The temperature shot into the high nineties, which, along with the sweltering humidity and lack of breeze, turned the afternoon into a gigantic sauna. The effect was like being trapped in an oven set on slow bake. J.R. urged me to stop and rest more often, his logic being, "A windless sea sails no ships." Plaintively I replied, "We're not ships. We don't even have sails—but I'll concede that we are windless." He replied snottily, "And stupid for being out here." I was too miserable to bicker.

He was nearer right than wrong though. The scorching heat had sapped my strength, leaving me doddery and nauseous. Sweat dripped onto the dusty path, marking my progress, and the ring of dark splotches made it easy to see where I had paused to catch my breath—a scary truth-teller, for as the weary afternoon's struggle dragged out the rings drew closer together. Rough going!

A tingly shiver swept over my skin and I caught my breath. Heat exhaustion? Another one, longer, more convincing. Alarmed, I realized the sweat wasn't trickling like it had just minutes before. The climb up to Dragon's Tooth had been bad, but this was downright scary. J.R. voiced the threat in grim tones, "If we get heat stroke up here, we're dead!" I couldn't have agreed more.

I plodded on a few yards until I reached a small shaded spot. Ignoring a patch of poison ivy—the least of my immediate problems—I slid to the ground, pack still on, and leaned against the tree. "Strange, Ego, but I feel chilled." He urged, "Drink some water. It'll help." I managed to maneuver the water bottle out of the pack's side pocket stared dully at the contents— over three-fourths gone! "Jesus, Alter, where'd all the water go?" he gasped. I squeezed the sweat out of the bandanna, wiped my face, and motioned at the spotted dirt beside my leg. "The Trail got it." Taking a tiny swallow, mostly to wet my tongue, which had begun to feel like a football crammed into my mouth, I croaked, "We gotta make it last. Can't get any more 'till we get to Maupin Field Shelter. That is, unless The Almighty sends some rain." For some reason, that struck me as funny—nary a cloud anywhere for Him to work with—and I cackled out loud.

"And just how far would that be?" he growled. I opened my mouth to take another sip of water and a gnat managed to sneak inside, getting all the way to the back of my throat before meeting its untimely end. Gagging, I swallowed water and flailed at the thin cloud that swirled around my face. "Dadblamed gnats, go find your own water!" He persisted. "How far?" I rubbed a gnat out of my eye. "Don't know. Probably no more'n a couple of miles. Just don't get your panties in a twist, Worry-wart. We're gonna make it." He growled, "We'd better," and I retorted, "Or else?"

A few clouds wandered into the blue overhead, creeping in from a dark band that rapidly rose on the near horizon—a thunderstorm in the making? Could we be so lucky! Without warning, a tantalizing zephyr stirred the air as a cloud moved across the sun, bringing immediate relief. I sat for a few more minutes with eyes closed against the gnats, waiting for the chills to subside. Then gritting my teeth, I pushed to my feet and muttered, "Okay, Marine, let's get it done. We're runnin' on spit and gnat juice now."

Before long I came down off the high ridgeline and entered an area of dense forest with its interior darkened by the thickening sky. Distant thunder echoed across the mountains, bringing hope, and wilted leaves started to come to life as the wind freshened. "Hot dang, Ego! It's gonna rain!"

Something began to fall, rattling the leaves. "It's rain!" I whooped. "We're saved!" He prodded me, "What're you waiting for? Let's collect some water!" I slid the pack off my shoulders, yanked out the tarp, and rigged it beneath a large limb so it could catch the precious drops. "All right, Marine! We're gonna guzzle a cloud or two!"

We waited expectantly—and then stared dumbly at the little black-green pellets that trickled onto the fabric. "Frass," he snarled with disgust. "We pray for rain and we get caterpillar poop."

I looked up. Clinging to the foliage, thousands of grayish-black, hairy, gypsy moth caterpillars frenziedly crunched, sending down a steady shower of tiny, dark beads as they worked to decimate the forest canopy. Dozens of frass pellets peppered my face, and I quickly lowered my head before the nasty stuff fell into my mouth—gnats in my belly were one thing but I drew the line at caterpillar poop!

Feeling like the victim of a cruel prank, I shook out the tarp and stuffed it back in the pack. "Hell's bells, Ego! Where'd all this come from?" It was as if a line had been drawn through the trees, for we'd had no warning. He asked the more important question: "How far do you think this goes?" Dejected, I shrugged and said bitterly, "I don't have the slightest idea, but it's the only 'rain' we're going to get." For like a wily sorcerer, the sun peeked through a hole left by the receding clouds, which now scurried off to the southwest taking the feisty breeze with them. I clenched my jaws and trudged on through the gently falling "rain."

By the time I neared Maupin Field Shelter, the thousands had multiplied into a plague and the "shower" had mushroomed into a "cloudburst." Also, the gnats had mysteriously disappeared. Searching for an explanation, I said, "Maybe gnats don't fly in the rain, whether it's falling worm crap or the real stuff." He thought it over, "Or it could be that caterpillars eat gnats—or anything else they can get their crummy little mouths on. Like hikers for instance, when they run out of leaves."

"Cripes," I muttered, catching a vision of an unsuspecting hiker grabbing a short nap beneath a worm-infested tree and waking up covered with the filthy things! "You're giving me the creeps! I'll trade worms for gnats any day!"

Something tickled my hair. Instinctively I smacked at it and my hand came away sticky, smeared with green, slimy worm guts. Gagging, I wiped the disgusting stuff off with the bottom of my tee shirt (making a mental note not to use that area to wipe my mouth or cook pot). The same thing happened again before I had gone a dozen steps. Without thinking I slapped and made instant gore out of another fallen caterpillar. Slap; squish. Slap; squish; and before long, my hair began to stink like a week-old roadside possum.

The Marine cut through the routine. "It's a sad state of affairs when the idiot I'm stuck with doesn't know enough to 'flick' instead of 'swat,'" he snarled. "Huh, what'dya say?" I only half heard him, busy as I was concentrating on the top of my head, waiting for the next "dropper." He repeated, "Just flick'em off, Dumbhead. It's a lot tidier than having worm goop smeared all over your moronic noggin." Irked at being called a "Dumbhead" (actually, mostly irritated for not thinking of it myself), I muttered, "Any 'dufus' that'd eat a garter snake shouldn't mind a little worm mush," but he'd had his say and didn't reply.

By the time we reached the shelter, I had pretty well gotten the hang of it: Let the caterpillar crawl from my head onto a finger, then flick it to the ground and stomp it several times with fiendish gusto. "More 'free' Trail entertainment?" the Dufus asked. I: "Hey, out here fun's where you find it. Let's find the spring."

It was a cesspool. Hundreds of dead caterpillars, bloated and black, formed a stinking mess on the sluggish surface. My brain screamed for water and my mouth was so dry I could hardly swallow. Desperate, I forced my eyes to look at the abomination and faced the grim realization that this was all we had. Thick gorge burned my throat, but I choked it back.

J.R. snarled, "Don't even think about it! We can't drink this crud." I snapped back, "Why the heck not? We've been eating gnats all afternoon. It's either this or death by desiccation, and I'm not ready to be turned into jerky yet." Praying I wouldn't barf in front of The Marine, I gritted my teeth and plunged the water bottle through the floating wormy hell, into the water beneath. Holding it there until the air bubbles ceased, I quickly yanked it up through the crust and eyeballed the dingy-brown liquid. Horsepiss or dark beer? Determined to make the best of the screwy situation, I quipped in my best Limey imitation, "I say, Old Top, anyone for a bit of exotic tea? Brewed in Nature's own cauldron, exclusively for us. Now, do you take one iodine, or two?" Facing the inevitable, his resistance crumbled. "Three if you please, Old Chap."

I began to giggle at our ridiculous situation, then so did J.R., and suddenly we started to laugh hysterically (though the sounds that spilled from my swollen throat sounded like raspy croaks). The harder we laughed; the more I croaked, which fueled more laughter. Finally spent, almost too exhausted to move and wheezing for air, I dropped four iodine tablets into the "tea"—an extra one just to be on the safe side. Shaking the bottle to hasten the process, I watched the iodine dissolve and waited impatiently for several minutes to let the purifier do its work. And then came the moment of truth.

"Bottoms up and cheers!" Closing my eyes, I filled my mind with a large, frosted tumbler of cold, premium lager; and drained the bottle. Trying to stay focused on the beer and not gag, I said, "Another round on me, Bartender, and hold the frass this time. My friend here's dryer'n a desiccated dingo." I chugalugged another one and then refilled both bottles. "Okay Old Top, let's go see what's in the pantry." So much for worms!

Another car whizzed by, then six in a row—all late models, expensive and polished to a mirror-like sheen. The elegant passengers, most decked out in finery suggestive of a night on the town, ignored my extended thumb.

"Well, chicken-nasty!" I exploded. Like a quick-change chameleon, I hurriedly switched the snarl to a smile as a blue Lincoln Town Car approached. It speeded up and roared past as if the driver were attempting to avert a cloud of pestilence. My smile decayed into anger and I shouted again, "Chicken-nasty on your car!" J.R. grumbled, "Without a doubt, that's the most pathetic cussing I've ever heard. If you're determined to swear, at least do it right. 'Chicken-nasty' is something a 'swabbie' might whimper if he mashed his pinkie."

"Okay, Pea Brain," I barked, "if you think you can do any better, go right ahead," but he growled, "Marine officers are 'gentlemen' by an act of Congress and do not swear." Horse's ass! "Yeah, sure, and I've got the combination to Fort Knox." Frustrated, I glanced at my watch—5:45 PM— as another string of traffic zipped past and vanished down the mountain. "Dang it all! Thirty minutes wasted!"

Rockfish Gap wasn't the best place to hitch a ride; but it was either that or walk the five miles down the mountain into Waynesboro—a necessary detour to buy enough food to get through the Shenandoah National Park and on to Linden, Virginia (my next mail drop), 115 miles away. Nope, there was no getting around it. I had to go into Waynesboro, and walking was out of the question for right now I felt like a limpid, useless hunk of flesh—weak, exhausted, with feet on fire. The only bright spot in the hot, torturous day: Soon after leaving Maupin Field Shelter early this morning, I had passed out of the caterpillar infestation (although the gnats had returned, which seemed to support The Ego's hypothesis).

A loud metallic screech jerked me back from thoughts of yesterday's misery. An older model, rust-splotched car pulled off the road a few yards in front of where I stood. "Please, let it be a ride," I silently mouthed. Yes! The driver was definitely waving at me. I grabbed my pack and hurried toward the car, praying it wouldn't take off down the road when the driver got a better look (although compared to yesterday, I looked almost human after an attempted cleanup at a small brook earlier).

The driver, approaching thirty, had a sallow, thin face that showed pock marks beneath a thin, scrubby growth of reddish whiskers—oddly out of place with his stringy, blond hair, which was topped by a faded, orange baseball cap turned backwards. He studied me for a long moment and then asked in a slow mountain drawl, "You goin' down th' mount'n?" I vigorously nodded my head. "Then git in." Motioning at the empty rear seat, he told his passenger, a six-year-old replica of himself (sans beard), "Git in the backend, Carlton, an' let this man sit up here." The boy glared at me sullenly, his eyes speaking what his mouth didn't, and then he obediently climbed over the seat and into the back.

"Whar 'bouts you aheadin'?"

"The fire station in Waynesboro." (*The Philosopher's Guide* stated that city officials allowed thru-hikers to pitch tents in a small grassy area at the rear of the fire station; also, hikers were allowed to use the station's shower and laundry facility!) "You going that far?"

He slowly dug a toothpick from his shirt pocket and pushed it way back inside his mouth. Contemplating the question for several seconds (as if he might be down-loading a computer program to access the right answer), he took a deep breath and spoke in mountain-ese, "Yeeep."

Destination confirmed, I scooted in, pack in my lap, and we headed down the "mount'n."

The jalopy screeched to a noisy stop in front of the fire station. "This air th' place," the driver said—his only words since I had gotten in the car.

Shaken, I got out, thankful to be alive after the hair-raising, spine-tingling, widow-making ride down the curvy highway. (My benefactor, doing his best imitation of Richard Petty, had tried to set a new course record—though I couldn't understand why his brakes screeched because he never seemed to use them! When we had hit the first curve, rubber squealed as the car almost soared off into the wild blue yonder and I squeaked in a frightened voice, "Jeez, I didn't know you were a pilot, too." He hadn't bothered to reply; didn't even give me a second look. His face was cast in stone, lips pursed with determination, the toothpick rotating in small circles—serious business—so I had shut up and hung on for dear life.)

Carlton scampered over the seat without being told and reclaimed his rightful place. "Thanks for the flight," I said.

Lifting the cap and scratching his head, the man pondered my implied critique of his attempt to straighten out the highway and finally grunted, "Yeeep." Carlton gave me a defiant glare and the clunker peeled rubber.

The Waynesboro Fire Station is a modern brick building beside a busy thoroughfare. A massive, shiny, red engine sat just inside the large entrance, ready to roar out into the street at a moment's notice. Two men in traditional fireman's uniform sat in a small glass-enclosed office near the main entrance. When I tapped on the glass, the older of the two motioned me in and asked, "You going to spend the night?"

"Hope to," I replied.

He handed me a clipboard. "Sign this. The hiker area is around back. Enjoy your stay." Feeling as if I had been blitzed with conversation after my recent experience, I thanked him, grabbed my pack, and made my way to the rear.

The small grassy plot was deserted, although there were signs that it had recently been used. Propping my pack against a large picnic table, I went inside to the small space behind the fire trucks that had been set aside for hikers. A spiral notebook that served as a hiker register lay on a small table, and I quickly glanced at the latest entries. "Shoot, J.R.! Wingfoot, Tripp, and Geek were here last night. We just missed them. No one else is staying here." Disappointed and suddenly swamped with loneliness, I said, "Just you and me—strangers in a strange town." He grumbled, "You've got your priorities all screwed up, Ace. Shower first and eat; and then read Trail drivel and feel sorry for yourself later. Just check that out."

A crude handwritten note had been pinned to a tilted bulletin board above the table: "Hikers! All You Can Eat at Bonanza!" A rough map had been scrawled beneath the wording. "All riiight! Ego, we're gonna pig out tonight!" Giddy and salivating with anticipation, I headed for the shower.

Bonanza's salad bar was a cornucopia of unheralded delight! I couldn't ever remember seeing so much food gathered beneath one roof in the cause of gluttony. Not only did Bonanza stock the salad bar with an overwhelming assortment of veggies, they tossed in such things as chicken tenders, gizzards, and wings. Off to one side, the dessert bar smirked knowingly at my unconstrained excitement. (Well, I *had* warned the manager, who stood near the cash register when I came in: "I'm a thru-hiker and you're going to lose money on me." He didn't blink an eye. "Come right on in," he had chuckled. "We'll make it up on somebody else.")

So be it! In a matter of minutes I intended to commit the act of premeditated gluttony! The only downside—some hiker company would have made the evening perfect.

I sat (hidden, I hoped) in a back corner booth, my back to the salad bar, trying to separate myself from the other diners as far as possible; but the restaurant was quickly filling up. The problem, simply put: Even after the shower I still reeked of Trail smell—at least my clothes did! And in this idyllic gathering of clean, smiling, well-dressed families who had decided to eat out on this warm June Friday evening, I felt like a loathsome piece of decaying flotsam as a weird potpourri of unpleasant odors (reminiscent of a stagnated swamp) emanated from my booth. So except for quick self-conscious trips back to the salad bar, I tried to remain inconspicuous.

Five plates used so far—five trips. (A sign at the salad bar asked patrons to use a clean plate each time when coming back for refills— Health Department regulations.) I was happy to comply, except The Ego got me worried when he asked, "Do you suppose there's a limit on how many times you can get refills?" I scanned the walls for notices, but the only other sign I saw asked patrons not to let non-paying people freeload off their plates. "Jeez, I don't know. Maybe we'd better really pile it high on the next trip." About that time, a waitress came by and asked if I wanted her to take away the empties. "Gladly," I mumbled through a mouthful of chicken gizzards, happy to have the telltale signs of gluttony removed from public scrutiny.

"Model-Teee!" I knew *that* sound! Skate stood next to the salad bar, waving her arm and pointing like she had just glimpsed Superman in the buff. Again it came, the high-pitched announcement, "There's Model-T!" and the entire patronage turned to stare at the commotion, following her outstretched finger over to the lone, beet-red hiker scrunched down in a booth. Ignoring the curious stares, she rushed unladylike through a family of four congregated at the chicken tenders, parting them like a hot knife slicing through butter, and dragged me out of the booth, engulfing me in a smothering embrace.

"Jiminy Jackrabbit, Skate! Everybody's looking at us!" And they were! "Fer Chrisake! Control yourself!" I spluttered, trying to get my breath. That gal had arms like steel!

She squealed again, "But I'm sooo glad to see you! Eco, it's Model-Teee!" Eco Warrior, his youthful face lit up in a broad grin, made his way past the crowded salad bar at a more respectable pace.

I managed to free myself. "Jeez, guys, it's been ages since I saw you last. Now let me think. Oh yes, all of two days ago; back at the Tye River, if memory serves me right." A faint blush crept onto Skate's face.

"Well, it did seem like a long time to me," she said, and the blush turned into a sheepish grin.

I knew how she felt. My hike across Three Ridges had seemed like a lifetime. "It's good to see you both, too, but let's sit down. We stick out like Santa at an Easter party!" People still gazed our way. "Are you still slack packing with Warren and his group?"

Eco replied, "Yeah. He's going to slack us clear through the Shenandoah's, even all the way to Harpers Ferry if my foot hasn't healed by then. But it's doing a lot better now."

"Are you staying at the Fire Station?" I asked hopefully. "That's where I am."

Skate answered, "No, we're camping with Warren's group just outside of town." My face must have showed the disappointment I felt because she added with a shrug, "They're getting an early start in the morning and our stuff has to be packed and ready. He's planning on a twenty-five mile day."

"Too rich for my blood! By the way, where is Warren and The Circle?"

She perked up. "They just came in. There, by the salad bar."

I glanced over my shoulder at the group and gave a casual wave, thankful for their presence. For, lost in the crowd of thru-hikers and no longer the "Lone Stranger," I could now relax and enjoy the meal because we all looked (and smelled) about the same.

Abruptly Skate pointed at my heaped plate (number six), from which I'd only managed to grab a couple of bites before her gregarious greeting, and questioned me in a concerned voice, "Model-T, you're not sick, are you? You've barely touched your food."

Trying to keep a straight face, I grimaced. "I don't know what's wrong. This stuff tastes weird, not at all like mac-n-cheese or ramen. But I'm trying to force it down."

Eco was getting impatient. "C'mon, Skate, let's check it out for ourselves."

With a troubled look clouding her face, she followed him to the salad bar.

By the time they returned—each carrying two plates loaded with small mountains of food—The Circle had set up camp at two booths in the adjacent corner, and the feasting began. Gluttony prevailed and, like the voracious caterpillars beneath which we had recently walked, we attacked the salad bar, leaving in our wake empty bins, sweating, harried waitresses, and an anxious manager.

And the stacks of plates grew higher. Across the room, The Circle amassed four two-foot, wobbly stacks (which made our puny collection of twenty-one plates seem insignificant)! And when we finally finished, the salad bar had been depleted, ravaged by gluttony! The poor manager gazed at the barren wasteland, which two hours earlier had been the pride of his restaurant, perhaps even of his city. Surveying the damage, his eyes glazed with shock, his face reflecting the agony of a victim who has just watched his home pillaged and his women raped, he muttered, "Good God A'mighty! Who would have thought thru-hikers could eat so gosh-awful much!" Shaking his head, shoulders slumped and mumbling to himself, he walked away.

Satiated and satisfied that we absolutely couldn't eat another bite (and cozy in the knowledge that we had gotten our money's worth), we walked out as a group. The manager stood by the entrance, ready to lock the door behind us. Pausing, I gave him a sympathetic pat on the shoulder and gently chided him, "Well, I did warn you . . ."

He barely managed a weak, sickly grin.

Warren gave me a ride back to the Fire Station. I went to the hiker area at the rear of the building, to find it still deserted. "Well, Old Top, it's just you, me, and the boogey man. And we stink too bad for him to bother us." I spread the Therm-a-Rest on the ground beneath the picnic table and covered up with the poncho liner. "What if it rains?" he asked. "What if it doesn't?" I retorted, pulling the poncho liner over my head. "Go to sleep."

About four in the morning, a loudspeaker blared. Almost immediately, the red giant rumbled to life and roared off into the night with its siren shrieking. Fully awake, heart pounding, I listened as loud, garbled transmissions erupted from the building. After a while the noise gradually subsided, giving way to early morning sounds as Waynesboro slowly awakened to face another day, and I dozed again.

But not for long! Without warning, raindrops splattered the picnic table; quickly grabbing up my gear, I went inside to a dark corner behind the remaining trucks and made my bed.

It was still raining at daybreak. I went to Kroger's and bought enough food to get me on to Linden and then headed to Weasie's Pancake House for a quick gorging before going back to Rockfish Gap. (Their "All You Can Eat" two-dollar pancake breakfast was too much of a temptation to pass up, even though I was still uncomfortably bloated from the "great Bonanza pig-out.") As I went inside the Worry-wart warned, "We're going to pay for this when we start hiking." I shrugged "Naw, it's only gas. We've got room. Heck, a few pancakes will chase the gas right out!"

By the time I got back outside the rain had stopped, and the sun was peeking through the overcast. Gritting my teeth at the pitched battle being fought in my belly between the churning gas and the obstinate, immovable lump that only minutes ago had been twelve of Weasie's pancakes, I stuck out my thumb and wished for the best. After thirty minutes, Lady Luck smiled and I caught a ride in a late model pickup with a middle-aged man who crept along at a snail's pace, talking the entire way back to Rockfish Gap about the local rednecks and their hot-rodding ways. (I thought, "Dang, mister, could I tell you a thing or two!" Talk about Yin and Yang . . .)

At Rockfish Gap the Blue Ridge Parkway becomes the Skyline Drive—same road, but motorists traveling on northward now have to pay a toll. At the juncture, the Trail crosses a bridge above busy U.S. Highway 250 and I-64 and soon meanders back up the mountain.

As soon as I started to climb, last night's overindulgence, aggravated by this morning's bad judgment, made its presence known. Explosive volleys of gas, loud and long, began to penetrate the silence. Disgruntled, J.R. snapped, "Dammit, Alter, that's disgusting." I asked, "What's your problem? Farting *is* a respectable Trail sound, you know." He growled, "It's downright embarrassing," to which I replied after letting go with a humongous barrage, "I don't see why, especially since we're alone, just us and the trees and the breeze. Besides, it's just like I predicted: The pancakes are pushing out the gas an' there's nothing like a good 'poot'—isn't that what you call it?" He, miffed: "Yeah, but I've never heard anything like this." I sniggered, "I believe it was you who said, 'A windless sea sails no ships.' Well, Old Top, are we ever sailin' this morning!"

I had him cold! Faced with such irrefutable logic, he shut up and we burped and farted and "sailed" on up the mountain.

If I were asked to describe the Shenandoah National Park (SNP) in one short sentence I would say, "It was an eating experience." But then I would feel obliged to elaborate: "Both for me, and a hundred gazillion caterpillars."

I felt as if I were walking in mid-winter. The once-proud oaks now stood naked, their leaves transformed by voracious jaws into little black-green pellets of frass, their bare limbs raised to the sun in futile surrender. The sun, given free reign on the forest floor, nurtured waist-high stinging nettle and other noxious weeds and turned the soft, leafy carpet into an impenetrable obstacle. Forget trying to find a backwood's campsite—unless a body were clothed in heavy coveralls and armed with a machete!

The stinging nettle was particularly noxious. The loathsome weed grew faster than the maintainers' sling blades could hack it down. In places, the nettle choked the pathway—often growing over waist high—and immediately caused a sharp burning sensation that lasted for several minutes wherever it happened to touch the skin. I twisted and contorted my way through the nettle jungle like a drunken exotic dancer, gritting my teeth against the fiery pain and swearing guttural oaths at the cursed plants while I shrieked at the caterpillars for eating the trees instead of turning this pestilence into frass!

For I was once again in caterpillar hell—Maupin Field all over again, except magnified ten fold. (Curiously, the caterpillars had suddenly reappeared shortly after I had entered the Park. And just as strange, the gnats had departed, except for a few hardy strays. Maybe there was some truth to The Ego's hip-shooting hypothesis after all!)

On the upside, places to eat abounded in the Park. The Trail passed through numerous campgrounds and waysides, and each had a camp store; some even had grills or restaurants! However, all were expensive, aggressively seeking the tourists' dollars; and the prices were beyond the average thru-hiker's meager budget, including mine. The most I could hope for was an occasional quart of ice cream and possibly a hamburger or two, so I resolved to push on through the Park as fast as my skinny butt would go (which at this point wouldn't have given a lame tortoise a lot of competition).

The following, taken from my journal, summarizes my trek through the Shenandoah National Park:

Day 1: Self-registered for backcountry permit at small welcome station/toll booth on Skyline Drive north of Rockfish Gap ("pooting"—a concession to The Ego—under control by then). Lunched on Bear Den Mountain with Wild Bill; sat in hot sun on one of several old metal tractor seats (burnt butt!) planted on hillside like exotic flowers, with stinky red bandana draped over my head as sunshield; great view of Waynesboro in valley far below. A mile north, spotted Warren and The Circle, who were several yards down the side of the mountain by a large rock, chanting and singing (no sign of Skate or Eco), getting hyped up for the next two hundred miles. Fought the world's tallest bear pole at Calf Mountain Shelter when I attempted to hang my food bag on bar at top with long metal pole; after numerous failures, tied heavy rock to a rope, attempted to toss it over bar and raise bag; bad aim; rock fell toward head of section hiker standing by pole watching me make a fool of myself; I yelled, "Don't look up!" whereupon hiker asked, "Why?" and did same—just in time to get his glasses knocked off; I apologized and slunk off to stash my food bag in shelter, figuring bears were less threat than angry hiker! Warren Doyle arrived at shelter pushing measuring wheel and wearing dirty brown skirt (no petticoat)—his way of making a statement (according to hiker rumor but neither confirmed nor denied by Warren) about SNP catering to tourists instead of campers/hikers; he took a nap and left at sundown to catch up with The Circle. At supper, picked two caterpillars out of my mac-n-cheese but left the frass, which caused The Ego to accuse me of becoming a vegetarian; that night, family of skunks rattled pots as they licked at leftovers left by hikers too lazy to clean up after supper; thankfully, skunk family had no competition!

Day 2: Encountered large black bear near Rip Rap Trail; stalked bear down Rip Rap a half-mile, hoping for a good picture; priority quickly changed from picture to saving my hide when bear decided it didn't want its picture taken and chased me back to the Trail, plus some—didn't realize I could run so fast! Spent night at Blackrock Hut with Wingfoot and Capt. Noah (who had been sucked into a magical place known as Rusty's Hard Time Hollow, where—his words, "hospitality takes on a new dimension"), and hordes of frass-spewing caterpillars. Flashlight bulb shot; potty break at 2:30 AM (no moon, but lots of frass); didn't realize I could pee so fast!

Day 3: Splurged! Bought ice cream, apple, and flashlight bulb at Loft Mountain Camp Store. One mile north of Loft Mountain, came within one step of rudely awakening large timber rattler stretched out across the Trail; moved back a few feet and tossed large rock near the rattler's head, which caused it to coil up beside the Trail and "sing" for ten minutes; after lengthy discussion, The Ego and I decided the snake had "squatter's rights," so we detoured through waist-high stinging nettle, legs afire, beating rocks with hiking stick and praying that its mate wasn't hiding in ambush on our side of Trail. An hour later, observed master yogi-er Wingfoot in action during break at Ivy Creek Overlook, where the AT touches the Skyline Drive. Car with Maine tags stopped and driver got out; Wingfoot asked if I was thirsty (dumb question!), then walked over and began talking with the man. Five minutes later he returned with cold cokes and a handful of oranges. Felt awed to watch "The Master" ply his skill—felt even better to enjoy the fruits of his labor. Spent night at Pinefield Hut where gypsy moth caterpillars had defoliated everything except for huge hemlock tree at rear of shelter; dumb worms had tried to eat the hemlock, which is poisonous, and carcasses had made two-foot pile around the base. Hooray for the hemlock!

Day 4: Stopped at Hightop Hut for the night; Wingfoot going another twelve miles—too much for me; Compass Rose, pretty brunette in her late twenties, already there (doing week-long hike in Park, preparing for thru-hike next year); soon became obvious she had some kind of obsessive-compulsive thingy about dirt, plus everything had to be laid out in the shelter just so-so; soon decided she didn't have a chance of an ice cube in Hell of making it off Springer unless she started wallowing in dirt and eating frass, but didn't say anything. Played "cat and rat" all night with a monstrous wood rat that tried to cart off my pack; every time I whacked at the big beast, Compass Rose squealed; by morning I was nearly deaf and she had lost her voice—and run her flashlight batteries dry.

Day 5: Reached Lewis Mountain Campground in early afternoon. Checked out the ice cream (too expensive), so opted instead for small chocolate milk and two apples. Met Hacker Hiker at store; he was slack-packing south with the help of his wife; his legs in bad shape, struggling to keep his hike going. He warned that the spring at Bearfence Mountain Hut (tonight's destination) was nearly dry and clogged with caterpillars, so I filled both my water bottles and another empty two-liter soda bottle that I dug out of trash bin. Fortunate to have been forewarned, for the spring was in bad shape! Read in the shelter register that Warren and The Circle were now a day ahead; saw nothing about Skate or Eco. Compass Rose arrived, then two section hikers. While we ate supper, a large female raccoon came up to the shelter and yogi-ed some food, and then entertained us with her repertoire of antics before finally waddling back into the woods. (Love that FREE entertainment!) Compass Rose hadn't known about the spring's condition, refused to use it, and soon ran out of water; shared mine, which put me short for breakfast. So I went to spring, filtered out caterpillars and frass with my bandana, and collected enough water for a couple of swallows before bed time and coffee the next morning. Offered her some of the horsepiss-colored liquid, but she hadn't yet enrolled in "Hard Knocks 101" and refused.

Day 6: A wonderful, pristine gift this morning! Three miles north of Bearfence Mountain Hut, hiked through herd of fifteen fawns (I counted) grazing on either side of the Trail; they paid me no attention, although nearby two large doe kept a watchful eye as I quietly padded through the group. Said J.R., "I'll be dippsied! A 'day care' for fawns!" A hundred yards up the Trail we glimpsed a turkey hen with a trailing brood of chicks flitting through the undergrowth toward the deer. Which caused J.R. to wonder if the deer also ran a daycare for turkeys—dumb! At Milam Gap (where the Trail crosses Skyline Drive before beginning a gentle two-mile climb to Big Meadows), a man asked if I knew Compass Rose; "Not far behind me," I replied. He: "Are you hungry?" I: "Do fish swim?" and he laughed, saying, "Then come with me." His car trunk was loaded with canned goods; gave me two large cans of Dinty Moore Beef Stew and two cans of chicken noodle soup— almost five pounds, but that was okay because I didn't plan to carry it far! At Big Meadows, decided the one-mile side trip to the Wayside restaurant was a small price to pay for the Big Splurge (I'd saved up for this one)! Ordered double cheeseburger and fries, which plunged my budget close to rock bottom; while waiting for my order, struck up conversation with friendly, middle-aged man and two women from Little Rock, Arkansas, who sat at the adjoining table; remarked in passing that I planned to buy a quart of chocolate ice cream at the restaurant's camp store and polish it off outside before I hit the Trail again. They left just as my meal arrived; the man soon returned with a paper bag and handed it to me, saying only, "Enjoy your trip," and walked out. Inside the sack was quart of chocolate ice cream! A big heart from a Little Rock! Went on to Rock Spring Hut for the night; lightened my load by eating one can of beef stew and both cans of chicken noodle soup.

While I ate, Compass Rose arrived; shortly afterwards, large black
bear sauntered out of undergrowth thirty yards away, began turning over logs and large rocks in search of grubs. I whispered,
"Photo op!" and grabbed my camera; The Ego hissed, "Not a good
idea. Where you gonna run to this time?" and he had a point, but
this was too good to pass up; got within twenty feet and snapped
picture, but bear paid no attention and somehow I felt cheated.
"Gonna get closer," I muttered. "Dumb move," he replied (but then
he never was much of a poker player); halved the distance (with
The Dufus screeching at me like stuck pig); bear licking at the bottom of a huge log it had just flipped, ignoring me. "Going for a
face shot. Be quiet so I can concentrate." I took two more steps—
now almost in the bear's face, so close I could smell its fetid
breath. Bruin looked right at me and I aimed camera, telling
Dufus, "See, this bear's just a big old baby. A perfect shot!" and
then put my finger on shutter button. Dropped camera as bear
charged; vaguely heard Compass Rose scream, "Run, Model-T,
Run!" Took her advice, scrambling for rear of shelter, with each
step expecting to feel claws ripping into my back, but nothing happened; cautiously stuck my head around shelter and saw bear
sniffing at camera; it soon lost interest and went back to hunting
grubs. Went down and retrieved camera an hour later (undamaged
but covered with bear slobber) after bear finally got its fill and left.
J.R. highly pissed.

Day 7: Sat on Mary's Rock, purportedly over a billion years
old, and studied the giant cloverleaf at Thornton Gap, nearly 2300
feet below, where beetle-sized traffic crawled off Skyline Drive
onto U.S. Highway 211; some of the "beetles" crept into
Panorama Wayside, with its fine restaurant and AYCE salad bar—
barely visible from my vantage point; thoughts of food turned on
saliva machine; thoughts of my empty wallet turned it off. Caterpillars and frass-rain mysteriously absent north of Thornton Gap
and trees untouched (wondered if maybe the caterpillar plague
moved like a giant tornado—random destruction at Nature's
whim). Real rain began as I neared Pass Mountain Hut, a mile
north of the Gap; barely beat nasty thunderstorm; two women, not
so lucky, arrived minutes later soaking wet, scared; told me they
were schoolteacher sisters headed north on first day of a week-
long hike—Mary, a bundle of energy and optimism packed into a
fifty year old body; Anna, five years younger, moaning about how
she had let herself be dragged into this God-forsaken wilderness

where she was probably going to die. (Wondered if she was having a premonition because I'd seen wet dishrags with more pizzazz.) Ate other can of beef stew, crawled inside poncho liner and put toilet paper in my ears to tune out Mary's constant chattering about all the fun Anna was going to have, while Anna continually lamented about her impending doom. Said J.R. sarcastically, "Isn't it nice to see someone having so much fun!" I: "Wait'll she hits the caterpillars!"

Day 8: Got away from shelter before sisters woke up, determined to put in a big-miles day to escape the pizzazz-less dishrag. Got to Elk Wallow Wayside by 10 AM; counted loose change (including some "trail pennies" I had found and planned to mail home for grandchildren) and had just enough for an order of fries; sat outside at picnic table eating fries drowned in ketchup when "hells angel" type roared in on big black Harley. He swaggered inside, came back out with cup of coffee and sat at table next to mine. Mean-looking hombre—heavy black beard, uncombed shaggy hair, grease-smeared jeans; drank his coffee without speaking. I scrunched down until my nose almost touched the ketchup, trying not to offend the guy by looking at him or breathing his way; suddenly he asked with a clipped, precise accent, "Where are you headed?" Taken by surprise, I choked on a fry; coughing, I spluttered potatoes on the table and gasped, "Maine. Walking." He grunted, "Long way." Encouraged, figuring it was my turn again, I said, "Doin' the Appalachian Trail." His turn now. "How?" (Was this a game about who could carry on an intelligent conversation using the least words? Okay . . .) "Foot; 2000 miles; Georgia to Maine." He: "Why?" I threw in the towel and began telling him all about my journey; when I finished, he reached over, shook my hand. "My name is Al, from Quebec. I'm on my way to a motorcycle convention in Pigeon Forge, Tennessee." Reaching into his pocket, he handed something to me. "Here, take this for luck. It's our new 'Loon' Canadian dollar." Thanked him, watched him roar away, then sat staring at the small golden coin that gleamed in the early morning sun, feeling as if I had stepped out of a Lone Ranger episode. The Ego quipped, "Who was that masked man?" and I replied, "Son, that thar was th' Looone Stranger! Hi-yo, Silver, awaaay . . ." Hiked on to Gravel Springs Hut for the night; two men and two women on a weekend hike already there. As sun was setting, Mary shuffled out of the dusk dragging Anna, who looked like something a cat threw up; with each step, Mary chattered,

"You're doing just GREAT! See, here's the shelter already. Aren't WE having fun!" Anna collapsed on the picnic table, gave her superhiker sister the "finger", and in a weak, ragged voice gasped, "Don't you even speak to me. Just let me die right here." A little later, when Anna had revived enough to walk, she and Mary went to the spring, about twenty yards away, and stripped to the buff— all dignity gone—and proceeded to bathe in our only water source. (Was I glad I'd filled my water bottles earlier!) Although the show wasn't as cute as the yogi-ing raccoon, it WAS different. The Ego chortled, "Saturday night live!"

Day 9: About three miles north of Gravel Springs Hut, watched Park Ranger wake family on peaceful Sunday morning and politely but firmly tell them they were in violation of Park regulations (had committed unforgivable sin of pitching their tent within sight of Trail); swift hand of Justice quickly descended on luckless, frustrated father in form of ticket, patiently written by unsympathetic Ranger, while hysterical mom pleaded her husband's case (which almost brought The Marine and me to tears but fell like caterpillar frass on Ranger's heart of stone). Little redheaded girl crawled from the tent opening and clutched her mother's leg, asking in quavering voice as Ranger proffered ticket for her daddy's signature, "Daddy, are we going to jail?" at which point her mommy interjected, "No sweetheart, YOU AND I are going home." Glaring at poor, deflated hubby/daddy and turning THE LOOK on him full barrel, she added, "Daddy's going to the DOGHOUSE." Little redheaded girl's bright blue eyes clouded with confusion and she asked, "Why is Daddy going to live with Jiggs?" The Marine blubbered, "Enough. I can't take anymore." Neither could I, and we beat a hasty retreat from the "crime scene." Late morning, flipped six-foot black snake off the Trail going down into Compton Gap, about two miles from SNP's northern boundary. (Almost flipped, I should say. The reptile was stretched all the way across Trail, taking siesta in sunny spot; I tossed rock at him but it didn't budge; in no mood to play games after seeing impartial swift arm of Justice in action, I eased the walking stick under snake's mid-section and flipped hard; miscalculated; snake slid off stick, chased me back up the Trail.) Fact learned: Snakes slither about as fast as bears run! Walked out of SNP at 11:55 AM, Sunday, 24, June. Hallelujah!

I spent the night alone at the new Denton Shelter (complete with a spring-fed, icy, wonderfully exhilarating pull-chain shower) nine miles north of the SNP and smack in the middle of Mosby country. John Singleton Mosby (a Confederate colonel who with his band of rag-tag cavalry had with daring and impunity pierced the soft underside of Union forces throughout the Shenandoah Valley) had encamped within a stone's throw of where I now sleeplessly tossed. Unexplained noises floated through the pale moonlight, and I could almost see gray ghostly figures moving across the clearing, stoic-faced as they plodded toward a futile destiny. In the wee hours of the morning, sporadic banging of wood-on-wood began to split the ominous silence and crashed into my ears, sending shivers through my body. The Marine said, "It's probably the privy door. Why don't you go close it?" Was he crazy? I wasn't about to go *out there!* Not even an over-full bladder was enough to make me go out into that unearthly assemblage of damned, distressed spirits!

I lay beneath my poncho liner, clammy, tense, needing to go pee, peering into the black void—fearful of what I might see, yet afraid to close my eyes. I waited for the next volley of mysterious banging—my heart racing, easy prey for my predator mind, now fully unleashed. "Why are we putting up with this nonsense?" he asked impatiently. "Just get up and go pee, and we can get some sleep. There's absolutely nothing out there but your silly imagination. Surely you don't believe in ghosts." Another "wood-hitting-wood" salvo invaded the silence. "Listen to that!" I hissed. "There's something out there! No siree! I'm staying put." Jeez! What was wrong with him? A body would have to be bonkers to go out there and mingle with Mosbys' ghosts!

The pain gradually got worse until it finally became unbearable, and I faced the inevitable. There was no putting it off any longer, ghosts or not, for my bladder had become one enormous mass of torment causing jolts of pain to stab into my abdomen every few seconds, leaving me nauseous and drenched in sweat.

Thankfully, the first hint of dawn had started to transform the ephemeral shades of vanquished warriors into trees, and some semblance of reality began to shackle my unhinged imagination. "Are the ghosts gone yet?" he asked sarcastically. "Do you think it's safe enough now to go pee?" The idiot! I snapped, "You don't see them unless they want you to. Plus, there's good'uns and bad'uns, and we don't know what kind we've got here. We've got to be careful." He growled, "Aw, grow up, for cryin' out loud. There's no such thing as ghosts."

Maybe The Marine was right; maybe ghosts didn't exist. Truth be known, I'd never seen one. "Okay, Killer, here goes." Cautiously, eyes checking the dark shadows for anything suspicious and ready to bolt back to the safety of the shelter, I slowly made my way toward the edge of the clearing, whispering with each step, "No such thing as ghosts," but I could sense their presence. And no matter how much I uttered the hollow words, the echo floated back, "Are you sure?"

Almost there—another ten feet. Without warning the darkness exploded in a flurry of snapping twigs and rustling undergrowth—right behind the tree I'd picked! "Mosby!" I groaned. "Dammit, Killer, do something!" I tried to run but my legs balked. The Marine yelled, "Hold on boys! We're for Dixie!" and I managed to croak, "Stars and bars! Long live Gen'ral Lee and the Confederacy!" Another commotion, and then we caught the white flash of the doe's tail as she crashed off through the brush. "Damn J.R., I think I just wet your shorts!"

Somehow I got my legs walking and stumbled on to the tree. Fiendishly, J.R. whispered, "I've heard that snakes like to feed just before dawn." Dang him! I shone the weak light around my feet. Snakes and ghosts! Shuddering, I finished and made my way back to the safety of the shelter.

When the sun was fully up, I went to the privy. The door was securely latched, and I shuddered again.

I picked up my food drop and mail (Judith had sent money!) at Linden, a sleepy community a mile off the Trail, and went another three miles to Manassas Gap Shelter (a safe distance from Mosby's gray-clad phantoms—I hoped), thinking that I might make a short day of it after last night's "wake." The shelter was run down, crowded by weeds—tolerable—but a note scribbled on a page ripped from the register and duck-taped to the wall warned of two large copperheads that lived in the rocks of the fire ring, just outside the shelter—intolerable. (I didn't fancy making a 3 AM potty run with copperheads lying around looking for an easy meal.)

Glancing at the fire ring I growled, "Danged if I'm staying here." He asked huffily, "Well then, Alter-man, just what do you propose? It's already 3 o'clock and the next shelter is thirteen miles away. I think we should stay here." I countered testily, "And I think we should go on and pitch a tarp," which made him snarl, "You do whatever you want, but I'm staying here."

Talk about a strange twist! But before I could find out just how he planned to manage that little trick, Volunteer and Hippy Man (his guitar long since relegated to a dusty corner at his parents' home) walked into the clearing. Hot dang! We had company! Maybe I would stay the night after all.

I hadn't seen either of them for weeks. Volunteer hadn't changed much—thinner, like all of us—and Hippy Man still had the dirty-blond ponytail, though now longer by a couple of inches. We whooped and hollered and bear-hugged like Russian Cossack dancers in a vodka-guzzling contest.

When the hug fractured, we all sat at the picnic table (only a few feet from the fire ring) and Volunteer asked about Wahoola.

I replied, "According to his latest register entry a couple of days ago, he's about a week ahead of me. There's no way that I'll be able to catch him."

Hippy Man said, "A week's about what we guessed, too. Volunteer and me have been bustin' our balls tryin' to catch him. A few twenty-five mile days oughta close the gap. You wanna go with us?"

I shook my head. "Too fast a pace for these skinny legs."

Abruptly Hippy Man said, "Still got some daylight left. We're goin' on to Rod Hollow (Shelter) for tonight," and they stood and put on their packs. Disappointed, with my plans for a fun-filled evening with a couple of fellow snake-watchers in ruins, I watched them to leave. "See you up the Trail, Model-T," Volunteer called over his shoulder, and they were gone.

I looked at my watch—a little after 5 o'clock. Clones of Ward Leonard! Feeling, puny and depressed, I stared at the fire ring, vaguely thinking I needed to get away from this snake den but suddenly too tired to put my pack on.

An hour or so later, I still sat hunched at the table, undecided to the point of not really caring, when a loud voice penetrated my funk. "Model-Teee!" and Skate and Eco Warrior, wearing broad smiles, emerged from the forest. She ran the last few steps and caught me up in a bear hug. I struggled to get my breath, at the same time wondering how someone so short and feminine could squeeze so hard, thinking, "Jeez! This gal could make a killing in wrestling!" Finally breaking her hold, I held her at arm's length—in case she decided one hug wasn't enough.

She laughed, her eyes shining with delight. "Model-T! We thought you might be here. The Postmaster at Linden said you were there a little before noon. We've been trying to catch up with you, now that Eco's foot is better." He stomped his bad foot to demonstrate that it was indeed mended.

What a tonic for my decrepit body! Right off I asked, "Are you planning to spend the night?" They assured me that if I planned to, so would they. "Great! By the way, did I mention yet about the unusual fire ring at this shelter . . ."

The next few days are best described as "serendipitous" as we blended into a trio of happy-go-lucky wanderers with nary a care or deadline, for we had entered "hikers paradise." Came the Gaps—Ashby; Snickers; Keys—each with a restaurant or store within a stone's throw. Came mile after mile of bushes laden with blackberries, and we gorged with juice-stained fingers, laughing with delight as the berries squished and flooded our mouths with liquid fragrance.

Came Blackburn Trail Center, a hiker oasis owned by the Potomac Appalachian Trail Club—thru-hikers welcome; hot showers, cold sodas, and a bed available for free (and even a meal, if the resident caretaker's wife is so inclined, which she was the evening we arrived)! Jake, wife Jan, and pre-teen daughter Jennifer were gracious hosts, well chosen to represent PATC in this mountain paradise. After supper, Jake invited us to come sit inside the large, screened-in porch. We talked quietly and welcomed the soft, pliant dusk, watching it yield to the encroaching night. Sipping a final beer, we shared experiences and memories and listened to the chirping of tree frogs. This was but a fleeting convergence of lives, a brief melding of minds; yet, the bond of friendship firmly bridged the chasm of unfamiliarity. On the far horizon, now hidden by the night, the lights of Washington twinkled like wee frantic fireflies—reminders of another world, another life. Serenity permeated the dusk, becoming a soothing balm for tired spirits, and for the moment I was at peace with God's creation.

The next morning, came Loudon Heights with its trenches and berms, hastily thrown up by Stonewall Jackson's artillery corps before he swooped down and snatched Harpers Ferry away from the Federal forces. My two companions had lagged behind, so The Ego and I stopped to take a break and gaze at the earthworks. Suddenly I was overwhelmed by a sense of *déjà vu* as, once again, spirits of gray-clad men seemed to swirl through the forest. My mind filled with rebel yells—so intense I could almost hear the neighing of frightened horses and feel the blasting roar as cannons, fired in anger, duty, and desperation, rained a lethal curtain of destruction onto blue-clad men far below.

Rock clinking against rock broke the spell. Startled, I looked around and then relaxed as Skate and Eco appeared through the trees. Shaking off the ghosts, I fell in behind them and began whistling "Dixie" for the benefit of my two Yankee friends as we, "The Serendipity Trio," headed down the mountain to Harpers Ferry.

Carl Sandberg once wrote, "Harpers Ferry is a meeting place of winds and water, rocks and ranges." An apt description, for the town sits between the confluence of the Potomac and Shenandoah Rivers—broad, rock strewn, enchantingly beautiful coursers that echo the country's history in each swirling eddy and each frothy rapid. The quaint, antebellum village is an anachronism amidst the babble of tourists who scurry in and out of unique stores and up and down the streets like frantic mice. Nearby, towering cliffs dominate the landscape—sovereign giants that lend a semblance of permanency to the small fiefdom, which exists solely at the fickle pleasure of the two mighty rivers.

Harpers Ferry is also the home of the Appalachian Trail Conference (ATC), and only a mightily rushed (or addled) thru-hiker would even consider bypassing this backpacker's mecca. Being in no particular hurry this sunny Thursday morning, June 28th (although some, looking askew at this ragged walking "skid row" known to a select group as Model-T, might wonder if I might be a tad "addled"), I followed Skate and Eco down a blue-blazed shortcut path to ATC.

Our "mecca" turned out to be a modest, two-story, stone building nestled beneath tall, stately trees in a quiet neighborhood. A long narrow porch extended across the front and "Appalachian Trail Conference," prominently displayed in bold yellow lettering on a rustic brown board, hung near the main entrance. Several packs (without owners) leaned against the wall and the entire porch area overflowed with opened packages, food items, and boots and clothes spread out to dry.

I asked my companions, "Where do you suppose everyone is?" Just then, the door opened and Volunteer, Tripp, and Hippy Man walked outside. (My heart leaped with excitement! Could they have found Wahoola already?)

I asked, "Where's Wahoola? Did you guys catch up with him here?"

Hippy Man shrugged. "We tried, darn it. But he's already in Pennsylvania, still at least three days ahead by our reckoning."

Disappointed, I digested the news and said thoughtfully, "Well, it's a long way to Maine. We all might catch him before Katahdin," but the others looked skeptical.

The front door opened and a middle-aged lady with short, slightly graying hair and the most motherly smile I had seen in a long while, walked out. "Hello. I'm Jean Cashin and welcome to ATC. I thought I heard more voices out here." She hoisted a Polaroid camera. "I was going to take their pictures (she pointed at Volunteer, Tripp and Hippy Man); now I'll get all of you. Just line up here by the sign, in groups of three."

So this was Jean Cashin! Over the years she had become a surrogate mother for thru-hikers—helping, mothering, lending a shoulder to lean (or cry) on, or just listening (if that's what was needed). For most hikers Jean was ATC personified, and I felt awed to be in her presence.

She took our pictures, asked if we had any special needs, and then told us to make ourselves at home and feel free to browse inside, where there was a hiker box, ice water, and scads of pictures in scrapbooks covering previous years as well as the current year. "And, lots of volunteer work to be done, if any of you are so moved," she added with a twinkling smile.

I asked her, "Where is a good place to spend the night?"

"Well, the nearest hostel is the American Youth Hostel across the (Potomac) River at Sandy Hook (Maryland), three miles from here, and it runs about twelve dollars per person. Then there's the KOA Campground a couple of miles out on Charles Town road. Four dollars a person." Looking apologetic, she added, "We don't have much in the way of hiker accommodations right here in Harpers Ferry—except for the Hilltop House Hotel, but it's more expensive."

Bummer! We thanked Jean, told Tripp and the others that we would see them later, and headed for the Post Office to get food drops and mail.

On the way, we discussed our limited options. Eco and Skate voted for the four-dollar campground—fine with me. That settled, we decided to go our separate ways for the afternoon and meet at the KOA Campground later.

I took my food parcel back to ATC and opened it, automatically checking first for a money order; then secondly for Snickers—lucky day, for I found both! Ripping a wrapper open, I stuffed half a Snickers in my mouth, mumbling, "Gotta hand it to you, Marine. You married a good woman." He chuckled, "Even if it comes with THE LOOK?" I: "Nobody's perfect. Snickers makes up for lots of shortcomings. Let's go see the sights in the Old Town." He replied gruffly, "Not looking like this." So we went inside and bought a new tee shirt with the ATC logo printed in big letters on the front, and then changed in the washroom. Without a second thought I started to drop the old stained rag in the trashcan, but J.R. stayed my hand. "We can't just discard it like a piece of trash," he said. "Think of all the tears and agony and memories embedded in this old friend that has served us so well." I held the cloth close to my nose, took a whiff, and growled, "Yeah, and there's enough caterpillar guts in here to start a Chinese apothecary. But you're right, it deserves a final gesture." Bending down, I used it to rub the dust from my boots, and *then* tossed it in the can. "Okay, now let's go do the town." The maudlin Jarhead . . .

Coming out of the washroom, I saw Wingfoot thumbing through the hiker register in a corner across the room. Our eyes locked and he motioned for me to come over.

We chatted for a few minutes and then he leaned close and said confidentially, "The man who's been doing *The Philosopher's Guide* is calling it quits and ATC wants me to take it over. So I'm going to have to cut my thru-hike short."

"Jeepers, Wingfoot, that's a big undertaking! But you've already done five or six thru-hikes, so it's no big deal."

"Yeah, but . . ." He spied an open door across the room. "Come on, I want to show you something." Curious, I followed him to a small room crowded with myriad items—packs, boots, camping gear, old clothes. He whispered, "This is the ATC Archives Room." Then lifting an old brown, wide-brimmed hat off a nail near the door, he gently placed it on my head. "Do you know whose this was?"

"Not the slightest."

"Look inside." I removed the hat and peered closely. On the faded band were the letters, "Benton McKaye." This ancient relic belonged to the man universally recognized as the founding father of the Appalachian Trail! Goose bumps pricked my skin and ran down my spine as I reverently replaced the hat on the wall. Wingfoot's eyes twinkled. "There's all kinds of history in this room, but I guess we'd better not push our luck. I don't think we're supposed to be in here."

A final glance around the room for memory's sake. "Thanks for the tour Wingfoot. "I've gotta go. Promised a Jarhead a tour of Old Town." Let him mull that one over . . .

KOA had set an area aside on the back part of the campground for the exclusive use of thru-hikers (where we wouldn't be an eyesore for their regular customers?). It didn't matter a whit to us, though, for in our small isolated area we could act like—well, thru-hikers. By the time I pulled J.R. away from the historical exhibits and got out to KOA (courtesy of Highpockets—a tall thru-hiker in his early sixties who had developed leg problems and was now hanging around ATC doing volunteer work and shuttling thru-hikers, including me, with his 1963 Comet sedan), Volunteer, Tripp, and Hippy Man had already pitched tents.

Tripp said, "Volunteer, Hippy Man, and I are going to slack-pack through Maryland tomorrow. Highpockets is gonna take our packs up to Pen Mar (a park on the Maryland/Pennsylvania border, forty miles from Harpers Ferry) in the morning. You wanna go?"

"You guys are crazy! That would put me in the hospital." I had a thought. "Is Highpockets going to drop you off down by the bridge?" (I referred to the Byron Memorial Footbridge—a pedestrian walkway attached to the side of the railroad bridge that spans the Potomac, connecting Maryland with West Virginia.)

He scratched his head. "There ought to be room. You might have to sit in Hippy Man's lap though. Highpockets is picking us up at six o'clock sharp."

I walked away shaking my head. Forty miles! I'd heard of thru-hikers doing a four-state marathon, leaving before sunup from Keys Gap, just south of the Virginia/West Virginia border, hiking all day and night, and reaching Pen Mar County Park sometime the following day—a distance of forty-seven miles!) Not my bag!

As soon as Skate and Eco arrived (again thanks to Highpockets), I asked them if they wanted to leave when I did. Eco said, "Gosh, Model-T, even roosters don't get up that early," (a guess on his part, because he'd never gotten up early enough to hear roosters ever since I'd been hiking with him)!

Skate chuckled, "And you know, Model-T, I don't dare let Eco run loose among civilized people by himself."

"Good thinking. No telling what he might get into." Eco feigned a yawn, pretending to be bored by our analysis of his social behavior. "Okay, I'll see you two in Maryland," and I went to find a phone and call home.

Judith answered on the second ring and I turned the phone over to J.R. After the usual "mushies," she said, "Mal Black (a good friend from Roanoke) wants to hike with you from Pen Mar Park to Duncannon (Pennsylvania) if that's okay." (Mal had been doing sections of the AT for several years.) "He and Jimmie (his wife) will bring a picnic lunch. What do you want me to tell him?"

The Ego and I did a quick huddle and he replied, "I'll be at Pen Mar Sunday at noon. Give me his phone number and I'll call him to work out the details."

That night I slept under the stars (no tarp) for a fast get-away in the morning. For once the roguish rain roamed other mountains; and except for a light blanket of dew, my night was unblemished. True to his word, Highpockets pulled up to the KOA entrance promptly at 6 AM and we piled in. (I didn't even have to sit in Hippy Man's lap!)

Soon afterwards I crossed over the footbridge and stepped onto Maryland soil, and then headed down the old C&O Canal pathway, slapping furiously at the thick cloud of vampire mosquitoes that rose from pools of stagnant water in the derelict canal. The three "slackers" hustled away into the early morning haze. The Ego asked, "Do you think we'll ever see them again?" and I answered, "I shouldn't be surprised. This forty-mile day is gonna take the wind right outta their sails. And, like you said, 'A windless sea sails no ships'!"

"Dammit all!" J.R. snarled, "I've plowed mules smarter'n you! Jeez!" Exasperated, I retorted, "I doubt that. You wouldn't know which end was supposed to pull the plow."

I could understand him being upset, but not angry. So we DID have a small problem—more of an inconvenience, actually—but I didn't plan on losing any sleep over it. His anger built, and he fumed, "If you hadn't been so all-fired anxious to save a few ounces by carrying a tarp instead of our good water-tight tent, we wouldn't be in this predicament!"

Our "predicament": The wind was whipping some rain (not much) beneath the small tarp and getting the edge of the poncho liner slightly damp—no big deal. (Unexpectedly, a king-size thunderstorm had swept in shortly after dark and now seemed stalled overhead. Stout gusts pummeled the tiny refuge, but I had anchored the tent pins deep into the soft earth and tied the guy-lines tight. Yeah, in spite of the wind's mauling, the tarp should hold.)

Determined to have the last word, I reminded him, "Ounces become pounds, and pounds turn into misery. Besides, for a Marine you're pretty darned finicky about getting a little damp. I thought you Jarheads had webbed feet and duck brains, which makes you part water fowl anyway." Ha! Top that!

Which touched a raw nerve and he withdrew in a huff—fine with me, for at least I could now enjoy the raw beauty of the storm without interruption. I lay on my back beneath the thin fabric, which flapped furiously just inches above my head, and opened my soul to the storm, letting the primordial forces play tag with my mind. Feeling immune to danger, almost immortal, I sighed contentedly. "Ahh! Nature at its best." Nah, this wasn't a "predicament"!

After a spectacular finale of lightning and earth-shaking thunder, the storm weakened and my mind began to backtrack along the day's happenings . . .

When I left Harpers Ferry this morning, Rocky Run Shelter had seemed like a logical stopping place for the evening (a sixteen-mile day). But after the early start, and helped along by South Mountain's gentle trail, I reached the shelter by mid-afternoon. "Darn, we could get a couple of more hours in before supper," I grumbled, opening up *The Philosopher's Guide.* "Lookee here. According to this, Dahlgren Backpackers Campground is only another mile and a half, and it's got free hot showers!" (The last shower had been at Blackburn Trail Center, three days ago.) "It doesn't say anything about a shelter, but we can pitch the tarp." He thought about it, weighing the pro's and con's, and said, "It's Friday. The place may be jam-packed. And what if it rains?" I looked at the sky, a brilliant, cobalt-blue rug. "It's not going to rain." He grudgingly acquiesced and we went on.

Dahlgren Backpacker Camping Area (the official name) turned out to be a pretty, grassy field dotted with sturdy picnic tables—absent of people. A small stone building sat at the far end of the field. "The bathhouse," I guessed. "Let's go check out the shower."

I dropped my pack by the door marked "men" and went inside. *The PG* hadn't lied! Holding my breath, I turned on a faucet in one of the shower stalls and was immediately rewarded. "Hot water, J.R.! Hot dang!" Excited, I walked over and flushed one of the commodes, overjoyed that it also worked! "Shower time!" I whooped and rushed out the door to get my pack.

I had just finished showering and was putting my sweaty clothes back on when seven Boy Scouts, ages twelve to fifteen, wearing nearly identical brown scout shirts, came through the door. They were cutting up, as boys that age are prone to do, but the group went silent when they saw me. "How you fellas doin'?" I asked.

The boys giggled like a bevy of young girls. One of the older scouts— a tall acne-pocked youth with long blond hair and the first sprouting of a fuzzy moustache on his upper lip—clutched the arm of the chubby boy next to him and propelled him, unresisting, toward the nearest shower. For some reason this caused the others to laugh, and some of the boys hooted and held their noses, which made the chubby scout grin sheepishly and blush. Suddenly my nose picked up a repulsive odor and instinctively I sniffed my armpits—not me this time!

"Jeez, what stinks?" I asked, and this triggered another round of laughter.

The blond-headed boy, apparently the leader, said, "It's dog-dooey. Jake here stepped in a whole pile of it while we was settin' up our tents." Poor Jake looked like he would gladly have sunk through the concrete floor into eternal oblivion if he could have. "An' he ain't gonna sleep in my tent, not stinkin' like that!"

The others chorused, "Mine neither!" Ol' Jake was at a crossroads in his life, whether he knew it or not. "Dog-dooey" on the shoe was tantamount to puking on the table at mealtime—maybe worse. Something had to be done to save poor Jake!

"What're you fella's planning to do?" I asked, hoping the Boy Scout Manual didn't require corporeal punishment for the offense of "dog-dooey on the shoe in the presence of other Scouts"!

The leader said, "We're gonna put him in the shower an' keep him there till he don't smell no more."

That seemed a little brash—and a waste of good hot water (or were they bent on washing Jake down with the cold stuff). I offered what seemed like a better solution. "Why don't you just put his foot in the commode and flush a few times? It would be a lot easier. Faster, too."

"Yeah," one scout said, "that's a neat idea, mister. Go ahead Jake, stick your foot in the toilet." Like a gaggle of geese honking, the boys began to exhort Jake to "go ahead and do it."

As I went out the door into the sunny, pristine afternoon, poor Jake was braced on either side by two of his comrades, one foot in the commode, his face screwed up in a tight ball like his foot was about to be amputated. The commode flushed, the scouts cheered, and The Ego chuckled, "If only all of life's problems could be solved so easily!" I laughed, "One thing's for sure. That kid's going to have the cleanest shoe in camp."

Sounds of repeated flushing and cheers followed us across the field.

Getting as far away from the Scouts' area as I could, I headed toward an isolated picnic table at the edge of the tree line. "Home for tonight," I remarked, and I set about making camp—being careful to check the area for "dog-dooey."

By dusk, several other Boy Scout troops had arrived at the campground. Tents sprouted like magical mushrooms, and sounds of youthful voices calling back and forth—friendly banter between troops—filled the clearing. Smoke from a dozen charcoal fires wafted through the air, releasing tantalizing smells of hotdogs and hamburgers—easy fare for fledgling chefs. Throughout the camp the Scouts did the cooking while the adults stood in small groups and talked, all the while keeping wary eyes on things.

From our vantage point on the opposite side of the clearing, J.R. and I watched the various activities, absorbing the sounds and smells, wishing we were part of the fun and camaraderie, until finally he said, "Let's go over and join in. At one time I was a scoutmaster, you know." I grimaced. "Yeah, so you've told me—several times. Jeez, I don't know, Ego. To them, we probably look like a grungy old, derelict down on his luck. They'd likely circle the wagons and call in the cavalry if we tried to join in." His voice was filled with nostalgia. "You're probably right. That *was* a long time ago . . ." So we sat and observed, isolated in our own small world.

A few minutes later, two adults detached from one of the groups and ambled toward us. "Looks like they're coming here," J.R. whispered with a hint of excitement. "What do you suppose they want?" I replied, "Beats me, but it's your show. You're the scouter-man."

Smiling broadly, the two men greeted him. The taller of the two, a scoutmaster, seemed to be the leader. Tall and slender, about forty, he had a hook nose set above a small mouth with thin lips. "Howdy. My name's Bob," he said for openers, "and this is John. He has a son in the Troop and volunteered to chaperone this weekend." J.R. shook hands with both men.

An opposite of Bob, John was stocky, in his thirties, and had piercing blue eyes and light-brown hair cut close to his scalp. (J.R. immediately pegged him as a military man.) John chuckled, "'Volunteered' is an understatement. 'Shanghaied' is more like it." He pointed a finger at the Scoutmaster, adding, "But when the Boss says 'jump,' it's only a question of 'how high.'" Both laughed, although the "Boss" seemed slightly embarrassed. John continued, "After all, he's a sergeant-major and I'm only a lowly major."

J.R. grinned. "Yep, I know exactly what you mean. (Sergeant-major is the senior enlisted military rank—a position of dignity, honor, and respect—while a major is half-way up the officer rank structure, between second lieutenant and colonel. So although a major outranks a sergeant-major, it's like mixing pineapples and peas, and J.R. immediately grasped the humor.) "I was in the service myself," he proudly announced. "Retired Marine."

And that touched off a ten-minute barrage of "sea stories" (akin to the lies fishermen tell when they get together). The bull session might have gone on indefinitely, except that a scout trotted across the clearing and, standing at attention, croaked with a puberty-skewed voice, "Mr. Bob, the hamburgers are done."

The Scoutmaster asked J.R., "Are you a thru-hiker?"

"Sure am."

"We thought so. How about coming over and have a burger or two and tell the boys a little about your hike?"

John smiled mischievously. "Yes, you'd be doing us a favor. And by the way, the boys were impressed with your solution to a certain problem that one of the scouts had—who happens to be my son."

The Marine gave a feeble grin and blushed. "I'm busted. Anyway, anything to help the Scouts." As he followed them across the field toward the

tantalizing aroma of burned hot dogs, he prattled, "By the way, did I tell
you about the time I ate a garter snake . . ."

Three hamburgers and an hour later (I did the Trail-talk), satiated and
happy, The Ego and I went back to our campsite. Checking the night sky, I
told him, "See, crystal clear, just like last night. Let's sleep on top of the
picnic table; better view of the stars." (And off the ground, away from
slithering and crawly thingies and dog-dooey!)

Unrolling the Therm-a-Rest, I spread the poncho liner on it and lay
down. "Nice," he grunted, an understatement, for the view was mind-
numbing—countless, brilliant stars; universe without end; unfathomable,
yet serene. A sudden freshening breeze, strong enough to be heard above
the muffled chatter of dozens of scouts, rustled the leaves. Perfect! I gave a
contented yawn and began counting the stars.

In minutes, a brief glow flickered on the western horizon and was
shortly followed by another flash, brighter this time, and the distant rumble
was unmistakable. "Darn! Where did that come from?" I muttered.
"Maybe we'd best set the tarp up—just to be on the safe side." Working
fast, I rigged it into a pup tent of sorts, staking the edges down and tying
the foot-end to the picnic table and the head-end to my hiking stick, which
I anchored in place with ropes staked to the ground. Then, barely beating
the first raindrops, I spread the Therm-a-Rest and poncho liner inside and
wiggled in. "You think it'll hold?" he asked. "Yeah, it'll hold. And this
stuff's gonna pass through pretty quick. It won't amount to much." Sealing
the opening at the head-end with my rain jacket, I said, "See? Snug as a
bug in a rug." He snorted, "Who the heck wants to be a bug?"

Without warning the storm intensified, spilling a deluge from the heavens
as if some celestial water main had broken, and I could feel water seeping
into the poncho liner at the foot-end, although the rain jacket seemed to be
doing a fair job at the head. "Need to turn over and get some sleep," I muttered, but as soon as I tried, I realized a weight was pressing against my
chest, holding me firmly against the ground. Worse, I couldn't take a deep
breath.

Groping for my flashlight, I flicked it on and immediately saw the
problem. The tarp had developed a sag right above my chest and neck and
had become a giant press holding at least a gazillion gallons of rain—and it
was about to squeeze the bejesus out of me (not to mention collapse our
shelter). "Dammit, Ego, we've got to get this water off the tarp!"

Frantic, I got my hands in the middle of the sag and shoved—hard. Suddenly, the stakes holding the walking stick came out of the ground and the entire head-end of the makeshift shelter caved in. A wall of water swept down onto my head and chest, under my back, and down the entire length of the Therm-a-Rest. Gasping from the shock, I rubbed water out of my eyes and snarled, "Chicken nasty! Crud-mamma'n freakin tarp! Dammit if that wasn't the stupidest thing I've ever done!" The words were barely out before his tirade began. "You make stupid look smart. Try 'idiotic,' 'moronic,' 'brainless,' 'dim-witted,' 'simpleminded,' 'asinine' . . ." He ran out of words and finished with, "Oh hell, what can you expect from a nincompoop imbecile of an alter-ego!"

I swallowed my anger, for *now* we had a "predicament." Appropriately contrite, I suggested, "How's about we go find a corner in the Men's Room. At least it'll be warm and dry." He said bitterly, "Anything will be better than lying in this lake." Shivering, I grabbed up the waterlogged Therm-a-Rest and poncho liner and headed through the heavy rain toward the bathhouse.

Inside, the floor of the Men's Room was crammed with sleeping Scouts and adults (victims of collapsed tents or tarps?). The rank odor of wet sleeping bags (much like a dog smells right after getting a bath) filled the room, supporting my speculation. I quietly closed the door and tried the Ladies Room—same situation. "What now, Bozo?" The Ego growled.

Wordless, I trudged back through the rain, now slackened to a heavy drizzle, untied the waterlogged tarp from its tangled cords, and threw it over the picnic table. Crawling inside the makeshift shelter, I lay down on the mattress and wrapped up in the soaked poncho liner. When I finally dozed off, J.R. was still ranting and raving, whipping himself up into a real tizzy; but I was way beyond caring.

The Ego sulked for a few hours, deflecting my overtures to make amends with stony silence. Then, as I cooked a late breakfast on the steps of the Washington Monument (an unimpressive, bottle-shaped edifice built in 1838—ten years before the *other* Washington Monument was begun), out of the clear blue he said, "Nice view, huh?" I grunted, "Sure is." (And it was, for the monument sits on a high knoll, giving an eagle's perspective of the broad plain that sweeps westward toward Antietam's blooded soil.) "Wet night, huh?" I replied, "Yeah, a little." Silence, then he asked, "Think it'll rain again today?" I eyeballed the sky—cloudless and pure blue. "Maybe, but not likely." Inanely, he mumbled, "You havin' grits?" I stirred the pot before replying. "Yep." He prattled, "Grits is good." Eyeing two buzzards that circled high above the monument, I said, "Yep," wondering what he was angling for, but he retreated back behind a blank wall. Maybe he was over his hissy-fit . . .

The rain had hatched a gazillion gnats, but I was ready for the little bastards this time. (A hiker once told me that gnats wouldn't fly beneath the lenses of glasses. So when I saw a cheap pair of non-prescription sunglasses in the hiker box at ATC in Harpers Ferry, I put them in my belt pouch—just in case.) And to my amazement they actually worked! The buggers swirled all around my head, but they refused to invade the small space between the glasses and my eyes!

Then came deer flies—nasty critters—a lot smarter than their tiny cousins, but just as persistent. Worse, these guys *bit!* I slathered on 100 percent DEET like it was sun block, but they buzzed right on through, thumbing their sharp proboscises at me before slurping up the DEET. (This stuff would melt nylon, but it wouldn't repel deer flies!)

I turned the plague into a game. (Yep! More free entertainment!) The back of my cap had a two-inch opening above the adjusting strap, and this small alcove, which led directly to the sweaty bald spot on top of my head, seemed to be almost magical in its power to attract the adventurous little beasts. I could feel them (sometimes as many as six at once!) crawl inside and settle in, licking their chops, anticipating a juicy, free, three-course feast of DEET, skin, and blood. Then when the meal was underway and the first biting stings started, I would gleefully grind the cap against their "dinner table," squashing the unsuspecting diners into pulp.

Then removing the cap, I would look inside at the havoc I had wrought, count coup, and unceremoniously dump the remains on the Trail.

"Just call me Deerfly-slayer," I told The Ego (who was acting as scorekeeper) after a particularly satisfying "run." He asked, "How many this time?" and I exclaimed, "Got ten! A prize-winning performance!" He tallied up. "All right! That makes one hundred and fifty-three for this hour— a record!" I immediately reset the dinner table and got ready to break my own record. Talk about fun!

Unfortunately, the deer flies finally figured out what was happening and started biting my shoulders through the thin tee shirt, at last zeroing in on an area around behind my pack straps where I couldn't reach. After several unsuccessful swats and a few bites scored by my adversaries, the fun began to disappear. "Doggoneit, Ego, this is getting to be an aggravation. My shoulders are starting to feel like pin cushions!" He considered the problem and said, "Lay a switch to the little bastards; keep'em shook up," and I asked, "Whatdayamean?" He said, "Break off one of those small sassafras branches. (Sassafras saplings grew in profusion along the Trail in this area.) I did as he suggested. "Now strip off all but a few leaves toward the end and use it like a horse's tail. Switch the heck out of the bastards!

It helped. We went on our way, with me beating my shoulders, left, right, left, right, in time to my stride, like I was part of some religious sect that used self-flagellation as part of its absolution rite. But after a few miles I finally tired of flogging myself (plus, my skin was getting raw). "Killer, I can't keep this up much longer. We need another plan. You got any more ideas?" He must have been one step ahead of me for he came right back with, "Try poking several sassafras branches down between the pack and back, but keep all the leaves on this time. Need lotsa leaves to spook the bastards! Get'em up there where the leaves will shake all around the cap."

It sounded weird, but why not? I defoliated a couple of small sassafras saplings and began poking; and in a blink I looked like a walking sassafras tree raised on some kind of wild-growth hormone.

In this manner, with the pesky deer flies angrily buzzing above the sassafras "fro" while they frantically tried to figure out how to sneak in for another free meal, The Ego and I churned the dust of Maryland beneath our boots.

CHAPTER 8

Tweakin'
the Devil's Tail

Pen Mar County Park is a charming place, well kept, its covered pavilions and concession stands sparkling clean; and on this sunny Sunday morning the fleet of picnic tables were aligned in neat rows like Mary the Contrary's silver bells and cockle shells, ready for business. A large American flag dangled from a tall flagpole—its symbolic power reduced to a limp shroud in the still air. Off beyond the pole the haze-rimmed mountains and checkered valleys of Pennsylvania formed a spectacular backdrop, beautiful to behold, yet somehow alien and forbidding to J.R. (who mistakenly considered his Kentuckian birthright to be a part of Dixie).

Yep, a pretty place, but barren of picnickers! A setback, for I had left Devils Racecourse Shelter—last night's "lodging"—at first light after eating the last of my food (a crumbly breakfast bar), pushing hard to reach Pen Mar in time to "yogi" any breakfast revelers. The Ego said, "All that rushing for naught. I told you it was a dumb thing to do." Disappointed, I replied, "It was worth a try. Anyway, the Blacks will be here in a few hours." My stomach gave a loud growl and I pacified it with a large gulp of water. "Jeez, I'm so hungry even ramen would taste good!" He said, "Well we might as well take a nap until they get here. Make the time go faster." A good idea for once, so I picked a table beneath a large maple, stretched out on the top, and closed my eyes.

I was having a fantastic dream! The tantalizing aroma of fried chicken wafted into my senses. And the dream came with voices, too—close by, hushed, almost funereal. Suddenly J.R. rattled the dream. "C'mon Alter, time to go to work!" I opened my eyes, sniffed the air again, and sat up.

Two women and a man sat at the nearest picnic table, about ten feet away, talking quietly. The man had brown eyes crinkled around the edges with grin lines, and flecks of gray sprinkled his brown hair like coarse salt on a Hershey bar. He chuckled, "My wife and daughter were wondering about you. They thought you might be a corpse, just waiting to be picked up by the Park Warden, but I told my daughter to take the cover off the fried chicken and wait a minute to see what happened. That way we'd know for sure."

Short and paunchy, his heavy jowls sagged and quivered like jell-o when he talked, and I suspected he had put away hundreds of fried chickens in his fifty-odd years. As had the daughter, a short, dumpy gal with frizzy blond hair. Thick glasses magnified her brown eyes and made them into two freak-like aberrations that took up the upper half of her chubby face. As if reading my thoughts, she smiled shyly and blushed.

I laughed. "Well, it did the trick. I didn't know if I was alive or dead myself, but after smelling fried chicken, I'm definitely alive or else I've gone to chicken heaven." Darn! I swallowed a mouthful of saliva and continued, "I've never seen any fried chicken that looked so good!"

The wife, an older version of the daughter—same frizzed hair style except cotton gray and wearing lookalike glasses (a two-for-the-price-of-one deal?)—smiled at the compliment and began setting out paper plates and utensils. Unlike the daughter, she had a washed-out aura that comes with years of toil and wear, although her face still reflected a motherly glow.

Absently, I watched as she arranged the paper plates, and then caught my breath. She had sat four places!

Scarcely daring to believe my eyes, I did a recount—definitely four! The Ego got excited and I was salivating so hard I almost choked.

The man said, "You look like you could use a good meal. Come on over and sit down. Martha cooked plenty, probably enough to feed half the county."

Martha looked pleased. "Now Elmer, you know that's hogwash." She gave me a kind look, adding, "But I did cook plenty. Elmer and Dorothy do like to eat."

"Ma'am," I said, making a beeline for the empty space beside Elmer, "I do believe I *have* died and gone to heaven!" and reached for a chicken leg, but then jerked my hand away when J.R. reminded me that the invitation to "dig in" hadn't been given. "By the way, my name is Model-T and I'm hiking the Appalachian Trail all the way from Georgia to Maine. Been on the Trail for almost three months."

Elmer said, "Yep, we figured as much. Martha an' me eat a lot of Sunday dinners here; Dorothy, too, when she ain't workin'. Always bring a little extra in case there's any o' you hikers around." Martha nodded.

Talk about Trail Magic! "Maybe I am dreaming," I thought warily, at the same time hoping that if it were a dream, maybe it wouldn't end until I had at least gotten in a few bites! Elmer passed the platter of golden-brown, crispy chicken. I speared a breast and reached for the gravy, which sat next to a plate of honest-to-gosh real homemade-from-scratch *biscuits!* I silently prayed, "If this is a dream, please don't let me wake up now! Please!"

"Model-T!" a voice called. "I've been looking for you."

I sat the gravy bowl back down and turned around as Mal Black walked up. His eyes shone excitedly, his bushy gray beard warped by a large smile—and he was dressed for hiking. Astonished to see him so soon, I sneaked a glance at my watch—11:05. He caught me in the act and grinned. "We arrived a little early, just in case you were already here. This is great! Now we can get some miles in before dark!"

Determined to salvage something, I bit off a big chunk of chicken breast, wiped my greasy paw on my ATC T-shirt, and shook Mal's hand, lying about how glad I was to see him. I included my hosts in the introductions, explaining, "This is Mal Black, and he's going to hike with me for a few days."

"These good people thought I was about to expire from malnutrition and are giving me first aid." That said, I ferociously attacked the breast again, cramming in as much as I dared and hoping I wasn't about to become the Park's next choking statistic. Finally able to speak, I asked, "Where's Jimmie?"

I started to reach for the gravy again but paused as Mal said, "She's up toward the entrance spreading out some lunch." He looked embarrassed. "Jimmie wanted to feed us before we took off, but you finish here and then come on over when you're done."

"That's okay, Mal," I said, dolefully eyeing the gravy and biscuits. "We'd best not keep Jimmie waiting." Apologizing to Elmer, I added, "We do need to get on the Trail as soon as possible." Martha looked crestfallen at the unexpected turn of events, so I reached for a biscuit, opened it like an oyster shell, and dabbed some gravy on the fluffy insides. "A biscuit sandwich to tide me over until I get to the next spread." I took a large bite, and Martha beamed with pleasure as my face exploded in sheer ecstasy. (What a joy to help my fellow man—and woman!)

True to my expectations, Jimmie had brought enough food—including fried chicken—to feed a shelter full of thru-hikers! In some ways she

resembled Martha—short gray hair (though not frizzy), same kind eyes
and motherly smile. She greeted me with two hugs, explaining that one
was from Judith, and then the eating began!

An hour later, absolutely unable to eat another bite, I rode with the
Blacks to a nearby market and bought four days of food to take me on to
Boiling Springs, 56 miles away. Then, after the quick ride back to the park,
it was time to leave. As Mal put on his backpack, Jimmie looked at me
with misty eyes and shook her finger to accent her words. "Now you take
good care of my Mal." I gave her my solemn promise that I would do my
best, and we were off.

Before we had gone a quarter-mile, we reached a small wooden sign
with "Mason-Dixon Line" inscribed in yellow lettering. Mal said, "We're
now in Pennsylvania. How many states does this make for you?"

"Six down, one in the works, and seven to go. Yippee!"

Through the afternoon, we hiked together, with me hot on his heels
(for I was determined to make good on my promise to Jimmie to take care
of "her" Mal). He was in excellent shape (for someone approaching seventy), and he set a fast pace. And Mal was fresh. (Unlike me, he hadn't
been abusing his feet on a thousand miles of mountainous trail, and I was
hard pressed to keep up with him.) Before long, a stabbing pain began to
plague the heel of my right foot but I wasn't about to let Mal show up this
veteran thru-hiker, so I gritted my teeth and stayed on his tail.

When we camped that evening, Mal poked gingerly at his right knee.
"I must have pulled something. But it doesn't seem swollen, just sore."

Relieved, I replied, "We'll have to keep an eye on it." (A swollen knee
could spell big trouble, even jinx his hike. On the other hand, a sore knee
was an annoying inconvenience, requiring pampering.) Jumping at the
opportunity to "save face," I suggested, "Maybe we'd best slow down
tomorrow. I don't want you to cripple yourself on my watch, else Jimmie
might call the law on me!"

He chuckled, looking grateful. "That's fine with me, but I wouldn't
want to hold you back." (Which caused me to wonder if that was the reason for his fast pace—him rushing to keep out of my way while I was
about to go lame trying to match his gait!)

"Tell you what Mal, why don't I set the pace tomorrow, and you prod
me if I'm going too slow."

The next few days went much smoother. I kept the pace slow, and we
took frequent breaks. Mal and I both coaxed our balky feet and legs
along the Trail, coddling them like newborn infants. Thankfully, the
pain didn't proliferate beyond the reach of a few ibuprofen. The Trail

gentled and the weather, boosted by a friendly southwest breeze, made for pleasant hiking, especially since the gnats and deer flies mysteriously disappeared.

For me, it was like being on vacation. Katahdin slipped from its role of domineering taskmaster to a passive trifle, and a festive air prevailed as we strolled along, enjoying sporadic bounties of wild raspberries, blueberries, and occasional patches of blackberries. Talk about fun!

Our journey was marred by one incident. Mal and I were eating lunch the next day at Caledonia State Park—an idyllic setting graced with large spreading oaks and maples and a clear stream. Carefree, fun-filled shouts filled the air as kids splashed in the nearby swimming pool; while in the stream, a fisherman attired in hip boots and wearing a fly vest stood thigh-deep in a crystal pool and made short casts toward a partially submerged rock. I watched his progress with interest, wondering if I might yogi a freshly caught fish should the man get lucky.

I noticed an older man crossing a small footbridge above the stream where the fisherman toiled. He limped toward us, waving, and I recognized Hacker Hiker, formerly of The Brew and Pizza Group. I waved back.

As he got near, I said, "Hacker Hiker, you're about the last person I expected to see here. This is my friend, Mal Black. We're hiking together to Duncannon."

They shook hands and he said, "Good to see you, Model-T. How's your hike going?"

"Just dandy. It couldn't be better—unless we had free beer and dancing girls for evening entertainment at the shelters. How about yours?"

He barely smiled, and his face clouded over as he answered, "It's not. This is the end for me, Model-T. Ever since the Shenandoah's my legs have been giving me fits, and it's gotten to where I can't even carry my pack." His shoulders sagged and he seemed to wilt. "My wife has been slack-packing me, but I have a hard time even making it from one road crossing to the next."

Saddened, I struggled for something to say, some words of encouragement to bolster his spirit and make it better for him, but my mind seemed filled with trite, empty snippets. So I simply said, "I'm sorry for you, Hacker Hiker," and I meant it with all my being.

His voice cracked. "There's nothing to do except go home." His sad eyes misted and he murmured, as if he were pleading with some inner demon, "If only the pain weren't so bad . . ."

A car horn sounded and we all glanced toward the parking area. Hiker Hacker mustered a weak, resigned smile. "My wife's honking for me. I'd better go."

Mal and I shook his hand. Fighting back tears, I said in a tight voice, "Good luck, Hacker Hiker," and impulsively we hugged. Then squaring his shoulders like a brave patriot who faced a firing squad, with nary a backward look he shed his "Dream" and hobbled away from the Trail, back to the intransigent masquerade of "Suburbia."

We watched until the car drove away, and then I said, "Mal, let's hike." The day had lost its gentle innocence.

I awoke, excited and straining at the bit, anxious to get on the Trail. It was Wednesday, July fourth, and Pine Grove Furnace State Park was square in my sights, just 3.7 miles away! Delightful visions of picnic tables piled high with food danced before my eyes. J.R. kept wheedling, "C'mon Alter, don't be a laggard, 'cause time's awastin' and with this perfect weather, the picnickers are going to be out early."

And so it was. The dawn came on softly, a soothing rose-colored potion that seemed to refresh aching muscles and listless bodies and renew languid ambitions. I breathed in deeply and exhaled, welcoming the morning aloud. "Ahh! The adversities of the Trail are wondrous to behold!" Mal chuckled at my enthusiasm.

As did Skate, who raised a hand in cheery greeting from her berth on the floor. Last evening while Mal and I ate supper, she and Eco joined us at Toms Run Shelters (yes, there were two of them, newly built, clinging to each other like twins as they stood apart from two decrepit shelters waiting to be demolished). Skate stretched, yawned, and announced sleepily, "You know, Model-T, today we will pass the halfway point."

She was right! In my exuberant "yogi-mode," that little fact had slipped my mind. "After today it should all be downhill," she declared.

"In a rat's derriere! The Trail only goes uphill." (For certain, it seemed like we *did* considerably more climbing than descending; yet, logic dictated that it had to equal out over the long haul, else a body would end up halfway to the moon.)

I slipped the last few items into my pack and put it on. "I'm outta here. Tell Eco 'Happy Halfway Day' if he ever wakes up. See you in Boiling Springs, if not sooner."

Mal was already packed and waiting at the edge of the clearing. I joined him, and we strode off into the beckoning folds of morning's gossamer haze.

Pine Grove Furnace State Park, like its neighbor Caledonia, is a marvelous playground where at every turn the pride and meticulous efforts of its citizens is reflected in the neat, well-kept buildings and spacious green fields. Here, children can romp to their hearts' content while parents sit at nearby food-laden tables and fill their bellies. Here, too, thru-hikers can strike it rich, for Pine Grove Furnace is the mother lode of yogi-ing! (In fact, rumors had flashed up and down the Trail about one lucky thru-hiker who had yogi'd his way through a maze of picnickers right here on the previous Fourth of July. Supposedly, he got caught in a frenzy of "one-upmanship" when picnickers began to vie for his presence at their table, with each trying to outdo the others in the amount of food forced on the poor soul! He finally managed to escape their maniacal clutches and staggered out the far end of the Park, a strange smile and satiated expression frozen beneath glazed eyes as he struggled like a beast of burden beneath a pack overflowing with a mountain of goodies "forced" on him by the zealous multitude.)

Such were my thoughts as I reached the Park's main entrance. "What time is it?" J.R. asked. I checked the time and replied, "Almost eight." He grumbled, "We're too early. There won't be any picnickers out this early." (The hypocrite! A spit and a holler ago he'd been complaining about not getting here early enough.) I replied, "Naw, it's the Fourth! People are gonna be here getting their places staked out. And this early, the only hikers will be Mal and me! Yeah, Ol' Chappie, we're gonna score big!"

I hurried after Mal, who was already a good hundred yards into the Park. Couldn't let him ruin our chances; after all, his yogi-ing skills might not be good enough to shake a stick at. The Ego said, "Maybe we should just let Mal go on ahead. He hasn't been on the Trail long enough to be starved, so he probably isn't even interested in yogi-ing." Sometimes The Marine made sense!

I yelled, "Hey Mal! I'm gonna stop and talk to some people if I see any. Catch up with you later." He turned around and gave me a thumbs-up, and then shouted something back. I was unable to decipher what he said, but it didn't matter anyway, because a hundred yards or so beyond where Mal stood I could see a man at some tables stacked high with what could only be coolers and picnic baskets!

I waved back for Mal's benefit, and he took off again. "Okay DaddyO, let's bag some game!" I growled, briskly striding toward the tables and whistling, "I'm a Yankee-Doodle Dandy." I could already taste the fried chicken!

There were four tables—loaded—and oddly only one person, who sat at the table with the "mostest." I sized him up: balding, middle-aged, short red beard, and a huge pot-belly that pushed out his faded coveralls like a pregnant woman in her last trimester. "This man likes to eat, Ego. He oughta know what it's like to be hungry. This'll be like stealing candy from a baby!"

The man gave me a dour look as I walked up. Confident, I smiled broadly and said, "Great day for a picnic."

"Yep."

"Lots of food for one person to eat."

"Yep."

"You gonna eat it all yourself?"

"Nope."

Dang it! I was getting nowhere fast. "Potbelly's" vocabulary wouldn't quite fill a porcupine quill.

"Who then?"

"Who what?"

Darn! There was probably room for his IQ alongside his vocabulary. Frustrated, I asked "Who's gonna eat it all up?"

"Me an' some others."

"Where th' others at?"

"Comin' after awhile." He stood up and yawned, obviously worn out by the intense conversation. Something about him reminded me of Ol' Bubba back at Moreland Gap. "Potbelly" pulled a dirty toothpick from his shirt, slowly stuck it between his teeth, and squinted into the sunlight, solemn-like, as if he were trying to decide if he could entrust me with a profound secret. After a long moment, decision made, he squared his shoulders, came to a close imitation of "attention," and proudly announced, "I'm th' guard." Finished, he sat back down.

I motioned at the coolers and baskets, reeking of fried chicken and God only knows what other delectable treasures, and asked the obvious. "Guardin' th' food?"

"Yep."

"Well, I hafta admit that you're doin' a great job," I grumbled and walked away, defeated, leaving "Potbelly" to his arduous duty of "guard."

The Ego was seething. "Of all the rotten luck! Given all the people we could have met on this most opportune day on this small planet in this limitless universe, we get Gomer Pyle!" I shrugged it off, telling him, "Problem is, that guy's dumber than rooster balls and doesn't know how to play the game. I shoulda told him I was the chicken inspector for the Park and had to take random samples from each table to make sure it met strict taste standards." Still furious, he began to mimic Gomer, "Well golleee, Sargint Carter, I'm th' guard fer all this here grub an' ain't nobody gonna git in these here baskets without *ofishul* permission. No siree, Sargint!" I said, "'Potbelly' was just doing his job. We'll score next time." He, grudgingly: "If there is a next time."

We did score—at the far end of the Park—though it wasn't quite what we expected: A man stood between two tables (the last ones inside the Park boundary) on which were stacked four coolers and two large picnic baskets. He could have been "Potbelly's" younger brother, except this fellow had no beard and his belly wasn't as prominent. He watched me warily as I approached. "You guardin' th' food?" I asked, trying to look important. I knew the routine by now!

"Yup."

"Waitin' for th' others?"

"Yup."

"Did you know that today is Hiker Appreciation Day?"

"Nope."

"Well, it is. Every Fourth of July is, by an act of Congress."

He looked worried. "Never hearda no sucha thang."

"Well, it is. People having picnics are supposed to do good deeds to hikers, regardless of race, creed, or occupation. You know, like offer them cold drinks and food, and do all kinds of nice things so the hikers will have a nice day."

"Little Potbelly" glanced around for help, but it was just him and me. For a moment I thought he was about to cry, his face was so screwed up in the agony of indecision. Finally, he exhaled with an explosive rush and repeated, "Gosh, mister, I never heard no sucha thang 'bout nothin' like that."

I stood silent, expectant, hands perched business-like on my hips, and waited. Slowly he opened a cooler and said, "I guess th' others won't mind if you get a chicken gizzert an' a soder, 'specially since it's that hiker thang day." Decision made, he handed over a cold, greasy gizzard and a can of soda.

"My friend, the hikers of America thank you, and a grateful country expresses its appreciation for your kindness. You are to be commended!" Greedily, I wolfed down the oblong obscenity and the drink and handed back the empty can, saying, "Always remember the Fourth, for God, Country, and Hikers!" and skedaddled before the "others" arrived.

Mal waited for me at the "official" halfway marker—a wooden post topped with two arrows, one with a large "S"; the other with an "N"; with "1069 miles" painted on each. (By my math, this totaled 2138, while the *Data Book* showed the Trail to be 2143 miles, a discrepancy of 5 miles. Actually, although the Trail's mileage constantly changes as sections are relocated off of roads and private land, the shuffling seems to balance out and the halfway point remains relatively close to the marker.)

Mal pumped my hand like I had just returned from a landing on the moon, and we celebrated with a handful of trail mix and some lukewarm water. The short festivity over, we mechanically resumed the hike, but my thoughts dwelled on picnic tables heavily laden with coolers and baskets . . .

Boiling Springs, Pennsylvania, is like a jeweled bracelet gracing the long arm of the Appalachian Trail. The town's pristine beauty dazzles the eye, as does the clear, sparkling waters of its focal point, Children's Lake—a large, shimmering gem surrounded by picturesque houses and stately trees. The lake is fed by a stream of frigid, crystal water, which boils out of the earth in a never-ending torrent. But, beauty aside, Boiling Springs is not a hiker town.

Mal and I hobbled (a mild description, for my right heel was throwing another tantrum and Mal's knee was beyond "sore," now starting to swell) along the white-blazed walkway that borders the edge of the lake. Needless to say, we drew a few curious glances from the scattering of adults and children going about the serious business of fishing. Along the lake's unsullied banks, large willows played host to myriad ducks and geese that languished in the midday heat. "What a beautiful view!" I exclaimed. "This is just like a painting by one of the great masters!"

Mal's artist eyes drank in the scene and he murmured, "I don't think anyone could capture this beauty on canvas."

The sidewalk ended at a large, wood-frame, two-story white house, identified by a sign on the front lawn as ATC's Mid-Atlantic Region Office. Parking our packs on the spacious porch, we went inside. The only person was a pudgy, middle-aged woman with gray-streaked hair and a harried look, who was frantically writing on a note pad and trying to talk on the phone at the same time. Glancing up, she rolled her eyes and motioned to a water cooler, mouthing, "Help yourself."

We smiled our appreciation and did, drinking greedily from paper cups, refilling them several times. Then we wandered along the numerous displays and posters until the lady finished her phone conversation.

"Now, how may I help you?"

Mal asked, "Is there anyplace in town where we can camp for the night?" (The next shelter, fourteen miles away, lay across the Cumberland Valley—a sprawling expanse of large, open farms covered with patchwork fields of knee-high corn and emerald-green meadows spotted with cows—and the first nine miles was a scorching road walk without any place to pitch a tent.)

She shook her head. "Unfortunately, we don't have a campground or any place set aside for hikers to stay here at Boiling Springs. There are a couple of bed and breakfast places, but they're expensive."

Mal's shoulders sagged (as did mine) at this unwelcome news. There was absolutely no way we could get to the next shelter before midnight, for it was already past three; plus, the afternoon was a sizzler. We were about done for.

I asked, "Well, where do the other thru-hikers stay? Surely some come through asking about a place to stay."

She looked perplexed. "Why, I haven't really thought about it. I'm a new volunteer and I haven't met many hikers." She shrugged and tittered nervously, "I suppose they go on out of town to wherever hikers go."

Mal said, "We really don't need much space. Do you know of anyone who might be willing to let us stay in their backyard. We'd be glad to pay."

"Gee. I can't think of anyone, but tell you what. Karen Lutz, the director, will be back in a few minutes. She knows many more of the local people than I do, and maybe she can help. I haven't lived in the area for very long."

"Kind lady," I pleaded with a look that must have bordered on the comical, "we throw ourselves on the mercy of the good people of Boiling Springs, specifically you and Karen Lutz. C'mon Mal, lets go get some ice cream while we wait for Karen to come back."

When we went out the door, Skate and Eco were sitting on the porch. "Where have you two been?" I asked. "I thought sure you would catch us before now."

"I wanted to," Skate informed me with emphasis on the "I". "But I couldn't drag Eco away from Pine Grove Furnace. The picnickers all wanted to 'mother' this poor little thru-hiker boy, feed him and blow his nose. And people were *very* generous—something to do with some kind of 'Be Good To Hikers Day.' We barely made it out of the park by dark."

Eco grinned foolishly at Skate's exaggerated account but didn't contradict her, so I surmised it was at least partially true. (I was tempted to reveal my "legacy" to the hiker community, courtesy of "Little Potbelly," but who would believe such an asinine tale!)

"We're headed for ice cream. You want to come along?" I asked. "By the way, there's no place for hikers to stay in the town. What are you planning to do?"

Eco rubbed his belly and smacked his lips for emphasis. "We already had ice cream. Hit the store first thing."

Skate answered the rest of the question. "We're going on and take our chances, even if we have to sneak behind someone's barn. How about you?"

I glanced at Mal, but his face was noncommittal so I shrugged. "Just play it by ear, I guess. Hopefully, we'll find a spot in somebody's back yard. Tell you what, how about we meet in Duncannon day after tomorrow, on Saturday, and have breakfast at the Doyle Hotel. Say at 8 AM? Mal and I should be able to make that okay."

"Sounds like a plan," Eco said, and Skate nodded her okay.

Mal and I headed to a store a short distance away to get ice cream— for me, a quart of chocolate; for Mal, a wimpy pint of orange sherbet, and we went outside and sat on a grassy plot to eat. "Darn, will you look at that!" During the short interval that we had been inside, the entire north- west horizon had turned an angry greenish-black streaked with bands of ominous gray. "Gee, Mal, this storm looks like a mean one!"

"It sure does. Maybe we'd better head back to the ATC place." His voice was calm; however, his eyes told a different story.

We reached the porch as the first gusts of wind hit. "Better put rain covers on our packs!" I shouted as huge drops of rain, pushed by the onslaught, sprayed across the porch. Fighting the wind, we finally man- aged to get the covers on, then grabbed the remnants of our ice cream and dashed inside just as a colossal thunderbolt lit the darkened sky and shook the earth. Immediately, the power went off.

The receptionist was on the verge of becoming hysterical, wringing her hands and breathing with shallow, rapid gasps, quickly hyperventilat- ing. Evidently they didn't grow these king-size summer thunderstorms wherever she hailed from. Mal and I gave her reassuring smiles. Darn, I hoped she wasn't about to faint! Time for some old soft shoe!

Ignoring the "No Food Inside Please!" sign, I spooned a big glob of melting chocolate ice cream into my mouth, rolled my eyes with pleasure, and on a whim let some of the brown liquid scandalously drool down my beard—though in the semi-dark room the effect was diminished. Like an imp, I grinned at the woman and did another spoonful, watching as her eyes followed the oozing brown clump into my mouth. She held her breath, her attention partly diverted from the storm, as another trickle eddied down my beard toward her spotless, polished plank floor.

"Golly Mal, this is great stuff," I chuckled, ambushing the brown slob- ber with the back of my hand before it made it to the floor. Offering the nearly empty carton to the lady, I grunted, "Didn't mean to hog it all, Ma'am. Be glad to share." She shook her head, so I drank the remains and dropped the empty container in the waste can.

A mighty gust shook the building, followed immediately by a loud thud against an outside wall—falling tree, or airborne garbage can—and involuntarily Mal and I ducked. The receptionist, her eyes glazed with panic, gave a terrified squeal. This gal was about two stitches from losing it! Time to pull another rabbit out of the hat.

I looked at Mal and grinned reassuringly. "The last time I hiked through one of these, the wind was so strong I used my pack cover for a sail and it pulled me right up the mountain."

Mal laughed, catching on fast. "Well, I've got to admit that's pretty strong. The last time I hiked through anything like this was up on Buffalo Mountain. It rained so hard it turned the Trail into a stream and I floated all the way to the bottom."

The woman stared at us with amazement and stammered, "You mean you actually walk in stuff like this?"

"Heck fire, Ma'am, this is just a little puppy dog storm compared to some I've hiked through." Mal nodded in agreement and she seemed to relax a bit.

I was just getting warmed up, ready to up the ante with a really tall tale, when a lady holding a flickering stub of candle came through a connecting door. Wearing a worried look (but without any sign of hysteria) she said, "This could spell big trouble for the Trail. There'll likely be lots of downed trees." She took our measure, giving us a no-nonsense once-over, and offered her hand. "Looks like you two got here just in time. Hi, I'm Karen Lutz."

So this was ATC's regional director. She looked to be in her early thirties (hard to tell in the dim light), and her short black hair may have been a practical concession to her job, along with her outfit—jeans and hiking boots. Karen seemed to exude confidence and leadership in every word and action.

When we finished introductions, she said, "I understand you're needing a place to spend the night."

Mal replied, "Any place large enough to put up a tarp would be great." The house shuddered as another gust roared past, causing hail pellets to pepper the windows. "Assuming this ever stops," he added.

Karen hesitated, as if she were wrestling with a weighty problem, and then seemed to reach a decision. "You both seem responsible. I have friends who run a bed and breakfast here in town. They're on vacation and the place is closed, but they sometimes let hikers tent in their backyard if I approve. Under the circumstances I don't think they would mind if you put up your tarp there tonight. Just leave the place the way you found it."

We both expressed our thanks, grateful for her trust in two strangers whose only link to her was the brotherhood of the Appalachian Trail. Then while we waited out the storm, we talked of environmental concerns and land acquisition problems—which seemed to have a calming effect on the receptionist (or perhaps it was Karen's calm, professional manner). And all the while, as the tempest howled and the house trembled, icy fingers of anxiety played with my mind. How were Skate and Eco coping with Nature-gone-mad?

At last the storm moved on and Mal and I followed Karen outside into the light drizzle. Many of the elegant trees, which shortly before had adorned the lake's edge, had been whimsically dumped into the water like so much chaff, their sunken limbs sluggishly gyrating like tethered serpents beneath the gunmetal surface. On the broad expanse of greenway, where only minutes ago children had played and sent carefree shouts echoing across the lake, fallen branches and downed trees sullied the landscape, while small groups of geese and ducks wandered aimlessly as though in shock.

Karen's eyes revealed the depth of her pain, but she shrugged and said, "There's a ton of work to be done. I'd better get some people together and see what we've got to do."

J.R. summed it up for Mal and me. "This lady has the right stuff." Amen!

Mal and I offered our services, and Karen put us to work gathering up fallen limbs. I paused with an armload of splintered wood and said, "Mal, I always heard the Good Lord takes care of drunks, fools, and thru-hikers, and it's no question that we qualify for two out of the three! It's amazing that we ended up in a strong building when the storm hit. Yep, we're lucky, all right." But his artist's eyes were still ravaged by the marred beauty of the lake. Staring through me, he just grunted and continued to pick up branches.

I understood.

Toward late evening, tired from our afternoon's labors, we made our way to Garmanhaus B&B's back yard and began to rig Mal's tarp. Suddenly he said, "Don't take this wrong, Model-T, but if you don't mind I'd really like to do three low-mileage days into Duncannon; just take my time and give my knee a chance to heal—not that I don't enjoy your company," he added with a chuckle. "That way, I can enjoy the solitude of the Trail and you can keep to your schedule and meet your friends Saturday for breakfast. I can call Jimmie from here in the morning and she can come to Duncannon on Monday and get me." (Jeepers, had I pushed Mal *too* hard!)

"Gee, I don't know. Jimmie's last words were for me to take good care of 'her Mal.'"

He assured me he would make it just fine so I reluctantly agreed, telling him, "Okay then, I'll leave as close to five in the morning as I can and try to get the road walk done before it gets too hot. How about if I sleep under your tarp?" (His was three times the size of the one I had.) "That will save me a lot of time in the morning." He agreed that it was a good idea.

Mal's tarp had seen better days and had numerous holes the size of match heads, with a few that I could easily have slipped a dime through! Tactfully, I asked, "Have you ever thought of investing in a new tarp?"

"It is kind of holey," he admitted with a sheepish grin. "But it's not going to rain anymore tonight." His prediction seemed right, for the skies had cleared late in the afternoon and a quick check of the evening sky turned up nothing that vaguely looked threatening.

We settled down on the lush grass. Even though Karen had given us permission to be here, I felt uneasy, like we were intruders. In the deepening gloom, the backyard soon became a foreboding place of mysterious nooks where unseen things lurked. Standing like a spectral matriarch beneath the stoic oaks, the old mansion harbored generations of memories—and ghosts?

Unbidden, images of ghoulish eyes peering from behind yellowed, lacy curtains rushed into my mind. By my side, Mal's soft snoring seemed bizarre in this inner sanctum of drifting spirits, where each unexplained noise caused my heart to skip a beat; where each sighing of wind through the leaves became the whispers of wandering wraiths; where the flashes above the trees illumined the vacant windows and transformed the myriad holes in Mal's old tarp into fleeting wobbly fireflies . . .

I flinched as a dazzling glare lit the entire overhead, barely beating the loud clap of thunder. Damn!

As the first drops of rain spattered the canvas, I reached for the small tarp of Kelly's—not large enough to fully cover Mal and me top and bottom—and growled at my oblivious tarp-mate, "Okay, Weatherman, you have a choice. Soaked feet or a wet head. What's your pleasure?" He answered with a loud snore-packed gurgle. Another brilliant flash, and in the brief flaring I glimpsed the rapid dripping from a dime-size hole right above Mal's mouth—conveniently centered for a refreshing drink!

"We can't let him drown," said the Ego, half jesting. "Yeah," I replied. "Guess that decides it."

Quietly, I spread the tarp over our upper halves, making sure Mal's head was covered, and went to sleep, happily secure in the knowledge that, indeed, the Good Lord surely watches over fools and thru-hikers—I didn't know about drunks!

The Doyle Hotel in Duncannon had seen better days. Built by the Anheuser-Busch people sometime around 1900, it must have sparkled with elegance during those fun-filled days of the early twenties when it graced the main street of the "jewel of the Susquehanna," as the town was once known. On this early Saturday morning though, the old Doyle's charm had long since faded for its red brick facade was tarnished by peeling paint anywhere wood showed, and a general aura of neglect lay like a murky shroud around its once-proud walls. Actually, I felt a certain kinship with the old hotel, for I was certainly jaded this morning after a hard four-mile push from Thelma Marks Memorial Shelter to make my 8 AM breakfast date with Skate and Eco. (I had spent the previous evening alone at the shelter and overslept after an uneasy night filled with wild imaginings of eyes watching from the shadowy depths of the moonlit woods.)

I paused at the double doors that served as the building's main entrance and glanced at my watch (only ten minutes late!) as I wiped the sweat off my face and arms with my soggy bandanna. The words "Hotel Doyle"—shiny gold at one time, now lusterless and nearly illegible, were imprinted on dirty glass above the lackluster entrance. The Ego echoed my thoughts. "Looks pretty sad. I'll be surprised if they even have a restaurant." I replied, "We'll soon find out," and pushed through the doors—into a beer hall!

The smell of stale beer and thick, pungent cigarette smoke nearly bowled me over. Two men sat at a dimly lit bar, wordlessly staring into space with bleary eyes, beer bottles loosely tilted in practiced hands. As the door closed, each flicked me an indifferent glance and then resumed their efforts to peer into infinity. The fat, balding bartender, his enormous gut covered by an apron that was even more disgusting than the shirt I wore, gave me a short nod and ran a rag across the section of bar in front of where I stood. "What'll it be?" he rasped.

A sign above the bar advertised the "house" draft beer for fifty cents! But at eight in the morning! Suddenly Mule's words, uttered with such muddled conviction weeks ago on the sandy beach by the French Broad, cascaded into my mind: "This is just the cheapest calories I could find." Heck, why not go for it! A triple whammy—thirst quencher, one-course meal, and a buzz—all in a glass! Vaguely aware that I still had my pack on, I grunted, "Gimmee a draft," and dug into my belt pouch for two quarters.

He pushed a mug filled with fizzing amber liquid into my hands, picked up the quarters, and I drained half the contents in a long, satisfying gulp. The Ego murmured happily, "Dang, I do believe Ol' Mule was on to something!"

"Say, I'm supposed to meet a couple of friends here for breakfast right about now—short gal with a long pigtail and a wet-behind-the-ears young'un, 'bout eighteen." I drained the mug and handed it back. "Refill, please. You seen'em?" I searched for more change but had to break out a dollar bill.

He worked the tap and said, "Yeah, they been in an' outta here a coupla times already this mornin'. They might be in th' rest'rant. Just go through that door an' it's across the hall. You can't miss it."

I bolted the beer down and ran my arm across my mouth. A long, resounding burp took me by surprise, so loud that it brought a flicker of life to the infinity seekers. (In fact, one even stared at me with glazed eyes and did a half-hearted thumbs-up. But the bartender didn't bat an eye; his cortex was probably calloused from constant exposure to far worse sounds!) I grinned and pushed the last two quarters across the bar. "One more, if you please, an' keep the change." Yeah, Mule was lots smarter'n he looked. And the Ol' Doyle was starting to look pretty good, too!

Skate and Eco were in the "rest'rant" (a small room that took a quantum leap of the imagination to identify it as such). True, there were a few tables and chairs, but no waitress, no sign of food, not even anything that faintly smelled like something to eat. No reflection on Mule or his bacchanalian diet, but my taste buds now yearned for a "real" breakfast, and apparently it wasn't going to happen here.

"Hi kids. Sorry I'm late, but I had to make a pit stop. Cripes but I'm hungry! Where're we gonna go eat?"

Skate, always the mother hen, clucked, "Right here. We had just about given up on you. After all, the Model-T is *never* late, so we went ahead and ordered."

"This really is a restaurant? Does it come with a waitress, too?"

Surprise! The food was delicious, ample, and inexpensive. When we finished eating, Skate said, "We still have our room upstairs, Model-T, and checkout time isn't until noon. If you want, you can leave your pack there while we go to the Post Office and do laundry." She added with a wry look, "And you can take a bath in our private, communal tub at the end of the hall."

"Gee, I don't know. I'm not used to such posh accommodations . . ."

The room would have made a great setting for an Alfred Hitchcock thriller—no door key (last night, Skate had propped a chair beneath the door knob), and the air conditioning didn't work (because it had never been installed—nor had fans. Eco admitted the temperature had been just slightly short of Hell.) But on the positive side, the single window did open, and the room's only light source, the 75-watt bulb that dangled from the high ceiling, hadn't added much to the stifling heat. And the price was great! Only ten dollars each, with towels thrown in!

I surveyed the room. "Well, maybe I can tolerate such luxury for a couple of hours. Where's the bath, or do I want to know?"

The bathroom (broken door lock) apparently served the entire block of rooms that made up this part of the building. It was furnished in early antique décor—ancient oversized, once-white porcelain fixtures and the centerpiece, a chipped, off-white tub with short, ornate legs that resembled lions' paws. The "ring" around the tub's interior looked as if it may have been there through two world wars and decades of other events!

J.R. balked. "I'll be doggoned if I'm about to take a bath in that, not even for a whole box of Snickers!" I growled, "Don't get your bloomers in a wad, Killer, 'cause neither of us is. That tub's dirtier than we are!"

The lavatory looked a little better. Chances are it had been cleaned once or twice since Watergate—at least its "ring" didn't look life-threatening. I scrubbed at the sink with a scrap of soap that someone had discarded and examined my handiwork. "This'll do for a quickie spit bath," I said. "Well, all right," The Killer grudgingly acquiesced, "but I'm not about to brush my teeth anywhere near that tub!" So much for luxury . . . (Had Eco and Skate actually taken a bath in that tub? Burning with curiosity, I went back to their room but was too embarrassed to ask!)

Came chores and an early lunch of pizza, and then we returned to The Doyle. I retrieved my pack and went back down to the restaurant to wait while Skate and Eco finished packing. I hadn't been there long when the door opened and a large German shepherd decked out in harness came in, closely trailed by a tall distinguished-looking man (definitely a hiker by his clothing) who gripped a handle attached to the dog's harness. A short, attractive woman followed him in and closed the door.

They sat down at a nearby table, and the dog flopped on the floor by his master's leg. The man had the lean appearance of a thru-hiker, and his close-cropped, slightly graying hair led me to guess his age at about fifty. Oddly, he had skinny legs, which ended inside the largest Merrell Wilderness boots (same kind as mine) that I had ever seen! Conversely, the lady wore street clothes, looked to be in her mid-thirties, and was definitely not a thru-hiker.

A waitress magically appeared with two glasses of water and menus, but the lady said that they wouldn't be staying.

Only one blind person hiking the Trail that I was aware of: Bill Irwin! And the dog had to be his dog guide, Orient! While I watched, he reached for the glass of water and nailed it dead on. "Amazing sense of perception," J.R. said, to which I replied, "Nobody could do that unless they could see a little." He, defiantly: "I beg to differ. That man is totally blind." I said defiantly, "Then how did he know *exactly* where the glass was, 'cause that was the first time he'd touched it? Just answer me that." He couldn't, of course, so he mumbled, "Well, maybe he *can* see just a little." Gloating at the small victory, I retorted, "Now isn't that what I just said?"

But he wasn't ready to throw in the towel. "There's one way to find out. Let's go over and meet him. Stick our hand out and see if he shakes it." "Fair enough," I agreed, and we went across the room.

"Hi. I'm Model-T," I said, extending my hand, but he had his out almost before I heard my own words. This man was fast on the draw! Feeling cheated, I shook it.

"Pleased to meet you. My name is Bill Irwin, and this is my friend, Carolyn Starling. And my other friend here is Orient." Hearing his name, the dog's ears perked up. "Together we call ourselves The Orient Express."

He explained that he had been in Duncannon for several days giving Orient a break from the Trail and having a veterinarian give him a thorough going-over; further, The Orient Express planned to get back on the Trail the next morning. "Carolyn here is my good right arm. She traveled all the way from Burlington, North Carolina, to check on me and bring me some new boots." (I soon discovered that the congregation at Bill's church in Burlington had offered to sponsor him on his thru-hike, and that Carolyn had volunteered to act as his coordinator.)

The door opened and Skate came in, followed by Eco. Bill turned at the sound and said without any hesitation, "Hey there, Skate. You, too, Eco-Warrior. You all headed out?"

J.R. nudged me. "How'd he know it was them? I bet he can see a lot more than he lets on." I muttered, "Isn't that what I've said all along?"

Eco replied, "Yeah, but we're planning to stop at 3-B's for ice cream on the way out of town. A dollar for two big scoops!" That was welcome news!

"Now that sounds like a good idea," Bill said. "If you don't mind, I'll come with you."

Delighted, I told The Ego, "Okay, this is the moment of truth! If he stumbles over curbs and steps in front of cars, I'll be a true believer."

Orient led the way, with Bill maneuvering over curbs and through intersections like he had 20-20 vision (while the rest of us had to do a semi-trot to keep up). "Just look at him go," J.R. gloated. "I *told* you he could see!" (Jeez! Not twenty minutes earlier he had tried to convince me that Bill was totally blind!)

At 3-B's we quickly gobbled large mounds of ice cream, trying to beat the heat before it melted. A rivulet of chocolate ran down Bill's hand and dripped on the pavement, but he didn't seem to notice. Silently, I handed him an extra napkin, which he ignored. But as soon as I said, "Here's an extra napkin, Bill," he reached right to the spot where I held it. "There," The Ego said ecstatically, "I knew all along that he couldn't see! His senses are so much more developed than most people's that he doesn't even need eyes to know what's going on." I growled, "Which is more than I can say about some people I know!" Criminy! What a hypocrite!

We bid Bill farewell, not knowing if our paths would cross again.

Rocks! *The Philosopher's Guide* warned hikers about the rocks of Pennsylvania, but ever since crossing the Mason-Dixon Line, all the way to Duncannon, the Trail hadn't been any worse than what we'd dealt with since leaving Springer Mountain. I had started to believe that this whole thing about rocks was a myth. The tongue-in-cheek quips about Pennsylvanians filing sharp points on the rocks with huge files—an exaggeration intended to depict the misery thru-hikers could expect as they passed through William Penn's turf—just hadn't happened.

Until now! "Gads! Why would anyone build a trail where it's so rocky?" I asked myself as I stared at a gazillion rocks that formed the treadway. All sizes—baseballs to beach balls; some anchored into the ground, most wobbly ankle busters—had tortured my legs for the past three miles without any letup. My neck had developed a crick from constantly looking down for secure footing and then checking ahead for snakes (none so far!) or poison ivy, which seemed to thrive among the rocks. My ankles throbbed and the pain seared up into my shins, bringing tears to my eyes. "Crud-mamma'n rock patch!" I yelled, then calmed down. "According to the *Data Book*, there's another hundred and twenty miles of Trail left in this confounded state." The Ego, acidly: "Yeah, but just like this trip, shit happens."

I hadn't seen Skate or Eco since leaving Duncannon four hours ago. They had quickly gotten ahead, mainly because they were fresh, having laid up at the Doyle overnight while I hadn't had any such break. (Of course, there *was* a slight generation gap . . .) I longed for their company—at least someone with whom to share the misery!

I followed the Trail up onto a stretch of large boulders, beating the rocks violently with my hiking stick to scare away any rattlers as I pushed along in near panic, crashing through low-hanging branches like they were spider webs. J.R. spat vehemently, "You're going to bust a leg if you don't slow down. You can't go tweaking the devil's tail and expect to get away with it, because you're gonna get tromped into the ground and then what'll you do? Besides, there aren't any snakes up here. Snakes eat mice, and mice don't live up here because there's no food or water. Wallah! No mice, no snakes."

Well, what he blathered did make sense. "Okay, if you're absolutely, one hundred percent sure that there's no snakes up this high . . ." I forced myself to slow down but still kept on pounding the rocks—just in case.

A few whacks later, an angry whir rose from between two rocks near my right foot. "Yeow!" I yelled, jumping three feet into the air, and ran for my life. "Blockhead!" I berated myself. "I should have learned by now not to listen to that idiot. There's mice everywhere, probably even on the moon!"

By the time I hobbled into the Earl Shaffer Shelter at dusk, totally spent, Skate and Eco had already settled in for the night, having gotten there two hours earlier. For once I was too tired to cook supper (The Ego was lying low after the snake scare and didn't hassle me any), so I ate a breakfast bar and drank some water.

From the far side of the shelter, Eco said drowsily, "Model-T, in a couple of days we'll be back in my territory." (He was from near the small burg of Port Clinton.) "How would you like to help me reclaim my hidden treasure?"

Hidden treasure out here in no-man's land? "What're you talking about?" I grunted, annoyed, for I wanted to sleep, not talk.

"A treasure I hid last winter, but that's all I can tell you now." Skate giggled like she was in cahoots but didn't say anything.

"You're nuts. Go to sleep." I downed four extra-strength ibuprofen, along with the last of my water, and drifted into oblivion.

We stood by the edge of a dirt road, its packed red clay base glistening in the misty rays of the early morning sun. Off to one side Rausch Gap Creek flowed into some kind of huge pipe contraption, then out again. A heavy metal grating covered the pipe, probably to keep enterprising thru-hikers from using it as a bathtub. The stream did look inviting though, so I decided to give my feet a treat and soak them for a few minutes. They were on the mend, mainly because the rocks (except for a few short stretches) had retreated back beneath the soil.

Skate and Eco watched as I removed my boots and inched my feet into the icy water, but neither made any move to join me.

Eco gazed down the road and said, "Well, we're here. The treasure's just down this road a little way. You coming?"

This was a surprise, for he hadn't mentioned anything about his "treasure" since night before last at the Shaffer Shelter, and I'd begun to suspect that he and Skate had cooked up a weird hoax to have some fun at my expense. Without another word, he took off down the road with Skate hustling along behind. The Ego said, "C'mon, Alter, get your boots on. I want to see what Eco has up his sleeve." I yelled, "Wait for me!"

By the time I caught them, Eco and Skate were standing at the edge of a small graveyard a short distance off the road. A few ancient, moss-stained tombstones protruded randomly from the ankle-high grass, leaning at odd angles without any sense of pattern, the names almost illegible from the ravages of years. Large old trees spread gnarled limbs above the time-worn stones, creating a solemn, ethereal cathedral over their grave-shackled dwellers. In a word, the place was "spooky"—certainly a proper setting for buried "treasure" (if it existed)!

A name on a nearby stone caught my eye and I peered at the dim, eroded lettering: "Andrew Allen, Died 1854." The faded words stated that the poor fellow had been killed in an accident at a nearby gold mine. I shivered at the thought of the mangled, worm-riddled remains just scant feet out of reach.

Eco knelt at the base of a battered stone. "Here it is," he announced, reading the name aloud, "John Proud II." The writing on the tomb showed the man had been born in England in 1802 and had died in 1854. (Same mining accident?) Eco poked the earth near the left side of the stone's base with a stick. "Yep, right about here," he grunted as he began to dig with his spoon.

About six inches down, he paused. Then grinning, he pulled a small plastic-wrapped bundle from the hole, laid it gently on the ground, and quickly refilled the hole. I looked at Skate, my face a question mark. She shrugged her shoulders and the puzzled look on her face led me to believe she was as much in the dark as I was.

We watched while Eco unwrapped the plastic and triumphantly displayed a small J and B Scotch bottle (airline cocktail size). His face glowed with euphoria as he kissed the bottle and blurted, "This is rum; 151 proof rum! People, we're going to party tonight!"

Trying to hide my disappointment, I looked at the tiny bottle and thought, "Not much." Oh well, beauty flourishes in the eyes of the beholder! "Say Eco, you didn't happen to bury a couple of Cokes up by old John Proud the Second's head, did you?"

"Sorry, Model-T. But I've got some cherry Kool-Aid mix in my pack though."

Skate chimed in, "And I have some lime Gatorade!" Things were looking up! R.I.P., John Proud II!

I tripped for the umpteenth time this morning and J.R. snarled, "Hell's bells! Why in the heck don't you look where you're going?" I was back in the rocks again—had been off and on since leaving Port Clinton yesterday morning, and this particular section just south of The Pinnacle was rough going—every step a potential disaster. Regaining my balance, I flung back, "I don't see what you've got to complain about, 'cause *you* have a free ride. If you think you can do any better, then *you* carry the pack." Silence. The Freeloader had a good thing going and he knew it!

I had been walking on rocks for miles, stumbling often, occasionally falling, and constantly swearing. I'd even made up a little ditty that I hummed now and then to help take some of the sting out of the ordeal: "Rocks! Rocks! They's hard on yo' socks. They chews up yo' boots and hurts yo' foots!" Dang'em rocks!

And they were wrecking my boots. Shiny-black and pristine when I left Springer, now they had become old battle-scarred veterans, with the rubber Vibram soles badly separated from the leather uppers at the toes—victimized by uncountable scuffs against the Pennsylvania rocks. Cracks had developed in the leather from the constant flexing; and the insides, exposed to permanent wetness, were rotting. A two-hundred-dollar pair of boots—trashed! "J.R., we're gonna need to do something about these boots when we get to Delaware Water Gap because they're never gonna make it to Katahdin!" No reply. (Jeez! Maybe the Freeloader had somehow vaporized! Naw, I couldn't be so lucky.)

A little after noon, I reached the blue-blazed path that led to The Pinnacle. "Good place to take a rest," I grunted, but all I got was frosty silence. I walked down the path and came out on a magnificent rock shelf that overlooked a broad panorama of checkered fields—dark green squares of corn and lighter squares of pasture. Heat waves rose out of the landscape like long transparent worms, shimmering in the still air as they wiggled upward toward the brilliant blue sky. "Yeah, a great place to rest!" I mumbled, picking a small shady spot by a large boulder. I slipped my pack off, sat down, and leaned back. "Too bad Ol' J.R. is missing all this," I said aloud, watching some buzzards that flapped in the distance, disrupting the wavy worms' heavenly migration. "Ahh! Best spot I've found all day," I sighed, closing my eyes.

I jumped, snapping my eyes open! Something had touched my boot! My brain screamed, "snake!" and I jerked my feet into my groin as I carefully scanned the ground and rocks nearby.

Nothing! The Ego said, "It's just your imagination playing tricks, Old Sport." (So he was back! And in a good frame of mind, at that!) "Yeah, I suppose," I slowly agreed after meticulously examining the immediate area again and seeing nothing. "Guess I'm just tired."

Suddenly I caught a slight movement from the corner of my eye and blurted, "Holy moly! Did you see that? I swear that rock just moved!" He chided me, "Alter, you *are* hallucinating. You'd better lay off the 'Vitamin I' (ibuprofen)." (A possibility, for I had been eating the little miracle workers like candy since hitting the rocks.) "Yeah, you're right. Rocks can't move by themselves," I conceded, stretching my legs back out and relaxing (with one eye open).

"Ha! See there, Dufus! That round rock down by my left boot. See how it's jiggling, like something's shaking it!" The rock was about the size of a small watermelon. "Jesus! If it's a snake big enough to move *that* rock, I'll croak!"

I reached for my hiking stick, ready to hightail it out if a snake reared its ugly head, and prodded the stone hard enough to roll it over. Absolutely nothing! The stone, now still, looked like all the others. "Man, I've really got the heebie-jeebies! I need to take a nap!" I leaned back and closed my eyes again.

And heard a whisper! It cut through the air, barely audible, a soft, hiss-like, unintelligible garble. My eyes flew open as the noise became louder, forming words: "Boots! Boots!" The unearthly chant seemed to be coming from the rocks! "Boots! Boots! Boots!" over and over, rising in tempo! I slapped my face hard, hoping this was all a nightmarish dream, but watched, horrified, as the rocks began to come alive, one by one, then by the dozens.

A harsher voice joined the cacophony and I looked around. On a large boulder above my right shoulder sat the Devil himself, an evil, malevolent smirk on his repulsive face, one talon-like finger pointing at me while the other orchestrated the rocks as he led them in the terrifying chant: "Boots! Boots! Boots!" The Devil's long, scaly, snake-like tail slowly coiled and uncoiled, its wicked point barely a foot from my head, as it shot lasers of energy at the stones, bringing them to life. The pulsating crescendo filled my head like a gigantic drum, booming, driving rational thought from my mind.

On some unseen signal from the Old Deceiver, the rocks now began to inch forward, pulsating and keening, "Boots! Boots! We's starved for boots! We want yo' boots!" Paralyzed, frozen to the spot, I watched with horror as the rocks crept closer, and then began to scream hysterically and flail my arms as the first of the faceless orbs reached my feet and started to gnaw at the leather!

The voices suddenly coalesced into one, this time softer, which somehow caused the rocks to retreat. "Wake up!" the voice said firmly, and an arm shook my shoulder. "Are you sick?"

I opened my eyes and stared wild-eyed at the tall, dark-skinned man who bent down and looked at my face with concern. "You were shaking and groaning, mumbling incoherently—something about eating your boots. You don't look like you have a fever though. Are you out of food?"

"Naw," I grinned sheepishly as realization that it had all been a dream slowly dawned. (Or was I still enmeshed in a nightmare with subplots!) Almost too scared to look, I forced myself to cast a furtive glance at the rock above my shoulder and nearly fainted with relief to find it bare. And the stones were no longer dancing! Seeking a final reassurance, I surreptitiously checked my boots but they didn't show any teeth marks! Darn, it had all seemed so real!

I rose to my feet and chuckled, "Guess I must have dozed off. Had this silly dream about rocks trying to eat my boots. Crazy, huh?"

"Well, if you're sure you're okay. By the way, my name's John. I'm doing a section of the AT from Delaware Water Gap to Port Clinton." We shook hands and he glanced at his watch. "Golly, ten till three! I've got to get a move on," he said.

Almost three! I'd slept for nearly two hours! "Give me just a minute to put my pack on and I'll walk back up to the Trail with you." ("Just in case . . ." I thought, eyeing the silent stones.) J.R. whispered, "Good move, Old Sport." Jesus!

Came Lehigh Gap, formed ages ago by broad, picturesque Lehigh River, which meandered through the valley like a blue paper ribbon, creating a delightful view. Then came the climb out of the Gap—unlike anything I had yet encountered—up a mountainous jumble of rocks towering several hundred feet above the river. A heart stopper in more ways than one, for the Trail weaved upward like a nightmarish Gordian knot into a phantas-magoric gray landscape, where scrubby shrubs barely clung to poisoned soil.

Saddened, we looked toward the base of the mountain where the culprit sprawled—now shackled, its furnaces lifeless like the mountain it had rav-aged, its smokestacks now silent like the sterile devastation it had caused—the zinc smelting plant at nearby Palmerton. Zinc pollution had poisoned the mountain (and the people) because environmental controls had not been in place. (EPA finally forced the plant to close in 1980, but the damage had been done. The mountain is now an EPA Superfund cleanup site.)

J.R. spoke with quiet anger. "Take a good look, Alter. This is what happens when greed, corruption, and total disregard for human life run unchecked." I replied softly, "Is this where pollution is taking us? Anyone who sees this would have to realize that the human race is doomed unless—" I choked, unable to continue, feeling like I just witnessed the execution of a friend. J.R. growled, "C'mon, let's move. We have enough misery already."

As we made our way across the plundered mountaintop, I glanced up at the cobalt-blue sky and the distant forest-covered mountains and thought, "God's gift of Earth, once pristine and pure; now sullied and soiled, how can it endure?" Yin and Yang . . .

Then came Wolf Rocks! Volunteer said, "This is about the snakiest-looking place I've ever seen." We sat on a large boulder, one of a multitude, eating lunch. Thick canopy rose out of dense growth on the forest floor, pushing in on the mammoth graybacks over which Trail passed.

"Yeah, this is a snake den if I ever saw one," I agreed, shuddering. "You can almost smell'em!"

I was thankful for the company. (Yesterday afternoon, when I had reached Leroy Smith Shelter, Volunteer was cooking supper. I couldn't believe my eyes, for I'd thought he was a week ahead of me, but he explained that he had taken several days off to visit a friend. While we ate, he caught me up on the latest trail gossip: Moleskin Meg was taking a couple of days off in Palmerton to rest her legs; Doctor Doolittle had developed a hernia and was off the Trail, pending surgery; Skate and Eco had gotten into Palmerton day before yesterday and were now traveling with Dog and Shug, whom I hadn't seen since back in Georgia. Hippy Man was hiking south for a week or so after doing a "mini-flipflop"; and no, they hadn't been able to catch Wahoola—still a week ahead.)

We finished lunch and started up the Trail (with me in the lead at The Marine's insistence—some wild hair up his behind about being a role model for this young wannabe Jarhead). We had only gone about a hundred yards when I spotted a small scrap of paper, weighed down by a rock, lying in the middle of the path. Curious, I picked it up, read it, and handed it to Volunteer. It was unsigned and less than an hour old (the author had thoughtfully scribbled the date and time down).

Volunteer read the note and handed the scrap back, and I replaced it in the middle of the Trail for the next person, although the information was definitely time-sensitive. "Hmm. So there's supposed to be a rattler coiled between two rocks fifteen yards ahead right on the Trail—according to this," I said with a frown. "It's probably long gone by now."

Slowly now, stepping carefully, I began to pummel the rocks with my hiking stick (much to Volunteer's amusement). "Is this how you kill rocks in the Marines?" he sniggered from his safe position behind me. Impertinent pup! J.R. thought it was hilarious and began guffawing so loudly inside my brain that I could barely hear the beating of my stick, much less the buzz of an angry rattler. I gave Volunteer a caustic glare and flipped J.R. a mental "bird," telling him to shut up unless he wanted to feed a snake, and continued to pound away, carefully checking for likely ambush sites.

"Uh, Model-T." Volunteer's voice was hesitant, almost apologetic. "You just stepped over that rattler."

I froze, and then slowly turned, heart stopped, gritting my teeth as I waited for the stabbing pain of vile fangs and the fiery throb of poison rushing into my leg. Nothing happened! I exhaled in a loud gasp and stared hard at the leafy bottom of the crevice between the two rocks that now separated Volunteer and me. "I don't see anything that remotely resembles a rattler, only these old leaves. Are you sure?" and to prove my point, I poked at the leaves. They suddenly stirred and began buzzing like crazy as the outline of a small rattlesnake, its color almost identical to the leafy bottom, abruptly took shape! The snake coiled, angry at being disturbed, ready to do battle!

"Yikes! It *is* a rattler!" I jumped backwards and almost toppled off the rock. "Damnation! How the heck did I miss seeing it? And it didn't even rattle when I beat the rocks." Volunteer shrugged and quickly detoured around some rocks to join me. "I guess it must have been a sound sleeper," I said lamely as we went on up the Trail.

Less than fifty yards ahead, another note lay on the ground, also in the same handwriting: "There is another rattler between two rocks twenty yards ahead on the left side of the trail." We both began whacking rocks! (The Marine wasn't guffawing this time.)

"Uh, Model-T."

"Yeah, what is it?" The hair on my neck began to rise, for he had that same apologetic tone.

"You're straddlin' that other rattler."

I gazed down between my legs at the leaf-covered bottom. Sure enough, barely visible against the blotchy-brown were *two* rattlers, loosely entwined, just lying there like they hadn't a care in the world! "Damn! I just peed all over those vipers!" I gasped as I leapt for my life.

We went on up the Trail, both pummeling the rocks like African hunters beating the bush for tigers—this time with Volunteer in the lead.

Finally came Delaware Water Gap! The end of the Pennsylvania rocks! My heart leaped with joy as Volunteer and I walked up the short driveway to the basement hiker's hostel of the Presbyterian Church of the Mountain, its aged brick facade mirroring the same fastidious care and pride of community that glittered throughout the town.

Four things of significance happened during my three-day stay:

First, I got a new pair of Merrell Leather-lite boots, *free,* courtesy of Merrell's rock-solid warranty—which is why I got to stay three days.

Second, I met Markus . . .

I beat Volunteer to the shower, and when I came out, curiously the lad had wandered off. He was easily found, though. I just followed the tantaliz-ing aroma of pancakes and bacon across the street to The Green Lantern, where I found him sitting at a bar attacking a stack of pancakes as big around as Cadillac hubcaps. A hedonistic fire glowed in his eyes and he seemed oblivious to everything except the plate, his piston-like arm, and his gaping maw. The sizeable pool of syrup that formed a moat around the stack had overflowed the plate and oozed onto the counter, forming a small, thick puddle. Fascinated, the half-dozen patrons paused in their dining to watch as he detached a large chunk from the mother lode, expertly speared it, and dunked it into the puddle on the counter; and a couple of gasps came as he crammed the dripping, sodden glob into his mouth. He exhaled with an audible sigh of sheer pleasure, licked the syrupy dribble from his chin with his tongue, and then stared, dreamlike, at the ceiling as his hand automatically darted back to the pancakes.

I walked up and poked him in the ribs, bouncing him out of his trance. "How much are you getting paid to perform your eating act?" I asked, pointing at the several customers who had been taking it all in.

Volunteer sneaked a glance over his shoulder and flushed bright red. I patted him on the shoulder and told his audience, "It's okay, Folks. He's harmless enough; doesn't eat humans, dogs, or cats, though he has been known to occasionally swallow shelter mice whole. My sincerest apologies. I thought he was tied up good, but he chewed through his leash and got away."

Smiling sheepishly, he bottomed out at deep scarlet as a sprinkling of titters floated across the room, causing him to hunker down close to his plate. "Aw gee, Model-T, I didn't realize I was making an ass of myself."

"Don't worry about it. Asses, too, have their place in the animal kingdom," I chuckled softly, motioning toward the middle-aged, corpulent patron three seats down from Volunteer—one of the "regulars," I guessed, since no one bothered to give him a second glance. His sagging jowls quivered and flopped as he noisily rooted at a platter piled high with sausage links, scrambled eggs, fried potatoes, and gosh knows what else, all covered with thick, white gravy. The man was off in his own little world.

"See. There's asses everywhere. They come in all shapes and sizes." I sat down next to Volunteer as the waitress, a faded rose in a lackluster dress, placed a menu before me. "I don't need a menu, Ma'am," I declared, pointing at the fat man's platter. "Just bring me what he has."

Her face clouded with uncertainty and she asked, "You sure you want what Markus has got? It ain't on th' menu 'cause nobody round here ever wants to eat that much at one settin'."

Like I couldn't put away the mound of food like Markus was rootin' around in! She must not know thru-hikers very well! "Yes'm, I'm sure.

And while you're at it, bring me what this young feller had, too," I told her, indicating Volunteer's nearly empty plate. "I haven't eaten since breakfast."

She rolled her eyes in amazement and yelled back to the cook, "Hey Sammy, one Markus special and one deluxe stack. You want coffee, too?"

Volunteer interjected, "Uh, Ma'am, could you make that two Markus specials?"

Markus glance over at us, respect written on his bloated face, and grunted, "Eatin's a right serious business, an' ah reckon you boys is gonna need some elbow room." Slowly, he shifted his huge frame down a space. "Afore th' forks start aflyin," he added. He was definitely serious!

I nudged Volunteer, and then said to Markus, "Thank ye kindly. We'll try to be extra careful, but it's really this young'un here who's a danger with th' eatin' tools; lack of experience, you know. Why, last week I watched him almost nail a fellow hiker's ear to a shelter wall with his knife when he got excited cuttin' on a hunk of fried possum. Knife just flew right outta his hand before he knew what was happening." I shook my head. "Coulda been bad!" Volunteer choked on a piece of pancake and grabbed for his water glass.

Markus pondered the picture in his mind for a long moment. "You boys maybe need a mite more room at that," and he retired to a table a safe distance away to watch the two asses do their stuff.

Third, SWAT-man taught me a lesson in "one-upmanship" . . .

Filled up to my gullet and barely able to walk, I went back to the hostel to overcome my misery with a short nap. It was empty, except for a stranger (not a thru-hiker, for he was dressed in blue jeans) who occupied a wingback chair. A short, scrawny guy, maybe thirty-five, he was clean shaven, although he had a long ponytail neatly collected with a rubber band. "How do?" he asked.

"Fair," I grunted. "Stuffed all the way to the ears, truth be known. My friend and I just finished a little meal at the diner across the street." Burping loudly, I laughed and said, "Guess they aren't used to thru-hikers, though, because three fellows were placing bets on whether my friend and I could eat the 'Markus special,' which is a whopper breakfast named after Markus, Delaware Water Gap's own Olympic-class eater. The 'Champ' himself was there, bettin' on us. Smart man."

"How'd it turn out?"

"Well, we didn't let Ol' Markus down. But I'd sure hate to go up against him." Changing tack, I probed, "Where're you from? You're not a thru-hiker."

"Does it show that much? I just finished a two-week section hike from Duncannon to here and I'm waiting for my ride to take me to the bus station. In fact, he should be here shortly. My name's SWAT-man."

He went on to tell me he was a member of a S.W.A.T. team in Philadelphia. Hot dang! I'd never met a real live S.W.A.T. man. Curious, I took a closer look and then shivered as he gave me a penetrating look with eyes of knife-blade steel that betrayed his ready smile, which he seemed able to turn on and off like a well-oiled lock. A hint of scar coursed up from his eye into his scalp—a battle scar? And when he spoke, I immediately thought of granite. This was a man to be reckoned with. Without warning, he pulled a long knife from a leg sheath and began to sharpen it with a small stone. It already looked razor sharp.

The granite voice grated against my ears. "You hike over Wolf Rocks?" It was more a statement of fact than a question—like an accusation. (Even if I hadn't, I'd have admitted to anything as the unwavering eyes above the smiling mouth probed my depths!)

"Sure did. Day before yesterday."

"See any snakes?" The stone slid back and forth across the sharp, shiny edge, making a soft, ominous swish that gave me goose pimples.

Time to establish my credentials! "Man, did I ever! Humongous ones, bigger'n my arm. In fact—" His eyes narrowed and Mighty Marine cut me off, hissing, "Watch out! He's setting us up for a snake tale and we definitely don't want to out-snake this man, not with him holding a knife. He could be a looney."

I wimped. "Well, they weren't all *that* big; just a couple of little ones, really." J.R. cautioned me again, whispering, "He *said* he was a S.W.A.T. member but he didn't show us his badge. Policemen *always* flash their badges when they identify themselves, even when off duty."

SWAT-man turned the good boy smile back on. "If you're not in any big hurry, I'll tell you what happened to me at Wolf Rocks." Assuring him that his time was mine, I sat down and he continued, "I started to step down onto a small ledge, and there was this big timber rattler laid out, sunning. I was wearing shorts and heavy wool socks that had fallen down around my ankles. I took a step backwards while I decided whether to kill it or chase it away and felt something tugging on my sock, so I looked down an' there was a big copperhead that had bitten into my sock and got his fangs tangled up." He grinned, though whether at the thought of wrestling with a couple of poisonous vipers or at the skeptical look on my face, I hadn't the foggiest clue. Talk about harebrained tales; this took the cake!

The Marine nudged me. "Careful now! This guy's fruitier than fruit cocktail. Think up an excuse to get out of here, and let's go find a policeman."

Common sense and past experience told me not to listen to The Idiot Jarhead, but he *did* know about these things, at least he'd had experience in military law enforcement. And jeez, a wacko with the world's sharpest knife! I'd never dealt with a wacko before (except The Ego)! My brain froze and I blurted, "What happened!"

Nonchalantly, just like he was ordering a Markus special, he continued, "I reached down and grabbed th' copper behind the neck and got it untangled, then pulled out Ol' Tucker here and whacked its head off." He affectionately ran the stone across Ol' Tucker's gleaming edge, a reward for faithful service.

"Yeah, J.R., this guy is nuttier than a pecan tree," I silently acknowledged. "He's just toying with us. I'll play along until you can think of something." Aloud, I said (not very convincing at this point, having decided that Wacko was simply making it all up to feature his best buddy, Ol' Tucker), "Sure sounds exciting. And what happened to the rattler?"

"Oh, he took off while I was terminating the copperhead. Here, you wanna see it?" He reached behind the chair and pulled out a long piece of cardboard. Tacked to the board, drying, was the skin of the largest copperhead J.R. had ever seen, and he was from copperhead country! "I skinned it, and I'm taking it back to show to the guys before I make it into a belt and a hatband." SWAT-man's face shone with pride, and his eyes softened as he let Ol' Tucker's pointed tip "kiss" its recent victim.

Dang that J.R.! Burnt again. Ashamed, I shook his hand—the hand that wielded such awesome fearlessness—and said, "SWAT-man, it is a pleasure to meet a real S.W.A.T. man!" Then the thought registered, leaving me weak as wilted lettuce, "This could have happened to me!" I confessed, "Damnation, SWAT-man, if that had happened to me I'd have died of fright on the spot, or else I'd still be running with an angry copperhead flopping from my sock!" He dutifully laughed, except for the eyes. Weak-kneed and slightly nauseous, I said, "Guess I'd better go sleep off this meal. Good luck."

I went toward the bunkroom, shuddering, muttering beneath my breath about crud-mamma'n snakes. A last casual wave at this master of "one-upmanship," but he was intent on caressing Ol' Tucker with the stone, over and over, and a faraway vision dulled his steely eyes.

Fourth, I got a free haircut! J.R.'s niece, Robyn, lived less than an hour away in New Jersey. A short phone call, and I had clean sheets and plenty of great food and company until my new boots arrived. And the haircut—with dog clippers. A first for her—and for me! Thanks Robyn!

On the third day Robyn and her three-year-old daughter, Shaye, returned me to the hostel in time to pick up my new boots from The Green Lantern waitress (who graciously accepted them from UPS for me). Many thru-hikers had trickled in, some whom I hadn't seen for weeks—The Moseys, Total Rec's, Tripp, Dog and Shug, and The Orient Express (Bill had been met back down the Trail by friends and was taking a couple of days off while a vet checked Orient out). I was particularly glad to be reunited with Skate and Eco even though I didn't get to see much of them, for her family had driven in from Ohio and whisked both away for a bit of luxury! I introduced Robyn to my friends, a delightful experience all around, and after a quick supper at the Delaware Gap Diner (her treat!) she left.

Late in the evening, Pastor Karen Nickels dropped by to check on things. Her motherly face shone with a dynamic spirit that surged from an inner well of "living water." Yet, beneath her kindness, I sensed a tough bulldoggish, no-nonsense strength similar to that which I'd seen in another Karen—the Director of ATC's Mid-Atlantic Regional Office at Boiling Springs. These ladies were two of a kind; and as had happened with Karen Lutz, J.R. and I were enriched by this brief touching of our paths.

Early the next morning, I quietly packed and maneuvered through the maze of bodies sleeping on the sitting room floor. (All the bunks had filled up fast the previous evening as more thru-hikers arrived.) Outside, a heavy overcast hid the first rays of dawn. I wolfed down two bologna sandwiches and an apple that Robyn had insisted I take and polished off a quart of water, neat, and was shouldering my pack when a car pulled into the parking lot. Skate waved from the open window. "I just *knew* you would be leaving early," she said as she climbed out, followed by her family and a sleepy-eyed Eco. "We wanted to leave with the Model-T. And my family wanted to meet you."

I was touched. The O'Leary's wished us well, gave Kate hugs (and shed some tears), and drove away. I said gruffly, "Let's hit the Trail," (mainly a call to action for Skate, who numbly stared at the disappearing tail lights and tried, without success, to blink back the tears).

As we crossed the Delaware River Bridge—a magnificent span of concrete and steel, yet shaking and bouncing like a flimsy footbridge in an earthquake as eighteen-wheelers roared past, only inches away from our narrow walkway—the rain began. Below, murky water eddied around hidden rocks in large swirling circles, ominous and threatening like the rock-inundated mountains of Pennsylvania.

As I stepped off the far end of the bridge onto New Jersey soil, The Ego boasted excitedly, "Well Alter, we did it! We tweaked that devil's tail and made him skedaddle right out of Pennsylvania!" I suppose he was bragging about how we had actually made it through the rocks without breaking a leg or feeding a rattler. "Don't count your chicken's before the eggs hatch," I growled out loud. "The Devil's bound to have a calloused tail."

A few yards ahead, Skate and Eco trudged through the steady downpour. She glanced back to see if I was talking with another hiker. I shrugged my shoulders at her curious glance. She frowned and then bent back into the rain and walked on.

CHAPTER 9

Tomorrow's Memories

"Dammit, I think I've got a new one," I groaned. "How many does that make?" J.R. asked. "Not sure," I replied. "Seventeen at last count. Dangit, I even have blisters under blisters!" It was true! Baby blisters were cutting up like misbehaving children underneath two thick-skinned parents, one on the bottom of each big toe. "Ouch!" I winced as my boot snagged on a stubby rock. "So much for new boots."

The Trail had turned sour since I left Delaware Water Gap four days ago. It had rained off and on for three straight days, and the morning's heavy overcast still drenched me with intermittent showers. So far the sun had been unable to penetrate the thick layer, even for a few minutes, and all my gear was soaked. Sadly, the new Leather-lites resembled muddy derelicts, not even fit for skid row (not to mention my feet). Ramshackle boots and wastrel feet—a shoddy affair!

New boots usually meant a few blisters, but combined with the constant wetness, a bumper crop had sprouted. I mused, "Wonder what the Trail record is for having the greatest number of blisters at one time?" He thought about it for a moment. "No way to tell, but I'll bet we've out-blistered Moleskin Meg. She'd be jealous as heck."

In spite of the pain, I chuckled at the thought of Moleskin Meg sitting behind that large rock back in Georgia yelling for duck tape. Thank goodness I still had some left! It didn't stick for long on wet skin, but if a body could wrap it around the blister so that it overlapped, the stuff would hold till hell froze over (or at least for several hours)! The big problem was, blisters had also formed on the heels and balls of both feet, and these were hard places to overlap the tape. Worriedly, I glanced at the dwindling supply spooled on my hiking stick.

291

I tripped on a rock, and pain surged up my right leg. (I was favoring my left foot, which for some reason had out-blistered the right. This caused me to limp, which put more stress on the right leg.) "Okay, that's it!" I snarled. "I've had it with rocks. The books lied! The rocks don't end in Pennsylvania! The freakin things are in New Jersey, too!"

It was a fact! Maybe the rocky treadway wasn't *quite* as bad here as back in PA, but the going was still frustrating, especially since I had expected something entirely different. (In my naïve mind's eye, I had envisioned a smooth, manicured, rock-free path leading over gentle, rolling hills.) Ha! All I had gotten from NJ was rain, blisters, and more of the cursed ankle-busters! Disgusted, I shrugged out of my pack and sat down on a butt-sized boulder.

"What do you mean, 'That's it'?" The Ego asked. "I mean I'm gonna kill some rocks. I'm gonna commit rockicide!" Picking up two fist-sized chunks, I began pounding them fiendishly against each other. It felt wonderful! I smashed the rocks together, harder, relishing the staccato cracks and the shock waves that hammered my wrists. Small bits of stone flew through the air and peppered my face, but I squinted my eyes into narrow slits and kept on smashing until no more flakes came off. Tossing the spent rocks aside, I picked up two more and began pounding again. "Hot dang, Ego! I shoulda done this weeks ago. Sonofagun! This makes me feel *good!*" He retorted sarcastically, "Well, it *does* make more sense than kicking them."

I grabbed a marble-shaped pebble and placed it on a flat rock. Really into it now, I smashed down viciously with a triangular stone the size of a misshapen grapefruit. "There!" I screamed. "Take *that,* you bloody bastard!" I stared at the crumbly remains and chortled with glee. Grabbing another victim, this one larger, I laid it on the sacrificial altar and demolished it with a quick blow. "Darn! That'n was a wimp. Need a bigger rock," I grunted, reaching for one the size of a miniature asteroid. "Okay Killer, now I'm goin' after the big ones!" I lashed down swiftly in a vicious attack.

"Ow! Sumabitch! Ouch!" I yelped, leaping to my feet and dancing, impervious to the foot pain, which had suddenly become absorbed into the throbbing of my smashed finger. Instinctively I stuck it in my mouth and sucked hard. J.R. snickered, "Them rocks not only chews yo' boots an' hurts yo' foots; they also screws up yo' thinkie an' whacks yo' pinkie. By the way, isn't that yo' 'potty hand'?" I brushed a tear away with my good hand and snarled, "Dammit, J.R., it's not funny. Go piss up a rope!"

Pain replaced anger, and I pulled the finger from my mouth and examined the end result of my fury. Not all that bad, considering the blow—slightly swollen, with a purple splotch that covered the entire tip of my right index finger, but no gash. It just hurt like the dickens! J.R. chortled,

"Now what do you have in mind? You finished with your tantrum or are you going to do some more rock bashing?"

Without bothering to answer, I gritted my teeth, removed my boots, and reached for the duck tape.

I hadn't seen Eco or Skate since the evening after we left Delaware Water Gap. My feet had already started to grow blisters by the time we reached Catfish Fire Tower, an abandoned ramshackle skeleton of rusty girders, after a thirteen-mile day. They wanted to go on for at least three more miles but my feet just weren't up to it, so I decided to camp near the tower (with high hopes that the weather would clear the next day). If the sun came out, I would be able to dry my boots. And if I managed to keep my feet halfway dry, I might be able to head off the blisters. Conveying a false lightheartedness, I'd told them to go on ahead.

Late the next afternoon, after hiking through steady rain most of the day, I reached Gren Anderson Shelter—a rundown affair that exactly matched my mood—only to find it overrun by a boy's club group of at least fifteen shivering, sullen kids out of their element. No sign of Eco and Skate, nor had they left a message in the register. Disappointed, I went to the cleared area behind the shelter and rigged my tarp in a heavy drizzle, covering the muddy ground with the thin plastic ground-cloth. I said, "It's gonna be a bad night." Then with pizzazz I added, "But just remember, Ol' Sport, the adversities of today become tomorrow's memories." He grumbled, "Not only do I have to endure the rain, but I have to put up with barnyard philosophy from a mush-brain." (Make that a *long*, bad night.)

Storms rolled in shortly after dark. Rain dropped in bucketfuls, sending water rushing beneath the tarp to pool in the shallow depression (a detail not noticed until the water oozed over the flimsy plastic ground cloth and rose to the top of my Therm-a-Rest) where I lay. Trying to make the best of our lot, I said, "Ego, we're gonna float down the hill if it gets any higher. You know, experiences like this are like money in the old memory bank!" He barked, "For cryin' out loud, Alter! Who in his right mind would want to remember *this?*" (Make that a *very* long, bad night!)

Thankfully, when the dawn struggled through the sickly gray drizzle we hadn't floated away. I awoke, soaked and shivering, with a morbid sense of déjà vu (Dahlgren Campground repeated, except this time the tarp hadn't collapsed). For once J.R. stoically accepted our lot and didn't add to my misery—else he was so mentally constipated with anger he couldn't talk.

I noticed a sagging tent nearby—a surprise, for I hadn't heard anyone come in during the night. Pinched with jealousy, J.R. muttered, "That person's probably drier than stale toast. At least someone had enough sense to pack a tent instead of a flimsy tarp," at which I automatically prattled, "Heavy pack; miserable hike." Wrapping the wet tarp around the sopping sleeping bag, I stuffed the sordid mess inside my pack and said, "Probably be a good idea to visit the privy before we get on the Trail." He, grumbling: "At least we'll be out of the rain for a few minutes."

In his dreams! The privy turned out to be a simple plywood box (no walls or roof!) topped with a wet commode lid. A small sign tacked to a tree told us to "Use a poncho if you feel the need for privacy." I chuckled, "Well, this is a first! You happen to have a poncho, Old Chappie?" but he was gripped by nostalgia and his ugly mood evaporated like gas fumes. "A one-holer! Doggone, I haven't sat on anything like that since Vietnam. C'mon, Alter, let's try it out!" he urged excitedly. "Jeez, Marine, I don't know. What if someone sees us?" (That tent was almost in the privy's backyard.) He said, "Who in their right mind would be out this early! Besides, it's one of those 'memory things.'" Put that way, why not; so we perched on the "throne."

Shortly, I heard the rasp of a zipper and Barbie Doll (a priggish plain-Jane thru-hiker I'd briefly met at Delaware Water Gap) poked her sleep-distorted face out of the tent. Wordlessly, her eyes big question marks, she took a long look. Equally surprised, I almost fell through the hole. Not knowing what else to do, I sent a benign smile and a nonchalant wave her way as if this was business as usual. She frowned (actually, it was more like "THE LOOK") and ignored my wave, so I shrugged my shoulders (after all, I didn't build the stupid thing) and, motioning at the sides that weren't there, crowed, "Look Maw, no walls!" Bingo! As she ducked back inside, J.R. chuckled, "I'll bet Barbie uses a poncho!" Laughing with delight, I replied, "You know it. An' talk about stackin' up the memories . . ." Suddenly, the morning didn't seem so glum.

That afternoon, the sun finally pushed through the clouds—a good thing, for I had run out of duck tape! My feet finally seemed to be accepting the new boots—at least no new blisters had formed. However, the current crop had reduced me from a lean, mean, hiking machine to a hobbling lummox.

Skate and Eco were now two days ahead and I was forced to face the realization that they had probably gone the way of Wahoola, who had widened the distance to nine days. "We'll not see them again, not on this Trail," I remarked ruefully. The Ego: "Cheer up, Old Chum. Moleskin

Meg's still behind us. She's always looking for someone to hike with." He sure knew how to make a fella feel better!

I had lost my urge to smash rocks, especially after doing that number on my finger. In fact, the entire personality of the Trail seemed to change with the coming of fair weather. Stretches of rocky treadway still hampered my progress, but they were not as lengthy, and the ups and downs had gentled, which lessened the toll my feet had to pay.

And then there were the pumps! In a few places, old-fashioned, long-handled pumps had been installed atop wells dug alongside the Trail—convenient water sources in areas where springs and streams were scarce. Yet, my first encounter with a pump had been a bust . . .

When I had happened on the first one, a day or so out of Delaware Water Gap, The Ego and I stared at the oddity with amazement. "It's a pump," he said. "Of course it's a pump, Dummy. What'd you think it was?" I snapped. (I wasn't in a good frame of mind because the morning had become a "Misery Contest"—me against the rain, rocks, mud, and blisters.) Undeterred, he prattled on, "This is the first one we've seen on the Trail since leaving Springer Mountain." He studied it for a few seconds, then declared, "It's gotta be a Yankee thing, digging a well right on the Trail. Let's see if it works."

He had to be kidding! We were right in the middle of a torrential downpour. Lightning played all over the sky—some of it close—and thunder-boomers rattled the air. "Why would you want to do such a dumb thing? Just raise your head and hold your mouth open and you'll get all the water you want without even having to pump a handle." But he had his mind set and insisted that we give it a try.

It was easier to just do it than to stand in the downpour and argue with the idiot, so I began to pump, willing the water to start gushing so I could get moving again. I pumped slowly at first, then faster and faster, willing the water to come. He suggested, "The seal's probably dried out. Just pour some water down that little hole where the thingamajiggie goes up and down. When I was a kid, sometimes Pap had to prime his pump and that's what he did." I hesitated. "Jeez, Ego, I don't know. We've only got a half quart and it's got to last until we get to the next fill up, wherever that might be." But he dug in his heels. "Heck, here's all the water we need, right in this well. All we've got to do is pour a cupful in and it'll be primed and ready to go. Guaranteed!"

To miserable to argue, I gave in and dribbled a dash down the "thinga-majiggie" hole. "A little more," he said, and I poured in another couple of ounces. "Okay, now try it." I pumped like the dickens. Nothing!

"You've got to give it some more water," he insisted. "Pour the rest in. It's *got* to work!" There wasn't enough water remaining in the bottle to make a good spit. "'Got' doesn't get thirsty, Mush-brain," I shouted, mad as a hornet—mostly at myself for being dumb enough to get taken in by his warped curiosity. "Aw, what th' heck!" Angry, I dumped the rest of the water down the "thingamajiggie" hole and pumped frenziedly. Nothing! Nada! Nary a dribble! Muttering obscenities, I kicked the pump and stalked away, slip-sliding down the muddy path through the deluge. Mush-brain mumbled, "It's gotta be a Yankee thing . . ."

Now came more days of fair weather and pleasant hiking, often through small fields of colorful wildflowers and rich, verdant valleys. My feet continued to heal and my stride regained its former bounce. In spite of being back in the old familiar hiker vacuum, I found joy in my renewed vigor.

Then came Tripp . . .

I didn't quite beat a late afternoon thunderstorm to High Point Shelter (a short half-mile north of its namesake—the tall obelisk monument that marks New Jersey's highest point). I rushed under the overhang and there was Tripp, hunched in a corner cooking grits like he hadn't a care in the world! He had lost weight, almost to the point of being emaciated. I would have hugged him, except I might have knocked over his grits and that would have been an unpardonable offense to an ol' Southern boy. Instead, I reached across the cook pot and shook his hand. "Tripp! Jeez, it's great to see you. How're things going?"

He smiled and stuttered a greeting, and then giving the grits a stir, he frowned. "Not so good. I had to get new boots back at the Gap and, what with all this rain, I've got some bad blisters."

Nodding sympathetically, I said, "Me, too. You show me yours and I'll show you mine."

"I don't think so. Wrong sex!"

I laughed, taking off my wet shirt and using it as a makeshift towel before hanging it on a nail. "Are you getting enough to eat?" Motioning at his bubbling pot of grits, I added, "Besides that?" Digging inside the pack for my dry shirt, I pulled it on and immediately felt better.

He thought for a moment and said, "Probably not; but then, I'm not all that hungry. I only eat when I get hungry."

"Not good," muttered The Ego. "If he loses any more weight, he's going to start losing muscle." I glanced at Tripp's food bag; it looked worse than a deflated tire! For whatever reason, he wasn't carrying much food. A thought: It wouldn't hurt to keep an eye on my Mississippi friend for a few days. (Besides, his presence might help keep The Ego out of my hair!)

"Tripp, what say we hike together for a few days? I could sure use the company."

"That's fine with me, but I've got to pick up my mail drop in Unionville tomorrow."

I hadn't planned to make the one-mile side trip into Unionville, New York, a small town near the New Jersey and New York border, but something other than trail-fare would be nice. "Works for me. Maybe we can find a decent greasy spoon and get a burger." That settled, I lit my stove and began cooking mac-n-cheese.

Unionville was larger than I had anticipated—at least the cemetery was! Tripp and I limped past an old wrought-iron fence that separated the living from the dead. Gravestones stretched as far as we could see, mostly old stones with elaborate, flowery lettering, although some of the tombs were ornately sculpted, replicating the deceased in marble. If the care this town lavished on its dead reflected its population, this would be a great place to live!

While Tripp went looking for the post office, I stopped in at Horler's General Store, a well-stocked grocery with Ben and Jerry's ice cream, bought a quart of something with "chocolate" in the name, and sat on the sidewalk curb to eat it. The townspeople who walked past smiled and said hello. Friendly people, great ice cream! Yep, a good place to live.

Tripp soon returned, a happy man. He waved an envelope at me. "It came!" I looked puzzled. "The money order. Twenty big ones, and the Post Office cashed it, too!" Beaming, he waved the picture of "Old Hickory" in my face.

"You didn't get any food in your mail drop?"

"Nope. I'll buy some here."

("Not much with a twenty," I thought.) Passing the carton of ice cream, slightly less than half full, to him, I said, "Eat the rest of this." (Time to start fattening this puppy up!)

"You sure?" he asked, grabbing the container and whipping his spoon out of his pack with greased-lightning swiftness. I watched with a satisfied grin (which almost matched his) as he quickly emptied it! "Thanks, Model-T. Now let's go find that greasy spoon."

"We'd better buy groceries first . . ."

From the outside, the Unionville Luncheonette looked shabby. Paint peeled in long strips from the aged clapboard siding, and the roofline sagged like a swayback mule. Faded signs on the front—neglected tattle-tale remnants from better days—had somehow escaped eradication through the years (or maybe they were historical heirlooms!) and silently heralded the Luncheonette's past heritage. "I wonder how it passed the health inspection?" I murmured, looking at Tripp. "You think it's open?"

"Well, it has an 'Open' sign on the door." He twisted the doorknob, stuck his head inside and nodded, so we stacked our packs beside the door and went in.

"Shabbiness" had metastasized throughout the interior: It had rickety plank flooring, a couple of plywood booths, and a small counter with assorted stools that segregated the eaters from an ancient grill. A groaning, scarred refrigerator tilted off-balance in a corner. (Compared to this place, the Doyle Hotel looked like the Waldorf Astoria!) Even the lights were off, which made the dim interior seem alien and deserted. A homely, acne-pocked girl in tight-fitting jeans, perhaps twenty, sat on a stool at the counter, squinting in the dim light as she read a romance magazine. I checked my watch—a few minutes before noon. Including the girl, we made three customers! The girl was engrossed in whatever she was reading and paid us no attention.

"Say miss, do you know where the waitress is?" I asked, rather loudly in order to compete with the magazine.

She glanced up, bored, chewing her gum rapidly as she shuffled her bottom, which generously overlapped the stool. "That's me. Y'all want somethin' to eat?"

At this point I wasn't sure if I did or not. Tripp answered, "It would be nice." She gave Tripp a flirty look, which made him blush.

The girl walked over to the wall and flipped a switch. "Boss man said to keep th' lights off unless we got customers." One dinky, dim light bulb dangled from the ceiling on a long wire, casting weak shadows across the room. Preliminaries out of the way, she fluffed her bleached hair and asked, "Y'all wanna eat at th' counter or you want a booth?"

"How much extra does the booth cost?" I joked.

Chewing furiously, she stared at me like I'd blown a fuse. Then working the gum with her tongue, she blew a small bubble and popped it before replying. "Boss man ain't never said nothin' 'bout chargin' extra." Before she decided to make a determination on her own, I grabbed Tripp and pulled him into a booth. Her face brightened as she asked, "Say, are y'all thru-hikers?"

My turn! I looked at her like she was bananas. "You found us out! How'd you know?"

"All you thru-hikers got skinny butts." Triumph spread like wildfire across her face at having passed the "test." She flashed Tripp an interesting look and winked, which almost sent him through the creaky plywood seat. "Now, whatcha gonna have?"

We ordered hamburgers, fries, and canned cokes (wary of trench mouth—at the very least) and were happy when the food arrived on paper plates. Two unordered slices of cheese had been added to Tripp's burger, and his pile of fries was noticeably larger than mine. Perched back atop her stool, our waitress chewed her cud with her eyes locked on Tripp's every move, but he stubbornly refused to look at her. I whispered, "Tripp, that gal has the 'hots' for you."

The poor guy blushed and whispered, "Let's pay up and get th' heck out while we can!"

Seeing that we were finished, she came over to the booth. "Y'all want some pie? It's on th' house, long's th' boss don't come in." She giggled and rubbed her finger in a small puddle of condensation on the tabletop beside Tripp's plate and batted her eyelashes.

Before I could ask "what kind," Tripp jumped up, nearly upending the booth, and mumbled, "We gotta get back to the Trail, thanks anyway." He tossed three dollars on the table and charged for the door.

With that possibility lost, she looked at me with some interest, though not nearly what she had lavished on Tripp. Hastily, I threw three one-dollar bills beside my plate. "My buddy has conniption fits. I gotta go check on him!" I hit the door running and didn't look back!

The afternoon became a contest of wills: Us against the sun. It soaked the pavement, sending up scorching waves that beat against our faces and sent sweat streaming into our eyes. For the past hour we had been walking along a lonely country road, its shoulders so narrow and weed-clogged that we were forced to stay on the searing hardtop most of the time. The breeze had died and there was no shade, for farmers had long ago chopped the trees from their fencerows. We walked side by side, sweltering in the oppressive heat, too miserably hot to carry on conversation, now and then moving to single file and crowding against the high growth when a vehicle zipped past.

At last the Trail left the pavement, took a sharp turn to the right, and began a boring two-mile stretch around the edge of a sod farm. Conditions improved slightly—still no shade or breeze—for we now walked on a non-reflective cinder track, which gave some relief.

Tripp hadn't said much since leaving Unionville. Suddenly he spoke, his voice a loud stutter against the quiet crunching of boots on cinders, "What kind of pie do you reckon she had?" (Did I detect a note of regret?)

"We could go back and find out. No tellin' what kind of 'freebies' she might have dragged outta th' fridge, 'long's th' boss man don't drop in.'"

Tripp giggled thickly through parched lips. "Yeah, and we were lucky to get out of there with our hides." He licked his lips, trying in vain for some moisture. "How much farther to that pump? I'm really getting dry." (A half hour ago we had drained the last of the two quarts we'd each carried out of town—sacrificed to the scorching sun—and my own mouth felt like sandpaper.)

Moistening my tongue with a tiny glob of saliva, I said, "It can't be far. About another mile, I'd guess. Dang, I sure hope that pump's working!" (If it wasn't, we were in *big* trouble for, according to the *A.T. Data Book*, there was no water at Pochuck Mountain Shelter, today's destination. *The Philosopher's Guide* recommended that hikers get water from the pump at the base of the mountain before beginning the climb up to the shelter.)

The pump didn't look so good. "Prime the pump" was lettered on a piece of cardboard tacked to a tree. Beneath the words, someone had scrawled, "This pump is a bunch of crap" in crooked letters.

"Dammit all, it's gotta be a form of Yankee torture," I muttered (glad that Tripp couldn't hear the string of vehement expletives that The Ego launched). "Well, lets see if we can get the darn contraption to work."

"What're we going to prime it *with?*" Tripp asked.

"Beats me. I guess we shoulda saved some water. Damn!"

Tripp stared at the pump like a little kid who had lost his candy money. "We could pee in a bottle and prime it with that, maybe," I suggested lamely, having nothing better to offer. Frustrated, I worked the handle a few times, but it protested with dry, rasping squeaks and refused to give up its precious bounty. "Crud-mamma'n piece of trash!" I slammed the handle down and glared at Tripp.

He grinned at my outburst. "I never heard that one before, Model-T. Did you learn it in the Marines?"

"It's a long story." The anger departed, mellowed by his smile.

Tripp spotted something shiny beneath a bush near my feet and picked it up. "Look at this!" He cradled a filthy plastic soda bottle in his hands like it was a magic lamp and he was about to "rub" all our troubles away with a single stroke. Inside, two inches of coffee-colored liquid showed through the dingy plastic. Unscrewing the top, he stuck his nose close to the opening. "Phew-wee. Rum and scum!" He held out the bottle. "Wanna drink?"

"Not on your life. I can smell it from here. No tellin' how long that stuff's been layin' there. You might's well pour it out and I'll carry it to the next trash can."

Tripp tipped the bottle and then hesitated. Fighting the heavy stammer that cluttered his speech, he said, "Do you suppose this is enough to prime the pump?"

Why not? It was liquid! But we'd need a smidgin more. Excited, I whooped, "We're in business, Tripp! Gimme th' bottle." Puzzled, he handed it over. "I'm gonna up the odds," and I walked behind a tree.

It was just enough! Tripp drizzled the "piss-cocktail" into the "thinga-majiggie hole" while I cranked the screeching handle up and down and bellowed exhortations for the obstinate pump to deliver. Suddenly, a thin, tea-colored stream began to flow with great effort from the rusty opening. "Quick. Get a bottle under it. Don't waste a drop," I shouted over the metallic groaning of the handle.

"Don't you think we should let it get clear first?" Tripp yelled.

"Fill the soda bottle. That'll be enough clearin'. Hurry up, fer cryin' out loud! This thing might quit at any minute!"

I needn't have worried. The old pump creaked and regurgitated the dingy-brown stuff until all our bottles were filled. Tripp eyed the water with concern. "D'ya think it's okay to drink?"

"I'm gonna," and I chugalugged a whole quart. "This isn't near as flavorful as worm-tea." I smacked my lips with satisfaction, chuckling at the revolting look on Tripp's face, and then watched as he took a tentative sip and then drank greedily. "Let's fill 'em up again and get on to the shelter."

We left the soda bottle filled with the "cocktail" sitting by the pump for the next desperate soul. As we walked away, The Ego mimicked, "Gollee, Sargint Carter, this crud-mamma'n piece of trash done saved our butts!" Sarcastic bastard!

Pochuck Mountain Shelter was crisply new, with stacks of scrap lumber still lying around waiting to be hauled away, but it lacked what it needed most—a water source. Why anyone would build a shelter where there was no water defied my intelligence! (How many thirsty hikers had kicked and cussed the balky pump and wept frustrated tears as they trudged on up Pochuck Mountain with a small glimmer of hope that *just maybe* the guide book had made a mistake and there *really was* water at the shelter?) Thank goodness Tripp and I had coaxed enough water from the cantankerous contraption to carry us through the night!

Dog and Shug sat on the floor, feet dangling over the side, preparing supper. (When I had first met these two back in Georgia, I'd mistaken Shug for a young boy.) Petite, close-cropped red hair, and a pert, turned-up nose that perfectly matched her saucy manner; she was definitely an original! On the other hand, Dog was tall and gangly, had a patchy black jaw-beard that simply refused to proliferate, and his appetite was phenomenal! They cooked and ate from a communal gallon cook pot, with Dog taking the lion's share—no doubt storing the excess in hollow legs for later regurgitation (like an extra stomach)!

Dog stirred vigorously, trying to keep the roiling boil from spilling over the edge of the pot—no water shortage for these two! I dropped my pack, bent over the pot, and sniffed the flaccid odor of macaroni, watching as the little elbows scurried away from Dog's spoon like minnows frantically darting from a hungry bass. "Mac-n-cheese, huh?" I asked. "I claim first dibs on leftovers."

Shug gave an impish grin as Dog shouldered me away from the pot with the finesse of an expert before I could swing into yogi mode. I winked at Tripp (a lost cause) and said, "I thought you guys were traveling with Skate and Eco. Where are they?"

"We took a day off at High Point (State Park) to go swimming, and they went on ahead," Shug replied. Drat! I was never going to catch those two!

At that moment, two hikers—strangers—arrived. The woman, slender to the point of being emaciated, looked wilted by the afternoon heat and her long, brown ponytail oozed drops of sweat. Narrow-faced, her thin lips pursed with discomfort, she could have passed for a middle-aged crone, although she was probably in her late twenties. Without so much as a "howdy-do," she flopped down on a stump and groaned, "Gawd, it's bloody hot. Tim, be a good lad and go find the spring. I will absolutely perish if I don't get some water." Even in her depleted condition, her English accent was refreshing.

Tim seemed much better off than his companion. Although trail-worn, his eyes glimmered with a mischievous twinkle, which perfectly matched his lean build, crew-cut hair, and boyish grin—a thirty-year-old teenager!

We immediately accepted them as family, for they wore the patina of the Trail—weeks of accumulated weariness to match soiled clothing and jaded eyes, not to mention essence of thru-hiker! Tim said, "If one of you blokes could point the way to the spring. Melanie and I ran out of water an hour past. She's had a rather hard time of it coming up the mountain, I'm afraid." His clipped accent was pure cockney—right out of Charles Dickens!

The silence was pregnant, an ominous harbinger of bad tidings. We glanced at one another, first with disbelief, and then embarrassment. Thru-hikers *always* knew about waterless shelters—a given, just like where the good eating-places were—but somehow, the fact had eluded these two!

The silence grew louder. Dog peered into his pot like a sorcerer seeing the future in a magic potion; while Tripp suddenly became interested in two ants struggling with a crumb on the ground by his feet. Shug began to peel an onion to drop into Dog's concoction, focusing intently on the task. Oh what the heck! Being The Model-T didn't come easy.

"Well, there's good news and there's bad news. Which do you want first?"

Melanie, her eyes pleading, whimpered, "Oh Gawd, don't tell us the spring has bellied up."

"Worse, I'm afraid, because somehow they overlooked the spring when they built the shelter, and that's the bad news." Tears brimmed, and she seemed to shrink right before our eyes.

I rushed on before she went over the edge. "But the good news is, I have a little water to spare, at least enough for a drink while Tim goes back down and finds some. There's bound to be some houses along the highway at the bottom of the mountain. And then there's the pump, if you can get it to work." I glared at my companions, daring them to *not* pitch in after making me do their dirty work. "Maybe the others can chip in, too."

We each divvied up a few ounces of water, and the grateful look in her eyes was ample reward. "Simply smashing of you to do this, Old Sods," Tim said, raising his cup in appreciation, while Melanie, fanning herself with a limp hand, echoed, "Smashing."

Tim headed back down the mountain with water bottles clanking in time with his whistling, and Melanie's world was once again in kilter. Unpacking, she smiled for the first time. "Tim and I call ourselves 'Thatcher's Children.'"

Almost instantly, the bonds of kinship bridged a chasm of cultural divergence, and harmonious chatter filled the clearing. Friendships forged by the simple sharing of Nature's lifeblood! What a delightful feeling!

Near dusk, just as we were settling in for the night, Mule came in, sweaty and smelling like a neglected compost pile. I hadn't seen him since Hot Springs! "Hey Mule, long time, no see," I greeted him. "Are you still drinking those high-cal cheapo breakfasts?" He grinned at the remembrance.

"Only every chance I get. Doggone, it's good to see you. It's a long way back to Club Geek." I introduced him to the others, and we pushed gear aside to make room. He pulled a bottle from his pack and took a long swig. "Geez! That's good!" Happiness floated out of his reeking body. "Man, Model-T, this is my lucky day! You aren't gonna believe this, but a gal back at Unionville gave me a free meal and a whole chocolate pie." Tripp's muffled snicker snaked across the shelter like a long piece of spaghetti, right into my ears, and I nearly choked trying to hold back the laughter. Mule took another long pull on the bottle and smacked with satisfaction. "An' back down at that last pump, somebody left a full bottle of rum in some kind of funny tasting mix. It's weak, but it's gooood! Here, have a nip."

"Thanks, Matey, but I've had my limit for today. Now Tripp here might like a snort."

Ahh! The adversities of the Trail—money in the bank!

"This is just plain crazy," The Ego complained. "Why bother with veggies when they have ice cream and baked goods. Veggies! Yuk!" I said testily, "Well, I happen to like veggies." Obviously, we were at a stalemate. "Okay, how about we get a couple of cups of chocolate ice cream and some corn on the cob," I suggested as a compromise. "We can carry the corn and have it for supper." My eyes drifted to the bin of zucchini, and it drew me like a magnet; it looked fabulous—it all did, for that matter. "And a zucchini," I added. "Only if we get a package of those cookies," he insisted.

I had already walked among the well-stocked bins and baskets of L and L Farm Market—a roadside produce place within sight of the Trail where it crosses lonely Warwick Pike—at least a dozen times, trying to decide what to buy. (The market was a joyous bonanza, for the climb over waterless Wawayanda Mountain had been a grueling ordeal, made worse by sizzling heat and high humidity—and J.R.'s constant jabbering about how "if you think this is bad, you ought to see what they make the Marines go through." I wondered briefly who "they" were but didn't pursue the matter, hoping that he would just shut up and let me enjoy my misery, for I had drained my water bottles well over an hour ago and was so thirsty that even the "rum and something" cocktail I had turned down last night at

Pochuck would have been welcomed. So when I reached a highway and saw the sign pointing down the road to "Fresh Fruits and Vegetables," I had gone scurrying to seek water, if nothing else.)

What to buy was a tough decision for I was down to my last two dollars, plus sixteen "trail pennies" I'd found on the Trail. My next resupply point was Arden, New York, a spot in the road a short mile from the Trail, just before it enters Harriman State Park. Barring bad luck, I would be there in two days, so I felt comfortable with blowing it all here. Darn! All this stuff, and all I had was two bucks and sixteen pennies! I went into the restroom and filled my water bottles while I tried to make up my mind.

We finally settled on the ice cream (a must!), an ear of corn, a small zucchini, two plums, two nectarines, and a single cookie (a peace offering for the tough Marine). A girl at the cash register weighed the plums and nectarines and then rang up the total. "That'll be two dollars and twenty-seven cents."

"Gee, Miss, I'm sorry," I said, handing her my bankroll. Pointing at the smaller of the two plums, I asked, "How much will it be if I put this one back?" Behind me, two well-dressed ladies waited impatiently, fidgeting, glaring at me like I had trespassed on holy ground.

The girl ignored the growing line—now there were three annoyed customers—and counted the change. "Let me see," she said, removing the plum from the assortment and then gently placing it back on the scales. "Golly, I'm sorry, sir, but I must have made a mistake. The total comes to two dollars and sixteen cents. Do you want a sack?"

Smiling my appreciation, I declined the bag; but, like she hadn't heard me, she put everything in a paper sack and handed it to me, saying in a low voice, "How I envy you. I've always wanted to hike the Appalachian Trail, what with it being so close. Maybe some day . . ." I thanked her and strolled outside.

When I reached in to get the ice cream, I also found a Twinkie and two wrinkled one-dollar bills! Angels are found in the strangest places!

Came New York's Harriman State Park, with its Lemon Squeezer (a narrow, white-blazed cleft in a giant boulder, *not* designed for fat people—or hikers wearing backpacks). Came the stunning full-circle panorama from the top of the stone tower on Bear Mountain, with the historic Hudson River a thousand feet below and tiny silhouettes of the World Trade Buildings on the hazy New York skyline nearly fifty miles away! Came Bear

Mountain State Park, with is inviting swimming beaches and its crowded picnic tables loaded with food, just begging for a hotshot yogi-er to show his stuff; but I didn't dillydally because The Ego and I were headed to see the monkeys!

According to *The Philosophers Guide,* the Trail went right through the middle of the Trailside Museum and Zoo. And it was *free* (a good thing, for I'd only gotten a twenty-five dollar traveler's check at Arden). On both sides of the paved walkway, exotic animals chirped, hooted, screeched, snorted, and growled from ecologically correct mini-landscapes. Children stared, wide-eyed, as they tightly clutched their parent's hands, occasionally letting out little squeals of delight—or fright—as the zoo's inhabitants, bored by their blah existence, blankly stared back. Along the walkway, markers identified trees and shrubs—a regular "botany classroom," especially for those who seldom trespass beyond city limits. But the display held no particular appeal for The Ego and me for we'd been living in a "botany classroom" for the past four months!

Three wrinkled, seedy pachyderms dawdled in a shallow pool, robotically spraying water over their backs. In another pool, alligators snoozed, uncaring, waiting for the next handout. J.R. grumbled, "This is all well and good, if you have all day to stand and gawk. But we're wasting valuable time. Let's find the monkeys!" He was right. Graymoor Monastery was still six miles away and it was already after one o'clock. Even monkeys weren't worth missing the "all-you-can-eat" supper that the friars offered thru-hikers!

We found the monkeys after taking a couple of wrong turns. Now these guys were *zingers!* They cavorted all over the place, arms and tails grasping limbs and bars, chasing and being chased, throwing instant, screeching temper tantrums from high perches when provoked, then quickly resuming their play as if nothing had happened. We laughed at their humanoid antics. Said J.R., chortling, "That old duffer over by the barrel looks like my English prof in college." He watched us with sly, calculating eyes, probably wondering if we were worth the short trip over to work us for a handout. Abruptly, he lost interest and went back to picking cooties off of his belly (probably having reached the conclusion that we were worse off than him)!

A woman and her small son walked up to the cage and the old geezer made a beeline for them—easy pickings! The kid tossed a peanut at him and he immediately grabbed it, cracked the hull with practiced ease, and tossed the two small pellets into his slobbering mouth. He screeched loudly and was rewarded with another peanut. In a flash every monkey in the cage rushed over and crowded to the front, pushing the old one to the rear, and began chattering and screeching and flinging themselves against the bars as they vied for the next peanut.

It never came, for the youngster became scared by the ruckus and started bawling. The mother screamed, "Shut up!" at the monkeys and rushed the boy away from the din.

"Reminds me of a bunch of hungry thru-hikers," The Ego growled as the monkeys resumed their play—except for the old one who now sat in a corner with his back to the world. I said, "You got that right. Let's head for Graymoor!"

The Bear Mountain Bridge, a mammoth suspension bridge nearly a half-mile long that spans the wide Hudson River, is an easy stone's throw from the Trailside Museum and Zoo. Back in the '70's, pedestrians had to pay a toll to cross. In fact, on his 1948 hike Earl Shaffer had to pay a nickel. (By 1990, the pedestrian toll had been lifted, but vehicles still had to pay.)

Bear Mountain Bridge is also the lowest spot on the entire Appalachian Trail—a mere 124 feet above sea level. Yet, striding along the narrow walkway—the lone pedestrian on the long vibrating span—high above the shimmering wakes of boats that scurried to and fro like tiny water bugs—I felt as if I were on a tightrope above a vast crevasse whose edges stretched from the beginning of time to infinity.

The Marine was on a high, buzzing with excitement as he crowed like an afflicted rooster at the passing vehicles (while I fought off dizzy, nauseous waves of acrophobia that had struck without warning midway along the span). When at last I stepped back onto terra firma, The Idiot shouted, "Today we have soared with the eagles!" Trying to keep from upchucking, I snarled, "Wrong, Doofus. All we've done is flap with the buzzards."

Graymoor Monastery, home of The Franciscan Friars of the Atonement, sits on a knoll overlooking the rolling hills that dip toward the distant Hudson River. A few ancient buildings, chapels mostly—works lovingly crafted by artisans long since gone—snuggle in quiet repose among modern structures, which bustle with activity. Busloads of curious tourists, hungry for adventure or seeking spiritual nourishment, eagerly debark and immediately scatter over the grounds and into buildings like confused ants when their anthill has been disturbed.

J.R. and I watched the activity with interest from a bench at the edge of the parking lot. Nearby, several "seekers" had gathered around a statue of the Virgin Mary, looking expectant and chattering excitedly as they waited for some scheduled happening. They were not disappointed, for soon a friar dressed in a long dark robe appeared from inside a large building with white clapboard siding—a strange anomaly against the brick and stucco of the other structures. He held a small, ornate cross and intoned a Latin chant as he slowly walked through the pathway that magically opened among the group. Then pausing, he knelt before the statue and quietly prayed as he fingered the rosary that hung from his neck. When he had finished, he stood and led the assembled in The Lord's Prayer, and then departed as he had come. The "seekers," now solemn and hushed, slowly dispersed.

A bus roared out of the parking lot spewing blue exhaust fumes, its windows filled with sated, subdued faces and unfocused eyes. Shortly, another bus pulled in, crammed with eager, wide-eyed faces. As the pilgrims debarked, some glanced inquisitively my way, but I refused to be drawn into the role of carnival freak and focused on a point above their heads, mimicking the bored expression that some of the animals had used on me back at the zoo.

Tripp suddenly stood by the bench, startling me from my little mind game. Sweat leaked from his shirt, dappling the concrete with splotches of dark gray as he eased out of his pack and flopped down beside me. "I didn't expect all these people," he said without preamble. "It's a real circus. Do you know where we're supposed to go?"

"To the main building, I think—wherever that is. According to the 'Guide,' we're supposed to be at the main building at five sharp to get checked in. I'd guess it's on up the hill." I looked at my watch. "It's already 4:30. Maybe we'd better mosey on up that way. By the way, where've you been? Back at Unionville trying for that chocolate pie?" (I hadn't seen him since Pochuck Shelter.)

"No way! I've been eatin' your dust. You sure have been truckin'."

Before I could think of an appropriate comeback, I noticed a tall, pretty blond—a hiker by her attire—wading through the crowd, evidently looking for someone. She spotted us and waved, then made her way over to the bench. "Hi, my name's Journalist. I was checking to see if any other hikers had gotten here."

"I'm Model-T and this emaciated specimen is Mississippi Tripper. We were just talking about where we're supposed to go."

Her blue eyes sparkled. "Well then, it's a good thing I came along. The bad news is, Graymoor is hosting a 'retreat' this week. The Old Friary, where they normally let hikers stay, is all filled up. The good news is, we still get fed. Father Cuthbert, the hiker coordinator, told us we could pitch tents beneath the water tower on top of the hill. There's a bunch of us there already."

"Sounds good," I said, grabbing my pack. "Lead the way."

Several minutes before the magic hour, eleven exuberant hikers—myself included—were assembled near the front door of the large modern brick building that housed the Franciscans. It was like a mini-Trail Days—Hollow-legged Dog and Shug; Thatcher's Children; Mule; Journalist and her companion, Journeyman (a solidly-built hiker nearing thirty, with a thick mane that blended into a heavy, black beard and framed his white face with ebony; and two thru-hikers I hadn't met, gangly Joe Wolfe and stocky Patrick. A festival air prevailed as we chattered with excitement—monkeys temporarily let out of their cage and about to be unleashed in the Garden of Eden—and waited impatiently for the "gatekeeper" to arrive.

At precisely five o'clock, the door opened and a gray-headed man wearing dark slacks and a polo shirt stepped from the air-conditioned inner sanctum. "My name is Father Cuthbert, and on behalf of Graymoor Monastery I welcome you. I apologize that we can't offer you the hospitality we normally do, but we will do our best to make you feel at home. Ordinarily you would have rooms in the Old Friary, along with showers and use of the laundry, but everything is filled with people here for our retreat."

His gentle tone and peaceful face perfectly matched the softness of the "real" Graymoor, away from the bustling crowd and the roaring busses less than a quarter mile down the hill. Here, tranquility lay like a soft shroud, soothing the mind and soul, easing pain and cares and restoring the human spirit like a lustral balm. "I have arranged for the washrooms in the auditorium, the large white building down by the parking lot, to be left open." Glancing at his watch he continued, "Dinner will be served in the dining hall at 5:30—that's twenty-six minutes from now. In the meantime, please feel free to enjoy our library and talk with the friars. And if you wish to eat breakfast," (this got a group chuckle) "serving begins at 7 A.M. sharp. Tomorrow being Sunday, we will have brunch until 9 o'clock. Are there any questions?" There were none. "Well then, please enter in peace."

We followed Father Cuthbert down a long corridor. The floor was so highly polished that it was like walking on a mirror, and I could sense the unease of the others as we trod lightly, trying not to mar the unblemished surface with boot marks. He stopped at the library entrance and told us the dining room was only a short distance on down the hall, and that he would join us there.

Most of us wandered into the library to wait out the (now) twenty-one minute ordeal until mealtime. Several friars sat quietly reading or writing, and except for a few quick glances, we were ignored. As a group, we took seats in a far corner and carried on short, whispered conversations, hardly daring to move for fear of disrupting the orderliness of our surroundings. The smells wafting up the corridor from the kitchen were driving me into a mental frenzy. Dang! Nineteen minutes to go! I whispered to Tripp, "What time you got?"

"Ten after five." Double dang! By his watch we had twenty minutes left.

J.R. whispered, "Father Cuthbert said we could talk to the friars if we wanted, and I want to. Let's mosey over to that couch and see if we can strike up a conversation." (There was a spot between two elderly friars, one dressed in street clothes, the other in the Franciscan habit.) He prattled on, "I've never talked to a real monk before, but I read about Friar Tuck in Robin Hood. He was a nice guy." Annoyed, I hissed, "What's the matter with you?" You wanna get us thrown outta here? These people don't want to talk to grungy thru-hikers. Besides, everyone knows you're not supposed to talk out loud in a library." Jeez, what an eight-ball, risking a *free* feast for idle chatter!

As if to protest J.R.'s stupidity, my belly erupted in a whopper of a growl, cutting through the silence like a buzz saw. Embarrassed, I looked around to see if anyone had noticed—maybe it only sounded like a jet's afterburner to me—and nearly croaked because everyone in the room was staring! Some eyes glowered, a few twinkled, and I thought I heard a couple of discreet coughs. Shug giggled as, mortified and flushing beet red, I tried to sink through my seat.

An elderly friar, possibly eighty, thin and balding, also wearing the habit, arose from a nearby chair and tottered toward me. "Uh-oh, J.R.," I silently groaned, "we're gonna get the boot!" The other hikers seemed to physically separate themselves from my "predicament," suddenly finding *objets d'art* worthy of whispered examination all around the room, except in my direction. The old gentleman stopped before me and I clenched my teeth, waiting for the ax to fall.

He said *out loud,* "Young man, many of your brethren have sat in this place waiting for dinner. I have listened to their sounds of hunger ever since the first hiker arrived seventeen years ago, but none has jarred the Monastery like that which just now filled the room." The ax was falling! Resigned to my fate, I peered into his tired, wise eyes, seeking any sign of compassion. Then his face crinkled into a wizened smile and the eyes sparkled. "I'm Father Bosco. Until last year I oversaw the hiker program here at Graymoor, but my health is failing and Father Cuthbert has assumed the duties." He reached inside his robe and extracted some small pamphlets, then handed one to each of us. (I was nearly too weak with relief to accept mine!) He seemed to reflect inward as he softly murmured, "Alas, if only souls showed the same signs of hunger that bellies do."

Several of the friars began to leave. Father Bosco said, "Now, it's time to feed the body, but perhaps the soul will be nourished later." He made it sound like a question. As a group, we followed the friars to the dining hall.

Dinner was a magnificent affair—the food excellent, with no limit on refills—and it was free! (Father Cuthbert did mention several times that the Order existed on the magnanimity of the public, and that donations were always welcome.) The monks—perhaps one hundred—were dressed in casual attire, except for a scattering who wore traditional robes. A small number never uttered a word as far as I saw, and I wondered if perhaps these had taken vows of silence. For the most part the friars were cheerful and talkative, readily accepting us into their monastic world, and earlier feelings of unease quickly disappeared in this atmosphere of pious camaraderie.

Surprisingly, most seemed to eat sparingly. However, we more than made up for the monks' meager repast as we blazed a trail of boot streaks on the highly polished floor, making our way, time and again, to the heavily-laden serving tables. Surely we put a terrific dent in Graymoor's store of provisions—and hospitality!

Late that evening, I sprawled beneath my tarp and listened to the rich, gentle voices of the monks float through the soft darkness as they worshiped at evening vespers. The ancient chants rose toward the heavens— strange, unknown melodies, yet hauntingly beautiful. Long after the voices ceased, the soothing strains echoed in my ears, lingering to caress my mind until at last I slept.

Brunch was without parallel! Everything customarily accepted as "breakfast fare" was ours for the taking, even eggs to order! Father Cuthbert joined us while we ate, again apologizing for having to put us beneath the water tower. And once more he subtly reminded us that donations were gratefully accepted, if we were so moved.

Most of us helped to close the brunch line, although by the time we finished committing the sin of gluttony there wasn't much left to close! We thanked Father Cuthbert for Graymoor's wonderful hospitality and bid him adieu. As we finished the meal, hikers wandered over to the small, discreet donation box and dropped tokens of their gratitude through the narrow slit.

The twenty and fiver tucked away in a plastic bag in my pocket—my entire fortune at the moment—felt like a sack of dirty rocks. All during brunch the donation box had danced before my eyes, a festering image that threatened to ruin the entire meal, if not the whole day. Kent, Connecticut, my next mail drop, was still several days away, and the small sum had to last.

All the other hikers had left and the dining hall was empty, except for a dozen workers (apprentice monks?) who stacked chairs on tables all around where I sat alone, nursing a cup of coffee, facing the "moment of truth." J.R. argued, "One good turn deserves another, and you have to admit that we've been well treated. Leave the twenty." The *twenty*, did he say? I retorted, "Are you crazy? That's almost the whole wad. We need to buy an additional two days of groceries to get us on to Kent. How's about I leave an I.O.U. and we'll send a donation when we get home." The *twenty!* Jesus! He said, "Naw, we'll feel like cheaters if we do that. I'd rather go hungry. Besides, you're always bragging about how great a yogi-ier you are. Let's find out just how good you *really* are." I squirmed like a fishing worm dangling in front of a hungry bass. What to do?

One of the workers, ready to stack the chairs at my table, politely asked if he could get me anything else, in effect telling me it was time to leave. I told him I was finished and stood up, my mind whirling with indecision, and walked slowly toward the box as I tried to ignore J.R.'s wheedling and think things through. A compromise! "I'll leave the fiver," I told him, but he wasn't budging. "You are a sorry specimen of the human race. These people have bent over backwards to make us feel welcome and have fed us until it hurt. It's got to be the twenty." Dang him! He knew how to make me feel like trash!

Woodenly, fighting the twinges of panic that spiraled into my chest and made breathing difficult, I got out the plastic bag, fingered "Old Hickory's" face, and quickly dropped the bill into the slot. J.R. beamed. "There now, that didn't hurt at all, did it?" Amazingly, it didn't! Once the money had left my fingers, it wasn't a problem anymore! I actually felt great! "Okay, Killer. Let's hit the Trail!"

We walked down the hill—two entities, one body, for the moment comrades—past monuments of stern, unsmiling saints and myriad shrines, past the parking lot where the tour busses were already discharging eager sightseers, and out into the secular facade of another dimension. "I feel twenty years younger, J.R.," I remarked as Graymoor disappeared beyond the bend. He chuckled. "Yeah, a dollar for each year. The cheapest therapy money can buy." Hesitating, he continued, "I remember Pap used to say, 'It's always better to slop th' hogs than to let'em root fer acorns. Makes better meat.' I always wondered what he meant, but that may have been his way of saying, 'It's always better to give than to receive.'" I added my benediction, "Amen to that! It's too bad we didn't see Father Bosco at brunch, 'cause I'd have told him our soul got fed as much as our belly. He'd have been pleased." He gave a short grunt of agreement, but his thoughts had drifted to long ago memories of a tow-headed lad and a gray-haired country sage who spoke of hogs and acorns . . .

The frustrating stretches of rocky treadway had all but disappeared! There were still plenty of long climbs and descents, but everything considered, the hiking was much easier.

On the other hand, water was fast becoming more precious than food! Summer had shifted into high gear, bringing hot, dry days and the beginning signs of drought to the New York countryside. Springs normally gushing had turned into balky misers. (Twice during the past week I had reached a dry spring, thirsty and out of water; then frenziedly digging a hole in the muddy earth, I'd watched impatiently as a few ounces of dingy liquid oozed into the bottom. Filtered through a sweaty bandanna and treated with a couple of iodine tabs, it was a short step above nothing, but in this arid season, water ruled! A stagnant pool was a "find"; a flowing spring a luxury!)

A case in point: Telephone Pioneers Shelter is a small six-person shelter high up on sprawling West Mountain, where the Blue Ridge capriciously switches to pastoral, rolling fields before gently entering Connecticut. A gorgeous view from a waterless vantage point!

I arrived late in the afternoon after a sweltering walk, to find many of my companions from Graymoor already there—and thirsty!

"Model-T! How much water do you have?" Mule asked as I came in.

"I'm dry as a desert sand dune." (I'd drained my water bottle about a mile back, secure in the knowledge that the spring here would be flowing, albeit slowly—at least that's what a "southbounder" had written at Morgan Stewart Shelter, where I had eaten lunch.)

Journeyman said grimly, "We have a problem here. Everyone's out of water, or just about, and the spring's just barely dripping. I put a pot under it, but it takes about ten minutes to get half a cup. There won't be enough to even cook supper."

Hell's bells! What were we going to do? Dog looked pathetic, like a small lad who had just dropped his sucker in a pile of cow manure. Even Tim of Thatcher's Children had lost his perpetual cocky smile. I tried to work up a little spit to moisten my tongue and suggested, "We can dig a hole in the mud under the drip and let water seep in, then scoop it out. I've had to do it already, a couple of times. Maybe we can get through the night."

Tripp spoke up. "I've got a cup or so left. Why don't we all pool our water, then we can ration it out, like a spoonful for each person every so often?" That made sense, and the group agreed. We all emptied our bottles into Journalist's—even those of us who had only a drop or two—and she was elected "Keeper of the Water" by acclamation. As a tail-end amendment to that piece of legislation, we voted to immediately give ourselves one spoonful of water each, so "The Keeper" carefully doled out a couple of ounces in a cup and we partied down!

"C'mon Dog. Let's go see if we can turn mud into water," I said, grabbing my cook pot. "And bring your water bottle. We might get lucky."

A half-hour later, the mud hole had given up almost a quart of nasty-looking, iodine-laced swill. Dog and I carried it back to the shelter, proud contributors to the commonweal. We'd done better than the balky spring, which had grudgingly leaked out a pitiful pint, and only half of that now remained, depleted by the latest round of "spooning" (which we missed).

"Okay, folks," I gloated, "not to worry. Dog and I have struck water! The 'Grim Reaper' might as well put away his scythe, 'cause he's not gonna need it tonight!"

Dog, all puffed up like a horny peacock, said excitedly, "And there's more where this came from! Handing the bottle to Journalist, he pointed at the brown layer that had settled to the bottom and cautioned, "If you're careful, you can pour the water off of the silt."

Melanie stared at the dingy contents like it was laced with dog dooey. "Oh Gawd Tim, I can't drink *that!* I'd rather *die!*" She was close to tears. "I want to go home!"

Tim shrugged, uncomfortable at Melanie's outburst. "It's buffo alright, Mel, but things have always been a bit of a bug here in the Colonies." He grinned, apparently relishing the use of the word. "It'll all come out."

Melanie glared at him, annoyed, and muttered with finality, "I *won't* drink it." Dog looked crushed.

Journalist held the bottle like it was filled with the "plague," undecided whether or not she should add it to the "good stuff," and then sat the bottle on the floor when no one offered any suggestion. "Maybe we should vote," she suggested.

"Aw, for cryin' out loud. I've drunk lots worse than this," I said, and I had! "Gimme th' bottle." I took a long, silty swallow and swiped the back of my hand across my dripping beard. "Prime vintage!" I growled. "Anyone else?"

Journeyman took the bottle and raised it to his lips—a show of bravado, I suspected, for he gritted his teeth. But before he could sip, Tripp groaned, "Oh no. Not another hiker!"

A stout, middle-aged man wearing long trousers and a floppy hat shuffled up to the shelter. "Hello folks. M'name's Bob and I'm the caretaker. You wouldn't be thirsty now, would you?" He gasped for breath, fighting to get the words out as he mopped heavy sweat from his face with a bandanna. "Didn't know if there was any hikers here tonight but thought I'd better bring some water up since the spring's not runnin'. Somebody help me out of this pack."

Dumbfounded, we watched Bob pull gallon jugs—six in all—of cold, bottled water from his pack! Melanie squealed with delight as she clutched one of the gallons to her bosom and then rubbed the cold condensation across her face. Heck, we all squealed! Journeyman immediately opened a jug and began to fill outstretched cups, which were quickly emptied. "A toast to Bob!" someone shouted. "To Bob!" we chorused in unison.

Bob, our hero, told us he carried water up to the shelter from the highway near the base of the mountain—at least a mile away—three or four times a week. He bought the purified water at a grocery with his own money (He was reluctant to reveal this!) and cooled the jugs in an old refrigerator. I did some quick math: A gallon of water weighs eight pounds, times six gallons, equals forty-eight pounds a trip, times four trips, equals almost two hundred pounds of water each week!

"Now, use what you need and I'll take the empties back down. If there's any left, you can leave it for the next hikers."

"Dog," I whispered, "you can have my share of what we got from the hole . . ."

Connecticut! The tenth state on the journey to Katahdin! Shortly after shaking the dust of New York from my boots, the Blue Ridge began to resurrect itself. It happened slowly at first—a softening of the overgrown hardwood forests as small groves of spruce began to appear; then a spring that flowed freely instead of eking out a dripping pittance. Soon came a freshness to the landscape, long absent, and then in a few short miles, mountains cloaked in a resplendent mantel of sylvan green and sequined with sparkling, rushing brooks, reached toward a robin's-egg blue sky. The wily Blue Ridge, a crabbed, frumpy jezebel in Pennsylvania and New York, had been reincarnated as a soft, seductive siren! Hallelujah!

J.R. didn't exactly share my enthusiasm for he was still ticked-off over the episode at the railroad crossing earlier this morning, before we had escaped from New York's parting gift—two miles of trail overgrown with waist-high weeds and briars. For the past hour, all he'd done was grumble about "the idiots one has to deal with even in this God-forsaken place." (I couldn't have agreed more—look who I was stuck with!)

"That guy was so dense he has lead for brains," he fumed. "What he needs is a good dose of Marine Corps boot camp. They'd get him straightened out in short order, by Gads!" (I didn't know if I agreed with the Jarhead's assessment, if he was any indication! Anyway, I didn't think it was such a big deal.) "Ho-hum," I yawned, bored stiff by his grumbling, trying to change the topic. "I wonder what Ten Mile River will be like? Darn, I hope we don't have to ford it!" From here on top of Ten Mile Hill, the distant roar resonated with the fury of a volcano—and the river was still more than a mile away!

"He's lucky I didn't jump on the train and punch him in the nose." I retorted acidly, "Lucky for *us* you didn't!"

In a way it was kind of funny: I'd left Telephone Pioneers Shelter really early, trying for a head start on the heat for today was supposed to be a repeat of yesterday, according to Bob the Caretaker. After the Trail wound down off West Mountain, it meandered through an area of low, rolling hills and mud bogs choked with noxious weeds and briars that all but obliterated the Trail. After two miles of pushing through this dew-drenched vegetative hell, I'd stopped to catch my breath and check my legs for ticks (This was Lyme disease country!) when The Ego exclaimed, "Well, just lookee over there. If my eyes don't deceive me, that's a railroad!" Sure enough, sunlight glinted off of two shiny ribbons, and right beside the track on the opposite side was a wooden platform with a single bench. I grunted, "Break time," and made a beeline for the bench.

Now this was weird. A neat sign on the platform read "Appalachian Trail Station." "Strange place for a train stop," J.R. remarked. "It surely can't get much business. Heck, I'll bet trains don't run past here except maybe once a week, if that." Climbing up the steps, I replied, "Yeah, but it does make a nice place to take a break." I slipped out of my pack and perched on the bench, and then began to munch a cookie. "If we had some shade, I might spend the whole day here."

I finished the cookie and was reaching for another when the rails began to vibrate. "Uh-oh, I think a train's coming," I said, squinting up the track, barely able to see the distant engine through the shimmering heat waves. He said, "You know, maybe we're not supposed to be loitering on railroad property," to which I replied, "Heck fire, Ego, we have as much right to be here as anyone else. Anyway, it's probably a commuter train, and you know it's not about to slow down for a rinky-dink whistle stop like this." He was silent for a moment, then said halfheartedly, "Jeepers, Alter, I don't know about—" but I cut him off. "Don't sweat it. That hummer will breeze right on past like we aren't even here."

The train was fast approaching, if two cars could be called a train. Wheels shrieked as it began to slow, and J.R. remarked, "Hmm, strange. Somebody must be getting off." The train screeched to a halt and the door of the last car opened right in front of where we sat gawking. "It's got to be a hiker," I mused, "for nobody else would be foolish enough to get off at this God-forsaken place."

We waited expectantly, and the time seemed to drag. "Whoever it is must have a lot of gear—or is handicapped," J.R. said.

Finally, a man in a blue business suit walked to the open door and stared at us. I threw him a friendly wave, which he didn't return, but I didn't really expect him to since we were in Yankee-land (people up here didn't seem to go in for that sort of thing). Darn! Whoever was getting off was slower than Christmas. I stuffed another cookie in my mouth and waited.

The man's stare slowly turned into a glare, and he boomed in a gravelly voice, "You're holding up the train. If you're coming, then get aboard. You can eat on the train." Holy cow! He was talking to me! "We have a schedule to keep and you've already cost us two minutes. We can't wait all day!"

He thought we were passengers, by gads! Buying time, trying to think up an excuse—anything to get this firecracker off my back—I blurted, "Where y'all headin'?"

"What do you mean, 'Where are we heading'? Any idiot knows this train goes to New York. What's your problem?"

Now, The Marine didn't cotton to being called "idiot" (although I thought the moniker did hit fairly close to the mark). I withered beneath the man's glower and stammered weakly, "I was just takin' a break."

He actually stomped his foot, and I halfway expected him to jump onto the platform and toss me off into the weeds. "A break! You mean we stopped because you were taking a break!" Spittle began to ooze from his mouth and his face swelled into a large, red glob. "Of all the idiotic, stupid, asinine things to do, sit here and stop the train because you're taking a break!" The eyelids flickered rapidly, like they were trying to keep time with the pulsating rhythm of the engine, and he slavered more spittle onto his chin. "Damn piece of hillbilly trash," he snarled, flipping us a "bird" as he stomped away from the door, which immediately closed with a hiss.

The train began to move, slowly, and then picked up speed. A few faces stared at me from the passing windows—one actually grinned—and then the train was gone. As it disappeared through the haze, The Marine muttered, "Did you see that? He ran one up the flagpole at us. I shoulda decked the bastard!" But I'd had enough excitement. "Jeez, J.R., let's get the heck out of this state before another train comes along! That guy might have a big brother!"

Two hours later, when the "Killer" and I crossed over the dirt road that masqueraded as the state line, he gave the benediction: "Damn shame the South lost the War . . ."

I picked up my mail drop at Kent, Connecticut, an elegant, upscale town featuring colonial-style architecture and bustling with tourists; had a pricey lunch with Tripp, Dog, and Shug; and returned to the Trail. After a stiff climb back to elevation and a dizzying descent down St. John's Ledges, I passed through one of the most beautiful sections yet as the Trail paralleled the picturesque Housatonic River for several miles. Tall, stately red pines cast a fairyland aura along the riverbank and added to the soul-softening delight of swirling eddies and deep, clear pools. Against the far bank, a trout fisherman stood in knee-deep current and flicked a fly, time and again, at a likely spot. The afternoon resounded with the music of the earth as Nature played a rhapsody with frolicking rapids and gurgling rocks, and I reveled in the harmony. Soothed in spirit, I reluctantly followed the Trail as it swung away from the river and commenced the long climb up to Silver Hill Cabin.

And found the two orphans! They had just finished supper when I reached the Cabin—a rustic hideaway complete with sleeping loft, a huge stone fireplace, and a porch swing—as the sun touched the trees. Eco Warrior sat in the swing, zoning, while Skate washed both their cook pots. After nearly two weeks of eating their dust, never expecting to see them again, here they were! (Either they had gotten slower, or like Tripp said, I was really truckin'!) We hugged and danced in circles, squealing like stuck hogs, as if we hadn't seen one another in years. Our bonds of friendship, forged by camaraderie and tempered by shared hardships, seemed as strong as steel! We talked the evening away; and when we finally ran out of words, we pitched our bedding on the loft floor and crashed.

The next morning I quietly packed and then whispered to my slumbering friends, "See you two puppies later today. This old man's gonna beat the heat while he can." Giving Skate a fond pat on the shoulder, I eased out into the misty gray of dawn just as the sun sent its first feeble rays through the trees, and headed north.

"I'm not sure I want to walk a mile for a beer, even if it is free," I told The Marine. We argued by the highway that led down to the small community of Cornwall Bridge where, according to *The Philosopher's Guide*, Richard and Patty Bramley gave bona fide thru-hikers a *free* beer, hiker's choice. The morning was still an infant—7:30—and Silver Hill was only a mile back. "Besides, it's way too early in the day to be thinking about drinking beer. Heck, they won't even be open."

"We're not going to drink it there, Stupid," he grumbled. "We'll carry it with us and have it for lunch. If the store's not open, we can just wait around. What's to lose?" I thought about it, not entirely convinced. "Yeah, but a mile down, then a mile back up? A long way to go for a lousy beer?" Another thought. "What if the *Guide* is wrong? What if they don't do it anymore, or what it the store's gone?" He said, "Naw, it'll be there. Just think! A cold, *free* beer for lunch! C'mon, get the lead out. I hear a car coming."

It was the only one. Fifteen minutes later—fifteen long minutes of J.R.'s nagging insistence—I headed off down the mountain in search of free beer.

Cornwall Package Store, a neat, white-sided structure more akin to a home than a purveyor of alcoholic beverages, sat at the end of the bridge that spans the Housatonic River on the edge of town. A sign in the window proclaimed for all to see that, inside its lily-white walls one could find (and buy, if so inclined) ninety-nine brands of beer. Just above the sign, a red neon light formed the word "OPEN." Talk about the early bird getting the worm . . . It was only a few minutes after eight!

"See, I *knew* they would be open!" J.R. gloated. (This guy led a charmed life. If only they had lottery tickets for sale!) I didn't bother to reply; instead, I quietly parked my pack by the door and went inside.

"Out early, aren't you?" The man, balding and heavy set with sagging jaws, was busy restocking a shelf in the wine section.

"Kinda," I replied, feeling somewhat foolish as I wondered if I had to ask pointblank for the "freebie." Somehow it just didn't feel right. "Are you Richard Bramely?" An opening gambit.

"Nope. Richard and Patty are on vacation."

Maybe I should buy something. Perhaps a Coke? "I'm a thru-hiker. Came down from the Trail. It being so close, I got a hankering for a cold Coke." Another good move—establish my credentials!

"In that case over there. Help yourself and I'll be right with you." I walked over and extracted a cold can from the case, then took it to the counter. "That'll be fifty cents for the drink and a nickel deposit."

I handed him two quarters. "I'm gonna drink it right here and give you the can as soon as I finish, if that's okay."

"Sorry, but I've got to collect the deposit. You can redeem it when you're through." I could sense The Marine's hackles starting to stir, and he muttered something about this being another Yankee absurdity. I dug into my belt pouch and found five tarnished trail pennies, which I handed to the man. He laid them on the register in a neat row and chuckled at my dis-gruntled look. "You can have 'em back, in case you got attached to them." Bad move! I had to keep my cool.

I stalled, sipping the Coke slowly, ashamed to ask the man about the beer. With Richard gone, maybe his helper wasn't even authorized to give away any free beers—just my luck! "Go ahead and ask him," J.R. insisted. Still I hesitated, not sure if it was worth the humility and burning ears and having to slink back to the Trail feeling like a beggar if the man should refuse. I was at a mental impasse. Stalling again, I asked, "You get many thru-hikers in?"

"Yep, a lot this time of year. Later, not so many."

"I'll bet they're a thirsty lot."

"Yep. They always are."

"Most of 'em buy beer and carry with them?"

"Some; not many." Dang it! I'd all but hit him between the eyes with "free beer," and he hadn't bit.

Okay, so be it. I hadn't sunk to the level of asking for handouts—yet. Yogi-ing was in a different category. Putting the empty Coke can on the counter, I told the man, "Well, here's the can." He grinned and handed me the same five pennies. "Thanks. I'd better get back to the Trail." I headed for the door, bracing myself against J.R.'s inevitable harangue.

"Say, hold on a minute. You get a free drink if you want it—soda or beer, your choice, any brand in the house. All you've got to do is sign the register." He pointed to a well-used spiral notebook on the counter. I opened the cover and found pages and pages of scrawled signatures.

Jiminy! I could have opened my own package store if I had all the merchandise the Bramley's had given away!

Relieved that I didn't have to face The Ego's wrath, I quickly added my name to the list and walked over to the beer display. Ninety-nine brands—a tough call! J.R. immediately spotted a giant twenty-five-ounce Foster's, the pride of "Down Under." "That's it!" he said excitedly. "That's what we want—Aussie beer. It's been ages since I had a Foster's." I grabbed the can and carried it to the counter. Beside its American cousins, it looked humongous! "This is about twice the size of those other brands," I said. "Does it cost extra?"

"Nope. Any brand in the house." I thanked him and started for the door. The man called me back. "I *will* need the deposit though." Chuckling, I handed him the five trail pennies.

Outside, J.R. chastised me. "You damned near blew it, Dorkhead. It's people like you who're afraid of their own shadows that caused The Great Depression." I insulated the Foster's by burying it down inside the polypro long johns and replied snidely, "I wouldn't know, Dufus. I wasn't around then. Were you? Anyway, we got the free beer so what're you griping about?" But he refused to be pacified and replied gruffly, "Dorkhead."

On the hot walk back up the mountain, he asked, "Did you pack the Foster's on end or lying on its side?" Now what? "Jeepers H. Clodhopper! I don't remember. What difference does it make anyway?" He retorted, "It makes all the difference in the world when you go to open it. If you laid it on the side, it's making fizz with every step you take, just like churning butter. The can could even burst from the pressure. You'd better stop and check."

I certainly didn't want beer all over everything so I halted, took off the pack, and opened the top. The can was standing at attention like any good Marine. I closed the pack and headed on up the road, grumbling, "This can of free beer is turning out to be a pain in the butt."

He still wasn't satisfied. "Why in God's good name did you insulate the Foster's in polypro's? Any mush-brain knows that polypro wicks moisture away from things, and we need the moisture for proper cooling. You've got to first wrap it in something that doesn't wick, like a sock, and then wrap *that* in polypro." I couldn't believe my ears! "What difference does it matter?" I asked angrily. "We're gonna drink the damned stuff in another hour or so anyway. It'll still be cold." He was starting to get on my nerves.

"I *hate* warm beer!" he yelled shrilly. "If you don't keep the moisture around it, it won't be as cold!" Jesus, a hissy-fit over beer? "Okay," I said, reluctant to get into a shouting match, and stopped again to redo the Foster's. "But I'm not about to wrap it inside one of these socks. They're too raunchy." (Since leaving Delaware Water Gap eleven days ago, laundry hadn't received very high priority, which put me in a situation of alternating dirty socks with dirtier ones; and the ones that now dangled outside the pack like obscene pennants barely beat out the ones on my feet as the "dirtier.")

We finally compromised. I wrapped the beer in the windbreaker, covered *that* with the polypro top, and we went on up the road. Dumb Jarhead Marine . . .

A little after four, I reached Pine Swamp Branch Shelter, a nice, clean place on a small knoll, to find it empty. I hadn't seen Eco or Skate since leaving Silver Hill early this morning, but I expected them to make it here for the night. "Say Ego, let's call it a short day and get some laundry done. We're way overdue." (According to the *Guide*, the shelter's water source was a stream that flowed out of a swamp a couple of hundred yards down a blue-blazed path.) "Good idea," he agreed.

The stream was a sad affair. Simply put, an upper swamp drained into a lower one, and the shallow channel in between was the water source. I partially filled the ice cream pail and stripped, washed and shampooed and rinsed clothes and one pair of socks (with the good intention of washing the other pair tomorrow)—in all, it took five refills—and put everything back on wet.

The shelter was still empty when I returned. "Now what do you suppose happened to Skate and Eco?" I mused aloud. "They should have been here by now, unless they slept till noon." Unwilling to wait any longer, I started supper.

The shadows lengthened as twilight crept into the small clearing. At each noise I anxiously peered into the forest, expecting to hear Skate's cheery greeting, but got only shadowy silence in return. "Well, it looks like it's just you and me again, Goob. Which side do you want?" I joked as I began to set up the mosquito net inside the shelter. J.R. chuckled, "The outside if you're sleeping inside." Then he said sharply, "Listen! You hear that?" I strained against the croaking of the tree frogs and heard a distant whine that seemed to emanate from the direction of the swamp.

"Yeah, but so what? It's just the wind picking up." I finished with the net and then inflated the Therm-a-Rest. "That's the funniest sounding wind I've ever heard," he declared. Sure enough, the whine now sounded like a muted buzz saw, and it was definitely louder. "It's more like a hive of stirred-up bees."

An angry menace seemed to penetrate the dim light as the whine drew closer. "Bees don't fly at night, do they?" I asked, now concerned. "It sounds more like—" He bellowed, "Mosquitoes!" as the first of millions suddenly swooped in and began to suck blood. I dove beneath the mosquito net and lay there, heart racing, watching as the vicious horde pummeled the net, seeking entry. A zinger sunk his siphon into my neck and I whapped it—one down, a gazillion to go!

Three or four buzzed around my head. I flicked on my flashlight and counted a small army crouching on the inside of the net, waiting for the reconnaissance mission to end so that a major attack could be launched. "Jesus, Killer! We've gotta get rid of these beasties, else they'll suck us dry," I muttered, and the battle began. Egged on by The Marine, I spent the next ten minutes squashing mosquitoes against the inside of the net, sadistically relishing the hunt until the last one was eliminated. (The Killer's bloodlust was now fully aroused and he urged me to let a few more in "for the sport," but my thumb was getting a blister.) I growled, "We'll have plenty of 'sport' in the morning when we try to get out of here. Let's try to get some sleep. By the way, do you still want the outside?"

Something woke me from the shallow, restless sleep (a falling stick or the rummaging of a curious mouse). The buzzing was still frantic and loud, and I felt two bites on my forehead. I turned on the light and checked my watch—nearly three AM. In the shadowy glimmer of the beam I saw the culprit clinging to the net near my head and swiped with my hand, and was gratified at the small blob of blood that marred the net. Immediately, the splotch was covered with its frenzied peers, and I shuddered and said a prayer of thanksgiving for the net.

Then began the ritual of tossing and turning, begging for sleep to return, knowing it wouldn't until I had relieved myself. "How fast can you pee?" J.R. asked. "Not as fast as mosquitoes can suck," I replied, thinking of Denton Shelter back in Virginia, although then it had been an imaginary fear that had caused me to lie in agony, afraid to go out into the dark. But this menace was real—winged sharks inches away craving my life's blood—and shorts and a ragged tee shirt didn't offer much protection. I could almost feel the fiery agony brought on by hundreds of mosquito welts! So wallowing in déjà vu, I suffered.

By four o'clock, the pain was so intense I felt like I might explode. "Okay, J.R., I can't take it anymore. We gotta make a run for it. Here goes!" I slipped from beneath the net and was immediately covered by the ravenous horde. Slapping wildly, I ran for the nearest tree, thrashing and flailing and stomping while I peed, and then made a mad dash back to the safety of the net. Then I spent the next ten minutes chasing down the two-dozen interlopers that rode my skin inside—and the next hour scratching. Exhausted, I finally fell into an uneasy stupor.

The sun was well up when I awoke. "Listen," J.R. said. Silence surrounded the shelter! The mosquitoes were gone! "Let's get out of here," he growled, but I was already packing—and clawing at the dozens of bloody smears all over my arms and legs where the winged feasters had met an untimely end. "Damn, we must look like squished liver," he complained. "Can't do anything about it right now," I replied, pushing the bloodsmeared net into my pack and buckling the top. "We'll wash up at the first water hole we reach." I hit the Trail running, scratching, and cussing.

Relief didn't come until I reached the spring at Belter Campsite, five miles away. I had just filled the bucket and started scrubbing at the bloody crust with my bandanna when Skate walked up. "My gosh, Model-T! What's happened to you? You look horrid!"

"A pack of wild hogs tried to steal my grub and I had to fight'em off." Seeing the consternation on her face, I said, "Actually, I battled Planet Earth's entire mosquito population last night."

"Not all of them," she said. "Eco and I had our share here. In fact, it was so bad while we ate supper that we had to put on our rain gear." Skate shook her head at my puny scrubbing effort. "We thought you would come on here for the night. Where were you?"

"I holed up at Pine Swamp Shelter, waiting for you to show up."

"We bypassed it. Eco had this humongous Foster beer he'd gotten at Cornwall Bridge and he wanted to cool it in a spring and have it for supper. You know how he is. His beer has to be perfect." She shook her head at my effort. "You can do that later. Let me do something about your face. You look deformed."

Surrendering my bandanna, I said, "Yeah, I know someone like that, too. They can be a real pain."

She dabbed at the dried blood like she might be applying makeup to a mannequin and said hesitantly, "Eco and I are taking tomorrow off and hitching a ride to Tanglewood to hear the Boston Pops. They play every Saturday evening during the summer. You want to go? Maybe stay over at a bed and breakfast?"

I considered her offer. "I don't think so, Skate, but thanks for asking. I've got to go into South Egremont (Massachusetts) Sunday to buy food; plus, I need to get on to Cheshire and pick up my mail drop. You kids go on and have a good time."

"Okay, Model-T." She finished working on my face and handed back the bandanna. Filling her water bottles, she said, "See you in a couple of days," and she went back to their campsite to awaken Eco.

As I renewed my efforts on my arms and legs, The Ego grumbled, "Doggone, we're going to be here all day at this rate. Can't you work any faster?" It *was* slow going, for the dried blood was like concrete. Frustrated, I snapped, "Yeah, I can work real fast," and began scooping up mud from the spring's runoff and smearing it over the blood. "You want fast? How's *this* for fast?" I slathered the black, stinking goop over all the exposed skin, including my face, slammed the bucket back in my pack, and strode off at a fast pace with The Ego mumbling about "attitude adjustment" and "swamp creature." I didn't give a hoot, for the mud felt wonderful!

After a couple of miles, the goop began to dry, then crack; and as I began a lengthy ascent, the sweat started to flow, streaking and splotching the crust and turning me into a walking horror show. J.R. harangued me constantly about my rash behavior (and I was having second thoughts, too, for this was like carrying my own personal swamp, complete with putrid odor). "Maybe I was a bit hasty," I conceded. "I'll wash it off at the first water hole."

I reached the top of the mountain and came around a sharp turn in the Trail—and met a young boy, about six, accompanied by a large Collie. The boy took one look at me and began to scream hysterically, causing the Collie to raise its hackles and bark furiously, which in turn brought a burly man rushing around the bend at full gallop! His heavy hiking stick was raised for business and he frantically tried to free a monstrous sheath knife from the scabbard belted to his waist—ready to fight to the death to save his son from this horrid creature!

"Daddy, it's a monster!" the boy wailed, pointing. "Don't let it get me!" He screamed louder. "It's the booger-man! Don't let him take me. I promise I'll be good!"

Abruptly, an overweight woman waddled around the turn. Gasping for breath, she clutched her son possessively and gave me a dark "I dare you" look. Thankfully the boy's screaming slowly subsided into racking sobs as he burrowed into his mother's ample bosom, and the dog stopped barking.

"Jeepers, I'm sorry," I stammered through the swampy muck. "I'm only a thru-hiker. Mosquitoes about ate me alive last night and the itching was driving me crazy. I thought the mud would help; you know, like putting it on a bee sting." The man looked dubious, but at least he stopped trying to free the knife (although his hiking stick remained at the ready). I added lamely, "I guess it looks pretty bad, huh?"

The boy calmed down at his mother's gentle "shushing," but the recriminating looks from momma and poppa told me I was still in hot water. I prattled on like a snake-oil salesman. "Yessiree, this mud's worked wonders, better'n any medicinal salve, an' I highly recommend it! Now if you'll excuse me, I'm gonna just skip on down this mountain and wash it off. Yessiree. Miracle stuff!"

I pushed past them and never looked back.

J.R. muttered, "Hell's bells! Now we've sunk to abusing six-year-olds. What other tricks do you have up your sleeve?" I retorted, "Aw heck, it'll just make him more alert to his surroundings. A couple of years in therapy and he'll be as good as new. Jeez, I hope we find some water soon. This miracle mud's starting to burn . . ."

The next morning, I crossed into Massachusetts at Sages Ravine, an enchanting place of tumbling waters and lordly pines. The caretaker there, a friendly girl with the healthy blush of outdoors living rouging her cheeks, offered me a large orange. I accepted it gratefully and tucked it inside my pack to eat later.

After a two-hour climb, I gained the summit of Race Mountain, a place where the rugged artistry of Nature's power is revealed in the seemingly endless granite ledges that form a stair-step toward the heavens. To the south, Connecticut faded away, overcome by the shimmering rays of the midmorning sun; while Massachusetts, green and beckoning, filled the northern horizon. "Celebration time. Another state conquered," I said, picking a ledge to sit on and slipping out of the pack. Reaching for the orange (which turned out to be a grapefruit), I ripped it open and burrowed my teeth into the ruby-red flesh, ignoring the juice that dribbled into my beard and dripped from my fingers.

Said J.R. somberly, "Katahdin's still up there, waiting for us." I replied with a quickening of my pulse, "Yes, I can feel its presence. What do you think it'll be like, seeing it for the first time?" He pondered the question and answered with another question: "Friend or foe?" Wiping the sticky juice off with my shirttail, I hoisted the pack. "Both maybe. Let's see what kind of mischief Massachusetts can toss our way," I grunted, eyeing the looming hulk of Mt. Everett across a deep valley—just another dip and hump on the long grind northward . . .

That night, I lay alone on the floor of Glen Brook Shelter—a weird-looking structure that seemed too tall for its small size and smelled of creosote—and listened to the beautiful, lilting melodies that poured from the tiny earphones of my radio. Boston Pops, coming "live" from Tanglewood! As the last strains faded and the tomb-like silence of the deep forest rushed in, I wished Skate and Eco "bon appetite" and went to sleep.

CHAPTER 10

Wimps, Humdingers, and Sumabitches

Massachusetts had plenty of mischief in store!

"Jiminy!" J.R. whooped as I half-slid down a slanted four-foot ledge slick as ice, saving myself from a bad tumble against a jagged pine stump by grabbing a puny sapling. Looking at the scarred bark, a generation of panicked hands must have made many such grabs. I recovered and managed to land feet first on a narrow shelf. "Whoever named this beast 'Jug End' sure knew what he was doing!" I spotted another drop off a few yards below and mentally started psyching myself up for it as I paused to catch my breath and tried to fend off the sinking feeling of despair. (Could it get worse? I'd already courted disaster a dozen times in the last half-mile with similar acrobatic contortions.)

Jug End was aptly named, since the earth appeared to drop off into a bottomless abyss! For at this place the mighty Blue Ridge momentarily capitulated to the broad Housatonic River Valley, now hidden in the depths by a spreading overcast. Worriedly, I looked at the overhead. (When I had left Glen Brook Shelter two hours earlier, the Sunday morning sky was an ocean of azure spotted with island-like fluffy clouds; but before long, a massive sinister shadow had shut out the sun and transformed the heavens into a gloomy sea of gray.) Clenching my jaw, I descended to the next drop off.

After I had maneuvered past several more "slip-slide-grab" obstacles (and busted my butt twice when my feet went their own way on the slip-

327

pery granite), the Trail suddenly gentled into a series of switchbacks. "Okay! We've beat the 'Beast'!" I yelled, relieved. "Let's get on down to the highway and grab a ride into the 'ville.'" (South Egremont was only a little over a mile from the Trail.) Suddenly craving a Cherry Coke float, I fairly flew down the switchbacks!

Five minutes later the pain started—a sharp twinge every few steps at the joining of the ankle and right shin, soon becoming a searing pain that spread up into the entire shin area. I slowed to a hobble and the pain subsided to a dull ache, aggravating but manageable. "I don't know what's going on, Ego. This is a first." He offered, "Maybe it'll go away if we slow down."

By the time I reached the highway, the pain was definitely an entity to be reckoned with, stabbing at the bone with each step. Its power took over my mind, screwing my face into a mask of agony and tossing any desire for a Cherry Coke float into the wayside ditch. J.R. said grimly, "This is no good, Alter. We'd better take on a full load of ibuprofen and get on to Tom Leonard Shelter." Heavy gray clouds hung low, promising rain soon, and the shelter was still a good nine miles away. I told him reluctantly, "That might be a problem. We've run out." He turned ugly. "What do you mean, 'out'?" I spat back, deciding I wasn't going to take the blame all by myself. "We didn't buy any back at Kent, if *you* will recall." He exploded, "Dammit all to hell! Now we've *got* to go into South Egremont for ibuprofen." I replied meekly, "No biggie. It should be easy to catch a ride."

In the next thirty minutes, at least two-dozen cars went by—mostly churchgoers—but none slowed. I fumed, snarling, "Chicken nasty! I can't understand why nobody will stop. It's not like we're criminals, for cryin' out loud! This close to the Trail, you'd think the locals would *know* we're hikers!" Calm now, J.R. said, "If you were on the way to church, would you pick us up? I sure wouldn't."

Without replying, I shouldered the pack and hobbled down the road.

The elegant village of South Egremont, with its manicured lawns and decorative flower gardens, was awash with late summer's colorful offerings. Yet on this dank, gloomy morning, the village's beauty was shielded from my pain-misted eyes as I limped along the sidewalk toward what looked like a convenience store.

The clerk, an older man who wore a bored, "Why me?" expression and went about his duties like a robot, ignored me until I managed to block him in a corner when he went over to the soda cooler to restock some drinks. "I need a bottle of ibuprofen," I told him.

He studied me for a long moment, probably wondering if I was trying to finagle a handout, then said, "I don't believe we sell anything like that. I never even heard of it."

Dang! They *had* to have ibuprofen! I tried another tack. "What about Motrin? You got any of that?"

"Oh, yeah. There's lots of Motrin behind the counter. How much you want?"

I asked to see a bottle, which he grudgingly got and set on the counter for me to pick up, probably scared that he would accidentally make skin contact and contract leprosy if he actually handed the bottle to me. It was a small bottle—only twenty-four 200-milligram tablets. "Better give me two bottles—and a quart of milk."

Outside, I took four Motrin tablets and drank all the milk, listening as Killer fumed, "That dingo's brain functions at the speed of fluff. Puppets have people pulling strings to make them go, and robots have computer brains and gears, but that poor sod has to rely on 'fluff.'" I ignored his tirade and asked, "What do you think? Should we hole up in a motel—if we can find one?" He didn't hesitate in his reply, "Waste of good money. I've faced lots worse than this in the Marines. Hellfire, we're not wimps!" I mumbled, "Maybe we'll get lucky and catch a ride."

We didn't get 'lucky', and after fifteen frustrating minutes I threw my arms up in disgust and yelled an obscenity at the blue Honda that breezed past. Still hurting (the Motrin hadn't done much for the pain), I snarled, "Dammit Ego, what's wrong with these people? We're gonna have to hoof it." He said, "What's the beef? It's only a mile." I groaned, "But to a miserable piss-ant, a mile is forever."

Just as the trailhead hove into sight the rain began, a few benign sprinkles at first, and then the clouds opened up in earnest. I turned off the highway and followed the Trail along an old weed-choked fence, then through a pasture overgrown with waist-high grass, which, made top-heavy by the rain, clogged the path and made the going difficult. At last I left the clutching grass behind and descended into a dark hemlock grove—and stepped onto a patch of water-slick clay. Without warning, my feet slipped and I landed on my butt.

Soaked, exhausted, numbed by self-pity, I tried to get to my feet but I just couldn't do it! "What're we going to do now, Ego?" I whimpered, but got no response. The hemlocks moaned as watery gusts contorted the feathery green branches. "Come on, J.R.! We're in this together. What in the world are we going to do?" He growled, "Be quiet, Alter. I'm trying to think." After a long pause, he said, "Okay, I read someplace that if you get into trouble in the backwoods, the best thing to do is eat something hot and calmly access the situation. It makes a body feel better and one can think more clearly and have a better chance at arriving at a workable solution."

He had to be kidding! It was pouring rain and I couldn't muster enough strength to stand, not to mention trying to cook. "You're nuts!" He replied, "If you have a better idea, I'm listening." I stared dully at the small puddle of water that began to form in the indentation around my bottom, vaguely aware of the rain splattering the top of my head. "Okay, I'll try." I managed to slither out of the pack and pulled out Kelly's tarp, tossing it like a blanket over my muddy empire. Finally, with a great deal of effort I managed to boil a pot of ramen. "Let's eat."

A few minutes later, after the pan was licked clean, I said, "Okay Big Man, we've eaten something hot. When do we start feeling better and come up the magic solution to get us out of this mess?" J.R. answered with a question: "How many times have we gotten lost since leaving Springer?" Confused, I answered, "Maybe once or twice, never for very long. What's that have to do with anything?" Another question: "And how many times have we fallen?" What was he getting at? Had he lost his marbles? "Jeez, I don't know. Maybe a half-dozen times, if that. Three times today for sure, counting where we're sitting right now, playing 'Twenty Questions' in a mud puddle in the middle of a rain storm like a couple of idiots."

"No, hang with me," he insisted. "How far have we hiked with our eyes closed?" Of all the stupid questions! I saw red! "What's wrong with you? Have you gone completely bonkers?"

He answered calmly, "Not yet. I just happen to think that you're a first class wimp, that's all. Bill Irwin and Orient are somewhere behind us, pushing on in spite of everything the Trail dishes out. Can you imagine what it must be like hiking blind, not seeing where you're going, not enjoying the sunrises and sunsets, or the mountaintop views? Have you any idea how disheartening it must be to fall dozens of times each day, or how frustrating he must get when he wanders off the Trail, helpless, at the mercy of strangers to get him headed back in the right direction? And think of the pain he has to endure, not only from the falls, but from facing each day with a cracked rib." (According to the "Trail grapevine," Bill had recently taken a bad tumble and broken one, possibly two, ribs, but he was still on the Trail!)

Too ashamed for words, I sat in silence and attempted to balance a lame leg against cracked ribs, knowing we weren't even in the same pain league with The Orient Express.

At last J.R. said, "Let's do it." I gritted my teeth against the pain and struggled to my feet. "Yeah, let's do it," I echoed grimly, and the journey continued.

Eight Motrin later, in a surreal gloom brought on by the pelting rain, I reached Tom Leonard Shelter. An angry-looking red spot had appeared above my ankle, just below the shin. Journeyman and Journalist were there, as were Thatcher's Children. Journalist remarked that I looked terrible, and I commended her on her excellent eyesight. Journeyman examined my ankle and diagnosed my problem as tendonitis, shin-splints, or a stress fracture. Tim put his money on lyme disease, while Melanie suspected it was a combination of one or more unknown factors. I thanked them all for their concern and excellent patient rapport, and agreed wholly with all conclusions, since in their wisdom they had covered all bases—and then some! After a lengthy discussion, Journalist sided with Journeyman and shin-splints won by a hair; but by this time I could have cared less. All I wanted to do was get off my foot and go to bed.

The next morning, the tender spot had a pronounced bulge. The rain continued, harder if anything, and I procrastinated, undecided as to whether I should hike or not (also wondering if I would be considered a first class wimp if I stayed). Undeterred, Journeyman and Journalist decided to brave the rain and departed. I felt smugly vindicated when Thatcher's Children made the decision to wait awhile and see if the rain abated. However, by late morning the rain showed no sign of slackening and Tim got fidgety; so after an early lunch, Thatcher's Children slogged off into the deluge.

To go or not? Finally The Marine assured me that it would be prudent, not wimpish, to remain at the shelter and rest the foot. Relieved, I said, "I've always tried to be a prudent alter ego," so we stayed.

About mid-afternoon, Dog and Shug arrived, thoroughly soaked, and dripped water in big puddles on the shelter floor. I was tickled pink to have company for the night—and then deflated when they decided an hour later to try for the next shelter some five miles on. I asked if they had seen anything of Skate and Eco, but they hadn't. Shug gave me a small bottle of Tiger Balm lotion before they left—smelly stuff, but did seem to provide some relief.

My afternoon soon settled into a boring routine of eating Motrin, rubbing on Tiger Balm, braving the rain to relieve myself when the urgency became undeniable, and reading the entire shelter register back to the first entry on December thirty-first, when three teenagers, accompanied by a

black Lab dog and a hefty bottle of Wild Turkey, braved two feet of snow
to spend New Year's Eve at Tom Leonard Shelter. I found Wahoola's entry,
eight days ago, and just below it was Moleskin Meg's. It looked like she
had snared a companion!

Names jumped out as I thumbed through the well-worn pages: Hippy
Man, bemoaning his missing guitar; Cup Cake, still connected to E Z
Strider like an umbilical cord; Chuck, another of the Brew and Pizza
Group, now traveling solo; Volunteer, his genial nature oozing from his
words like honey; Dead Ahead and Wild Bill, still sharing the same bear-
damaged food bag; Gypsy, a gangly hiker with a ready smile whom I'd met
at Trail Days, still traveling with Pablo, a small black and white mutt that
had followed him out of Erwin, Tennessee, and had eventually adopted
him—all just days ahead! Ward Leonard (no relation to Tom as far as I
knew) had gone through weeks before, chronicling his passage with a brief
"Ward Leonard, Northbound". I sighed, wishing for companionship to ease
the dreary afternoon.

Heavy rain fell during the night. Said J.R., "At least there are no mosquitoes," to which I replied, "Of course not. They all drowned."

Dawn came slowly, hampered by a steady drizzle. Close by, out of
sight, a swollen runoff played a watery dirge. I asked The Marine, "What
would a 'prudent' hiker do today?" He considered the question and
answered wisely, "Stay another day or two. Give the foot a chance to heal."
I shuddered at the thought of even one more hour imprisoned by boredom.
"Or, we could try for the next shelter. A *very* slow five miles," he added. I
tested the ankle again (for the umpteenth time this morning). It seemed
slightly better. "Okay, let's try it," I said, now anxious to be off. After
spreading on a heavy coat of Tiger Balm, I swallowed four Motrin, quickly
packed, and then limped from the waterlogged clearing without a backward glance.

"I signed on to hike the Trail, not wade it," J.R., the "Killer" Marine complained. Ignoring his outburst, I absorbed the rooftop colors that splattered
the trees around Tyringham, a pastoral hamlet clearly visible a mile away.
The small village sat at the end of a wide valley, now flooded by the twelve
inches of rain that the hurricane had dumped on New England (according
to a "local" I'd talked to earlier at a road crossing). When we'd left Tom
Leonard Shelter yesterday morning, I'd been prepared for the worse, and
although there had been a few places where the path was inundated above

boot tops, it hadn't been all that bad. But this valley equaled a dozen yesterday's!

I stood waist-deep in muddy water on what I hoped was the Trail, about halfway across the flooded valley (and I still had to cross the culprit stream that had overflowed its banks). Searching for the rutted path with my feet, I slowly waded towards high ground, still a couple of hundred yards distant. "I thought this was a Marine's prime element," I joked, trying to keep my mind off "things" that might be lurking near my legs. He retaliated, "Any deeper and we're going to need snorkel gear." A stone's throw to the right, a small wake, magnified by the sun's noonday glare, disturbed the surface. I cowered, heart racing in near panic. A snake? I knew cottonmouths didn't live this far north, but we were still in copperhead country. The wake disappeared as its engineer sunk beneath the surface, and goose bumps crawled across my skin at the thought of venomous fangs headed my way. "A frog," The Marine said with authority, and I didn't argue. A frog was easier on the mind!

The water obstacle did have an upside: My ankle seemed to benefit from the prolonged cold soak. "A doctor would have prescribed the same treatment," I told The Marine as we finally made landfall, thankfully without incident. "We're getting 'free' therapy." He: "You forgot about 'bed rest,'" and I replied, "True, but the foot rests every time it disconnects with the ground." He growled, "A shame the same corollary doesn't follow for your mouth, since it is usually disconnected from your brain." Wise guy!

Reaching dry terra firma at last, I unloaded the pack and spread things out to dry, and then dumped the water out of my boots and wrung out my socks. A movement about fifty yards offshore caught my eye (the same wake I'd seen earlier?), and I made out the oversized head of a large wood rat frantically paddling toward us. The rat suddenly began to backtrack, swinging in a wide arc, and then seemed to change its mind as it again turned our way. We watched the erratic maneuvers for some time, watched as the rat's paddling became more useless and labored. Finally, it ceased to clutch at the water and slipped down into a watery grave.

J.R. broke the long silence. "Now that rat was a first-class wimp. It just gave up. It was so close, but it just gave up." (I knew all about "first-class wimps" and couldn't help but feel a twinge of sadness for the rat.) I let the remark pass and lay back with my eyes closed against the bright sunlight, waiting for my gear to dry.

On a whim, I sat back up and stared at the water, perversely hoping to see the wake reappear, but the dingy surface was unmarred. I said, "When you think about it, I guess wimps come in all shapes and forms." He grunted, "You got that right."

Came Upper Goose Pond Cabin, where for a $3.00 donation a hiker could get a bed, kitchen privileges, and, if so inclined, a dip in the icy waters of the pond—really a sizeable lake. Peter and Mary Fitzpatrick, the season's caretakers, threw in a blueberry pancake breakfast—wonderful hosts!

And then there was the cold macaroni salad . . . The next evening at Kay Wood Shelter, two miles shy of thriving Dalton, Massachusetts, I was reviewing the contents of my food bag, trying to decide what to have for supper, when two southbounders (the first I had met) arrived. Clevis and Nalgene were in their twenties, wore the jaded look of thru-hikers, and were obviously devoted to one another. I soon learned that they had finished college, and that after they completed their hike, they planned to take jobs out West, working with special needs children. Nice kids!

I had just fired up my stove and put some water on to boil when another man, lots older and not a hiker, came up to the shelter. "How do? My name's Tom, and I'm the caretaker for the shelter." Glancing at my steaming pot, he said, "You might want to put a hold on that fire when you see what Kay sent, in case there were any hungry hikers here." He removed the cover from a large plastic bowl and a delicious aroma spread through the shelter. "Cold macaroni salad," he announced proudly.

"We meet both criteria. Hungry and hikers," I chuckled, moving to head off Clevis before he could take possession of the bowl. (Dog had taught me well!)

While we ate, Tom explained that Kay Wood, our generous benefactor (and the lady for whom the leanto was named), had herself thru-hiked the Trail two years earlier and knew how hungry thru-hikers could get. "She woulda come herself," said Tom, "but she had a meetin' to attend. I need to get back to th' house. If you want, I can leave the bowl."

"No need," Clevis said, divvying up the remains between the three of us and handing the bowl to Tom. "Tell her it was superb." Nalgene and I added our thanks and Tom left, mission accomplished. We talked until dark, and then Clevis and Nalgene retired to the loft. As I crawled beneath the mosquito net, The Ego remarked, "That lady makes a great macaroni salad." I: "Yeah, but I'm glad Ol' Dog wasn't here waggin' his tail."

I awoke early, anxious to get on to Cheshire, eleven miles away. Threatening clouds—angry-looking black-gray blobs fringed in wispy white—hung low, portending a miserable day. As I was getting ready to leave the shelter, I overheard Clevis trying to awaken Nalgene to another day of adventure. "Wake up, little mouse," he murmured gently, his voice filled with tender affection; and her sleepy reply came back, "Mice don't get up this early. Go away."

I called up to the loft in a soft voice, "Have a great trip."

His reply, seemingly trite at the time, floated down. "Each day is a great trip." As I walked away, his words were already fading to a distant echo. My destiny lay to the north, theirs south, and our paths diverged, never to meet again. But we had shared a great macaroni salad . . .

Late that afternoon, I crossed over the Hoosic River and hobbled up the main thoroughfare of Cheshire to the hiker hostel at St. Mary of the Assumption Catholic Church, hurting but happy. This hiker was *not* a wimp!

Father Tom Begley greeted me. An avid hiker, having himself completed a large section of the AT, Father Tom took an immediate interest in my limp. After I had explained the symptoms, he examined my boot insoles—thin as a pauper's purse—and pronounced, "Shin splints." Suggesting that I get new insoles, he said, "The nearest outfitter is The Mountain Goat at Williamstown, about fifteen miles north. The bus runs hourly, and there's a bus stop out front."

The next morning, I caught the first bus to Williamstown. For several miles, Massachusetts Highway 8 followed the Hoosic River northward, paralleling Mount Greylock, the highest point in the state, over which the Trail passes. I watched with sinking heart as the mass rose upward and disappeared in the clouds. "Dang, Ego, how are we ever going to get over that beast with this ankle?" He said waspishly, "Like we've done for the last 1500 miles, by putting one foot in front of the next—that is, unless you can grow wings. And don't start going wimpy on me again." Enough already! I growled, "You wanna talk about wimps, how about the big, brave Marine who trembles at the first sign of THE LOOK?" to which he replied, "That's not wimpy. That's plain scary." He had that right, so I let him off the hook.

The moment my feet touched the new insoles, renewed life seemed to surge into my legs. Afraid the feeling would go away, I took a few anxious turns around the store, but the sensation remained. Elated, I paid the clerk, and we went off to find a pay phone to call Judith. "I can't believe what a few extra millimeters of padding can do," I gushed, feeling something akin to the old spring return to my stride. I still had pain—and the limp—but I sensed better days ahead!

Alyson answered. "Mom's gone to the grocery, but she should be back in an hour or so."

"I'll call back," J.R. promised after a short chat, and we went looking for a small café to while away the time.

Williams College was close by, and flocks of students roamed the streets—perfectly natural for it was a Saturday, August eleventh. The date hit me like a slap in the face. "Hey, Ego, today is the four-month anniversary since we left Springer Mountain! Celebration time!"

More Goodies Café—the name sounded promising—was filled with tantalizing odors and only a scattering of students. Somewhat embarrassed by my squalid appearance, I took a table against a back wall and before long a youthful-looking waiter (college student?) wearing a white apron that had been splattered by a culinary mishap, walked up, gave me a quick once-over, and smiled. He placed a menu on the table and said, "Hi. I'm Joe and I'll be your waiter. Be back in a minute to take your order."

I was ravenous. "Hold on, Joe. I can give it to you right now." In a flash I scanned the menu and ordered pancakes—at three dollars, the least expensive for the most calories—and coffee. "I'm hiking the Appalachian Trail," I told him to allay his curiosity. "Just came in to Mountain Goat to get some insoles for my boots. I've been on the Trail four months today." Giving him a wry grin, I added, "A person can get pretty grubby after four months in the woods."

"Wow!" You're the first real hiker I've ever met. Four months today!" He began to ask the usual questions, which I readily answered, although with as few words as I could because the food smells were driving me crazy! Abruptly he got to his feet and said, "I'd better get hopping before the boss lady grabs me. I'll bring your food in nothing flat."

A few minutes later, a lady a couple of years my senior, her gray hair frizzed with the sweat of honest labor, made her way toward where I sat sipping the coffee, which Joe had brought right away. Flour smudged her dress, an incongruity considering her no-nonsense, all-business look. The owner? "Uh-oh, J.R., this could spell trouble."

When she stopped at my table and gave me a curious, appraising look, I held my breath, waiting for the eviction order. Instead, she said, "Joe tells me you're hiking the entire Appalachian Trail and that today is your four-month anniversary." Her face relaxed into a warm smile and I breathed deeply.

I grinned. "Sure is. I'm kind of off the beaten path, but it looks like I got lucky and landed in a little spot of Paradise. The food smells wonderful. By the way, I'm known on the Trail as Model-T."

She actually shook my hand! "My name is Verena and I own More Goodies. We cater mostly to college kids and town people, but to my knowledge you're the first hiker we've ever had." She glanced toward the kitchen. "I'd like to stay and talk, but things are kind of busy."

"Don't worry about it, and thanks for the welcome."

"Enjoy yourself. And your meal is on the house." With that startling revelation, she moved off toward the kitchen.

Dazed, I asked J.R., "Dang! Did I hear right? Did she say it was all on the house?" He, excited: "That's what it sounded like to me."

Just then, Joe brought the platter of pancakes. "Uh, Joe, come back in a few minutes. I might want a coupla other things . . ."

The next afternoon I climbed to the top of the War Memorial, atop Mount Greylock (as high as I could climb in this mischievous state that had almost done me in). To the north, as far as I could see, the rugged, rippled Green Mountains of Vermont—somehow darkly ominous—went on and on, finally falling off the horizon. Unconsciously, I shifted weight to my good foot, although the ankle had survived the trek to Greylock's summit surprisingly well. "J.R., do you think we're really going to make it?" In my mind, I could see the rat sinking beneath the muddy water. Sensing my mood, he took a long time to answer. "A lot of people will be disappointed if we don't."

"Yeah, they will," I grunted. Then descending the Tower, I started down the steep, winding path toward Vermont.

What a difference a couple of days can make! Since leaving Cheshire, trepidation had courted each step, causing me to choke with fright each time the offending ankle nagged at my nerve endings. My anxiety caused J.R. to hold forth in a stern, stentorian voice with one of what he referred to as "Warren's postulating proverbs for a successful thru-hike," presumably to rein me in some. (The Singing Horseman had sent J.R. a handout—a collection of maxims intended to bolster the faint-hearted—that he had gotten when he attended Warren Doyle's A.T. Institute in preparation for his '89 thru-hike. He had presumably sent the handout on to reinforce his "three-packs-of-dry-ramen-each-day" philosophy, and Ol' Ego had swallowed it all, lock, stock, and barrel, as gospel, being so impressed with the upbeat sayings that he had memorized the entire list for "insurance.")

Happily, thanks to the new insoles, I could feel the old, familiar stride (that seemed to eat up the miles) lingering on the edge of the limp, which had all but disappeared. The reddish, swollen aggravation was quickly fading into a pinkish-brown memory, though it still sparked an occasional spasm. The ordeal of the past few days seemed to seep from my soul, down through my boots and into the dust, and eager anticipation again gripped my mind.

Which brought on a "maxim." Reaching the border, I bellowed out a couple of humongous "ooogas," sniffed the air, and spurted down the Trail

like a hound closing in on a fox's lair. The ankle immediately rewarded my
rash impulse with a twinge of déjà vu, causing me to wince, and The Ego
socked me with a "Doyle-ism" (*my* term for the aphorism): "It is far better
to be a strong hiker than a fast hiker," to which I replied, "As any idiot
knows." But I slowed down.

We were now hiking two trails at once. (At the Vermont border, the
Appalachian Trail joins the same rutted path as the Long Trail—considered
to be the nation's first long-distance hiking trail—for about one hundred
miles before swinging east at Sherburne Pass toward New Hampshire,
leaving the Long Trail to fend for itself on its long run north to the Canadian border.) "Double fun," J.R. quipped. "Double trouble," I grumbled.
Compared to the Berkshire Mountains of Massachusetts, where the Trail
seemed to cross a road every couple of miles, the Green Mountains were
more akin to the southern Appalachians—wild and isolated, with road
crossings few and far between. But so far, the ground afforded far easier
passage than its southern kin.

I came to a particularly benign stretch and instinctively poured on the
coal, which brought a rebuke in the form of another "Doyle-ism": "Your
chance for injury is directly related to your pace . . ." Jiminy June bugs!
How long was I going to have to endure this sermonizing? His abrasive
recitations were beginning to bug me. Waspishly, I replied, "Warren also
said, 'Leave your emotional fat at home.'" Chalk one up for the Model-T!

I reached Congdon Camp at noon the next day. The ramshackle building, at one time a hunting cabin, contained an ancient wood stove and a
small window with half its panes missing. At some point, the structure had
been turned into a hiker shelter with the addition of built-in bunks.

Three mice played tag all over the place in broad daylight, brazenly
moving ever closer to my food bag while I ate lunch and thumbed through
the register. I quickly saw through the little critters' strategy and carried the
bag and register outside a safe distance from the building to resume my
scanning, noting that somehow Skate and Eco had scooted past and were
now a day ahead. Wahoola had also widened the gap—now nine days
away—and was still accompanied by Moleskin Meg.

Suddenly disheartened and lonely, I said, "Doggone it, Ego, we keep
getting further behind. We need to hike faster or put in more hours, else
we're never gonna catch up. No one knows where we are, or even gives a
mule's kick, for that matter."

He immediately reeled off another "Doyle-ism": "You can't make a
mountain any less steep or an afternoon any colder or a morning any
warmer or daylight any longer." Before I could reply, he tossed out another:

"Don't expect any favors from the trail. It knows no prejudice, nor practices discrimination." I retorted bitterly, "The Trail is diabolical, unforgiving, vindictive, and fickle. Look what it did to us in Massachusetts. It almost sent us home with our tail dragging." He fired another salvo: "Don't waste you energy complaining about things you have no control over." I, irritably: "For cryin' out loud! Are you gonna go through the whole list?" He, fiendishly: "Yeah, there's a bunch of 'em left, and then we can do reruns."

Sadist! I felt a twitch of envy at Wahoola as I put the register back inside. At least he could stuff plugs in his ears when Meg got on a verbal binge. As for me, they didn't make earplugs big enough to silence the annoying jabberer inside my head!

Goddard Shelter sits near the summit of Glastenbury Mountain. From the front of the shelter, the view is an eye stopper. Mountains ripple the landscape like green, frozen waves as they stretch toward the southern horizon, where Mt. Greylock, reduced to a small hump by the miles, might be a lifeboat on the vast wooded ocean—with a short leap of the imagination.

As I entered the clearing, a large Doberman dog at the top of the steps leading up to the shelter raised his hackles and growled. Alarmed, I paused in mid-stride and grabbed for the pepper spray clipped to my shoulder strap, and then forged ahead slowly, talking softly, but his stance didn't waver.

A man's voice boomed, "Bruno! Get over here and lay down," at which, sentry job finished, the dog's hackles flattened and his tail wagged a couple of times before he disappeared into the shelter. Again the voice rang out, "He's harmless enough, unless you're a piece of meat on a bone. Then there might be a problem."

"I'm the next closest thing—a skinny thru-hiker," I chuckled, climbing the steps. "Is it safe?"

"Maybe for the time being. He just ate." The man grinned, relishing the banter. Half rising, he shook my hand and then settled back between two piles of assorted food items. He frowned at the clutter, uttered a mild oath, and said, "My name's Jan and this brute is Bruno, and we're hiking the Long Trail." Running his hand over the larger pile, he smiled wryly and said, "As you may have noticed, I went slightly overboard on the food. My pack's killing me, so I decided to lighten my load." I nodded sympathetically.

Jan was probably a couple of inches taller than me, lean and muscular, with a look made stern by clear-rimmed glasses but betrayed by friendly brown eyes. I put his age at somewhere in the late thirties, though it was a tough call because of his mustache, which barely missed being called a "handlebar."

J.R. immediately zeroed in on his short haircut and military bearing, pegging him as a Marine. (Of course, the Marine Drill Instructor campaign hat adorned with the Marine Corps globe and anchor emblem and a military rucksack with staff sergeant insignia pinned on the front, both lying nearby, were strong clues!)

"My name's Model-T. Are you going all the way to Canada?"

"Yep, hope to."

J.R. got into the act: "I noticed the D.I. cover. You wouldn't happen to be a Marine, would you?"

"Staff sergeant in the Marine Corps Reserves. I've been planning this trip for a long time and thought I'd better take it now while I could. Rumor has it my unit may be activated since the Gulf is heating up." (The Ego and I had been out of the news circuit for several days, so it came as a shock to find out that Iraq had invaded Kuwait!) He added grimly, "War is a strong possibility."

That set "Killer" off. "I'm a retired Marine myself. Jeez! Maybe I'll get called back to active duty!" Jan's eyes crinkled at J.R.'s outburst, and his look said the Corps was a long way from having to scrape the bottom of the barrel (though J.R. was too caught up in the moment to notice).

While he prattled on about the "Old Corps," Jan went on with his sorting, nodding in agreement and occasionally throwing out noncommittal grunts. But my attention was on Jan! He was discarding MRE's (Meals, Ready to Eat)—precooked food mainly used by soldiers and Marines in the field. (Although MRE's carried a powerful calorie load, they were generally shunned by thru-hikers as packable food because of their heavy weight and high cost—unless, of course, they happened to be free!)

My pulse quickened as I took stock: Spaghetti with meat and sauce; omelet with ham; chicken with rice; pork and rice in BBQ sauce; frankfurters with bean component (what did a "component" taste like, not that it really mattered?); corned beef with hash; and crackers, cookies, cocoa, on and on—all neatly packaged in heavy plastic pouches. "Lord love a duck," I gasped to myself, swallowing hard to keep from drooling. "Double dang, with a humdinger to boot!" (For us ol' boys from south of the Mason-Dixon, "humdinger" holds a place of honor among superlatives, falling just below the granddaddy, which is a long, low whistle followed by "sumabitch.")

"What're you going to do with what you don't want?" I asked, cutting off J.R.'s reminiscing.

Pointing at the larger pile, he said, "Leave all this for other hikers, I suppose. Help yourself if you want any." He started to stuff the smaller stack into his rucksack.

"Yeah, I might take a little," I said, trying to appear nonchalant as I scrambled for my food bag before he changed his mind. Then cramming my bag and pack to the hilt (and ignoring J.R.'s vehement protest that "A Marine officer is *not* greedy"), I explained, "It's probably not a good thing to leave anything behind 'cause when mice get used to 'people food,' it makes 'em really aggressive. Bad critters, those aggressive mice."

Pushing hard, I got the last of the pouches in, except for three entrees and a couple of desserts. Grinning happily at my handiwork, I said, "Done! The Marines have landed and the situation is well in hand. Happy to solve that little problem for you."

"What about these?" Jan asked, indicating the entrees and desserts.

"Gonna eat 'em right now."

"All of that?" he asked, his voice filled with skepticism.

"Child's play," and I chuckled inwardly when his incredulous gaze turned to awe as I wolfed it down.

Jan: "I'll be damned!"

I: "Burrrp."

The Ego, groaning with disgust: "Shithouse mouse!" . . .

Before I got to the top of Glastenbury Mountain, I knew I had made a grievous error. I sank to the ground at the base of the abandoned fire tower and swore at the MRE's that festered in my gut like a wicked gremlin, sending up long, hollow belches mixed with reminders of the recent binge—great going down, but nasty in its present form. The Ego added to my misery, bitching about how I'd ruined his professional image in front of another Marine—unforgivable—not to mention how stupid I'd been to take on all the extra weight (at least fifteen pounds), which he predicted would cause us to end up in worse shape than when we'd come off Jug End. Finally he ran out of steam and ended his tirade, lapsing into stony silence.

When the hot poker quit trying to punch a hole in my abdominal wall, I got to my feet and headed up the Trail, hoping that I could manage to keep ahead of Jan, who had still been fiddling with his gear when I left the shelter. (It wouldn't do to let him see what an ass I'd made of myself!) J.R. jumped on that, saying sarcastically, "Pap once told me about this old goat he had that ate the lead core out of an old busted car battery. Dropped over stone dead. Pap said that it had to be the dumbest animal that God ever put on this green earth to do something so stupid, but if he'd seen you poking down those MRE's, he'd likely have changed his mind." Wisely, I kept quiet.

By the time I hiked the eight miles to Story Spring Shelter, the calories had been "sucked up" and the "gremlin" was now gone, but so was my appetite for more MRE's.

A stranger leaned back in a corner of the shelter, reading a thick book through heavy horn-rimmed glasses. He was tall and gangly, and already tending to baldness even though he couldn't have been more than twenty-five. I soon learned that his name was Jim, and that he had recently graduated from college and was getting a last fling in before starting graduate school studies in archaeology.

His build was similar to Dog's, which immediately gave me an idea. I began to unload MRE's on the floor, saying, "I don't know what got into me, carrying all this stuff. I've *got* to lighten my load, but I don't want to leave it behind either. 'People food' drives the mice crazy and they can go berserk tryin' to get more. Why, I even heard of mice attacking a hiker in his sleep to get at the ramen crumbs in his chest hair!" I sneaked a look at Jim's face to see if any interest had sparked.

Jim looked up from his book and his eyes began to shine. "Say, feel free to help yourself," I urged. Timidly, he took a pack of crackers, cocoa, and a pouch of spaghetti with meat sauce. "Now don't be bashful, take all you want, the whole lot if you're so inclined."

"You sure?" he asked hesitantly, and when I nodded, he loaded the pile into his pack. Gratified, I began cooking a pot of mac-n-cheese.

I had just started eating when Bruno bounced in, friendly to me now that I'd been accepted as part of his pack (though he growled at Jim until I passed him off as one-fourth Doberman). Still suspicious, Bruno sniffed at Jim's crotch a couple of times. Then satisfied that I hadn't lied, he flopped down on the floor to slobber away the time until his master arrived a few minutes later.

After introductions, Jan opened his rucksack and began to unload MRE's. "How're you fixed for food?" he asked Jim.

"Pretty fair, thank you."

"Hmmm. I have some extra MRE's if you can use them."

"I don't think so, thank you."

"Darn, my pack is still too heavy. I've got to get rid of some food, but I don't want to leave anything behind either. 'People food' makes mice very aggressive, you know. They get so crazy they've been known to attack sleeping hikers." Jan glanced at me and I smirked, giving him a covert "thumbs-up."

Jim sat silent for a long moment, deep in thought. Then he chuckled, "Say, are you two fella's in cahoots? You're putting me on, right?" Jan looked confused, and I had a hard time keeping a straight face. Jim peered hard into the undergrowth at the edge of the clearing. "Hey, am I on Candid Camera?" Again, I wisely kept silent.

A thunderstorm swept in shortly after dark, spewing fireworks all over the sky and rattling the shelter rafters until it finally settled into a steady rain. Sometime during the night, Bruno took a liking to my Therm-a-Rest and eased me off onto the floor while I slept. I woke up, aching, and tried to push him back over against Jan, but somehow he seemed to have gained a couple hundred pounds. Finally, I gave up and let him have the mattress.

A noise awakened me about three o'clock and I listened for several minutes. Nothing, except the rain beating against the shelter and Bruno's contented snoring next to my ear. I tried to get back to sleep but eventually gave it up as a lost cause and made the inevitable potty run out into the rain. Dashing back into the shelter, I slipped on the wet floor and fell. Ol' Bruno leaped to his feet, ready to defend his master to the death—mainly by barking his lungs out—which jarred Jan awake, and he sprang up, ready to do battle. In the confusion, I dived for my Therm-a-Rest, barely beating the Doberman by a crow's feather. Still sleep-dazed, Jan shouted, "Friend or foe?" Snickering, I replied, "Friend." (J.R. growled, "How about 'Idiot'?") Satisfied with my response, Jan shoved Bruno off his sleeping pad, grunted, "Semper Fi" and was asleep before Bruno eased Jim onto the floor. (Jim never woke up.)

Three things of note happened at Manchester Center. First, I set two new records: The longest walk from the Trail into a town (5.5 miles), and the largest quantity of ice cream eaten at one sitting (a half gallon). The walk took forever; the ice cream disappeared fast!

Secondly, I caught up with several friends (who seemed to be enjoying a free vacation, courtesy of Zion Episcopal Church members, who, under the watchdog eye of pastor Jim Rains—himself a backpacker—turned their Parrish Hall into a hiker hostel in season). Mule, Tripp, Eco (without Skate), Thatcher's Children, Dog and Shug, Dead Ahead (now separated from Wild Bill—whereabouts unknown—who had retained possession of the infamous bear-clawed food bag), and Gypsy (Pablo was tethered outside), along with some new faces! When I got a chance, I asked Eco about

Skate. With a hangdog look he said, "She left yesterday," and that's all I could get out of him.

Third, Wahoola and Moleskin Meg must have had a wonderful interlude here. They were now only five days ahead!

That evening I went looking for a pay phone. (Back at Cheshire, Judith had sent an itinerary of places and friends she intended to visit on her way to Maine. According to her schedule, she should have arrived at Virginia Beach for an overnight stay with the Klines, close friends from military days.) She was there all right, bubbly now that she was at last on her way. After ten minutes of "mushies," J.R. came away from the phone kicking up his heels. "Let's go get some ice cream," I suggested. "Chocolate," he insisted, and we ended up carrying a half-gallon back to the Parrish Hall, managing to finish it before it started to melt. Even Dog, salivating like he had rabies, was impressed.

I was scraping the bottom of the carton when Jim arrived. Right off, he headed for the corner where the "hiker box" was half-filled with cast-off food and assorted items. I went over to greet him and watched as he began to unload MRE's—considerably more than I had dumped on him. Grinning sheepishly, he said, "A gift from Jan."

The Trail north of Manchester Center tickled my soul—magnificent, undulating panoramas and verdant mountains beneath a clear sky—and the day was special, warmed by a gentle breeze that tempered the hint of autumn. Best of all, I had friends to share it with!

Dog, Shug, Eco and I leapfrogged back and forth, eventually ending up together in mid-afternoon atop Baker Peak, a solid slab of granite that rose upward until it seemed to brush the azure canopy of sky. We perched on its noble peak and idled an hour away, snacking and letting the magnificent view nourish our trail-weary souls until reluctantly we surrendered the crest to the coursing hawks and began the long descent to Big Branch Shelter.

"Hungry thru-hikers or porcupines?" I asked jokingly as we stared at the two jagged holes in the floor—each larger than a beach ball.

"Porcupines, I'd guess," said Shug. "Even Dog hasn't gotten hungry enough to eat floors." He grinned at the inference.

Big Branch Shelter was old, but it did sit beside a rushing mountain stream, which more than offset its stodgy appearance. This was the first sign of porcupine damage we had seen. (*The Philosopher's Guide* warned hikers to beware of porcupines' insatiable desire for salt—found in treated wood and sweaty boots, as careless hikers were apt to discover if they failed to hang their boots out of reach of voracious teeth.) "Dang! I had no idea . . ." I mumbled, marveling at the damage the porkies had inflicted on the plywood, suddenly realizing how easy it would be to become "de-shoed" in this country.

"Piranhas on legs," Eco said. "We'd better lay in some ammo." No dissent, so we stacked a goodly supply of fist-size rocks into each corner for the night's ordeal—if it came to that.

This was definitely Porky-land! Not satisfied with a diet of "floor," porcupines had also eaten away the lower half of the privy door and part of the seat. (The door had been repaired with a jagged piece of tin; but alas, the seat bristled with splinters—let the sitter beware!

As darkness came on, so did our "jitters." We had plenty of "ammunition," so we peppered each noise with a volley of stones—just in case. And then there were the holes in the floor, which looked like two giant evil eyes and stretched our frazzled nerves to the breaking point—but we couldn't do anything about that. Dog and Eco volunteered to sleep next to the holes, and Shug and I had a good supply of stones at the ready—just in case. A scurrying sound in the undergrowth; we launched missiles in a pre-emptive strike (followed by a resounding kick near the holes)—just in case.

Abruptly, Eco spoke up from his "sentry post." "You guys interested in having a tequila party? A man gave me a bottle of tequila on top of Stratton Mountain, and I've been carrying it ever since; never opened it."

"You've been carrying a bottle of tequila for the last twenty-five miles?" Shug asked incredulously.

"Yep, sure have. I was saving it for a special occasion, like now. How about it? A 'porcupine party,' you know, like a hurricane party. That's special."

I frowned at Eco, his face only a pale orb in the deepening gloom. "Naw, I can't drink that stuff plain. It's nasty—worse than gin. You gotta have lemon and salt to do tequila up right."

Eco chuckled, "Now Model-T, remember the rum?" How could I forget his crestfallen look at the foot of John Proud's grave when I asked if he had thought to bury some Coke to go with the rum!

Without waiting for a reply, he delved in his pack and brought out a twenty-ounce screw-top Coke bottle, a lemon, and a small plastic bag—presumably containing salt—and arranged the items neatly on the floor. Chuckling, he said, "Darn, I forgot the cocktail glasses."

I exclaimed, "A person's got to adapt in the wilderness! We'll have to 'wing it' with cups. Now, if I may be permitted, here's the proper procedure," I continued, taking charge and turning on my flashlight. "Pass your cups to Eco . . ." and I walked them through the process. Eco carefully doled out a fourth of the bottle into each container, while Shug cut the lemon into four parts. That done, I went to the next step. "Okay, watch carefully. Wet your finger and stick it in the salt, then lick it off and take a swig of tequila. Then without breathing, suck on the lemon. Wah-la! Margaritas in the wild!"

They easily mastered the lesson, and before long the cups were depleted. Feeling pretty darned good, we chucked rocks into the darkness and spun alcohol-fogged yarns, kicking the shelter floor now and then, until at last the words slowed and the rocks ceased. "Thanks for the porcupine party, Eco. I had a blast," I told him drowsily. Dog and Shug echoed my words, and we crawled into our bags, the jitters temporarily eased by the soothing liquor.

"My pleasure," Eco mumbled, and we gave the night over to the incessant melody of the stream and the salt-seeking porkies.

But I went to sleep with a respectable rock in each hand—just in case.

A huge blackish-brown mastiff with red saddlebags hitched across his shoulders guarded the entrance of the pedestrian suspension bridge that spans Clarendon Gorge, a deep cut etched into the earth over the eons by the ceaseless gnawing of Mill River. (According to *The Guide*, the bridge—a wobbly affair of wire rope and cables holding up a narrow wooden walkway—had been built after a young thru-hiker named Robert Brugmann drowned at the site in 1969.) Even now, although the river was in the clutches of summer's dry spell, its roar filled the air as it chewed at the steep walls of the rocky channel with frothy teeth. "A tough one to ford," I commented to Eco.

We had been hiking together all day—slightly hung-over drinking buddies bonded by last night's tequila blast—since leaving "Porcupine Lodge" (as Shug had renamed the shelter, although no porkies had showed up) well after sunup.

"Yeah, an' we might have to if we can't get past that mutt. He looks mean."

The dog bristled, giving a low growl as we stepped toward the bridge. We halted and Eco asked, "What now, Model-T. Any tricks up your sleeve?"

"Yeah, I'm gonna stare him down, like Davy Crockett used to do with bears'n coons. Us good ol' Southern boys learn how to do that at an early age, along with chewin' an' spittin'." I walked up and patted Bruno on the head and let him slobber all over my hands. "See, there's nothing to it."

"How'd you do that?"

"Easy, if you got the 'gift'," I bragged. Then as Jan stepped from behind a clump of trees, I added, "And know the owner."

The next morning, I quietly packed, mindful of the sleeping forms, and waved silently at Bruno, who wagged his stumpy tail in reply and grinned contentedly from the tattered sleeping pad occupied earlier by Dog, who now huddled on the bare floor next to Shug. Dog groaned in his sleep, twisting like a wounded caterpillar, and I smiled knowingly. Been there, done that! Hoisting my pack and favoring my ankle, I left Clarendon Shelter and headed up the Trail in the rosy softness of a perfect dawn. Today I planned to be a loner, for trying to match steps with Eco—who had dogged Skate's piston-like legs for hundreds of miles—during yesterday's eighteen miles had been a mistake.

The Trail gradually wound upward, now and then dipping down into a small valley but never veering for long from its ultimate goal of Killington Peak. After a quick lunch at Governor Clement Shelter—a narrow, depressing structure with vandalized rock walls and an ash-filled fireplace—the climbing began in earnest. I soon left the unhampered openness of towering hardwood forests and entered a dense red spruce dungeon where low branches crowded the narrow path, clutching belligerently, and slippery, exposed roots tried to dump me on my butt. At last I came to grassy ski runs—now idled and patiently waiting for the first snows to fall—that cut insolently across the Trail. Finally, the narrow path swung to the left and followed the mountain's contour not far below the Peak itself, from whence the faint calls of joy-seekers floated down.

I took a break at Cooper Lodge—an ailing stone shelter nearly as old as J.R.—that sat a few hundred feet down from the summit. The Lodge's claim to fame rested on the exploits of a rambunctious family of huge wood rats that were prone to clatter unwashed pots at midnight and nibble food crumbs from exposed beards and chest hair (at least according to some of the entries in the tattered register).

"How about it, Killer, you wanna stay and watch tonight's show, maybe toss a few stones?" I jested, having no desire to spend the night in a place infested with rats. He immediately replied, "I've got nothing better to do. Let's go get some rocks and we'll have a ball. I got lots of practice knocking off rats in 'Nam." Was he off his rocker? My spine prickled at the very thought of a huge, red-eyed rodent poking in my beard, and I shot a furtive glance at the rafters. He added, "We might even get lucky and bag some fresh meat for breakfast. Rat meat tastes like chicken, you know." I gagged and growled, "I think I'll leave that delicacy to the Marines." When he began snickering, I realized I'd been had and snarled, "Anybody that would eat a garter snake would probably eat a rat, too. Let's get out of here," so we pushed on to Pico Cabin (hopefully absent of rats)!

Pico Cabin perched precariously on a steep slope that dropped dizzily to the valley floor, now dark and filled with haze as the sun set. Crooked block pilings higher than my head propped up the front and somehow kept the structure from tumbling down the mountainside. (The cabin immediately reminded J.R. of a picture he'd seen years earlier of the old shanty back in the "knobs" of central Kentucky where his great-great-grandmother had lived—and died at the ripe age of ninety-four—when he was just a babe in his momma's arms.)

I climbed steep, rickety steps and entered a single room worn out by generations of hunters and hikers. Double-deck bunks had been built against two of the walls, while along the front wall, three windows with several missing panes looked out on verdant mountains that stretched in endless succession toward Canada until they faded into the twilight-haze at earth's end. A grand view!

Jan and Bruno arrived just as the ruby-red fire on the western horizon was about to be extinguished by approaching night. Bruno licked my hand and slobbered all over my boots, and then checked the lower bunks for my Therm-a-Rest. Disappointed (for I'd outfoxed the bed stealer by picking a top bunk!), he growled his displeasure, gave me a malevolent look, and then flopped on the floor while he waited for Jan to make HIS bed.

Tripp stumbled in after dark, after we had gone to bed. Oddly, Bruno hadn't made a sound when he came through the door. I whispered a greeting, and he told me that he had left Cooper Lodge at dusk after mice began doing acrobatics around his pack (obviously the opening act for the main event of the evening, The Wood Rat Competition)!

"You have your choice of berthing," I said. "Beneath me or above Jan and his dog."

"Oh man!" he sighed, his soft Mississippi voice filled with relief. "I was afraid there'd be a full house. And I get a bottom bunk to boot!"

"Yeah, sometimes fortune smiles." I didn't say for whom, though.

In the wee hours, I was awakened by Tripp's grunting and heaving—the same kind of sounds made by a wrestler struggling to break an opponent's headlock—except, I'd never seen a wrestling match where a contestant hissed, "Be gone, I say. Be gone, you hound!"

When I awoke the next morning, Tripp was on the other top bunk, balled into an uncomfortable wad inside his sleeping bag with his head buried. Bruno rolled triumphant eyes up at me from Tripp's sleeping pad, now crookedly rearranged to meet a canine's taste. I reached down and gave him a scratch behind the ear.

Tripp soon awoke and gave Bruno a searing glare, which would have buckled a man to his knees but went unheeded by the Doberman. As he switched the glare to Jan's unmoving back, I smiled wryly and said, "And I thought he only liked Therm-a-Rest's."

Tripp's eyes filled with understanding. "He got you, too?"

"A couple of times."

Jan woke up at the sound of our voices and stretched. "Man! What a great night's sleep!"

Tripp rasped, "That dog sure had one, too." His stutter became more pronounced as he struggled to get the words out—a sign I well knew.

Bruno slobbered on the sleeping pad, marking his territory, and then rolled over and showed us his back. End of discussion for him!

Jan chuckled, "That dog knows a good thing when he sees it. Gosh knows, I've tried to teach him better." He shrugged apologetically. "How about I buy you both breakfast at The Inn (The Inn at Long Trail, at Sherburne Pass) to make amends? I'm supposed to meet my wife there this morning and pick up a few supplies."

At the offer of a free meal, Tripp's sour mood vanished and we began packing (although Bruno would have slept the day away on Tripp's pad if Jan hadn't forcibly removed him).

Halfway down the mountain, Tripp asked, "Do you think they'll have grits on the menu?"

"Are you kidding?" I scoffed. "This is Vermont!"

Jan's wife, Jenny, was waiting in the parking lot when we walked out of the woods and crossed the busy highway. After a wifely hug (given with a wrinkled nose!) and introductions, she told Jan the bad news. "Your unit has been activated for deployment overseas. They want you back right now." To knowing ears, that meant events had escalated in the mid-East and war with Iraq was imminent—and that Jan's hike was over for the time being.

We went in to breakfast, but a pall hung above the table like a thick, oily vapor, squelching our appetites, dampening our conversation, polluting our thoughts. Jan bragged about how he couldn't wait to get over there and kick butt and show what the Marines could do, but J.R. knew the inner turmoil that Jan's bravado covered—for himself as much as his wife—

because for a Marine, such talk was ingrained from a recruit's first reality check with a nail-crunching drill sergeant.

Breakfast finally ended, and Jan split his remaining foodstuff between Tripp and me. Bruno sensed the mood and whined, nuzzling Jan's hand and looking pitiful as he slouched against his master's leg, somehow knowing that he had come to trail's end. With a lump in my throat, I shook Jan's hand and wished him Godspeed, bid adieu to Jenny, and scratched Bruno behind the ears. There was nothing left to be said, so I followed Tripp toward the Trail's opening in the tree line a few yards away.

My last glimpse of Jan and Jenny just before the forest engulfed us: They stood like statues, immobile, gazing toward the continuation of Jan's dream, now demolished by a fanatical despot halfway across the planet. Bruno strained at the unyielding leash, which was anchored by Jan's steely-muscled arm. He barked once, and then gave it up as a futile cause. On impulse, I yelled, "Semper Fi!" Jan came to a rigid position of attention and saluted me, and I returned his salute as the echoing refrain came floating back: "Do or die!" Blurry-eyed, I followed Tripp into the woods, warmed by *my* Marine's "Well done." We never saw Jan again.

A mile beyond Sherburne Pass, the Appalachian Trail abruptly departed from the Long Trail and swept eastward, carrying us toward New Hampshire's border, forty-five miles away. Trail life quickly blossomed into a tranquil jaunt, almost idyllic, with gentle, switchback trails sweetened by sun-drenched days. And the nights! Ink-black skies exploding with countless stars, overwhelming the imagination as the mind tried to accept the vastness of creation—a futile effort! Each evening my soul was magically rejuvenated, and with each dawning I awoke refreshed, eagerly anticipating the coming day's gift of life renewed.

Dog, Shug, Eco, Tripp and I leapfrogged back and forth, sometimes walking in pairs, sometimes alone, almost always coming together in the evenings to share in quiet, comfortable conversation—often swapping tidbits of supper's cuisine should something interesting creep into a menu. Mysteriously, Thatcher's Children had disappeared, swallowed by the immense swell of verdant earth.

Strange blazes, "tiger paw" orange and black patterns—someone said they blazed winter ski and snowmobile trails—began to appear among the familiar white AT blazes like an alien culture. And with the unorthodox markings came long, thin, hose-like contraptions favoring immense earthworms, hundreds of them, wiggling through the trees until they connected to the mother hose, which then disappeared off down the mountainside. "Conduits for maple sap," J.R. replied to my unspoken question. I grunted, "Strange country!" and my opinion was reinforced when we passed a tiny cabin-like shelter and peeked through the door, gawking at the four small bunks and a miniature table. Astonished, The Ego quipped, "Dwarfs, gnomes, or hobbits?" Equally baffled, I muttered, "Strange people!"

We were getting close to New Hampshire! I could almost smell the crispness of the White Mountains hiding just over the horizon. I paused and sniffed the air, jealously realizing that the distant scudding clouds must be brushing their lofty tips even as I watched. Magically, a clarion call seemed to echo above the forests, and its pull as it guided my feet toward the awesome heights would not be denied!

At West Hartford, population about 190—not counting dogs which, from the noise of their barking, probably outnumbered the two-legged residents—I found Tripp binging on veggies at a produce stand. Oblivious, he sat on a bench gnawing on an ear of corn with his nose buried past the nostrils, slurping and sucking at the juicy kernels like a starved hog.

"Doggone, Tripp, if it's that good I'd better get in on the action." He jumped, startled, and pulled his nose out of the cob. He gave a guilty grin when he saw who it was, which caused J.R. to remember the time Pap got busted by Granny when the old fellow sneaked a pint of Jim Beam into a tent meeting revival.

Tripp made a slovenly attempt to wipe the whitish, sticky juice from his smeared face. Then pointing at a small shack a short distance away, he mumbled, "Just see the boy inside," and resumed his swine imitation.

I bought three ears of corn, two tomatoes, and a cantaloupe, which after some thought I decided to split with Tripp for it was huge. While we gorged, Tripp asked, "Do you know what time the post office in Hanover closes?"

I got out *The Philosopher's Guide* and checked. "Five o'clock. And it's ten miles." I looked at my watch—nearly noon. "Why?"

"Got money in my mail drop," he grunted, spitting cantaloupe seeds into the dirt. "I thought about grabbing a good meal in Hanover tonight, but . . ." The "but" was obvious.

"Me, too." After paying for the veggies, I was down to some change. "It'll be a close race to get there in time. Plus, I can't go ten miles without a snack."

Tripp thought about it for a moment and then stood and put his pack on. "I'm going."

"Me, too," and we charged off up the road, faces and hands sticky with assorted juices—momentarily forgotten in the heat of the challenge.

The last four miles were done in an hour—a record for me! We literally ran across the Connecticut River (briefly pausing to chronicle our entry into New Hampshire on film) and sped up a long hill, barely beating the postal employee who was headed toward the doors of the Hanover Post Office to close up shop for another day. Glaring, he relented and let us in after glancing over his shoulder to make sure none of his co-workers were witness to his act of mercy.

Thankfully, the Postal Service functioned normally and our packages (mine contained my tent and winter clothing, plus food and a money order) were waiting. The same employee who had granted us entry now eased the door open and let us out, opening it barely enough for us to squeeze through, like he might be expecting a sneak attack. We thanked him and went looking for the Theta Alpha Fraternity House, which (according to *The Philosopher's Guide*) welcomed thru-hikers—donations accepted.

"You ever stayed in a frat house?" I asked Tripp, and he shook his head. "Me neither," I went on. "If anybody asks us what college we attended, we can now truthfully say we've been to Dartmouth."

We meandered through the campus, past stately buildings reeking of knowledge and students whose eyes reflected ivy-league solidarity. After asking directions a few times, we finally entered an area of sedate brick buildings. But which one was Theta Alpha? We saw no quirky Greek letters or bona-fide words, not even a paltry banner.

A flashy, brunette coed came down the sidewalk and I asked if she knew which house was Theta Alpha. She looked us both over (her eyes asking, "What business is it of yours?"). Then she pointed at the nearest building and said with frost in her tone, "I'm not really *sure*, but you *might* try that one," and hurried off before I could grill her further.

I said wryly, "Jeez, that one was more brittle than the Dead Sea Scrolls." Tripp's grin was as flaccid as month-old celery.

When we reached the door, Tripp said, "Model-T, you do the talking." No doorbell, so I knocked loudly. On the fifth try, the door opened and a short, thin-haired man seeming to ooze wisdom from his pores looked us over carefully, as if he were examining a laboratory specimen before slicing with the dissecting knife. A quizzical expression warped his face, pulling his eyebrows into a high arch that seemed almost comical, rising as they did above owlish eyes magnified into large, brown orbs by thick, horn-rimmed glasses. The Ego nudged me. "And they said Einstein was dead!"

Apparently we passed inspection because the expression faded and he said unenthusiastically, "You may come in," and we followed him into the inner sanctum. He pointed to two sofas pushed against the wall of the large sitting room. "The sofas unfold to make beds. You may sleep there. The showers are upstairs; quiet hours after ten." Without another word he walked from the room, leaving us with mouths agape.

"Weird," Tripp muttered. A pall of musty silence lay over everything—no students, no other hikers, no background sounds denoting people at work or play.

"Yeah," I agreed. "Spooky. Maybe thru-hikers enter through the front door and go out the back on a gurney, and wind up as a cadaver in Gross Anatomy at the Medical School." I said it in jest but neither of us laughed. "Speaking of thru-hikers, I at least expected some of our friends to be here."

Tripp shrugged, baffled, and repeated, "Yeah, really weird." We set up housekeeping at the two sofas and went looking for the showers.

Afterward, cleansed and refreshed, we were working with our food boxes and talking about going off-campus to find a restaurant when "Einstein" walked through the lounge, this time accompanied by two squat, ugly coeds. I rushed over to head them off before they escaped out the door, saying, "We want to thank Theta Alpha for letting us spend the night."

"Einstein" and the girls looked at one another oddly, and he said (rather haughtily I thought), "This is Phi Tau. Theta Alpha is next door." (His expression plainly said, "Are you sure you're smart enough to be hiking the Appalachian Trail?")

"Oh heck," I groaned, looking at Tripp, "we're in the wrong place!"

One of the girls—large buckteeth set her apart as the uglier of the two—said, "It isn't a problem. Gordy decided that you may stay."

Gordy (aka "Einstein") added, "Yes, I thought it interesting to have two adventurers as our guests for the evening." I shuddered at the way he said "interesting" and what it might entail (grad students armed with clipboards and pencils taking notes through the night, recording the garrulous behavior of two "adventurers"?). "Yes, you may stay," he again affirmed as they walked out the door.

When they were out of sight, Tripp said, "These people sure use 'may' a lot."

"Yeah, and did you pick up on how he said 'interesting'? We're probably guinea pigs for some weird behavioral experiment Gordy and his cohorts cooked up while we were in the shower. Heck fire, I'll bet 'crudmamma' isn't even in his vocabulary. Let's go eat!"

EBA—Everything But Anchovies—looked like an off-campus hang-out for hungry intelligentsia, but with EBA's "all-you-can-eat" spaghetti dinner on Monday's (which it just happened to be), it suited us just fine. Tripp chuckled, "At least they didn't say, 'all-you-*may*-eat.'"

Unable to resist the opportunity, I asked for anchovies with my spaghetti—on the side—and received a bored, "We don't serve none of that," from a slouching waitress who showed an uncanny resemblance to a trashed Phyllis Diller, crazy hair included.

"Then how about sardines?" I retorted, at which she rolled her eyes, almost bringing her face to life. I let it slide.

We were each on our second plate of spaghetti when I heard a voice cut through the racket: "Model-Teee! Tripppp!" Skate skipped across the room, jerked me out of my chair and caught me in a bear hug, causing me to dump a big twist of noodles headed for my mouth onto the table. It landed close to Tripp's plate, and he quickly scooped it up and popped it into his mouth.

"Gad, Skate, I can't breathe!" Her arms, crushing like the tentacles of a giant octopus, squeezed harder and then eased up slightly.

"Model-T! I'm so glaaad to seee youuu!" Déjà vu of Waynesboro all over again—people gawking and pointing! As soon as her arms relaxed, I broke free and slunk into my seat, mightily wishing I could crawl under the table and hoping we hadn't disturbed the peace—at least not enough to get ejected or hauled off to jail before getting a crack at one last plate of spaghetti.

Pacified for the moment, Skate grabbed a chair from an adjacent table and sat down, which triggered some primeval stimulus in "Phyllis," where-upon she stalked over to take Skate's order. "Don't ask for anchovies," I advised.

"Are you and Tripp staying at Theta Alpha?" she asked, and added before either of us could reply, "I didn't see you there."

Tripp answered, "Naw, we're next door at—what's it called?"

"Phi Tau," I filled in. "We called ahead for reservations." Tripp nod-ded, a ready partner to my tomfoolery. "Barely got in, at that. That's where the intellectuals hang out, you know." She looked skeptical and I grinned. "Jeez, it's good to see you, Skate." In spite of the gruff reception, I was tickled pink. "Have you seen Eco?"

She frowned and said, "He pulled out this morning." I waited for more, but she changed the subject. "Dog and Shug, Thatcher's Children, and a few others are at Theta Alpha. Do you want to join us? I hear it's party time every night there."

"Not me," Tripp said. "I'm leaving early in the morning."

"Me, too, but why don't you visit us this evening. Maybe Gordy will also find you 'interesting,'" and I told her about our "hosts" while we gorged on spaghetti.

Skate did come for a lengthy visit later. Gordy and company passed through the sitting room while she was there, hardly acknowledging our presence as they walked past (although Gordy did stop at the far door and peer back for a long moment, his owlish eyes unblinking; and his lips seemed to form the word "interesting" before he disappeared down the hallway.) We saw him no more.

For a long while after Skate left, loud sounds of merrymaking came from next door. I tossed restlessly on the couch until at last the revelry weakened into soft gobbledygook that floated senselessly among my thoughts. Suddenly J.R. asked, "I wonder if Gordy finds those people 'interesting'?" I replied, "Even bird poop is 'interesting' to a birder. Go to sleep."

I awoke feeling washed out after a restless night and pulled myself off the sagging sofa. On a whim, I went over to the large writing table and composed a note of thanks to Phi Tau in the form of a ditty: "Last night Phi Tau; Took the place of my maw. I didn't wet the bed; Or dwell upon the dead. But I did dream of a wiggly thing; Do you find that 'interesting'? Thanks, Gordy." J.R. said, "He'll blow a fuse trying to analyze that." I chuckled, "Yep, and if he works his cards right, it should be good for a sizeable government grant." I shook Tripp awake, packed, and went looking for Thayer Hall and it's famed "all-you-can-eat" breakfast. College life had its good points, too!

Over breakfast, Tripp and I listened to the other hikers, red-eyed and listless, as they complained about the noisy revelry at Theta Alpha and their lack of sleep. Again, in my mind, I heard Gordy's authoritative "You may stay" and felt a twinge of guilt about the ditty. Too late now to do anything about it. I grabbed two apples and a banana on the way out of the cafeteria, and headed for the Post Office to mail home my summer gear.

The next three days were a mélange of memory makers: A star-studded evening with Skate and Tripp atop the bare-rock summit of Moose Mountain's South Peak, when the heavens seemed to press so close that the juncture between space and earth withered into a dark, dew-shrouded quilt. Early morning sun glinting against a swooping peregrine falcon while I ate breakfast at Holt's Ledge with my feet dangling in the white sea of early morning mist that sprang from the deep valley below, its cottony billows rising until the surface was just level with the edge of my rocky table. The throat-squeezing thrill when I first glimpsed Mt. Washington—New England's highest—a small hump among the northernmost ripple of mountains, still days away. The sparkling, icy waters of South Jacobs Brook, where I skinny dipped, goose-pimpled, in a shallow pool beneath the footbridge, and then modestly sank into the pool's frothy surface when Melanie and Tim yelled down at me. Then the dash for my shorts as they made their way down the steep, rocky bank to join me, and Tim's hooting laughter when, shivering and too hurried, I stuffed two feet into one leg and tumbled back into the pool. And later that afternoon at Hexacuba Shelter—yes, it had six sides—when we teased Tim for carrying a gallon and a half of water from South Jacobs Brook up the mountain to the shelter (well over a mile), where a clear stream flowed. And our sadness when, that same evening, Melanie broke out in a severe rash and he decided they must leave the Trail in search of treatment. Wonderful days; wonderful friends! Even The Ego couldn't find anything to complain about!

Then came the first of the mighty Whites.

"If we keep climbing, we're going to punch a hole in the moon," J.R. growled. "Likely," I muttered, gasping to pull the rarefied air into my heaving chest and beginning the old ritual, not used since the long ascents of the lower Appalachians and almost forgotten: Silently count, "One, two, three, four, five steps," and then pause briefly to let my innards garner enough strength for another labored count. Adding to my misery, a persistent drizzle eddied down from the dense cloud layer that smothered Moosilauke's summit, not only making the steep path slippery, but also forming a harsh potion with my sweat, stinging and blurring my vision as it seeped into my eyes.

"Damn good thing the Trail's well marked," I wheezed, "because I can't see much through this blur." I ran my sleeve, soaked with the same wicked mixture, across my eyes, trying to wipe away the haze, and then flinched as the water-salt mix ate at my eyes. "Damnation!" I groaned out loud.

Tripp, barely a hand-reach ahead, was grappling with an outstretched limb to use as leverage over a slick boulder that blocked the ever-narrowing steep upgrade. Hearing my epithet, he glanced back to see what was wrong and lost his footing. I heard a squawk as he launched at my spindly legs like a well-aimed bowling ball. He upended me before I had time to dodge and we slid on down a few feet, out of control, and finally came to a sudden stop against a tree—a tangle of arms, packs, and muddy boots.

"Dang, Tripp," I spluttered, squirming to unwind from the human knot, "we have got to quit meeting like this."

Tripp roared, "Begone, I say. Begone!" And then we began to laugh uproariously as we wiggled to a sitting position, not giving a hoot about the mud or the rain, whooping and gasping as we tried to spit gooey, black globs of Moosilauke back onto the Trail where they belonged. I tried to imitate a whip-o-will, but it came out more air than whistle; still, Tripp caught the gist, and we whooped and hollered until we were drained.

J.R. scoffed at the nonsense, but I told him, "At least now I can see. It purged my eyes." He, dryly: "Too bad it didn't do anything for your brain." Sad sack! Play time over, we helped one another up and resumed the struggle.

Eventually the Trail reached what had been a stagecoach road that once led to a summit lodge—now long gone—and the going became easier (but colder, for we had climbed above timberline and were now exposed to an icy wind).

Abruptly, the mist thinned, exposing a weathered signpost just ahead, and Tripp exclaimed, "We're on top!"

A voice from close by filtered through the haze and I recognized it as Skate's. "It's Model-T and Tripp," I yelled. "Where are you?"

"Down here." Skate, Dog, and Shug were huddled together in a rock pit no more than a good spit away, sheltered from the wind and eating lunch. Skate motioned, "Come on in. The more, the merrier."

The "pit" (actually, a slight depression with rocks heaped up into a three-foot wall) looked inviting, but I was chilled and said, "I think I'll wait until I get down below timberline before I eat lunch. Got no view in this mist anyway." Tripp had already squeezed into the pit, so I waved and made my way toward the rock cairn several yards beyond the pit.

Buffeted by the gusty wind, I walked fast, anxious to reach a gentler clime. I followed the cairns through the opaque curtain, which hid the Trail like a tricky swami. After a while, The Ego commented on the condition of the markings. "They sure look different, not really white at all. They're more like a washed-out blue." I stopped and looked closely. "You're right, but this has to be the Trail. The color must be from some quirky effect of the weather." He chuckled, "Or cheap paint."

The Trail led down into the trees—thick, impenetrable stands of scrubby red spruce—and I began looking for an open glade to eat lunch; but the forest pressed in with soggy branches loaded with beaded drizzle that left me soaked. Suddenly J.R. muttered, "Alter, I think we may have a problem. These blazes are definitely blue!" And they were! "Well, chicken nasty!" I squawked, angrily slapping my forehead. "We've been following faded blue paint all the way from the top. Dammit, we've come at least a mile." He said stoically, "Nothing to do but go back to the top and try again." Glumly, I turned and slowly began the long hike back to the summit.

Tripp, now alone in the pit, was just putting away his stove. (He had cooked something hot!) The craving was overpowering, so I crawled into the hole. He chuckled, "I knew you'd be back. I just didn't know how soon."

"How'd you know?"

"The others went that way," and he pointed across the humpy crest in a direction perpendicular to the path I'd taken. "How far did you go?"

I grinned sheepishly. "Only two miles, down and back. Jeez, I'm starved. I'm gonna cook some ramen."

Tripp watched as I unpacked my stove. "Maybe I'll have another meal, too," he said, reaching for his pack.

"Okay, Tripp, do you think they went this way?" We'd finished eating and were ready to get off this infernal mountain—if it would let us!

"Yeah, I watched them go across the top until they dropped out of sight." His words broke up, partly from the bone-biting wind.

I peered at the subject of our discussion. The path followed a broad arm that lead away from the crest—a clearly defined treadway with a few sporadic rock cairns.

"I don't see any blazes. Do you?"

"Maybe it's a relo, not marked yet," he replied.

"Well, it's the only trail I see. Let's go."

We followed the cairns through the misty swirl, walking as briskly as the rocky path and our packs would allow, anxious to be away from this foggy nightmare. Tripp dogged my footsteps, his only communication an occasional grunt when his foot snagged on a rocky stub. After a good half mile we reached a rock ledge, and the trail simply petered out without warning. We peered down into a deep abyss—with him scratching his head in confusion while I squeezed my eyes shut as The Ego started to harangue me about people who couldn't even follow a simple path without getting lost.

"Tripp, we've been had."

"Maybe we're caught in a time warp."

I was dumbfounded. (J.R. muttered that I was never founded, just dumb, and I was starting to think he was right.) "Okay, let's backtrack.

There has to be a way off this mountain, unless Skate and the others sprouted wings, and I don't see any angel feathers lying around." We headed back.

Right before we got back to the crest Tripp spotted a small white blaze—at least it looked white—on a scruffy, knee high shrub beside a barely visible path that entered a small stand of brush. Feeling foolish, I took off my pack and got down on my knees, and examined the paint as if I were a forensic pathologist searching for clues. "Yeah, it's white all right." I stood up, satisfied that *at last* we were about to exit the summit— and was nearly blinded by the sun as the velvety, white veil impetuously swept upward as if it were being raised by a celestial host. Within seconds, Moosilauke shed its grim disguise and revealed its true glory!

I dashed back to the crest, with Tripp hot on my heels, and gazed, spellbound, to the north. Across a gigantic, shrouded gulf, Franconia Ridge sprawled on the edge of the earth's rim like a naked sleeping giant, its profile exalted by Mount Lafayette, which rose majestically into the base of the clouds—a stairway to the beyond!

The veil dropped as quickly as it had risen, and the ethereal scene faded from sight. But it was enough! In one trembling, rushing moment, we had glimpsed the raw might of the Creator's handiwork. Tripp said in a hushed voice, barely audible above the insistent wind, "Doggone! That's a 'humdinger' if I ever saw one," then as the stark truth of reality set in, he exclaimed, "We have to go over that!"

Reverently, I said, "Good God A'mighty," and my voice broke as butterflies filled my belly from the terribly beautiful picture that had just seared my mind. Instinctively, I gave a long, low whistle. "Sumabitch!"

The path down Moosilauke's north side was really a controlled fall! Metal handholds and precarious wood block-steps held in place with metal pins anchored deep into the sheer rock made impassable places passable. The builders had done a skillful job, intricately joining Nature and Man, creating a masterpiece beautiful to behold like the patterned skin of the fer-de-lance; yet, as deadly as its sting to the careless foot. Down and down the Trail went in a dizzying descent, defying the gray granite upswing of the mountain. For a long way, it descended alongside the steep rush of Beaver Brook with its myriad waterfalls, spectacular and puny, and its runaway flow that twisted and cut into the rock. Always down, down, down!

Somehow we made landfall at the bottom without serious injury! I looked at my watch and told Tripp, "It's only four o'clock, but my legs are done for. You want to go on or spend the night here?" I pointed at Beaver Brook Shelter, clearly visible down a short side trail.

"Here's fine with me."

The shelter was rundown and damaged. Planks had been ripped away from the floor in places (used for firewood?); worse, a log had been pried from the left wall like a poorly extracted eye tooth, and its raped end lay charred on the edge of the fire ring. A disgusting odor, akin to a mixture of urine and essence of vomit, rose out of the ocean of trash that littered the area—a loathsome legacy bequeathed by uncaring, slothful dullards too lazy to carry out what they packed in. The place was an obvious favorite of vandals and guttersnipes, probably because it was so easily accessible. (We could clearly hear the sound of traffic just beyond the trees.)

"Dang, Tripp, what a dump! A person could catch the crud just looking at it!"

Tripp was so upset he could hardly get the words out. "Horse whipping is too good for some people." I couldn't have agreed more!

We found a tent spot a few yards off the Trail, out of range of the shelter's lethal epicenter and the resident rats, and far enough away so that the putrid odor wouldn't ruin our evening. After we had put up our tents, Tripp said, "I could sure go for a beer." He was serious. "How's about I hitch into North Woodstock (five miles east) and get a six pack?" and things escalated from there.

I said, "Jeez, I could go for a hamburger. And a big can of baked beans!" The Ego prompted me to add, "And how about some bacon and eggs for breakfast?"

I gave him some money and he left, drooling and whistling, to catch a ride.

An hour later he returned, still whistling and drooling, this time carrying a large paper bag. Grinning, he pulled out a six-pack of beer, an onion, two pounds of raw hamburger, buns, a bottle of ketchup, a large can of baked beans, a pound of bacon, and a dozen eggs. "Tripp, you done good!"

He chuckled, "I almost didn't get the beer. When the gal rang it all up, I was short three bucks, so I told her to keep the beer. Then when I went outside, a man followed me and said, 'Friend, I saw what happened in there. Go back and get your beer,' and he put a twenty dollar bill in my hand and walked away before I could say anything." Darn, talk about "trail magic"! He became so excited that the stammering was like an Edsel with fouled plugs. "I've got almost as much money as I left with!" and he pulled a small wad of bills from his pocket. "Here's your share."

"Mississippi luck," I said, pocketing the bills. "Let's cook!" And we feasted and drank into the twilight.

We awakened to rain squalls sweeping through the valley, causing the rain to drum against the tent with staccato-like brittleness. I stuck my head out of my sleeping bag and shouted, "Hey Tripp, it'll be a chore to cook our bacon and eggs right now. What say we break camp and hike on to Eliza Brook Shelter (seven miles away) and cook there, unless the rain stops and we find a better place? I'll carry the bacon and you bring the eggs." He agreed, and when I walked off into the rain, he was trying to find a safe place inside his pack for the precious cargo.

The rain stopped in a couple of hours, and shortly thereafter the sun peeked through the clouds. By the time I had gotten over Mt. Wolf—surprisingly a gut-wrenching, nasty climb wholly out of proportion to its height—the day had become pleasant and I began searching for a place to cook. About a mile before the shelter the Trail crossed beneath a power line, and not fifty yards away in an open area rested a large boulder with a broad, flat top. Said The Ego, "Now isn't that swell. A considerate glacier dropped off a table thousands of years ago for our exclusive use today," and I headed for it.

"I might as well cook the bacon while we wait for Tripp. Then we'll have the bacon grease ready for the eggs as soon as he gets here."

I cooked the bacon in my pot, six slices at a time, frequently casting an anxious eye back up the Trail for Tripp. Fifteen minutes passed, and then thirty, and finally the bacon was cooked and stacked—sixteen crisp, slightly scorched slices—on a plastic bag, and the grease half-filled my cook pot, awaiting the arrival of the eggs. Almost an hour had passed and there was still no sign of Tripp. He couldn't have gotten past without me seeing him! I forced my eyes away from the Trail and let them caress the bacon. It was driving me crazy!

J.R. said, "We could eat ONE of our slices." A great idea! I divided the stack into two piles and snatched a slice from "our half," dunked it in the grease, and gobbled it down. Heavenly! "I hope nothing has happened to Tripp," I said. "Or the eggs," he added.

Fifteen minutes later, at J.R.'s constant coaxing, all of "our half" was gone, except for one slice, and I was reaching for it when Tripp walked into the clearing. "Darn, Tripp, I'd about given you up for missing in action. Where've you been?"

"Wolf Mountain was a humdinger! It really beat me down and I had to stop and rest several times." It had been hard, but not *that* hard. (I had been worried about Tripp becoming emaciated and had "fussed" at him several times about not eating enough. He simply wasn't getting enough caloric intake to offset energy expended, and I suspected he had reached the point where his body was starting to feed on his muscles. In some circles, they call that "starvation"!)

"Let's cook the eggs," I said, pouring all the grease into Tripp's cook pot and then watching as he broke them, one by one, letting them drop into the fat. I watched impatiently as he stirred the mixture with his spoon and exhorted it to cook faster. And I cussed with him when blackened, stinky globs began to flake off of the scorched, sticking bottom. But for two famished thru-hikers, this was only a minor aggravation, and we ate it all!

We found Left Handed Commie at Eliza Brook Shelter, huddled inside her sleeping bag while she read a romance novel. I hadn't seen her for weeks, and she looked ready for euthanasia (but then most of us did by now)! Worse, she had been there for two days, wallowing in a deep depression that had all but immobilized her, and she wasn't sure if she would—or could—go on. We tried to pump her up but she was so deflated that we gave it up as a lost cause, wished her well, and left before we got zapped by whatever had grabbed hold of her.

Kinsman Mountain! As I climbed, phrases kept pounding in my ears: "a real test of willpower"; "the first 'real' climb on the Trail"; "makes Albert Mountain look like a 'weenie'"; "separates the men from the boys"; "humdinger." It was certainly all of these! I stared at the small two-by-six-inch white splotch halfway up a vertical twenty-foot sheer wall (no metal rungs or block steps here; only a few puny roots and well worn scrubby limbs along the wall's edge for handholds!) and decided to add a phrase of my own: "crud-mamma'n, idiotic place to put a trail"!

After another thousand feet of elevation gain, I finally glimpsed the outline of the summit barely visible in the mist, which had moved in as the day again deteriorated. "We're almost there, Ego," I croaked, gasping out the words like a "holy-roller" glimpsing salvation. Then a hundred yards on, I was brought up short by a shoulder-high rock boulder (no scrubby limbs here)! After several fruitless attempts to scale it, I gave up. "We'll just have to wait for Tripp," I said. (He lagged somewhere behind, though I had no idea how far.) So I settled back against the rock, waiting for "salvation" in the form of a boost.

Within minutes, a barrage of scuffling sounds came from below, and "salvation" clambered into view in the form of a stocky Tennessean. "Sakes alive," Patrick said without preamble. "This mountain is one 'humdinger'!"

"I can think of a better term. Damn, Patrick. Am I glad to see you! Did you pass Tripp?"

"Yep, he's a good ways behind." I'd suspected as much, after his slow progress over Mt. Wolf earlier today.

"Well, I need a boost up." I got into position and he shoved hard, then I pulled him up and we continued on our way, gabbing about the latest news running up the grapevine, but my mind dwelled on Tripp. Who would give him a boost?

I got to Kinsman Pond Shelter at dusk, exhausted to numbness, soaked from the persistent drizzle and chilled to the bone. At first glance, the shelter appeared full. Two large, freestanding tents overflowed the floor, and five frightened women paused in their cooking chores, watching warily as I slipped out of my pack and flopped wearily on the edge of the shelter. I gave them a reassuring grin and said, "Ladies, I have good news and bad news. The good news is, it's not raining inside the shelter so you won't get wet when you take your tents down. The bad news, there's more like me on the way."

They grumbled about "wild animals" and "muggers." I assured them thru-hikers weren't "muggers," although some might fittingly be called "wild animals," which got a laugh and seemed to ease their fears. While they turned to and struck the tents, I found out that the women were from New York City, where there *were* muggers and "wild animals" of the two-legged kind; that this was their first exposure to the backwoods, taken on a dare from one of the gal's "Archie Bunker-type" husband (who claimed that they "were too chicken to go"); and that the women were terrified. They seemed amazed when I told them I had walked all the way from Georgia—not so much from the actual feat, but that I had actually lived to tell about it!

Patrick came in not long afterwards, and then Skate. She hadn't seen any sign of Tripp, which really buffaloed me. I asked her, "How in the world did you get over that big boulder by yourself?"

Her response was, "Which boulder?" which drew a chuckle from Patrick and a whistle of amazement from me.

Tripp straggled in well after dark, beat to a frazzle, too tired to cook. Skate boiled him some ramen and I began to hassle him about not eating enough, but his hangdog look pierced my resolve so I let him be.

The "New Yorkers" huddled in a clump at one end of the shelter, talking quietly, while we exploded, thru-hiker style, hanging dripping clothes from anything that protruded, and covering the floor with bedding, gear, and food (placed within easy reach of stoves readied for cooking). All the while, we chattered like a swarm of magpies as we closed out another day. Sadly, the few inches of floor separating the novice adventurers and us was as wide as the Mississippi River and as barren as the Sahara Desert.

When I crawled into my sleeping bag, the "New Yorkers" were still isolated against the far wall in self-imposed exile—a small band of women too frightened to sleep, victimized by imaginations where muggers and wild animals roamed at will. I slapped at a bold mouse that scurried past my head toward "the other side," probably to meet its buddies for an evening of pillage inside the women's food bags (which had been left neatly stacked on the floor for the mice's convenience). I grinned into the friendly darkness, half-listening for a scream, and told The Ego, "Life can certainly be a 'humdinger.'" He chuckled, "Yeah, when it's not a 'sumabitch.'" Amen!

CHAPTER 11

Only Daring and Insolent Men

S hortly after the turn of the century, when the fledgling gold rush surged past Colorado's Pike's Peak to the gold-covered banks of isolated Cripple Creek, miners accumulated so much of the precious metal that pack mules couldn't keep the flow moving fast enough to line the pockets of speculators back East. A railroad was the obvious solution, so the Short Line Railroad was built over the mountains to Colorado Springs. The railroad meandered alongside winding mountain streams and tenaciously gripped the high rims of precipitous canyon walls in its short journey, and some said the trip was more beautiful than the golden cargo. Teddy Roosevelt, out tromping the Rockies to expend some of the tremendous energy that seemed to propel him in (and out of) trouble, had to see for himself. Near journey's end, as the train slipped over the crest of Cheyenne Mountain and began its descending run along the edge of Cheyenne Canyon into tiny Colorado Springs, Teddy groped to describe the beauty he had witnessed. Failing, he simply said, "Boys, I have no words. This has bankrupted the English language."

I think I knew how he felt! Skate and I stared, dumbstruck, at the mind-boggling grandeur of Franconia Ridge as we climbed out of the spruce forest and reached timberline. Like imperious monarchs, the mighty "Presidentials" dominated the earth! Just ahead, Mt. Lincoln seemed to bow in humble servitude at the feet of lordly Mt. Lafayette, whose crowning summit was starkly etched against the royal blue of the cloudless sky.

Mt. Garfield poised on the horizon behind Lafayette's right shoulder like a quixotic knight paying homage to the ruler.

Standing there with mouth agape, I wondered if Teddy had been privileged to gaze out on *this* magnificent vista and, if so, had his vocabulary once again been bereft of fitting adjectives—as mine now was? Somehow, my low whistle and softly grunted, "Sumabitch!" didn't seem adequate, and suddenly the words of King David's nineteenth Psalm filled my mind and I recited aloud, "The heavens are telling the glory of God; and the firmament proclaims His handiwork." (Had young David, too, searched for words when he stood among the mountains of Israel and gazed in awe at "His handiwork"?)

Skate looked at me funny-like, even surprised. Grinning with embarrassment, I pushed past my impromptu eloquence, quipping, "Which president was Lafayette anyway?" That broke the bindings of enchantment, and we went on across the ridge toward the nearer, smaller mountain named for a great president.

That morning, the sun had pushed through the misty curtain and was well up by the time we left had Kinsman Pond (accompanied by sleepy groans from the "Big Apple" gals). Our late departure was intentional, though, for we had cooked up a scheme to "yogi" some extra food . . .

Lonesome Lake Hut—the first of several large buildings operated by the Appalachian Mountain Club (AMC) as hostels for hikers, reservations required—was slightly less than two miles away. And according to the "Trail grapevine," the "croo," as the hut workers are affectionately known (most are college kids on summer jobs), would sell leftover food to thru-hikers for a pittance—if anything remained after the paying guests had eaten. On the surface it sounded great, but there *was* a rub. Menus were carefully planned to make sure there *wouldn't* be anything left, because supplies had to be packed in on the backs of the croo, and lugging a huge load four or five miles up the mountainside wasn't fun, even for the most dedicated. (Some croos made the chore into a contest, which often turned into amazing feats of strength. To see a 110-pound girl striding up a mountain path with 150 pounds of supplies attached to a huge, wooden packframe larger than her entire torso defied the basic laws of physics!)

We discussed our chances of hitting it lucky as we descended the mountain:

Skate: "Timing is everything. We need to get there after the people finish breakfast but before the 'croo' begins cleanup."

Tripp: "I think it's a waste of time. They probably don't even know how to cook grits."

Patrick: "If they did, nobody would eat'em. That's nasty stuff." Skate agreed, but Tripp and I were shocked at this blatant blasphemy, for Patrick, being from Tennessee, was one of *us!*

I: "I agree with Tripp." (Us good ol' "grit lover's" from the South had to stick together!) "It's like baseball—you strike out lots more times than you score."

We didn't even get out of the batter's box. The breakfast platters had been licked clean, so we went on our way, disappointed, but already anticipating our next time "at bat."

When we got to the highway at Franconia Notch (where hikers get another crack at North Woodstock before beginning the long climb up Liberty Mountain to Franconia Ridge, Tripp began to brag about the friendly folks there "who palm twenty-dollar bills off on you like it's play money." In a flash, Patrick had his thumb out, trying to flag down a ride, and Tripp quickly joined him. (Skate and I didn't see them again for several days!)

After a joyous reunion that evening with Dog and Shug at Garfield Ridge Campsite—first-come-first-served-pay-the-caretaker-four-dollars—we reached Galehead Hut the next morning a little before nine—and got to "first base"! Breakfast was over and the paying guests had departed. We propped our packs on the narrow porch and went inside.

A young, bearded man, the only person in sight, sat at a table in the kitchen peeling potatoes. Voted as spokesman for the group, I said, "Howdy. We're thru-hikers. You happen to have any leftovers for sale?" (Best to let him know we weren't freeloaders.)

"I think there may be some oatmeal left. I'll go check."

Within seconds, he returned with a large pan that contained at least a gallon of congealed oatmeal. "How's this?" Without waiting for a reply, he sat it on a table. (This fella knew thru-hikers!)

"How much?" I asked, flashing a grin at the others.

"How about a dime each?" We paid up, and he said, "You'll need some sweetening," and he fetched a canister of brown sugar. We delved for more money but he cut us off. "It comes with the oatmeal." Then brushing away our chorus of thanks, he went back to the potato bucket.

Dog already had his spoon out, ready to do major damage. "Hold on a minute," I said. "Let's do this fair," and I carefully drew deep lines on the surface, splitting the oatmeal into four quadrants.

We emptied the canister of brown sugar onto the lumpy surface and dug in. Jason (our benefactor's name, as we soon found out) returned before long, carrying a plate of large pancakes, enough for each of us to have two. "I found these squirreled away under a towel. You might as well have them." He chuckled as we quickly emptied the plate. "Sorry, but the syrup's all gone," he apologized, quickly adding, "The pancakes are on the house." Base hit to first!

That afternoon, the four of us soaked and frolicked in the tea-brown waters of Ethan Pond—really a lake—and I bathed for the first time since leaving the hallowed halls of Dartmouth. Said The Ego, "Dang, Alter, we're batting a thousand today!" I grinned, splashing water into Skate's face and laughing as she squealed. "Yeah, and that should bring our average up to about .005."

The Presidentials, though challenging, didn't prove as tough as I had expected. The climbs out of the Notches (what we called "Gaps" down south) were long and often steep; but once back to elevation, the Trail stayed fairly close to the map contours. Small, discreet signs above timberline spoke of the flora's delicate nature and warned hikers to keep to the pathway, for a single footprint could destroy in seconds what Nature had taken half a century to create. But then, why would anyone want to wander away from the Trail? Sharp, abrasive rocks of all sizes and shapes covered every inch of soil; and I, for one, had gotten my fill of rocks in Pennsylvania!

Most of the mountains top out in the 4000 to 5000-foot range, except for Mt. Washington, which crests at 6288 feet—a paltry 355 feet shy of the Smoky Mountains Clingman's Dome, the highest point on the Trail. Yet, the difference between the Presidentials and their southern Appalachian cousins is spectacular. Here, wind and weather join in a quirky union to lower the timberline to about 4000 feet, above which only gnarled shrubs and alpine plants manage to adapt—a sharp contrast to the gentler southern clime, where forests flourish atop North Carolina's Mt. Mitchell (at 6684 feet, the highest point east of the Mississippi River).

Here, walking the high, barren slopes of the Presidential range, I felt as if I were on the rooftop of the world, and I doubted that the windswept, snowcapped peaks of the mighty Himalayas could have stirred my soul any greater!

Came the perilous climb out of Crawford Notch to the summit of Mt. Webster (done alone, for I had left the others sleeping at Ethan Pond Shelter), all the way fighting a feisty wind that raked the mountain with pesky gusts and nearly spun me off a narrow shelf and into a void that ended 2000 feet below. Fighting panic, with fear-aroused blood crashing against my eardrums like a jackhammer, I inched my way to safety. By the time I reached the top, the gusts, denied a human sacrifice, raced away to spread mischief elsewhere, and a gentle breeze moved in. Impulsively, I turned toward the void and bellowed the loudest "oooga" my lungs would support. Back came three echoing "oooga's," the first one strong, filled with a palpable southern essence, the others diminished by the mountains but recognizable. "Now, what made you do that?" The Ego asked, taken by surprise. I replied, "This 'sumabitch' is a 'four-oooga' mountain." He chuckled, "But you only did one." I: "True, but I got three back, and that's a bargain!"

I reached Mizpah Spring Hut about four o'clock. "Let's see if they have anything left from lunch," J.R. suggested. "Not likely," I said, "but it won't hurt to try."

One of the croo—a pretty redhead—sat behind a counter checking guests in for the evening. I identified myself as a thru-hiker and inquired about lunch leftovers. She said, "I'm so sorry, but everything's gone."

I thanked her anyway and turned for the door. "Wait a minute," she called. "Just let me check in the back." She soon returned with two thick slices of bread wrapped in a paper towel. "Last night's fare," she explained with a faint smile. I offered to pay, but she shook her head. "It would just get thrown out." I thanked her and went outside to feast, only to discover that the bread was still warm from the afternoon's baking!

A gray-headed lady (one of the guests who had been near the desk) followed me out the door. I stopped a short distance from the building and inhaled the delicious odor of fresh-baked bread, silently discussing with The Ego if we should eat it now or save it for supper. The woman paused a few feet away, glancing toward me a couple of times like she wished to say something but was unsure. Finally, she made up her mind and came over. "Excuse me, but you're hungry, aren't you?"

"Yes Ma'am, I am." It was the gospel truth!

"Well, I want you to have these," and she pulled a small bunch of wilted carrots from her jacket pocket and quickly thrust them into my hand.

What a magnanimous gesture! The lady had probably carried them for snacks on her day outings. I wanted to tell her I was neither homeless nor a freeloader, but the act had been so unselfish, so spontaneous, that I didn't have the heart. I simply said, "Thank you kindly, Ma'am. This means a lot." And it did! She walked away richer for the act, and I was blessed by her kindness.

We decided to eat the bread now but save the carrots for supper.

At nearby Nauman Tentsite—another four-dollar fee—I went looking for the caretaker, hoping to rent one of the wooden platforms for the night. The only person around was about twenty, with a dark jaw-line beard trimmed in "Menonite" fashion, which melted into an untamed, thick shock of hair the color of swamp muck. He was furiously jabbing a pickaxe at the rocky soil (mostly rock, for so far he had only managed to open up a hole the size of a cantaloupe). He stopped swinging when I approached and mopped his face with the front of his yellow tee shirt, which carried the AMC logo on the left breast.

I chuckled, "If you're digging for oil, you need a different plan."

Glancing wryly at the fruit of his labors, he extended a sweaty hand. "My name's Mark. Gads, this ground is harder than my girlfriend's pancakes!"

"Mine's Model-T. If you're the caretaker, I need a spot for the night."

"You're a thru-hiker, right?" I confessed that I was guilty as charged. "How would you like a *free* site?" There was that "F" word again! But then came the catch. "I'm leaving in the morning to go back to college, and I'm transplanting some red spruce seedlings into a couple of spots that got too much wear. If you'll help me, you can have a free site. It shouldn't take over an hour."

I looked around but only saw three wilted transplanted seedlings, and I wondered how long had it taken him to do that much. An hour of work for a four-dollar fee—and blisters to boot! "Jeez, I don't know. It's been a long day."

He went for the jugular! "I have all this food stashed in my tent— spaghetti, salsa, sardines, and lots of other stuff—that I'm leaving behind. It's all yours if you'll give me a hand." This kid knew how to play hardball!

I didn't hesitate. "Three friends of mine should be here shortly. Will you give them the same deal?"

"Sure will," he said, and I grabbed the pickaxe.

Mark found a mattock, and we were both hard at work, shooting sparks into the air as metal clanged against rock, when Skate, Dog, and Shug arrived about thirty minutes later. I explained the deal to them, and soon we had an organized effort going: Mark and Dog brought seedlings from the forest; Skate and I dug holes; and Shug laid a seedling in each hole, poured in some water, and pushed the soil in, firming it around the roots with a few soft pats of her foot. We finished the job within the hour and went to claim our reward!

We invited Mark to eat supper with us—the least we could do for our new friend. Dog cooked four pounds of spaghetti noodles in his large pot, and Skate and I heated copious amounts of sauce in our smaller ones. We consumed all that, along with several small cans of grated Parmesan, plus a large can of salsa mixed with pineapple chunks, finally wrapping up the meal with some apples that Mark had scrounged from the hut's croo.

Later, as we luxuriated in the soft twilight, Mark spoke quietly, "I believe this is the night Betsy is supposed to visit."

"Who's Betsy?" Shug inquired curiously.

"Several years ago, the body of a young girl named Betsy, who had drowned in a nearby stream, was brought to Mizpah Hut to wait for the authorities to come and take her away. Then late one evening a few weeks later, a young girl wearing a torn dress appeared in the doorway of the Hut, asking if anyone had seen her mother. Without warning, she just turned around and disappeared into thin air. Scared the dickens out of the croo. They said she looked like her skin was beginning to decompose; plus, she could have been the twin sister of the girl who had drowned."

"Why tonight?" I asked, feeling the shivers rake my skin.

"She first appeared on this date, August 28th, and several croo workers claim to have seen her in recent years, wandering the basement corridor and upper hallways, calling for her mommy—always on this date."

We sat quietly in the near dark, musing over Mark's story. Unable to help it, I glanced in the direction of the Hut, not three hundred yards away, from whence the faint clatter of pans and garbled chatter floated through the trees. Was the decayed apparition at this moment adorning herself as a "living" dead, ready to slip across dimensions to continue her restless search, somehow hoping to find her mother among the guests? I asked Mark if she was known to roam outside the Hut, and he replied, "Not to my knowledge." But I suspected she would surely haunt my dreams tonight, if not my tent!

I soon called it a night and retired to my tent, but sleep wouldn't come, for Mark's chilling account had given free rein to my imagination. Wide-eyed, I stared at the ceiling of my fabric tomb, unwilling to surrender my consciousness to dreams, where a decomposing waif in a tattered dress could wander at will until dawn.

The heavens suddenly rumbled, and then without warning a dazzling flare lit the sky, shortly followed by a tremendous clap of thunder—and Betsy was immediately preempted by a fire-breathing thunderstorm! Rain fell unbridled, threatening to sweep the tent off the wooden platform.

The Ego growled, "This is ideal Betsy weather. I wouldn't be surprised if she floated in and joined us for a nice, damp soiree." But I had more to worry about than playing host to a soggy ghost. Water oozed into the tent in a dozen places, creeping through seams and soaking my Therm-a-Rest and sleeping bag.

The deluge finally eased and I resigned myself to a wet night. As soon as J.R. launched his usual tirade, I snarled, "Get over it, Jarhead. A little water is a lot easier to deal with than spooks." The Jarhead retorted,

"Mules are a lot easier to deal with than jackasses, but I don't like either one." (I had to give him a point.)

During the night, Betsy remained with the "dead" dead, as far as anyone knew. At least no one confessed to coming face-to-face with her, nor did any bloodcurdling screams pierce the night. The Jarhead callously jeered, "I guess she got rained out—for a second time."

Dawn came slowly. Heavy, gray clouds hung low, throwing down a thick drizzle that hid the views like an ill-humored skinflint. I called to Skate, whose tent was next to mine, "I'm leaving in fifteen minutes. It could be a nasty day. You want to walk with me?"

A muffled, "Sure," came from her tent. I packed, wolfed down two breakfast bars, and waited another ten minutes in the drizzle for Skate to finish before we set off to climb Mt. Clinton. J.R., in better fettle this morning, quipped, "Now let me see, was Clinton president before or after the Civil War?" Going along with the twaddle, I replied, "Never was. These Yankees just have a strange sense of humor."

When we reached the top of Mt. Clinton we were met by icy, violent gusts—stout enough to rock us on our heels and sting our skin with drizzle. I had read about the fierce storms of the White Mountains, which could hatch at a moment's notice and send an unprepared hiker into a shivering, hypothermic tailspin, often ending in a numbing, cozy demise. I yelled at Skate, "Do you think we should go back?" Let her make the call.

She shouted in my ear, "What do you think?" deftly passing the decision back to me, then continuing, "It's no worse than some of the other stuff *I've* been through." (She made it sound like I hadn't!)

"We have our tents and sleeping bags, if it gets so bad we can't go on." A vicious blast suddenly swept her words away like chaff. ". . . set . . . up . . . the Trail." I struggled to fill in the blanks, couldn't get it, and shrugged. She screamed, ". . . tents." I nodded, although I couldn't fathom how one would go about setting a tent up in this wind, not to mention staking it down on sheer rock.

She stood braced against the wind, watching me, waiting for a decision. What the heck! Lakes of the Clouds Hut was only four miles away, no more than a healthy buzzard's swoop. "Let's go for it! Stay close," I bellowed. If things got extreme, we could always get inside sleeping bags and roll up in the tents like cocoons.

As I began to thread a path through the wind-whipped whiteout like an oversize needle with legs, The Marine growled, "A valorous, though stupid, decision." Already besieged with doubt but now committed, I growled, "It figures. Look who I had for a teacher."

After battling the elements for two hours, we came to a battered yellow sign anchored in a pile of rocks. Its black letters were faded to peaked gray by the thick fog, and the single upright wobbled in the gusty blasts like some weird Dr. Seuss character, which he might have called a "wobzoggle" had he been privy to what we now saw. The sign told us in no uncertain terms: "STOP"! We did, and read on: "THE AREA AHEAD HAS THE WORST WEATHER IN AMERICA. MANY HAVE DIED THERE FROM EXPOSURE EVEN IN THE SUMMER. TURN BACK NOW IF THE WEATHER IS BAD."

"Great place to let us in on the news!" I yelled.

Skate added, "Halfway between nowhere and nothing."

J.R. made the snide comment, "It's comforting to know we've been strolling in the 'temperate zone' for the last couple of hours." Somehow, I didn't feel "comforted"!

Lakes of the Clouds Hut emerged out of the opaque blanket like a ghostly mirage, suddenly so close that I could have hopscotched to the door in a dozen leaps. The wind had lost its strength an hour earlier, finally departing with an apathetic whimper, and now the fog lay sullen and unmoving. I grinned triumphantly at Skate, immensely relieved to reach safe harbor. We left our packs by the door and went inside to throw ourselves on the mercy of the croo leader, hoping we would be allowed to stay and work until the weather improved. I wasn't anxious to tackle Mt. Washington's fickle summit—a mile away and hundreds of feet higher—until things got better.

The hut overflowed with impatient hikers who waited for the weather to run up a flag of truce so that they might yet salvage a snippet of alpine adventure from the day. (Some had already dared the Fates, as evidenced by dripping jackets and soggy daypacks hanging from pegs just inside the door.) I quickly scanned the crowded lounge and dining area, where guests grouped around the tables playing cards or just chatting while they sipped at steaming coffee. "No thru-hikers here," I commented. ("Our kind" would have easily stood out from these "hutters," who strolled through the Whites with only daypacks, their daily trips fettered by the need for accommodations at strategically placed huts.) Some watched our entrance with puzzled eyes, but any curiosity quickly faded.

The croo leader, a hefty girly with long brown hair plaited into a ropey pigtail, vigorously kneaded a large lump of dough, her fingers squeezing the floury mound with undisguised fury as she covertly eyed the loiters who should have been long gone from the Hut so she could prepare for the next arrivals. I asked, "Any chance of us working for our keep until the weather breaks?"

She paused briefly and relaxed her stranglehold. "Gee, Mizpah Hut just radioed and arranged for two thru-hikers to work." She glanced at the crowd. "But this is going to be a busy day, and we're full up for tonight. Even the Dungeon is taken." (The Dungeon, as it is unaffectionately known, is the Hut's storm cellar—a dank six-by-eight-foot hole with an outside entrance. It is usually reserved for thru-hikers' use if they are willing to cough up the hefty rent of six dollars a night. Most pay without complaint though, since the next possible place to *legally* spend the night is The Perch, a campsite nine miles beyond Mt. Washington, if one counts the mile-long side trail that leads below timberline.)

"But I can't send you out in this weather. You'd have to sleep on the dining hall floor."

"Fine with me. Any port in a storm." Skate agreed, and we rolled up our sleeves and went to work—after disposing of a large pile of leftover pancakes and unlimited hot chocolate, all free since we were now on the Hut's "Payroll"!

Skate went to work grating a humongous block of mozzarella cheese, and I trudged out onto the dreary mountainside to clean the grease trap—a job despised by members of the "croo" and at every opportunity tossed off on whichever thru-hikers wandered in looking for room and board. I found a pair of heavy, black rubber gloves, solely dedicated to the mean task, and a grease-encrusted pail, and went at it. The Jarhead sneered, "Well, Ace, remember *The Peter Principle*?" (He had read the book shortly before we took to the Trail.) "My congratulations! You've finally got us 'promoted' to our natural place in the 'pecking order'—lard dipper." I could see some perverse humor in his sarcastic remark: A lieutenant colonel of Marines collecting grease on a drizzly, high mountainside, while the "hutters" dawdled in relative comfort not thirty feet away. "A lesson in morality, Ego. Remember, the Bible teaches that the meek shall inherit the earth." He considered what I said. "Well then, 'lard dipper' should make us a shoo-in for King of Spam, next time around."

I skimmed nearly a bucketful of greasy, nauseating scum from the holding trays, amazed at the quantity of filthy coagulate that could gather in a day—unless the trap hadn't been cleaned for awhile—and poured it into a fifty-gallon drum (which was destined to be remove by helicopter on a calm, clear day). Finally finished, I went back inside and scrubbed away the fat-crusted places where scum had splashed on my arms and clothes despite my best efforts to be careful. (But only time would scrub the lingering odor from my clothing—and my memory!)

The croo leader said, "After you finish eating lunch, I'd appreciate if you would stack chairs and sweep the dining area. Skate can give you a hand."

"Fine," I said, and walked over to where Skate was just finishing up with the mozzarella. "You ready to eat?" I asked. "I'm going to grab my peanut butter and some cookies out of my pack."

Skate said, "Model-T, we eat *free!* Remember? The croo made a big pot of soup and cornbread for the guests—and the worker bees. It's almost ready."

Dang! I liked this place! "Bzzzz," I hummed, establishing my new place in the "pecking order"!

We tackled the dining area once lunch was finished, scooting disgruntled guests into the small lounge as we preempted their seats by stacking chairs on tables. This done, we began sweeping the floor. I happened to glance out a window, only subconsciously seeing the panorama that filled the glassy frame, and returned my attention to the task at hand. "Nice view," J.R. remarked mischievously. His comment boomed like a thunderclap, and I looked out on an awesome, unbelievable sight! The clouds were gone! The Whites had been liberated and Mt. Washington's summit now lay exposed like a bleached skeleton! The infamous Carter range, a rugged stretch of mountains which some said was the warm up act for Maine, loomed on the far side of a yawning gulf with its heights half hidden and still grappling with the retreating clouds.

"Skate! It's clear outside! Look, the clouds have lifted." She rushed over to see for herself and I exclaimed, "Now's our chance to get over Mt. Washington. Let's hike!"

We turned in our brooms, apologizing to the croo chief for our rapid departure, and left our refuge behind (keeping our fingers crossed that we hadn't been taken in by a "sucker hole"). Dog and Shug were coming in the door as we went out and Skate told them, "We're headed over Washington. You guys want to come?"

Shug replied, "No can do. Mizpah radioed and arranged for us to work here tonight." So they were the ones! I felt a twinge of reluctance about our rash departure, for an evening with these two would have been like chocolate pudding—sweet and easy on the soul!

We bid them farewell and began the mile trek upward along the rough path. Before long, we began to encounter small, white, wooden crosses, well over a dozen, sprouting out of the rocks on both sides of the Trail like mutant edelweiss, each marking the site where an unwary hiker had died of exposure. We fought our way up toward the summit where, on a blustery day in 1934, anemometers clutched at a monster wind and then let go as it spun the cups to 231 miles per hour—the greatest speed ever recorded on land. On we went, gasping like fish out of water, toiling equally hard against gravity and the thin air as we pushed toward the roof of New England— where jet streams collide and can send the wind into cataclysmic, triple-digit spurts in the space of minutes. Up here, snow has been known to fall at the drop of a hat during any month of the year, and a balmy day is considered to be anything above fifty degrees. Not a place for the faint of heart!

Lady Luck must have hitched a ride on our packs, for we reached the top without joining the ominous collection of white markers on the rocky slopes. The summit was anything but "balmy"; in fact, the wind stubbornly held at forty-five knots and subverted the day's fifty-two degrees into a mean adversary. In spite of the wind's sweeping effort, a smoky pall and the stench of burning coal lay on the peak like a noxious curse.

We soon identified the culprit. On the rail platform in front of the Summit House a one-car locomotive hissed and clattered and belched black pollution into the crystal air as it slowly crept forward to begin the three and a half mile trip down the twenty-five percent grade to the valley below where summertime reigned. The Ego purred enticingly, "Say, Alter, we could ride it down to the highway and hitch into Gorham. Save at least two days." Insulted that he would even suggest such sacrilege, I stormed, "In that soot-farter? Never!"

We went into the warmth of the Summit House—a squat structure built back into the downslope with its front arcing around half the crest like a huge, partially-eaten doughnut. Right away I spotted the postage stamp-size Post Office. It was open, so I bought a stamped postcard. "Who are you sending that to?" J.R. asked. "You, Jarhead," and I scribbled, "Hope you're having as much fun as I am!" I finished it off with a smiley face, signed it "Model-T," and dropped it in the mail slot; but not before Skate had gotten a peek.

She laughed. "You've been on the Trail far too long." And she was probably right!

On a nearby wall were listed the names of all the people who had died in the White Mountains from various causes since record keeping began in 1876—103 in all, double the population of tiny Gravel Switch, Kentucky, where J.R. was born. The last fatality had happened in 1986, only four years previous. I searched for someone named "Betsy" but drew a blank.

Lugunatic, whom neither Skate nor I had seen since Neels Gap, sat in the basement of the Summit House (a place where hikers could stash packs and rest, though spending the night was strictly forbidden) waiting for thru-hikers to show so she could continue her interviews. She was glad to see us, and vice versa, especially since she had a bag of treats to share. She apologized for her clean, non-hiker image. "I drove up the auto toll road this time. But I did it your way last year, so I'm entitled."

We talked in front of her camera for a few minutes, answering questions about how our hikes were going. I chuckled, "I can sum it up in a few words: *It's like walking on the happy side of misery.*"

Skate laughed. "Actually, I've seen him slip over to the other side a couple of times."

"We all do," Lagunatic said, and a shadow darkened her face as her voice suddenly turned serious. "So many have given up and gone home. I guess one could say they mostly walked on the 'miserable side of happy.'"

She followed us out into the cold when we left and let her camera capture our struggle over the pile of boulders that established the absolute zenith of this mammoth mountain. A cloud swept across the summit, enfolding us in its misty, chilling grasp for a frozen moment, then scudded on its way, leaving the sun to sparkle once again on the slopes.

Came Madison Springs Hut the next morning, after a sunny, blustery hike from The Perch. Perfect timing! AYCE gingerbread left from the previous evening for a quarter, washed down with steaming hot chocolate—twenty-five cents a cup. I tossed two quarters in the kitty, emptied several packages of "Dutch Treat" cocoa mix until the paper cup was nearly filled, and began to add free hot water. Then I slowly worked my way to the bottom, adding water as I went. Skate remarked about my uncouth behavior, but I defended my action, saying, "Well, the sign *does* say a quarter a cup, and that's all I've used."

"And ten packs of mix!"

One of the croo radioed Pinkham Notch Camp at our request, to arrange for us to "work for stay" that evening. Approval came back, and we went on our way.

Pinkham Notch Camp turned out to be a tourist "mecca" just off busy New Hampshire Highway 16, a major thoroughfare for vacationers. When we arrived, two other thru-hikers, Dandelion and John the Baptist, were waiting to see the Director. It turned out that they, too, had been promised jobs—a case of the left hand (Director) idly doodling, while the right hand (able Assistant) scribed the "plan of the day." Skate and I offered to leave but the other two wouldn't hear of it, so we waited.

Soon a stern-faced lady (the scribe?) walked into the large commons room. "Here's the situation," she began. "Policy is, we only have two thru-hikers working at any given time." She noticed our disappointment and hurried on. "But somehow we approved four to work, so four it will be. What we'll do is, two of you can do cleanup after dinner, and two can work at breakfast. Now, who wants to work when?"

Double pleasure for half the work! Skate and I deferred to our new partners, and they chose the evening shift so that they could get an early start the next morning. We thanked the lady and everyone walked away satisfied.

The next morning at 6:30, after a hefty breakfast, Skate and I reported to Dave, the head chef—a reticent potentate who ruled his army of pots and pans like a three-star general. He assigned Skate to help with the chopping and dicing for omelet makings and positioned me at the sink. After ascertaining that I didn't have a social disease and knew the difference between wash water and rinse water, he gave me my orders:

"Don't let the pots 'n pans stack up."

"Yessir!"

"Get'em clean."

"Yessir!"

"Get at it."

"Yessir!"

I went to it, attacking the mountain of egg-crusted, batter-smeared, grease-coated pots and pans like I was engaged in mortal hand-to-hand combat. (A piece of cake, really, for J.R. had often faced worse than this in the cafeteria where he worked during his years at Western Kentucky State College!)

Undaunted, I scrubbed, nonstop, until 9:30, by which time the flow had dwindled to an occasional pot. "General" Dave walked over and growled his approval, "Best damn job I've seen in a long time. Collect your friend and come with me."

"Yessir!" I grabbed Skate, who sat on a stool by the wooden chopping block. "Boss man wants us."

We followed the "General" into a back room, and he opened the door of a giant reefer, motioning us inside. "You two did a great job. Anything in here is yours, sandwiches, rolls, cake, fruit, anything. Take whatever you want. Here, you can have this hunk of roast beef. And this bag of oranges."

"Yessir!"

We walked outside, loaded for bear. I took a few steps and said, "For cryin' out loud, Skate, I can't tote all this." Across the highway, less than two miles distant, Wildcat Mountain's steep ruggedness mocked my predicament; and beyond that, the Carters' tortuous profile stretched across the horizon like a sharp-toothed saw blade.

"Well, just don't expect me to carry it for you, Model-T. It was *your* idea to clean out the reefer. I can hardly carry my own pack."

I looked among the tourists ambling toward the main lodge, hoping that Dog with his hollow legs would magically appear. Disappointed, I took off my pack and sat on a bench beside the sidewalk.

"Now what?"

"I'm gonna eat a pre-lunch; lighten my load."

Skate looked skeptical but joined me. "I doubt we can eat *that* much."

I opened my pack and began pulling out food, determined to prove her wrong.

We had begun in earnest, much to the amusement of several people coming from the parking lot, when Patrick walked over. Hallelujah! A substitute for Dog!

"What are you doing with all that food?" he asked.

"Havin' a picnic," I mumbled through a mouthful of roast beef. "You care to join us? We might be able to spare a bite." Skate almost choked on a hot dog, trying to stifle a giggle. "Where you been?"

He pushed half a roast beef sandwich into his mouth. "Worked at Madison last night. Good place."

"Yeah," I agreed, remembering the gingerbread and hot chocolate. "You gonna climb Wildcat today, or try to stay here and work? I give it two thumbs up."

"Nope. I just checked and the jobs have already been taken. Since it's Friday, I think I'll hitch into Gorham and pick up my mail drop. Post Office closes at noon tomorrow and there's no way I can get over the Carters and into town by then. Got to get it today or be stuck in Gorham till Tuesday, what with Monday being a holiday. How about you all?"

Doggone! I'd forgotten that Monday was Labor Day! Both Skate and I had mail drops in Gorham. I did some quick calculating: Hitch in; get mail drop; leave it and nonessentials at The Barn (a hiker hostel). Then hitch back to Pinkham Notch with bare necessities and be over Wildcat, maybe even beyond Carter Notch (a deep abyss where the last of AMC's huts going north is located) by dark. Ambitious, but possible! I answered, "I'm going with you," and quickly explained my plan to Skate.

She said, "I'm with you, Model-T. Care for some pickles, Patrick?"

J.R.: "Good grief! You must have forgotten to take your 'dumb pill' this morning! This actually makes sense." A warped compliment?

The plan was executed with military precision, a fact that was duly noted by my Marine counterpart. With lightened packs, Skate and I fairly flew up Wildcat Mountain and by sunset had negotiated the plunge into Carter Notch. We had left our tents behind (trusting the dubious forecast of "clear skies the next few days" by the girl who had given us a ride into Gorham in her small sports convertible). However, a worrisome layer of high clouds had begun to dull the sky, and I suggested to Skate that we stop by nearby Carter Notch Hut to see if we could work for stay. She agreed, and we made the short side trip along the shore of a pretty alpine lake, its surface flawlessly mirrored in the soft twilight, and reached the Hut just as the guests finished supper.

The croo scurried frantically about, trying to get the place ready for the night's entertainment. Shug scrubbed dishes and pans at the sink, while Dog rinsed and dried. They saw us and smiled, throwing a harried wave our way. Obviously we were not needed here so we mouthed, "Later," and went back to the Notch to find a level spot to sleep. J.R. preened, "Did you see that? It takes *two* people to do half of what we did this morning!" I replied, "Yeah, but they're not 'killer' Marines."

Skate and I conquered the Carters without getting wet, but it was tough going, possibly the hardest yet. I told Skate, "If this is the warm-up act for Maine, we'd better load up with Vitamin I before we get to the border." The words were trite, but her silence disturbed me and I wondered if we were really ready for the "toughest of the tough."

When we got back to The Barn (an inexpensive, spiffed-up garage loft attached to the Gorham House, a "bed and breakfast"), a hiker "fest" was in full swing. Old friends and new faces! We joined in the partying (mostly eating and resting) until the evening became jaded. One by one, tired bodies left the party's epicenter to claim soiled, worn out mattresses laid haphazardly on the floor, or to pitch sleeping bags in darkened corners. Gradually the revelry ceased, and blessed silence brought sleep.

"To be perfectly honest, Alter, when we left Springer Mountain I never believed we would make it to Maine." The Ego's airy confession took me by surprise; even so, it was no more than dandelion fluff falling on

calloused ears. "And look at us now! We're here! We're 'Two-thousand
Milers'!"

"Not so fast with the six-shooter, Cowboy. We don't reach the 'two-
thousand mile mark' until we're five miles north of the Kennebec River,
and that's another 148 miles. I checked."

"Heck! That's nothing compared to what we've already done!"

I studied the faded brown sign sturdily tacked to a white birch marking
the Maine—New Hampshire State Line and stirred my boot in the hard
Maine soil, grateful that I had reached this milepost, yet dreading what lay
ahead. "That's not what I heard," I muttered. "Eighty-five percent of the
distance finished but fifty percent of the work left."

"Well, we got to Maine, and that's something," he persisted, somewhat
peeved, but I let it slide. The spice of argument had dissipated in the dregs
of my energy after a grueling seventeen-mile day. "Yeah, I can agree with
that. A pity there's no one here to take our picture."

(I had managed to beat the hiker-gaggle out of Gorham this morning.
Reaching through the semidarkness, I had shaken Skate awake and told her
I was headed out. She grumbled, "This is *not* a decent hour for even *fools*
to be out. I'll catch up with you later," and she promptly went back to
sleep. So I packed and went across the street to stand in the chilly gray
dawn with my thumb extended, hoping I wasn't the only fool up so early
on Labor Day. Within a few minutes, a security guard going home after the
midnight shift at a local plant stopped and gave me a lift back to the trailhead, four miles out of town.)

"Yeah," I said, fingering the sign, "It's good to get here." Shifting the
forty-odd pounds on my back I stepped into Maine!

Skate didn't make it to Carlo Col Shelter by dark, and I spent the night
with two men about my age. Dyed-in-the-wool "Mainers," they were
southbound on a forty-mile jaunt from Andover to Gorham. They spoke of
"their" mountains as though these gargantuan upthrusts were actually
alive; and oddly, their talk left me with an eerie feeling. It was as if I had
entered a mystical mountain kingdom where I trod at the pleasure of forces
not understood; as if this were a place where I might be swallowed whole
if I displeased these immortal titans. The thought plagued my sleep.

My unease moderated in the light of day. I hiked out of the Col and
made the formidable climb to the top of Goose Eye Mountain's East Peak,
where I paused to eat a chilly breakfast of instant oatmeal. What beautiful,
brutal country, this contorted Maine landscape, which grimly and unrelent-
ingly stroked the fluttery synapses of my mind! Overwhelmed by the sheer
immensity, I remarked to J.R., "The Presidentials don't begin to compare

with these Herculean Mahoosucs." He replied, "Apples and oranges. You can't compare Queen Victoria of England with Czar Alexander of Russia. Both were royalty, but one ruled with stately majesty; the other with raw power." The analogy fit.

Far below, on the broad saddle that bridges Goose Eye's East and North Peaks, a barely perceptible movement caught my eye. A southbounder? Curious, I gathered up my utensils and went to meet the stranger.

The distance between us shortened and the shape took form, increasing in size until I recognized the legendary man from a long-ago photo. Yet even without the familiar Appalachian Trail Conference badges on his sleeve and hatband, I would have known he was Ed Garvey! He wore full-length blue twill trousers and a like-colored, long-sleeved, heavy cotton shirt. A badly weathered brown (or gray, for it was too weathered to be sure) felt fedora sat, business-like, squarely atop his graying head. Sadly, somewhere between the years of his 1970 thru-hike and where he now stood, the powerhouse exuberance of yesteryear had somehow slipped away with the seasons. Standing before me was the man so deeply in love with the Trail that he had checked the condition of every shelter between Georgia and Maine on that earlier hike, regardless of how far the "blue blazes" took him from the white rectangles, and had carried away bags of trash. This was the man who had written *Appalachian Hiker: Adventure of a Lifetime*, which became the "bible" for aspiring hikers, including myself. I was about to meet my mentor, whose wise words had taught me that I *never* had to wash my cook pot!

Ed greeted me by thrusting a small tape recorder up to my face and saying, "If you would, please state your name and hometown." I did so and told him how much I admired him for fulfilling the promise he had made to himself after he finished his first thru-hike at the age of 55—to do it again in twenty years if his health held. (Judging by his appearance, it was going to be a close thing!)

"I'd really like to get a picture of us together, Ed, but my camera doesn't have a timer. If it's okay, I'll take yours and the next time our paths cross, maybe you'll autograph this one and we can have another taken together."

He posed by leaning on his hiking stick, bent and frayed like its owner, saying "Katahdin" as the shutter snapped. I asked him, "Do you still carry it?"

"Now what might that be?"

"The never-washed pot," and I outlined my clean-up technique, taken from the pages of his book (though slightly modified).

He chuckled, "It's in my pack, still unwashed." His look turned serious. "I had to 'flip-flop' from Harpers Ferry. I just kept getting further behind my schedule and saw I couldn't finish before Katahdin closed down. Now I'm headed back to Harpers Ferry, but I'm so tired." The way he said it made my soul weep. He gazed up toward East Peak, which I had just descended. "Does the Trail go over that?"

"Ed, I'm sorry, but it does."

"I think I'm going to have to quit at Gorham. I'm so tired."

We shook hands and wished one another well, and went our separate ways: Ed to Gorham and home and I farther into this land of brutal beauty. Ed shuffled away, encumbered by his seventy-five years as much as by the large external frame pack that sagged his shoulders and sapped his spirit.

I mused, "Jeez, Ego, there goes one hell of a man! Would you have the audacity to attempt the Trail twenty years hence?" He thought about it. (In twenty years J.R. would be the same age as Ed now was.) "Who knows, Alter? Life is like a vintage red wine—usually robust in the early years, destined to become a mellowed treasure as the years work their magic. Sadly, some wines lose the magic along the way. Who knows?"

I ate a heavy lunch at Full Goose Shelter, garnering strength for the ordeal that waited a scant two miles away. Somehow, the planners had managed to push the Trail through a mile-long ravine crammed with huge gray monoliths. Many were larger than houses, piled haphazardly into a nightmarish obstacle course that would turn the legs of young Marine recruits to jelly. Then they had fiendishly slapped white paint blazes on some rocks, named the maze Mahoosuc Notch, and claimed it for generations of hikers to come. Horror stories abounded about the "Notch"—tales about myriad cave-like crevices beneath terrifying jumbles, where the only way to pass was to push or pull packs through the ridiculously small passages. And the death-defying, terror-gripped jumps across deep chasms, whose bottoms were hidden in the gloom of perennial shadow! We hadn't even gotten there yet, but J.R. had already pegged the Notch as a "sumabitch"!

It was worse than a "sumabitch." I stood at the beginning of the ravine and searched my vocabulary but failed to find a higher superlative. My legs started to turn rubbery as I looked at the intimidating tangle. "J.R., this beast is gonna chew us up and spit us into a crevice." He snapped, "Get a grip. If Ed Garvey made it through here, surely we can. Let's get on with it." Without another word, I took a deep breath and descended into the Notch, feeling like a lunatic ant lost on a monstrous rockslide.

The massive granite slabs tilted at crazy angles, their surfaces icy slick from the beaded pearls that formed from the moisture that crept up from a subterranean stream, which had blazed its own trail long before the hikers came. Clawing and grappling, wiggling and twisting like a cavorting eel, I fought my way through this Chinese puzzle, often on my belly as I pushed or pulled my pack through low-topped, mud-bottomed crevices more fitting for earthworms than human worms. Otherwise, I was sliding down the side of grating boulders toward narrow perches—a temporary way station on a descent into hell, where faded white blazes beckoned from the ravine's bottom—frenziedly digging my fingers into the unyielding hardness of the granite as I futilely tried to slow the skids. On and on it went: A death-defying slide into a capricious, contorted crevice, followed by a wild, snot-dribbling scramble out of the depths and a panicky search for the next white blaze—my key to unlock this rock-bound prison! Over and over . . .

The Notch was an anomaly, unlike any place I had ever been! Ice from the previous winter still lingered ominously in sun-starved pockets. And hidden beneath my feet, I could hear the woeful dirge of the stream as it coursed along the subterranean channel. Its ceaseless rhythm seemed to pulse with my racing heart, rippling the fabric of silence like an immense swell.

Adding to the melancholic pall, deep within the Notch I came across the partially decomposed carcass of a moose, lying like a discarded brown towel in a deep pit. J.R. remarked, "Now there's a mystery. How could a moose possibly get in here?" I thought about it. "Perhaps it floundered in deep snow this past winter, and just melted its way down to where it now lies."

Thus I made my way through the rock-bound hell. Miraculously, I emerged two hours later, spent and withered, but surprised and grateful that I had escaped with nothing worse than a muddy belly, a few scrapes, and a bruised "ego"—no pun intended!

Then came Mahoosuc Arm! It thrust upward from the Notch like an enormous phallus, insolent and ready to despoil at the first misstep. How far it rose I couldn't tell, for its head was hidden in low, leaden clouds that had quickly moved in from the west. I took a lengthy break, waiting for life to return to my muscles, and then started to climb.

I had been at it well over an hour, all the while keeping a wary eye on the sky, when without warning the angry gray overcast began to spill down the steep slope like a giant waterfall. I soon became engulfed in an opaque blanket of drizzle, which quickly became a pelting rain. Slipping on a rock, I went to my knees and cursed, "Dammit sumabitch! Things went to hell in a hand basket when humans lost their monkey genes." Pushing to my feet,

I clambered up the edge of a twenty-foot wall imitating the monkey I wished to be, grabbing dwarfed, twisted branches and roots of anything that offered support. "I need a monkey tail," I grunted, filled with envy for the zingers we'd watched back at the Trailside Zoo. J.R. said, "Yeah, but we got cheated when 'homo' went 'erectus.' In hindsight, we probably got a raw deal."

I didn't have time to pursue the topic further because pellets began to pepper my face. Sleet! And the temperature was plummeting! I struggled a few more yards and without warning an icy blast nearly bowled me against the ground. The tip of the "phallus"!

Icy needle-laced rain shut out the world and brought numbing cold. J.R. yelled, "It's a nor'easter! We've got to get off of here!"

I couldn't have agreed more! I could already feel hypothermic shivers begin their deadly rippling, for my shorts and tee shirt, so recently allies against heat exhaustion, had now become an Achilles' heel in a dangerous game. Our only hope was to reach Speck Pond Shelter, a scant mile away, and get into the sleeping bag. In a few short minutes, my fingers had become numb and I shook as if possessed by demons.

The race for survival to Speck Pond Shelter is a blank page in my memory, for time ceased to exist. Reality returned as I shed my wet clothes, tossing them aside like soiled rags, and struggled into dry long johns and socks. When my fingers refused to grasp the zipper on the sleeping bag, I manipulated it with pursed lips until the opening was large enough to slide into. Then squirming inside, I found I couldn't get the zipper back up. So I stuck my fingers beneath tepid armpits, drew my body into a tight fetal position and lay there shivering uncontrollably, willing life to return to numb fingers and toes.

Suddenly The Ego began to laugh. "What was it you told Lagunatic? About walking on the happy side of misery? I think you lost your way today!" I answered wryly, "Just be thankful that the lips are the last to go."

I finally thawed enough to get my stove working and cook some ramen. The hot liquid restored my body and mind, and I lay in the sleeping bag, dry, warm, and snugly content, listening to the blustering wind beat the rain against the shelter and dash choppy waves against the rocky edge of the glaciated lake—the highest in Maine—only a few feet from the rear of the shelter.

A noise startled me, and a stranger stepped into the shelter. "Bad afternoon. I'm Jonathan, the Caretaker. You by yourself?"

"It sure is and I am."

"I need to collect the fee. Four dollars."

"I'm glad to pay it tonight." And I was! We talked for a few minutes, and he told me before he hurried back to his tent that I had the entire campsite to myself!

"Well, J.R., I don't know what's happened to Skate and the others, but I hope they didn't get caught in Mahoosuc Notch or on the Arm in this weather." The image of the rotted moose carcass flitted across my mind, but I pushed it away, adding, "We got lucky today. How about some mac-n-cheese for supper?" He replied, "Sounds super. How about a couple of English muffins to go with it?" I chuckled, "You got it!" I was back on the "happy side"!

After Mahoosuc Arm, time became subservient to the spacing of Maine's earthly behemoths, and I found my days ending in early and mid afternoon rather than chancing another six or seven miles of rugged country to the next shelter—and the opportunity to spend the night on a steep hillside tied to a tree. This was "all or nothing" country, where the soul could soar to unheralded heights on the wings of unparalleled beauty while the mind dealt with verbal bankruptcy. Conversely, a capricious decision or frivolous attitude could jettison a person from the Trail in an eye blink. I still walked alone, with only my taciturn Ego to share the beauty while my feet consumed the arduous miles, mountain after mountain.

A journal synopsis:

Wednesday, 5 September: Climbed Baldpate Mountain's two massive above-timberline domes of granite, slick as rime ice, in a cloudy drizzle. Atop West Peak, the "Hand of God" swept the Heavens clean in one bold stroke, and my cup overflowed at the beauty that met my eyes. Later, as I descended East Peak, the "Hand" gently brushed the mountaintop and all disappeared into a soft, white void.

Thursday, 6 September: A day of people, the first hikers since leaving Ed Garvey to his uncertain fate at Goose Eye—met a Freshman Orientation Group (about twenty boys and girls, wet and bedraggled but in good spirits) from Harvard; then a few miles on, came upon another group, these from Gould University. Gypsy (without Pablo) at Hall Mountain Leanto when I arrived; almost in tears as he told me that Pablo had chewed through his rope at The Barn and disappeared. I told him that Pablo had probably "adopted" a southbounder with lots of food, and was now headed back to the warmer climate of Tennessee. Also a day for a miracle: Earlier, while scrambling up steep Wyman Mountain, I grabbed for a handhold on a narrow ledge and my hand closed on a perfectly good large, yellow onion. Trail magic is found in the strangest places!

Saturday, 8 September: Picked up mail drop at Rangeley, got money order cashed, and went to Doc Grant's Restaurant—according to a sign it was "half way between the North Pole and the Equator"; 3,107.5 miles each way—and feasted (in moderation!) on the best pancakes on the Trail, even better than Weasies at Waynesboro, Virginia! J.R. disagreed. "These are just like Weasies. We're a lot hungrier now and that's what makes them tastier." Remembering the food orgy on THAT occasion and its unpleasant aftermath, I replied, "I don't think so. It's mainly that we're a little older and a lot wiser." Spent a peaceful night at Sabbath Day Pond Leanto with Gypsy. Loons haunted the twilight with their mournful, lonely cry, and I was soon lulled to sleep.

Sunday, 9 September: Easiest day in a long time. Reached Piazza Rock Leanto (decrepit with crippled foundation and listing floor) shortly after 1:30 PM, but next ten miles supposedly a bug-a-boo, so decided to call it a day. Thought about climbing up a blue-blazed path to see Piazza Rock, but The Ego easily convinced me it would be a wasted trip. ("You seen one, you've seen 'em all, and we saw enough big rocks in Mahoosuc Notch to last for the rest of our days, plus there's more to come.") No argument! Later Curly and Larry, whom I had met briefly in Gorham, arrived. Curly, tall and slender, his pate a miniature of Baldpate Mountain's East Peak, was a retired Marine lieutenant colonel aviator—a fact J.R. had learned belatedly that evening at The Barn. His wife, Larry, a short, vivacious lady who had hiked with him from Springer, had developed foot problems and was off the Trail but had walked in from Maine Highway 4, one and a half miles south, to spend the night. In the meantime, she planned to help Curly "slack pack" at every opportunity until her foot healed. J.R. was absolutely "bananas" as the B.S. flowed between the two Marines. The hour got late and I finally managed to tuck the old "has been" into my sleeping bag. An exciting note in the register: Wahoola spent last night here!

Monday, 10 September: A bitter fight across Saddleback Mountain—above timberline, lashed by storm with all the trimmings: gale force wind, whipping sleet-packed rain, and the inevitable gray-white curtain—the works! Could hardly follow the rock cairns. On a whim, picked up a good-sized rock and added it to

one of the cairns—my legacy to Saddleback. Finally made it to
Poplar Ridge Leanto (first shelter going north with a "baseball bat"
floor—red spruce saplings roughly the size of a baseball bat, split
lengthwise, and the halves nailed, round side up, as planking for
the floor—not conducive to a good night's sleep though the
Therm-a-Rest helped). Had just gotten into dry clothes and was
thawing out in the sleeping bag when Curly arrived, wet and flirt-
ing with hypothermia. Within the hour, another thru-hiker, Pennsylvania Creeper, a gray-headed, spectacled, retired physics
professor from Penn State came in, same condition. Right before
dusk, a thru-hiker named Serendipity, stocky and macho—no tent,
only a piece of clear plastic to roll up in—arrived. Curly had met
Serendipity back down the Trail and told J.R., "This makes three
of us." J.R. quipped, "Three dummies to be out here?" but Curly
shook his head. "No, three jarhead officers meeting happenstance
in the backwoods of Maine. Two light colonels and a grunt
(infantry) major." J.R., flabbergasted, went ballistic, and we used
up half a roll of film recording the historic event. The crowning
moment of the evening: In the wee hours Curly, sleeping next to
me, had some weird amorous fantasy; murmured "Larry" a couple
of times, and before I could escape had me in a "back seat"
squeeze. I fought my way out of his embrace and whacked him a
good one on his face, which awakened the errant Romeo. I snickered in his ear with gushing falsetto, "Not tonight, Dearie, I've got
a headache." Curly lit up the shelter with his red-hot blush, mumbled, "You sure felt like Larry," while J.R., disgusted, growled, "In
the name of Chesty Puller, what in the world is my Marine Corps
coming to?"

On Wednesday, impeded by my ankle, which had decided to act up, I
pushed through rainsqualls, slipping and sliding up and down Crocker
Mountain's twin peaks, and at last came to Maine Highway 27. (A lonely
stretch of road in the best of times; in today's steady rain "Godforsaken"
seemed appropriate!). After ten minutes, two hunters in a pickup (the first
vehicle to come along) stopped, and I rode the five miles into Stratton
hunched in the open back, along with three drenched, smelly hounds that
tried to lick my legs. I gave up and let them have a go at whatever it was
that gave them the small pleasure. J.R. was uppity about it. "This is about
as low as you can go, entertaining a bunch of mutts with your legs. We'll
probably be charged with indecent behavior contributing to the delin-

quency of hunting dogs." I scrunched my shoulders against the sheeting rain, grinding out the words through chattering teeth, "A bit of hedonistic delight for our flop-eared brothers can't hurt. Lord knows, I could sure use some pleasure in *my* day."

The hunters dropped me off in front of The Widow's Walk, a fabulous, white-clapboard, three-story Victorian house, complete with a large dome-topped turret and a prominent widow's walk that let one look down at the treetops—more like something from a Walt Disney set than a small town bed and breakfast. The hounds whined as I hauled my slobbery legs beyond the reach of their long tongues, and their eyes begged me to ride on for a little longer! J.R. asked, "Are you sure *The Philosopher's Guide* stated that hikers are welcome here?" I assured him that it did, and at a reduced rate! Then acting like I knew exactly what I was doing, I gave the hunters a confident smile, blew a kiss at my adoring canine friends, and dripping water, walked toward the front door.

Indeed I was welcome! Curly and Larry were there, already cleaned up, and ready to "do the town," which translated into "go eat." I showered, made arrangements to meet them later for a good meal, and headed to the nearest place with a washer and dryer—the Stratton Plaza Hotel, a favorite haunt of the younger thru-hiker crowd.

I walked up the steps, nodding at a thin hiker with a long, red scraggily beard, and opened the door. He spoke. "Model-T?"

I paused and stared, and then recognition dawned. "Wahoola? Is that you? Wahoola!" Skate could have taken lessons from our bear hug!

That night, we feasted at Cathy's Restaurant, a noisy, bustling enterprise where food was ample, even for thru-hiker appetites, and the service excellent. Between mouthfuls, I counted twenty-two thru-hikers, some whom I hadn't seen since Hot Springs, North Carolina, including the Mellow Woodsmen. This was more like a mini-Trail Days than a chance gathering in a small Maine village.

Skate came in late, saw me, and did her usual squeally, squeezy hello, much to the amusement of the entire clientele, and then berated me for keeping half a day ahead of her all the way from Gorham. Moleskin Meg, still Wahoola's shadow, overpowered the thru-hiker din, and I was somehow comforted to know that some things didn't change! "J.R., we're gonna make a quick get-away in the morning," I vowed. "Smart move. Ask Skate if she's going to eat the rest of her French fries."

"Who was the first '2000-miler' on the AT?" Journalist asked.

"Easy," answered Dog. "Earl Shaffer."

"Wrong. Shug?"

"That's what I thought."

Skate chimed in. "Myron Avery, 1936. Earl was the first 'thru-hiker,' 1948."

I knew that tidbit, having read much about the man who was the driving force behind the Trail's layout and construction; plus the plaque at Avery Peak on top of Bigelow Mountain, just north of Stratton, had refreshed my memory.

The correct answer made it Skate's turn: "How many calories in a regular Snickers bar?" She gave me an impish smile.

I had that one nailed and beat Wahoola to the draw by a split second. "280!"

We were crowded into tiny Pierce Pond Leanto on a rainy Saturday afternoon—ten of us—idling away the time by playing "Trail Trivia," waiting for Journeyman to get back. He had pushed on from Carey Pond Leanto yesterday afternoon, timing it so he would reach the Kennebec River by 8 AM this morning and be able to ford across before the water began to rise. He had been talking about fording for several days now, trying to screw his courage up for the crossing. (Water, which spilled across the turbines of an upstream hydroelectric dam, was "theoretically" timed so that it wouldn't reach the fording place until *after* 8:30. In 1985, victimized by the fickle nature of the river, a hiker drowned while trying to cross; since then, the State of Maine and the ATC have subsidized the operation of a canoe to get hikers safely across. Yet, some of the "purists" still insisted that fording was the only right way to get to the other side—even though ATC had a white blaze painted on the bottom of the canoe to keep the "purists" happy.) Journeyman planned to meet us here at Pierce Pond Shelter, crossing back over by canoe.

Trail Trivia gave way to Charades, a difficult undertaking in the crowded space, but we were having a ball! Our five-hiker team—Skate, Thatcher's Children, Pennsylvania Creeper, and myself—was down "one" from the opposition, which consisted of Journalist, Wahoola, Meg, Dog, and Shug. It was our turn. We huddled and decided on "A Funny Thing Happened on the Way to the Forum"—a cinch to even the score—when Journeyman arrived loaded for bear and grinning like a coon dog with a hog bone. In addition to his pack, his arms were locked around a doubled, large paper sack. He said, "I hope you all are hungry, because it's picnic time!" and he began to unload items that made our eyes bulge: Two six-packs of beer, two half-gallons of ice cream (still frozen!), two pounds of hamburger meat, hot dogs and buns, *and* mustard! We tossed Charades out into the rain!

Journalist asked, "How was the canoe ride?"

He answered nonchalantly, as if it were an everyday occurrence, "I decided to ford back across. The water wasn't all that high." Two times in one day! And he had lugged that large sack of groceries for four miles!

J.R. nudged me. "Ask him if he's ever thought about a career in the Marine Corps," but I "sshed" him and reached for one of the special beers—possibly the only ones ever to have forded the Kennebec!

Later, we "elected" Tim (of Thatcher's Children) to go to Harrison Camps—a half-mile from the shelter down a side trail—and make reservations for the "Hiker's Special" breakfast: Bacon, eggs, juice, coffee, toast, and *twelve* pancakes, all for $4.50, tax included.

The afternoon wore on and we consumed all that Journeyman had brought, and some. We sang parts of many songs, snatches of lyrics dimly remembered, but it didn't matter for our mismatched, off-key voices were joined in something far more harmonizing than the mangled golden oldies that slaughtered the twilight—the entwining of souls!

A brisk, frigid wind sent the clouds scudding and soon stars appeared, slowly filling the inky void. Emotionally satiated, we brought an end to a remarkable day.

The next morning dawned sunny, and as a group we made our way down to Harrison Camps, singing and frolicking like school kids dismissed early from school. Owners Fran and Tim Harrison greeted us as if we were visiting royalty instead of muddy thru-hikers. Moved by their friendly welcome (and in deference to the discreet sign by the door), we removed our boots and shuffled across the polished linoleum carpet toward tables set with linen and good china. We were immediately beset by culture shock, and our normally zestful banter and uninhibited laughter quickly dissolved into inaudible, self-conscious whispers. We fiddled awkwardly with the silverware, trying to remember not to place elbows on the table, timidly grinning at one another while we sniffed the bacon-egg-pancake-scented air and kept one eye on the kitchen door. Even Moleskin Meg was subdued!

The food was delicious! I surreptitiously counted my stack and got thirteen! Wahoola, sitting next to me, whispered, "They gave me thirteen pancakes!"

"Me, too," I said. "You gonna give one back?"

"You crazy? It's not my fault the cook can't count!"

Like miserly ragamuffins, most of us ate each pancake separately, savoring each bite, letting the flavor linger and caress the senses before ten-

derly forking the next piece into a generous puddle of syrup for its moment
of glory, unwilling to squander the experience in one carefree, gluttonous
fling.

    And then it was over, platters licked clean, second cup of coffee nur-
tured while the memory etched itself into an indelible scratch on the brain.
Like a giant nucleus of symbiotic parts, we arose as one, thanked our hosts,
reshod our feet, and headed toward the fickle Kennebec.

Things were getting bad! Ever since crossing the Kennebec River in the
battered aluminum canoe two days ago I had been craving fats. It didn't
matter what form—margarine, peanut butter, skunk lard, fish guts—anything greasy would do! The lust for lipids was so intense that I had started
drinking Squeeze Parkay right from the plastic container, which made me
feel like a butterholic. Stuff a hunk of bread in the mouth and chase it with
a swig of the yellow liquid. Goood! J.R. chided me: "It's pretty bad when
you start guzzling it like a wino." I swallowed hard to empty my mouth in
preparation for another go and said, "Yeah, it's a nasty habit all right." I
crammed in more bread and hoisted the yellow barleycorn to my lips.
"Cheers!"

    The sad fact: My fat reserve was depleted and I was now running on
empty. My body would begin to consume my muscle if I didn't keep packing in enough calories to replace each day's expenditure. And I couldn't go
very far without muscle!

    Which brought the image of Tripp's scrawny body to mind. I hadn't
seen him since Gorham. How was this brutally beautiful land treating him?
Shuddering, I opened a jar of peanut butter (large size) and ate a couple of
heaping spoonfuls, washing it down with the Parkay liqueur.

    I peered at the northern horizon. "Supposedly, one can see Katahdin
from the top of Moxie Bald on a clear day, but all I see are a bunch of little
humps." Still, I felt a tingle of excitement just knowing that one of those
small knobs might be the mighty peak, the one the Abenaki Indians had
called "Kette-Adene—"greatest mountain" (which the white intruders bas-
tardized to "Ktaadin"). According to the *AT Data Book,* it was still nearly
130 "trail miles" away, although only half that distance as the crow flies.

    My exhilaration evaporated, besmirched by thoughts of stringy, mal-
nourished muscles. "Gotta lot of eatin' to do," I hummed to a meaningless
tune. Well intentioned, I dug my spoon deeper into the peanut butter, then
changed my mind and downed a shot of Parkay—neat—and then followed

it with the gooey brown paste. "Amazing," I chuckled, immensely pleased at the results. "What's amazing?" queried J.R. "Lubrication. Everything works best if it's well oiled, even peanut butter. It slips right down the gullet." He grunted, "Yep, it's amazing what a little grease will do. Just look at those pistons go."

A couple of hundred yards away, Skate was making her way across the broad, rock-cluttered summit toward me, her legs churning up and down like a well-oiled, gravity-defying machine. He said glumly, "That gal's eating up the Trail. She sure isn't in any danger of starvation." His bittersweet comment reeked of jealousy and admiration. I replied, "Yeah, but it's a stacked deck. God gave women a head start when it comes to fat."

Skate dropped down beside me, huffing from the pull against gravity. "Nice view. Which one is Katahdin?"

"Can't tell. Heck, I'm not even sure I'm looking in the right direction. You gonna eat?"

"Just some trail mix I think, and enjoy the view. I'm not all that hungry."

Not hungry! That beast constantly nipped at my innards like a live piranha. I nudged The Ego. "See what I mean. We've got to even the score." Morosely, I raised the container toward Skate. "Here's to fat," and I downed a jigger's worth.

"Model-T, what ARE you doing?"

"Making amends for a Celestial mistake."

"Did you just drink Squeeze Parkay right out of the bottle?"

"Yep."

"Might I ask why?"

"It's a long story. Goes all the way back to Adam's rib."

She blinked quizzically, almost concerned, and then stated her opinion. "Nasty."

"Yeah," I admitted, lubricating my throat with another swig of Parkay before digging my spoon into the peanut butter. "Nasty."

Skate winced as the peanut butter, its track now nicely greased, easily slid down my gullet. I finished off with a piece of bread, swallowed some water, and packed up. "See you down at the shelter," and I ambled toward the first ledge of several that would take me off the heights, wondering if I had consumed enough fuel to get me to the bottom.

Sad news arrived that afternoon at Moxie Bald Pond Shelter, carried by Slim Chance (a thru-hiker whom I had not met before) who was fast-stepping it into Munson. "Did you hear about the hikers who were murdered near Duncannon (Pennsylvania) at the Thelma Marks Shelter?" We hadn't. "They were a couple of southbounders, Clevis and Nalgene. Word has it that he was shot and she was stabbed."

I couldn't believe what I was hearing! Not the two wonderful kids I had shared the macaroni salad with a month ago at the Kaye Wood Shelter in Massachusetts! A chill seeped into my soul as a macabre scenario ran its course in my mind, turning the food to sawdust and the evening to ashes. Too sorrowful for company, as soon as I finished eating I told my friends goodnight, grabbed up my gear, and pitched my tent down by the water's edge. As I drifted into troubled slumber, the words "Wake up little mouse, wake up" echoed in my head and haunted my restless night.

Shaw's Boarding House at Monson, a neat, two-story building with white clapboard siding and windows trimmed in blue, was a hiker's mecca. Twenty-five dollars got a body a bed, shower, and two all-you-can-eat meals! Shaw's was the favorite jump-off point for the final stint to Katahdin, a rugged, isolated area descriptively known as "The Hundred Mile Wilderness," because that's exactly what it was. (Owners Keith and Pat Shaw had begun their business as a home for the mentally retarded, but one day in 1977 they let a thru-hiker spend the night. Word of the "refuge" quickly spread along the Trail grapevine, bringing hikers in droves to the Shaw's door, and by the next year hikers had replaced the patients. According to Keith, Shaw's had hosted about 12,000 hikers since.)

As Skate and I paid our money, I declared officially, "Make that 12,002!"

Then came a fun day. Showers, mail drop, gossiping with friends— and watching Moleskin Meg deal with a "dilemma"!

By noon all of the "trail trivia" crew from Pierce Pond had filtered in. Moleskin Meg made the three-block trip to the post office several times, returning each time laden with packages until her stash of seventeen boxes rose like a small mountain on Shaw's lawn. Then she went to work like J.R.'s Granny plucking a hen for Sunday dinner, ripping open packages and dumping their contents on the ground, then squealing with delight as each treasure was revealed. Her penetrating shrieks splintered the stillness of the small town and caused consternation among some of its citizens at the Appalachian Trail Station restaurant (beside the post office), where I sat sipping a cup of coffee and enjoying the easy role of onlooker.

Said one gray-bearded old-timer decked out in green and red flannel, his Maine speech slow and syrupy like cold sorghum molasses, "When I was a young'un, I heard a sow makin' those sounds while she was bein' drug away by a catamount. Never heard anything like it since. What'der ya reckon it might be? Ain't been no catamounts seen in Maine for years."

His sidekick, grizzled but clean-shaven, replied, "Maybe it's a loon that done got caught in Murray's fish trap over at the pond. It's a strange'un alright." I kept silent, unwilling to spoil the excitement that had spiced up their day.

When I returned to Shaw's, Moleskin Meg's small mountain had eroded into a scattered pile of plastic bags, tin cans, and cartons; and the squeals had been replaced by frantic pleading: "Ohmigosh! What am I going to do? Here, Model-T, help me get rid of this! Pleeease!"

I surveyed the pile. "You got anything greasy? Or Snickers bars?"

"Wahoola grabbed off all the Snickers. Got a canned ham, though, and a box of crackers. And cookies. Lots and lots of cookies!"

"Yeah, that all sounds like a winner." Gratefully, she loaded up my arms. "Glad to be of help, Meg," and I went searching for a quiet place to help correct the "Celestial goof."

Meg called after me, "Send me hikers. I need lots 'n lots of hikers!"

"What you really need is a dump truck!"

Thru-hikers being what they are, Moleskin Meg needn't have worried. By suppertime her pile had dwindled to a few skimpy pickings. (I returned three times to help the distressed damsel—and collected enough food to supplement my mail drop with enough supplies for a ten-day cruise through The Hundred Mile Wilderness! (Or so I thought.) J.R. reminded me that we didn't have near enough cookies to carry us through The Wilderness since we'd eaten most of Meg's during the afternoon. So I traipsed down to the Monson General Store and checked their shelves.

"Lookee there," Ol' Eagle Eye piped. "A cheap cookie special!" It was exactly what I was looking for—lots of lard, chockfull of calories, and ninety-nine cents a pack. I did a quick count—54 cookies per pack. Times three would equal 162. "Sixteen cookies a day; five each meal, plus one to grow on. That should be enough, I'd think." The Ego, now happy, grunted, "Yeah, as long as you keep on budget."

We returned to Shaw's and called Judith at Robyn's home in New Jersey to make sure she was on schedule. She informed J.R. that she had made reservations at the Pamola Motel in Millinocket, the closest town to Baxter State Park, for the nights of 28 and 29 September. He told her to meet him at Katahdin Stream Campground early on the 29th so she could be there when he climbed Katahdin. Then followed the usual "mushies and gushies." When Keith, working nearby, began to blush, I got embarrassed and gave Lover Boy a mental jab. "C'mon, for gosh sake. You're gonna melt the phone and give Keith heart failure." The horny old goat!

Supper at Shaw's far exceeded our expectations: Half a baked hen each, a bowl heaped with steamed veggies, assorted pies, and unlimited cold milk! Keith recorded the meal with his camcorder while we ate, and I thought, "He probably has the most complete archive of hikers than anyone!"

That night I tossed in a sagging bunk, trying to find relief from a huge gas bubble brought on by greedily quaffing seven glasses of milk at supper. I groaned, "Mankind's curse." The Ego: "Gluttony?" I, nearly in tears: "No, free will."

The bubble had dissipated by breakfast, leaving in its wake only a dull memory, and I grinned at Keith's cheery, "I'll fix anything you want, as much as you want, but the rule is, you have to eat it all."

I asked timidly, "How about six scrambled eggs, half a pound of bacon and six pancakes, plus coffee?"

Keith said, "Sounds reasonable. If you want more, just let me know." What a guy! Throwing caution to the wind, I said, "It's gonna be a long day. How about a couple of doughnuts, too?"

About 9:30, after all the hikers had been fed and the kitchen cleaned, Keith drove Skate and me (none of the other hikers seemed to be in any hurry to depart) the two miles back to the trailhead. We dragged our packs from his battered pickup and I asked, "How much for the ride?" He replied, "No charge. Just send me a postcard." We thanked him, shouldered our monstrous packs, and headed into The Wilderness.

During the next days my journal read like a Laurel and Hardy comedy:

> Thursday, 20 September—Stopped for lunch at Little Wilson Falls, beautiful tumbling stream. Pulled one of two gallon plastic bags crammed with cookies from pack, carefully placed five on a rock, put bag back, and ate them slowly, almost religiously. Skate eyed proceedings with interest but made no comment. In late afternoon, forded waist-deep Big Wilson River. Bottom covered with slippery stone basketballs. Lost footing but saved from watery demise by well-oiled hiking machine. Twilight coming on by time we found campsite a half mile up the Trail—a good thing

as feet and fingers numb from icy crossing and dropping temperature. Remembered Skate's predator look at lunch, so ate 6.5 cookies inside tent.

Had heart failure at midnight when the ground began to shake and a fire-breathing, earth-shattering dragon charged straight at my tent. Almost peed in my shorts when double-engine train roared past. "Killer" was highly miffed, but how was I to know Canadian-Pacific Railroad tracks were hidden barely twenty yards beyond my tent? The "dragon" rumbled past twice more before daylight. Ate breakfast cookies inside my sleeping bag.

Friday, 21 September—Found out first hand that the Barren-Chairback range is first class "sumabitch"! (J.R.'s impulsive summation.) Fell twice; no serious damage. Viewed first AT blaze in Maine on Third Mountain at Monument Cliff—1932 vintage, even older than the "Killer". Suffered first cookie casualty at noon. Came a loud squawk, and thieving Canadian jay swooped down and grabbed a cookie quicker'n greased lightning. Got more to worry about now than predatory thru-hikers!

Made it to Chairback Gap Leanto at dusk after trying sixteen-mile day, last eight miles best described as "ludricious"—steep ups and downs. Red (a red-headed art teacher turned thru-hiker I'd briefly met at Shaw's) was there. Cookie master plan went out the window when, without thinking, I passed bag to Skate. She grabbed a handful and in thru-hiker tradition passed bag on to Red. Cookie strategy now in shambles.

Saturday, 22 September—Cold and overcast; threatening rain. Ate breakfast in gray dawn and reevaluated cookie situation while others still slept. Tally not good—down to nine cookies a day. Ate three and headed up Chairback Mountain, also "ludricious." Past summit, I glimpsed a spruce grouse in low red spruce; got camera right in its face but the critter never moved. Easy meal! But J.R. said, "No," because their diet made the meat taste like turpentine. I'm not that hungry—yet.

Forded West Branch of Pleasant River—another Big Wilson, except wider and deeper. Tempted to take side trail through Gulf Hagas (a deep slash in the earth abounding in diverse flora), but rain now threatening and feet still numb from fording the river so kept to the Trail. Reached Carl Newhall Leanto shortly after noon, just ahead of rain; decided to stay. Buzzy and Tag Along, husband and wife thru-hikers on the high side of thirty—he reticent, she bubbly—came in later, brought rain with them. By suppertime,

Skate, Red, Dog, and Shug had trickled in, seven hikers with gear crammed into six-person shelter. Braved rain to eat three cookies behind shelter. That night, when one rolled over we all did. J.R. complained, "Sardines have more room!"

Sunday, 23 September—Rained hard all night. Got late start waiting for weather to moderate. Slogged up Gulf Hagas Mountain on flooded treadway, water above boot tops. An hour later going up Hay Mountain, startled by movement in dense birch thicket just off the Trail; monstrous bull moose crossed path in front of me, not ten feet away, bowling over three-inch saplings like they were wheat stems; he ignored me but got MY attention! Stank worse than a thru-hiker!

Atop fog-covered summit of White Cap Mountain, ate early lunch by myself. Meal included six cookies (wisely, I kept breakfast ration hidden while in Dog's presence). Sun pushed the fog away while I lunched, providing me with a glorious view to go with my cookies! A milepost: This is the last big mountain until Katahdin! Ahead is a sixty-mile stretch of forested lowland abounding with ponds and bogs—a welcome change!

Reached Logan Brook Leanto at one o'clock and decided to stay; ankle throbbing. Dog, Shug, and Skate kept me company. A whopping 6.7 miles today. Hope the food lasts!

A catastrophe at supper! Without thinking, pulled the last bag of cookies from my food bag to get at the peanut butter. Dog spotted bag and immediately started whining that he didn't have any cookies; nagged at me, finally wore me down and I passed him the bag, saying, "You can have ONE." Should have known his brain hung out inside one of his hollow legs instead of in his head where normal people keep theirs. He passed the bag to Skate and Shug, and then grinning mischievously excavated another large handful before handing the bag back.

Crunching noisily, he said, "These are okay, but have you ever thought about carrying Oreo's?" (Not in the same state with you, Buzzo!) Thirty cookies left and not half way through The Wilderness! Chicken nasty!

Monday, 24 September—Tough ford across East Branch of Pleasant River; water swift and chest-high from all the rain. Made it safely across but cold and wet—again!

The four of us stopped for the night at Cooper Brook Falls Leanto (beautiful setting with a glistening waterfall that drops into a dark pool right beneath the shelter's front). Days now very

short; dark by six, in sleeping bag by six-thirty; cold and nothing
to do, but it's okay—warm and dry there. Cookie bag has become
a white elephant—a hassle trying to keep them hidden from Dog
and the others. At supper I passed the bag around and we finished
them off. "Fool's gold!" J.R. snorted, and I felt as if a huge stone
had been rolled off my tawdry soul! Hallelujah!

We got an unexpected windfall the next day at Antlers Camp (site of a
long-gone hunting lodge on the shore of Lower Jo-Mary Lake). Inside a
large screened cage, we found several cans and packages of food carefully
stacked on a board, along with a note: "Thru-hikers! Sorry you missed our
big 'feed' this weekend. We left the remainder, courtesy of LL Bean.
Enjoy. 'Cowbird and Caper.'"

It's amazing how good spaghetti with mushroom soup/tomato paste
sauce topped with sardines in mustard can taste to hungry thru-hikers—
even if the stuff looks like what squirts out of squashed grasshoppers!

We cleaned the pot!

Hiking alone late that afternoon, I got my first look at "the greatest
mountain," still forty miles away by Trail. As I rounded a copse of birch
along the rock-covered shore of Pemadumacook Lake, there it was!
Katahdin in all its glory! It lay like a massive lazy turtle humped against the
northern horizon, its top hidden from prying eyes by thick clouds. I whispered reverently, "There lies the giant, Ego. It's expecting us." He answered
with quiet finality, "It has been since our first steps from Springer." Even
from this distance the mountain was an aggrandized contradiction: Foreboding; yet pulling me toward its mysterious heights like a fluttering moth
toward a candle flame. Olympian shrine; yet usurper of dreams, feasting on
the wrecked hopes of the "nine in ten". Majestic; yet terrifying. The words
of Thoreau, written after his failed attempt in 1846 to scale Katahdin,
floated on the breeze like a poignant whisper: "*Only daring and insolent
men, perchance, go there . . .*" Giving a low whistle, I murmured, "Sumabitch!" and wondered at the sanity of "daring and insolent men"!

That evening, rejoined with my companions at a small tent site
beside a soothing, burbling stream, Skate reminded us that we had finally
made it to "page 1." (The *AT Data Book* pages are numbered from North
to South, and we had departed Springer Mountain on page 78!) The first
entry on page 1: "Katahdin (Baxter Peak); Miles from Katahdin, 0.0". A
bittersweet pang tempered my excitement.

For the past couple of days, ever since descending into the lowlands, autumn colors had slowly seeped into the foliage. Now, as if the artist had been jolted into fierce action by an inspired vision, broad splashes of brilliance suddenly illuminated the landscape: Yellows, oranges, reds, even purples, jumped out of the coniferous background to tease our eyes with delight. Across the myriad ponds, lakes, and rolling hills, the miracle of seasonal transition became like manna to green-stifled senses.

Today marked the seventh day in The Wilderness. My food bag had become alarmingly light and I still had two days left before reaching the Abol Bridge Campstore, just across the Penobscot River. When Skate and I stopped for a meager lunch break at Wadleigh Stream Leanto, I dumped what remained on the shelter floor.

"What's wrong, Model-T?" she asked.

"Takin' stock. It's gonna be close."

"Are you yogi-ing me?" She smiled mischievously.

"Naw, this is serious. I've got to be careful or I'm gonna run out of food." I surveyed the depressing pile and listened to J.R.'s silent carping: "This is like Jan in reverse. If only we had some of his MREs now!"

I partitioned the foodstuff into two scant clusters—days one and two—and took enough off each pile for supper tonight. It would be meager fare: Half a pack of ramen, a taste of peanut butter, a small swig of squeeze margarine, and one-third package of instant chocolate pudding. I put everything back in the food bag, drank some water—the ultimate diet food—and got ready to plod on.

Skate reached into her food bag and extracted a Snickers bar, and then held it out in plain view where I had to see it. Dang, torture by chocolate! She gloated, "Now let me see. Should I have this now or later?"

The temptation was strong to commit mayhem; instead, I grumbled, "Better not let Dog see that."

Her look softened. "Actually, I carried it all the way from Monson just for you, Model-T. Something to celebrate the end of the Trail. But we can replace it at Abol Bridge."

Saliva flooded my mouth. "You sure you want to part with this?"

"Yes, I'm sure," and she passed the bar to my eager hand.

Overwhelmed by the gesture, I could only say, "Thanks, Skate." My eyes said the rest.

She laughed. "They should have named you 'Snickers.' It fits better than 'Model-T.'" I couldn't argue with that! I tucked the Snickers inside my belt pouch, determined to make it last as long as my willpower would hold out. What a warm, caring friend!

That night at Rainbow Stream Leanto (another "baseball bat" shelter), I tossed on the corrugated floor with a restlessness born of gnawing hunger, vividly aware of the food bag that dangled so near, yet was isolated beyond my reach by the searing words, "That's all." Like a man tossing on a raft in the middle of the ocean, thirsting to death while his hands play helplessly in the tantalizing waves, this small remaining hoard within arm's reach teased my senses without mercy. Wahoola, sleeping next to me, groaned softly and turned over. Was he, too, awash in hunger spasms?

He and Meg had come in right at dusk, shortly behind Dog and Shug, and supper, normally cheerful and animated, had been subdued. Skate and I had already finished our meager meal and gotten inside our sleeping bags, so I had no idea how low on food they were. At least everyone had eaten something. I sighed and drank lustily from my water bottle, and then began the age-old ritual of counting myself to sleep. This time it was an endless line of Snicker bars with little legs vaulting over a low fence, their tidy wrappers imprinted with smiley faces. Each gave me a roguish smile and a knowing wink as it cleared the top bar before dropping into a huge, waiting mouth, and I finally dozed.

"How much farther to Abol Bridge?" Dog asked. He had asked the same question time and again over the morning.

"The same as thirty minutes ago. The rest of today and a wakeup," Shug replied testily. I could hear his stomach rumbling ten feet away.

The six of us—last night's boarders—had hiked together during the morning, our mood festive as we chatted like carefree troubadours and joked back and forth. Not long after leaving the leanto, as we rounded the west end of Rainbow Lake, the plaintive call of a loon echoed across the misted surface. Dog, in the lead, immediately asked, "What do you think roasted loon tastes like? I'd try one right now, no questions asked."

Wahoola said, "It's just another form of goose. You'd have to hang it for a week though, until the meat begins to rot a little for it to get the proper flavor. I think it has something to do with enzymes. I did eat a goose once."

I piped up, "I drank a bottle of 'Cold Duck' at a party once all by myself, but by the time it was finished, I was pickled. It also had something to do with enzymes, 'cause my head felt like it had been hung for a week and my brain was rotting."

Moleskin Meg asked, "Is Donald Duck a duck or a goose? I'd like to pluck his carcass and pop him in an oven."

Shug groaned, "I'm glad I'm a vegetarian."

Skate, bringing up the rear, laughed, "If we had one more weirdo, we could be known as 'The Seven Dwarfs.'"

J.R. chimed in, "I'm stayin' put!"

That night at Hurd Brook Leanto—our last shelter in The Wilderness—"The Seven Dwarfs" (unbeknownst to the others or him, I had awarded J.R. the role of Dopey) feasted on the last of the food. Abol Bridge Campstore lay just beyond the reach of our hunger pains—only 3.5 miles to breakfast!

What a sight! I could hardly absorb what my eyes feasted on: Penobscot River eddied and swirled through a mystical fairyland, dazzlingly vibrant in its autumnal cloak as it shimmered at the breeze's gentle touch. High against the northern sky, just above the tree line, "Kette-Adene" diminished everything within sight—except a small log building topped with a metal roof, its facade graced by a giant red and white Schlitz sign. It squatted just beyond the pea-green metal bridge, which connected The Wilderness with civilization.

"Gads! Look at Katahdin!" Skate's words, spoken with awe, almost went unnoticed. "And the summit! It's clear!"

"Beautiful," I murmured, again bereft of adequate words. (Verbal "bankruptcy" had become a way of life lately!) But at this moment we were praising different things. My eyes were fixed on the Abol Bridge Campstore! Katahdin would get its due in proper order—strictly a matter of priorities!

Sitting outside at a picnic table, I washed nine donuts down with two cups of coffee in quick succession, and then got down to serious business: a can of pork and beans, an apple, half a small jar of peanut butter with half a loaf of bread—and stalled out on the verge of upchucking the whole mess.

Skate warned me, "You'd better slow down before you do serious damage."

"You're right." I watched as Wahoola ran across the bridge toward the store, followed with more dignity by Meg, who merely trotted. Still hungry, I pushed through the door behind them and grabbed two Snickers (smarting at Wahoola's smirk, for my "habit" was still very obvious), paid the clerk, and hid outside behind a tree away from accusing eyes to eat them.

More footsteps clanged across the bridge. Dog spurted past my hiding place, dumped his pack by the door as if it were filled with hot ashes, and then dashed inside. Shug strolled past, lady-like. Spotting me, she smiled understandingly at my frenzied chocolate binge. I pointed at the door and mumbled, "I shoulda warned the clerk about Dog. You need to keep him on a leash when he's around people."

"We're people," she said.

"Naw, I mean real people."

"Oh." She quickened her pace, whether concerned about getting at the food or about Dog, I couldn't be sure.

J.R. said, "Uh-oh. Wahoola and Dog are *both* in there together." Panicked, I dashed back inside to stake my claim on the few remaining Snickers!

The Trail meandered alongside the Penobscot River for the first few miles, serene and gentle like the first poignant, lingering kiss of two lovers. Occasional glimpses of Katahdin stirred my soul, sweetening the day, and I lapsed into a surreal, dream-like trance.

Alone with my thoughts, I stopped for a long break at Big Niagara Falls, slightly over a mile south of Daicey Pond Campground where I would spend this last night on the Trail. Suddenly, everything seemed to be shifting into warp speed! Katahdin was no longer the abstract destination of 2100 miles ago; *it was here and now!* Abruptly, the journey was rushing to its end, sweeping bittersweet memories across my mind and coursing its torrent of awe into my soul, just as the roaring falls near where I sat cascaded its turbulent waters to the sea. I realized with a start that neither J.R.'s nor my existence would ever be the same.

Reluctantly, I shouldered my pack and headed up the path.

When I walked out of the woods at Daicey Pond, the others lay on the ground near the water's edge. They were unmoving and silent, each caught up in a private journey, eyes fixed on the mammoth hulk that filled the sky and mirrored its image in a masterful display of illusion on the pond's placid surface. Katahdin's craggy roughness seemed to rip into the tranquil veil of blue, just as it tore into the fabric of my comprehension. Thoreau's words pierced my thoughts, playing over and over: "Only daring and insolent men, perchance, go there . . ." Did I dare? For tomorrow, "there" would become "here"!

Wordlessly, I removed my pack and joined the pensive supplicants, opening my soul to this moment of veneration. J.R. whispered, "I can't ever remember being this moved. It's beautiful, almost like a religious awakening." Mellowed, I struggled to respond. "You've come a long way, Marine. Nay, WE have come a long way—together," and I wiped the mist from my eyes.

I sneaked a glance at Wahoola, then Skate. Moistened eyes? A mystical renewal or spiritual regeneration? Two thousand miles of soul-stomping adversity, or six months of mind-spicing enchantment? Tears threatened to spill out to make room for the myriad thoughts that churned my innards and I told the others gruffly, "I'm going up to the Ranger Station to check in." But the spell lingered.

At the Ranger Station, I filled out the mandatory registration form and paid the four-dollar fee for enough floor space to spread my Therm-a-Rest in one of the two tiny four-person shelters set aside for thru-hikers. The pretty lady Ranger looked over my form and asked, "You're Mr. Tate, trail name Model-T?" I acknowledged with a nod and she continued. "Headquarters in Millinocket radioed with a message from your wife. She's arrived at the Pamola Motel and will be out here early in the morning."

"Great news!" J.R. answered with a grin. "Could you send a message back?"

"Sure can. Write it down, if you don't mind, and I'll call it in right away. Why don't you check back in an hour or so, to see if there's a reply?"

"Fine," and J.R. wrote: "Meet me at Katahdin Stream Campground (the jumping off spot for the climb) at 8 AM. Hungry! Bring food and nose plugs!"

"That's not very romantic. Wouldn't you like to sweeten it up some?"

"Sure. Add, 'Hot coffee with six sugars, too.'"

The Ranger shook her head, clucking like a mother hen. "With the 'nose plugs,' it should make for interesting reading."

Eco Warrior had joined the group when I got outside. We traded bear hugs. "Jeez! It's good to see you, Eco. I thought you'd be long gone by now."

He chuckled with embarrassment. "I can't get enough of Katahdin. Been here almost a week and climbed it three times. Might do it again!" Jiminy! And I fretted over climbing the beast once! His youthful exuberance jolted my weak-kneed resolve like a shot of caffeine and the butterflies departed. "How would you like a cold beer?" he asked.

"You're kidding!"

"Got a cooler full at the shelter. C'mon!" Dang! I had sure missed this fella!

The reply came back: "Food and coffee, okay. No nose plugs. Are you going swimming?" J.R and I both chuckled as I sniffed my armpit, relishing the "essence of trail." Ha! Was she in for a surprise!

As twilight fell, the shelter banter became filled with nostalgia mixed with anticipation. In spite of our cheery conversation, a stubborn sadness lay just beneath the surface, nagging, seeking expression, tacitly ignored, for this would be our final night together. After tomorrow, bonds forged over these past many miles would be stretched by time, distance, and cultural divergence. Sadly, some would be severed. I choked back a maudlin comment and ate another Snickers—"A one-sided trade," J.R. said, but he didn't elaborate on which side was the loser.

By seven o'clock we had rolled up the sidewalks and gone to bed. Tomorrow, the mountain!

The Seven Dwarfs, now joined by Eco Warrior, walked into the early dawning, joking and laughing, carrying on as if a circus had come to town, which in a way it had. To sweeten the day, shortly after leaving Daicey Pond we had seen a bull moose on the far side of Elbow Pond pulling vegetation from the bottom, submerging his massive head, then bringing up a clump of dripping, mucky greens. Delighted, we watched him go through his repetitive ritual for several minutes—some of the "dwarfs" had not yet encountered a moose in the wild—then went on.

We had already covered one of the two miles from Daicey Pond to Rainbow Stream Campground and were now spread out along a dirt connector road between the two facilities. I lagged behind, conserving my strength for the ordeal to come, not even trying to keep up with the younger generation. Suddenly from around a bend up ahead came a piercing squeal. "Holy cow! That's Moleskin Meg," J.R. muttered. Another shriek, louder, this time accompanied by shouts. He said, "Sounds like murder's being committed. Let's get up there. Quick!" I took off at a run, wondering what in the world could have spooked Meg into making such a racket. Bear or moose attack? Or worse!

I rounded the bend lickety-split and stopped dead in my tracks. Moleskin Meg had Judith in a strangle hold that made Skate's technique look like child's play. Another screech: "Mrs. Teeee! Mrs. Teeee! I'd know you anywhere! Model-T's told us so much about you!" I had?

Wahoola came to Judith's rescue and managed to separate the two. She smiled warmly at her savior and hugged him. "David, you've changed."

"It's the beard."

Moleskin stared at him. "David? Your name is David?" He grinned with embarrassment.

Judith greeted the others in turn, naming each as if she were welcoming long-known friends or family, to each hiker's delight. "You must be Skate. Model-T has told me so much about you. And you would have to be Shug. Who else could have such beautiful red hair?" Shug nearly melted from her own blush, which matched her hair perfectly. "And where Shug goes, so goes Dog, which must be you." Dog would have wagged his tail if he had one.

A puzzled look crossed Judith's face. Skate said, "This is Eco Warrior."

"Oh yes, you're the one who broke his foot near Roanoke. Model-T wrote me all about it. And you made it all the way!"

Eco shuffled uncomfortably and mumbled, "Aw, it was nothing. Just a little break."

J.R. lingered at the back of the pack, leaning against the blue coolness of their Buick Skylark, waiting his turn. He and Judith stared at one another for a long moment, searching for familiar landmarks, trying to bridge the gap left by months of separation, a ritual made necessary by the chasms dug into their marriage by lengthy stretches of military absence. Satisfied, she walked into his arms.

After a quick kiss, she pushed him away. "I should have brought those nose plugs."

Later, as we tailed after the Skylark—no yellow blazing this late in the game—J.R. asked, "What's happening? When we met Judith just now, it seemed as if the gap between you and me sprang shut like a mousetrap. For a moment, we could have been a single entity." He said it without rancor and I replied, "Yeah. I felt it, too. Scary!" But, I couldn't deal with amateur psychoanalysis now, not on this, the Big "K" day. "How about we tackle this another time?" and he agreed, for there was no telling where *that* road might lead.

Judith had brought food! Donuts—enough for everyone—and a large thermos of coffee (plus ample sugar), but best of all, she had a half-bushel of New Hampshire's prime Cortland apples! How rapidly the fortunes of mere mortals change!

J.R. told her, "We'll be gone for several hours. What do you want to do? There's a nice library at Daicey Pond if you get bored." The summit, Baxter Peak, was 5.2 miles from where we stood, and counting the return trip we didn't expect to be back before two or three o'clock. I cast an anxious eye toward the mountain. Heavy gray clouds were already forming an ominous curtain beyond the top, but I shrugged off the twinge of anxiety.

The forecast on the board at the Ranger Station indicated a Class II day—summit visibility possibly limited. Nothing life-threatening!

"Eco Warrior can entertain me." (He had decided not to make the climb due to the summit prognosis; instead, he promised to have cold beers waiting when we got back.) "Go finish your hike." She kissed J.R., longer and more intimate this time. Maybe she had adjusted to the hiker scent! "Be careful up there." He hugged her and hurried after the others.

The Trail, gently winding upward at first, soon turned nasty, then dead serious. Huge granite boulders, grayish-pink, were stacked, scattered, jumbled, or scrambled in a confusing hodge-podge that sent the mind reeling in chaos! Thick fog had moved in by the time we reached timberline, reducing progress to a snail's pace. Before long, we came to a rat's nest of rocks unreasonably called "The Gateway," for nothing faintly resembled a "gate," and the going really became treacherous. Now and then, where a particularly dangerous boulder barred the way, a metal handhold had been added, but these were few and far between. (By my way of thinking, every boulder deserved a handhold, for this mountain made Mahoosuc Notch look like a summer outing!) J.R. grumbled, "I read somewhere that Thoreau called mountaintops the unfinished parts of the globe. He must have been looking at this jumble when he thought that one up!" I couldn't have agreed more!

We carefully picked our way through the rocky maze, taking our time as we slowly worked our way upward through the fog, ever aware that Katahdin, beautiful from a distance, was deadly in the buff. Over the years at least fifteen hikers had sacrificed themselves on its malevolent slopes. *Only daring and insolent men . . .*

Suddenly I crawled up onto a flat plateau! "The Tableland?" I shouted at Skate, who had paused there to let me catch up. She nodded. "Wahoola and Meg?" I asked.

"Gone on. They left a few minutes ago." I looked back but there was no sign of Dog or Shug—they must still be entangled in the maze of rocks. Skate walked off through the dense fog, putting a halt to further conversation, and I followed.

Before long, we reached a battered sign: "Thoreau Spring, named for Henry David Thoreau who climbed this mountain in 1846." Beneath the words, "Baxter Peak one mile" leaped out like a heaping plate of pancakes! I whooped, "This is it, Skate, the last mile!"

She laughed excitedly. "I can't believe it!"

"Believe it. I'm going to drink a toast to 'daring and insolent men.'" I quickly added, "And women." She stared at me with a quizzical expression. "Thoreau's own words," I explained.

"That's not what I meant. What are you going to toast with?"

"Thoreau's own elixir. It should be pure this high up." I cupped my hands and scooped a handful of the crystal liquid from the small struggling spring, which so strongly favored a rutted, water-soaked section of trail that I wouldn't have given it a second glance were it not for the sign. I intoned, "To all who followed Thoreau's dream and dared to walk on the happy side of misery, present company included, and to the great man himself, whose words cushioned our adversities and gave hope!"

Skate used her cup. "To Thoreau, and to thru-hikers everywhere!" We drank greedily, refilled, and then drank again. "Okay," she giggled, "are you ready?"

"As soon as I eat a Snickers—in memory of Thoreau."

J.R., belatedly: "I hope your hands were clean!"

We glimpsed the terminus sign through the thick haze—rustic-tan with white routed letters, the largest scripted in striking boldness: "KATAHDIN"—secured to sturdy stanchions anchored by the grayish-pink rocks, which covered the summit like an infestation of giant granite insects. A multitude of people—twenty, maybe thirty—sullied the summit. All appeared to be day hikers except for Wahoola and Meg, who quietly stood gazing at the sign.

I tuned out the crowd as best I could and pushed in beside Wahoola. Hesitant, besieged with emotion, I touched the sign and paid homage to the mountain. Beside me, Skate wept silently—tears of joy or sadness, or both? Her face sought my shoulder, and we joined to share the moment—happiness or consolation? Wahoola gripped my arm, and suddenly we became a circle of four, laughing and whooping and pounding each other on the back and hugging and dancing! Bystanders retreated before our hysterics, giving us room and respect, for we were not of their world—not here on this wild, unfinished part of the globe. We were *thru-hikers!*

When Dog and Shug arrived we held our hiking sticks high with pride as we stood together, and then singly, behind the terminus sign so that the occasion could be recorded for friends, family, and the rocking chair days of old age. Pictures finished, I walked to a nearby cairn—a monument of tradition started years earlier to raise Katahdin's elevation another twelve feet to an exact mile—and reverently added my Springer pebble to the pile.

Emotionally spent, our tears now dull stains on the rocks at the base of the "altar," we sat in a tight group while the crowd eddied around us like the swirling mist, and shared our last meal together. We talked in hushed voices, as if we were gathered at the coffin of "Friendship," and wondered at the inner conflict as feelings of exhilaration, happiness, sadness, relief, and fear roamed unfettered. (Yes, fear, for when we walked off of this mountain, we would step back into reality. Would we be able to adapt? Tomorrow's worry!)

We had beat the odds! We were one-in-ten'ers! The last white blaze had been conquered and there were no more beyond where we sat. I finished my last Snickers bar, stuffed the wrapping in my pocket, and told the others, "Well, it's back to the real world. See you guys at the bottom." Bellowing out *five* "OOOGAs," I growled, "C'mon Marine, Judith's waiting." Then, without a backward glance I headed back down the mountain.

Cup Cake managed to dog E Z Strider's steps all the way to Katahdin, but couldn't make the giant leap to New Zealand.

Hacker Hiker never made it back to the Trail. Ambushed by cancer, his dreams died with him the following year.

Wingfoot published *The Thru-Hiker's Handbook*, the replacement for *The Philosopher's Guide*, the next year and in succeeding years. He eventually moved to Hot Springs, North Carolina, where he continues his work on the *Handbook*. Soon after settling in Hot Springs, he began expanding on a long-held dream and soon planted a sign in his yard: "Center for Appalachian Trail Studies." He continues to devote his efforts toward this end.

Journeyman and Journalist went their separate ways, meeting briefly on transcontinental bicycle trips the next year—she headed west and he east. (They passed each other somewhere in Kansas.) Journalist finally married her childhood sweetheart, an Air Force jet jockey, settled down, and raised a family. Journeyman, still filled with wanderlust, talked about plans to cycle to Alaska and then sail from there to Greenland, via Cape Horn. Whether or not he managed to fulfill this dream is unknown.

The Orient Express, having been persuaded to climb Katahdin weeks earlier before the weather closed the mountain down, pulled into Katahdin Stream Campground the day before Thanksgiving and finished their "great adventure" there. Bill, who had fallen an estimated 5000 times during his journey, said he walked with "God's hand on my shoulder." He remarried, and now lives near the Trail in Maine. Each fall, when the leaves begin to turn, Bill and volunteer friends take ORV's down logging roads into The Wilderness and set up camp on the Trail, where they ply surprised, ravenous thru-hikers with massive amounts of spaghetti and pancakes. Orient died in the fall of 1999 and is sadly mourned by the hiking community. Bill now tours the country, taking his inspiring message of faith to those who wish to listen. The story of his thru-hike is chronicled in his book, *Blind Courage.*

After Katahdin, Mule returned to his native Stone Mountain, Georgia, where he replenished his body with copious amounts of "cheap calories" and nurtured a dream to hike the Pacific Crest Trail. His letters grew fewer, until finally the bond was severed.

Mississippi Tripper made it to Katahdin without a wheelchair. The following year, while out for a mere 500-mile stroll on the Trail from Springer, he fell in love with a thru-hiker. Assaulted by Cupid's arrows, he forsook his grits and followed his gal to Vermont. They settled not many miles from Dartmouth's Phi Tau Frat House, where Gordy's "You *mays*" still echo in the rafters.

Thatcher's Children climbed Katahdin on a beautiful October day. They bought a clunker for $500, toured the "Colonies," drove it back to New York City, and sold it for their initial investment before returning to Mother England. Wedding bells rang shortly thereafter, and they settled into a static existence.

Geek carried Ziggy to Katahdin, and he became the first cat to cover the AT. Fattened by shelter mice and cat food, Ziggy grew from a measly three pounds to a hefty fourteen by the time Geek dumped him onto the rocks at the northern terminus. We all agreed Geek's intelligence was inversely proportional to Ziggy's. That was one smart cat! Disturbingly, according to the hiker grapevine Ziggy used up his ninth life this past year.

Eco Warrior made good his promise and had cold beers waiting at Katahdin's base. His heart remained in Maine, and today he lives in beautiful Bar Harbor—close enough to climb Katahdin when the urge arises.

Skate wandered in and out of jobs, and finally returned to her real love, the German language. While working on her master's thesis in Austria, she, like Tripp, found romance. She and Kirk, a non-grit-eater from Atlanta who is finishing double master's degrees in history and international law, were married this past summer. They plan a belated honeymoon by hiking Vermont's Long Trail—some day, because it will take the wee hiker due in June a few months to break in its baby boots. Will they name it "Model-A"?

Shug never learned how to cook, but Dog married her anyway. After returning to school and wading through a mountain of books, they got masters degrees—and their boots de-soled by a visit from the stork.

Armed with a glowing letter of recommendation from J.R., Volunteer was accepted into the Marine Corps Officer Candidate School the following spring, received a commission as a second lieutenant, and went to Pensacola to learn how to fly. Eventually he received his wings, married, and is now one of Uncle Sam's finest! (Said J.R., "At least *something* good came from that hike.")

Moleskin Meg returned to Hawaii and became a Park Ranger, and then a teacher. She recently married—according to rumor, a man who failed his last hearing test. The rumor has not been substantiated.

Wahoola got a double whammy: Still restless like a caged monkey, he worked at menial jobs for a while and talked of hiking other trails. He finally settled into a college curriculum and got a masters degree in reconstructive ecology. Then he met a girl headed for Alaska, fell head over heels, and followed. Long after the romance faded, Wahoola stayed to savor the wild fascination of the Alaskan wilderness. He eventually moved to Vermont, staying close to the Trail that so enriched his life.

All of the others faded into obscurity.

With the Trail's mark indelibly etched on our soul, in the spring of 1994 I easily persuaded J.R. (with some inadvertent help from THE LOOK) to again take to the mountains. Judith let The Ego and me off at Amicalola Falls in early April, and we scaled Katahdin on September 29th, this time joined for the final climb by Kelly, who flew to Maine for the occasion. Once again, maudlin with 1990's déjà vu, we stood before the shrine in a heavy fog laced with sleet.

Then one snowy morning in early 1998, J.R. surprised me. "I wonder what the view from Katahdin is really like?" I retorted, "Better than THE LOOK." Although that demon had mellowed to a mere resemblance of its former self with the passage of years, it still made an occasional appearance. So once again Judith dumped us at Amicalola Falls with the admonition, "You realize you need a support group, don't you?" This time we reached Katahdin's majestic crest in flawless sunshine, again on September 29th. As we stared in amazement and absorbed the beauty, J.R. murmured, "Thoreau was wrong. This *is* the finished part of the globe. Nothing could improve on what we see here," and he was right!

I chose my words carefully. "Do you think we'll ever do it again?" He squinted at the long path winding southward and chuckled. "I haven't heard the fat lady sing. Have you?"